AN
APPALACHIAN
NEW DEAL

WEST VIRGINIA AND APPALACHIA

A SERIES EDITED BY RONALD L. LEWIS, KEN FONES-WOLF,
and KEVIN BARKSDALE

VOLUME 11
Other books in the series:

Transnational West Virginia
Edited by Ken Fones-Wolf and Ronald L. Lewis

The Blackwater Chronicle
By Philip Pendleton Kennedy; Edited by Timothy Sweet

Clash of Loyalties
By John Shaffer

Afflicting the Comfortable
By Thomas F. Stafford

Bringing Down the Mountains
By Shirley Stewart Burns

Monongah: The Tragic Story Of the 1907 Monongah Mine Disaster
By Davitt McAteer

Sectionalism in Virginia from 1776 to 1881, Second Edition
By Charles Ambler;
Introduction to the second edition by Barbara Rasmussen

Matewan Before the Massacre
By Rebecca J. Bailey

Governor William E. Glasscock And Progressive Politics in West Virginia
By Gary Jackson Tucker

Culture, Class, and Politics in Modern Appalachia
Edited by Jennifer Egolf, Ken Fones-Wolf, and Louis C. Martin

AN APPALACHIAN NEW DEAL

West Virginia in the Great Depression

JERRY BRUCE THOMAS

WEST VIRGINIA UNIVERSITY PRESS
MORGANTOWN 2010

West Virginia University Press, Morgantown 26506
© 2010 by West Virginia University Press

All rights reserved.

Paperback edition.
First published 1998 by University Press of Kentucky.
Printed in the United States of America.

17 16 15 14 13 12 11 10   1 2 3 4 5 6 7 8 9

ISBN-10: 1-933202-51-3
ISBN-13: 978-1-933202-51-8
(alk. paper)

Library of Congress Cataloguing-in-Publication Data

Thomas, Jerry Bruce, 1941-
An Appalachian New Deal : West Virginia in the Great Depression / Jerry Bruce Thomas.
p.   cm.
Includes bibliographical references and index.
ISBN 978-1-933202-51-8
1. West Virginia—History—To 1950. 2. West Virginia—Politics and government. 3. West Virginia—Social conditions   4. West Virginia—Economic conditions.
5. Depressions—1929—West Virginia.   6. New Deal, 1933–1939—West Virginia. I. Title

F241.T47   1998
975.4—dc21   98-15701

Cover image: Carrying water to one of the houses in abandoned mining community, Marine, West Virginia. Photograph by Marion Post Wolcott, September, 1938

Cover Design by Than Saffel

*Dedicated to the memory of my father and mother,
John B. Thomas and Edith Marie Steele Thomas.
They lived it.*

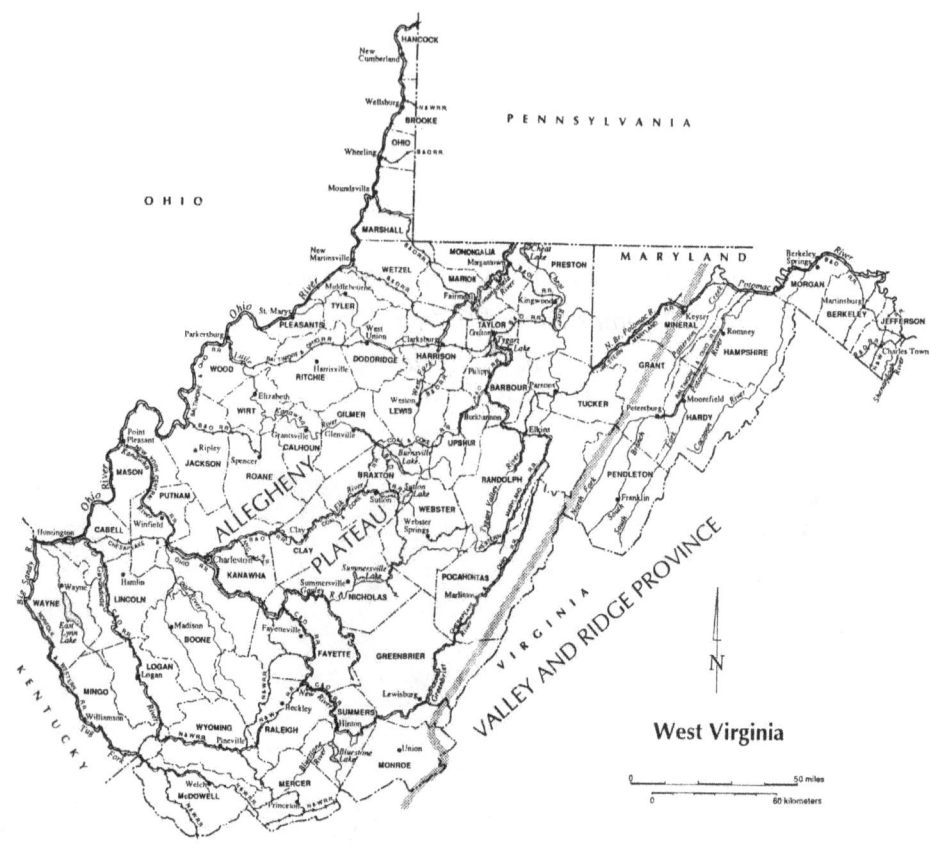

Map showing West Virginia's counties, major cities, railroads, and principal waterways. Reproduced from Otis K. Rice and Stephen W. Brown, *West Virginia: A History, Second Edition* (University Press of Kentucky, 1993).

Contents

Preface to the Paperback Edition viii
Acknowledgments xii
Introduction 1
1. On the Eve 6
2. Drought and Depression 27
3. A Search for Order 42
4. A "Jump in the Dark" 70
5. The Blue Eagle 91
6. A Failed Experiment in Federal Relief 112
7. Reshaping the Welfare System 136
8. The New Deal and Mountain Agriculture 160
9. The New Deal and Families in Distress 189
10. Reluctant New Dealers 211
Epilogue: From Nearly Perfect to Almost Heaven 234
Notes 241
Bibliography 285
Index 300

Illustrations follow page 100

Preface to the Paperback Edition

In 2008, ten years after it had first appeared, the original edition of *An Appalachian New Deal*, following the typical cycle for an academic book, went out of print, leaving it largely unavailable in bookstores or at online dealers. At about the same time, I began to receive more inquiries about the book than I had during its in-print life. The reason for the renewed interest, of course, was the economic downturn that began in 2007, a slide that seemed shockingly similar to the Great Crash of 1929, an event that the New Deal reforms presumably had made obsolete. In the last two decades of the twentieth century, however, in the interest of deregulation, Congress eliminated many of the financial and banking regulations of the New Deal, some of which might have moderated or prevented the recent downturn. In any case, with the new economic crisis, the worst since the 1930s, people wanted to compare the present with the past and to seek the lessons of history.

Of course history never repeats itself exactly, and the eight decades since the Great Crash of 1929 have made the United States, West Virginia, and Appalachia very different places with some problems similar to that bygone era but with other issues that would have been inconceivable in 1929. Also, some vestiges of the New Deal era, such as social security and unemployment insurance and other aspects of countercyclical economic policy make it unlikely that the current recession will reach the depths of the depression of the 1930s, a time when unemployment in Lincoln and Wayne, counties dependent on subsistence agriculture, reached 84 and 70 percent. The coal mining counties Raleigh, Mercer, Marion, and Mingo all had more than 40 percent unemployed. Public employees throughout the state such as policemen, firemen, and schoolteachers sometimes had to work without pay as municipalities and the state fell short of funds to pay all their obligations. Some school districts

Preface

dismissed women teachers, preserving teaching jobs for men, based on the notion that men were heads of families, and women just worked for pin money. State administrators slashed school and college budgets. Many retail businesses had to close their doors. County poor farms filled to overflowing, and private charities like the Red Cross and Community Chest had insufficient funds to meet the needs of the unemployed.

Another characteristic of the Great Depression which we would hope to avoid in the current or future recessions is its persistence. Though the New Deal in West Virginia provided much-needed help to those who suffered most, helped vanquish nearly medieval forms of welfare such as county poor farms, encouraged the growth of professional social work, established the setting that allowed working men and women to organize, and built many roads, bridges, and public buildings still in use today, it failed to bring complete economic recovery before World War II.

This reprinting has made it possible to correct errors in spelling or misprints that somehow slipped through the original editing, but it is not a rewriting and therefore incorporates no new research. The basic content remains as originally published in 1998. As I noted in the original introduction, my goals were to write a brief narrative synthesis about West Virginia during the Depression era that would be useful to students and interested readers and to put the story in a regional and national context so that it might contribute to the emerging literature about the era in Appalachia. I also hoped it might contribute as well to the state and city studies that added depth to the understanding of the New Deal's impact. Reviewers generally recognized that the book fulfilled those goals. Taking as my model other state and local histories of the New Deal, I focused a good bit on government and politics, tracing the internecine struggle in the state between the more conservative statehouse Democrats and the pro-New Deal federal Democrats, a conflict which is part of the broader story of the nature of the federal system and the kind of constraints Franklin D. Roosevelt and the New Dealers faced in seeking to bring change to the country. Also, mindful of the experiences of my parents (to whom this book is dedicated) and their generation, I sought to tell the important story of what happened to ordinary people as they faced the challenges of the Depression. Some reviewers, not unreasonably, felt that the political history overshadowed the social history, and for those students who will inevitably expand upon or revise my account, social history will likely be a larger part of the focus. I felt some frustration in not exploring more deeply the story of subsistence farmers, for example, a group that, unlike others facing the challenges of the era, failed to organize and for which few sources other than government documents existed. There is much, also, that might be done in further studies of the Depression experience of counties, towns and cities and of women and women's organizations. Eleanor Roosevelt has not lacked attention from biographers, but she had a special interest in West Virginia and spent a good bit of time in the state, another story not fully explored.

The acknowledgments section remains as it originally appeared in the 1998 edition, but my administrative friends would want me to mention that Shepherd College has become Shepherd University in the new century. I must add a special thanks to Carrie Mullen, Director of West Virginia University Press, and her staff, who have been so helpful in making *An Appalachian New Deal* available in this new printing.

Acknowledgments

It is a pleasant duty to acknowledge those who have helped ease the tasks of researching and writing this book. I am grateful to the many scholars from whose works I have borrowed, and I can only hope that I have given proper credit where due and that the views of others have been faithfully represented.

Though teaching is the primary mission at Shepherd College, the professional development committee and the administration have generously supported my research and writing, granting me a sabbatical in the fall semester of 1989 and two summer stipends that helped defray the costs of research forays. The West Virginia Humanities Foundation also helped, providing me with a grant that allowed me to spend a summer free of other academic obligations.

I have relied heavily upon the assistance of librarians and archivists, beginning with Joseph Barnes and his staff at the Ruth Scarborough Library, who cheerfully filled many requests for interlibrary loans and kept the microfilm readers rolling. Much of the research for this book required that I consult primary sources, and I gratefully acknowledge the help of archivists at the National Archives; the Library of Congress; the Franklin D. Roosevelt Presidential Library; the Eastern Regional Coal Archives in the Craft Memorial Library, Bluefield; the West Virginia State Archives; the West Virginia State College Library; the Special Collections Division at the James E. Morrow Library, Marshall University; and the West Virginia and Regional History Collection at West Virginia University. Debra Basham of the West Virginia State Archives and David Ware of the West Virginia and Regional History Collection were especially generous with their time in helping find appropriate illustrations.

Ronald L. Lewis, of West Virginia University, a leading historian of Appalachia, read the entire manuscript and called my attention to several areas that needed rethinking. An anonymous reader who helped the University Press of Kentucky evaluate the manuscript also made

Acknowledgments

useful suggestions. My colleague John E. Stealey III read an early portion of the manuscript and encouraged me to believe the project was worthwhile, and others in the Shepherd College history department—Walter Hanak, Anders Henriksson, James Holland, Ralph Sherrard, and Robert Willgoos—have consistently provided an atmosphere congenial to scholarly pursuits. Paul Salstrom, then at West Virginia University, generously gave me a copy of his dissertation and offered help and hospitality, as well as stimulating ideas, to the visiting researcher. At the annual meeting of the West Virginia Historical Association at Marshall University in the spring of 1996, members responded to a paper based on research for this book with useful criticism. For the help of all these fellow historians, I am most grateful. A former student, Kathy Shambaugh, helped find information about recorded music of the Depression era.

My family deserves my most heartfelt thanks. Without the constant support, good humor, and love of my wife Vicky, I could not have written this book. My son John has affectionately tolerated my preoccupation with the thirties. Most important, both helped me to persevere, even in the face of the loss of our beloved Alicia as the writing of the book neared completion.

Introduction

Some years ago when a colleague who usually teaches the West Virginia and Appalachia history course went on leave, I was drafted to stand in for him. In preparing for the assignment, I was struck by the lack of information about the Depression in West Virginia. Despite the crucial nature of that era for the state, almost nothing had been written about it beyond the brief summaries in the standard textbooks.[1] In teaching the part of the course about the Depression era, I confess that I relied heavily on notes, practically primary sources themselves, taken during the early sixties, when I sat as an undergraduate in Festus Paul Summers's class at West Virginia University. Though Dr. Summers's lectures were quite thorough and thoughtful, much historiographical water had gone over the dam since those days. A whole genre of national, state, local, and regional New Deal histories had been written. Moreover, scholars had raised many interesting questions about Appalachia, although at that point, there had been but slight consideration of Appalachia in the Depression.[2]

As a native West Virginian whose parents grew to maturity in the state during the Depression, I had a great curiosity about their generation's difficult time, and because the state has suffered continuing economic difficulties, I wondered about the connection between the Depression and New Deal era and more recent problems.

With the intention of gathering a few materials and writing a brief narrative synthesis, perhaps of article length, I set out on a scholarly journey that soon eclipsed its original goal and after several years led to this book. Now, if my colleague goes on leave, I will have something more than notes of Professor Summers's lectures to share with students, and I hope what I have produced may interest anyone who is curious about the impact of the Depression and New Deal era on the people and government of West Virginia.

Because West Virginia lies wholly or almost wholly within Appalachia, this study may also contribute to an emerging literature about the Depression and New Deal in Appalachia, although I do not suggest that conclusions about West Virginia necessarily apply to other parts of Appalachia. Recent scholarly literature has properly been at some pains to decry past claims of Appalachian exceptionalism and to note the variety of experiences and conditions within Appalachia. The term *Appalachia* is itself somewhat ambiguous as scholars continue to disagree as to the precise borders and whether all of West Virginia should be included in southern Appalachia. It is certain that West Virginia is the one state most completely within Appalachia.[3]

An important pioneering work on the depression era in Appalachia is Paul Salstrom's *Appalachia's Path to Dependency*. Relying on a blend of neo-Marxist and neo-classical theory, Salstrom asks important questions and offers many stimulating ideas in covering the broad sweep of Appalachian economic history from 1730 to 1940. My concern, of course, is with questions he raises in considering the impact of the Depression and New Deal legislation. He maintains that New Deal programs such as the National Recovery Administration, the Agricultural Adjustment Administration and the Works Progress Administration "harmed" the region by undermining the competitive position of its industries, especially coal (by driving wages and prices upward) and by turning subsistence farmers away from their traditional noncash systems toward cash (by making available to them "high" relief payments). Arguing *post hoc ergo propter hoc*, Salstrom traces many of the problems of Appalachia to Franklin D. Roosevelt and the New Dealers, who, he charges, followed policies that were "not only economically unsound, but inhumane."[4]

My study of West Virginia leads me to somewhat different and more charitable conclusions about the New Deal. The advance of industrial capitalism and destructive agricultural practices wrecked subsistence agriculture well before the Great Depression. New Deal relief payments in West Virginia, often less than half the national average, generally were desperately needed by the recipients, whether farmers trying to coax a living from eroded mountain lands or industrial workers left abandoned by closed mines and mills. The National Industrial Recovery Act, though a failure as macroeconomic policy, brought recovery and needed reforms to the state's coal fields, leading to substantial reemployment of miners. The Agricultural Adjustment Act provided little help to West Virginia's small farmers, but other New Deal legislation tried to help low-income farmers save their farms.[5] Although the New Deal failed to foster a complete recovery

Introduction

for either the nation or West Virginia before World War II, it did much to make the Depression more tolerable and to encourage in the American people a sense of compassion. That it fell short of its goals is not surprising, given the severity of the problems it faced, the nature of the federal system, and the inconsistency and lack of continuity in the New Deal itself.

Almost three decades ago, James T. Patterson called for a refocusing of New Deal studies away from national government toward the states. The state and city studies that followed have tended to conclude that, despite the popularity of Franklin D. Roosevelt, the New Deal recovery and reform initiatives often fell short of their goals or even had conservative consequences, because local issues and powerful interest groups stood in the way. With few exceptions, the state and local studies have emphasized the lukewarm or unenthusiastic response of state and municipal officials and the relatively limited long-term impact of the New Deal.[6]

West Virginia's experience confirms the distracting influence of local issues and economic interests and the difficulty of persuading state politicians to follow national leadership, even in the Hoover era. Did the voluntarist, privately oriented approach of the Hoover administration hold promise for resolving the Depression? Despite an impressive outpouring of private efforts under the auspices of such organizations as the Red Cross, the American Legion, Community Chest, and American Friends Service Committee, the Republican governor, William Gustavus Conley, came to believe that increases in both state and federal relief spending were imperative, and Conley's director of public welfare, Calvert Estill, became an outspoken advocate of federal relief. Did the activist, federally oriented approach of the New Deal find unquestioning support among state Democratic leaders? Governor Herman Guy Kump and his successor, Homer Adams Holt, although eager to bask in the glow of Franklin D. Roosevelt's political charisma, thought the New Deal threatened state power, and Kump especially resisted the urgent blandishments of federal relief administrator Harry Hopkins to increase state relief spending. Despite the handicaps imposed by the Tax Limitation Amendment of 1932 and the narrow perspectives of statehouse leaders, the New Deal did bring long-term changes to West Virginia. It did not, however, provide enduring solutions to the state's basic economic dilemmas.

This study has been especially influenced by the state and city studies that examine the era as an episode in the transition of America from individualism to a more complex organizational society.[7] The organizational approach encompasses the history of not only the political system and the economy but also of ordinary people: workers, farmers, women, families, and minority groups. Using the organizational theme in her study of Baltimore in the Great Depression, Jo Ann Argersinger finds that the New Deal programs stimulated community organization and citizen participation, even among "the more marginal groups traditionally ignored by two-party politics."[8] Similarly, Thomas Coode and John Bauman, in their study of Pennsylvania, contend that the New Deal "altered the social relationships binding individuals and groups to their communities and the nation."[9] Like these authors, while not eschewing political and institutional history, I have tried to tell the broader story of what happened to ordinary people as they sought order for their lives in the disorder of the Depression. Two major steps toward an organizational society in West Virginia during the Depression era were the United Mine Workers success in organizing the coal miners and the movement away from nearly Elizabethan methods of care for the indigent toward a more bureaucratic and professional system of relief and welfare.

It has also been useful to have at hand for purposes of comparison accounts of the era in other neighboring states. Ronald L. Heinemann describes the traditionalism, balanced economy, and political conservatism that moderated the Depression and the New Deal in Virginia, and George T. Blakey relates a different situation in Kentucky, where the economy was rather narrowly based on agriculture, distilling, and mining. Part of West Virginia's problem was that its governors consciously tried to govern like Virginia conservatives, but the economy in West Virginia was even more narrowly based than Kentucky's.[10]

What follows is organized both chronologically and topically. Chapter 1 summarizes conditions on the eve of the Depression. Chapters 2 and 3 trace the early years and both public and private responses to the crisis. Chapter 4 focuses on the untimely Tax Limitation Amendment of 1932 and its many unintended and largely unfortunate consequences. Chapter 5 analyzes the impact of the National Industrial Recovery Act and the rise of the United Mine Workers as a political as well as an economic force. Chapters 6 and 7 examine efforts to modernize relief and welfare and the clash between the statehouse politicians and agents of federal relief policy. Chapter 8 assesses the

Introduction

impact of New Deal policies on mountain agriculture, 9 focuses on issues of family, gender and race, and 10 traces the bitter contention between the statehouse and federal factions of the Democratic party, culminating in the election of 1940, one of the most bitter intraparty fights in the history of the state.

1
On the Eve

Editors and commentators in West Virginia newspapers and journals met 1929 with the kind of hyperbole that was typical of the twenties. In the *West Virginia Review*, a statewide monthly business journal, Commissioner of Labor Howard S. Jarrett claimed that the records for the past year would disclose "a period of growth unprecedented in the state's history." The outgoing governor, Howard Mason Gore, took satisfaction in the "marvelous changes" in the state during the twenties, and the incoming governor, William Gustavus Conley, promised "a progress and development during the year 1929 rarely experienced in years past."[1]

It had long been the style of West Virginia business and government leaders to speak of business in glowing terms and to ignore or to obscure inconvenient or painful realities.[2] Beyond the formulaic incantations of boosterism, however, lay deep concerns. Even before the fall of 1929, the conventionally recognized date for the beginning of the Depression, crises plagued almost every sector of the state's economy, including the coal industry, agriculture, timber, banking, and construction. West Virginia, nevertheless, had shared in the modernizing transformations of the decade, which had led to improved communications and transportation, broader commercial and cultural opportunities, and increasingly complex organization and bureaucratization in both the public and private spheres.

Gore (1925-1929) and Conley (1929-1933) were the last two governors of a lengthy Republican era. Since its beginning in 1897, coal, railroad, power, and chemical companies with out-of-state headquarters had come to dominate the state economically and politically. This protracted Republican reign had been interrupted only by the wartime governorship of a conservative Democrat, John Jacob Cornwell (1917-1921). While Republican regimes elsewhere had promoted progressivism during the first decade of the century, the West Virginia

Republicans generally served the interests of the economic powers of the state, although they occasionally paid lip service to progressive concepts.[3]

Like much of West Virginia's twentieth-century history, the twenties have received little critical attention from state historians. A recent notable exception is John Hennen's *The Americanization of West Virginia*, which analyzes the period 1916 to 1925, emphasizing the efforts of state elites to inculcate "Americanization," a doctrine that promoted support of both American intervention in World War I and industrial capitalism.[4]

Just as state leaders sought to keep West Virginia in the mainstream of the nation's social, economic, and political currents during the wartime and postwar periods, they also shared the heady atmosphere of the Roaring Twenties as the state underwent some remarkable changes. The size and cost of government grew substantially as the probusiness Republican regime of the twenties, more inclined to neo-mercantilism than laissez faire, provided more public services such as building, maintaining, and policing a system of highways; expanding the department of public safety; building up a state agricultural bureaucracy; overseeing a state system of worker's compensation; increasing the functions of the state auditor; expanding the department of mines; and supporting numerous health and educational institutions. In response to women's suffrage and in acknowledgment of other Republican constituencies, the regime put together the elements of a state welfare system with the establishment of the Bureau of Negro Welfare and Statistics, a Veterans' Service Officer, and the State Board of Children's Guardians. The regime also undertook the building of a costly new capitol on the banks of the Kanawha in east Charleston. Though some of these efforts were sparingly funded, they nevertheless indicate a willingness to expand the power of state government. Part of the motivation, no doubt, was that the patronage generated by expansion provided a means to reward faithful supporters.[5]

An important consequence of the expansive mood of the twenties was an increase in public debt. The state and its subdivisions paid for new schools, government buildings, and roads with proceeds from bonds, taking on what seemed at the time a reasonable burden of debt. When personal and corporate incomes declined and then, in some cases, collapsed in 1927 and afterward, something of a mood of tax revolt against "the high cost of government" grew.[6]

Because many West Virginians depended either directly or indirectly on mining and farming, the concurrent problems of the coal industry and agriculture set the stage for the Depression in the state well before the infamous crash. Coal mining employment peaked in 1923 at 121,000 and then fell to 107,000 by 1929. Production reached high tide at 146 million tons in 1927 and began to recede. West Virginia nevertheless became the leading coal producer among the states in 1928, and state newspapers cheered this news as they might a victory of the university's football team. The Clarksburg *Exponent*, however, pointed out what the boosters preferred to ignore—that during 1928 production actually declined, mining companies failed, and employment in the industry shrank. Coal was a sick industry, the *Exponent* declared. The Charleston *Gazette* sought the silver lining, explaining that the downward trends "cannot mean anything but that the coal business is readjusting itself and lopping away the deadwood."[7]

In the face of bad news, coal industry spokesmen still grasped for superlatives in characterizing the current state and future prospects of coal and West Virginia. In July 1929 an official of the state coal operators association described West Virginia as the leading industrial state of the South, with "riches that surpass the fabled wealth of Croesus." In early October, pioneer coal operator John Laing told a Charleston Kiwanis Club meeting that because of its rich coal supplies, "the eyes of the world "were upon West Virginia, and the state faced "a wonderful future."[8]

In truth, coal in the twenties provided the classic case of an industry beset with overcapacity and its associated ills: market gluts, chronic losses, frequent bankruptcies, and low wages. The industry expanded beyond the capacity of its markets not only because of the demand generated by World War I but also because railroads offered low rates to encourage the buildup of coal traffic. West Virginia, historically something of an interloper in the coal industry, competed with producers nearer to industrial markets by maintaining nonunion operations, and in the case of the Pocahontas and New River fields, by shipping a high grade of low-sulphur coal favored by the metallurgical industries. The success of West Virginia operators in defeating postwar organizing efforts of the United Mine Workers of America (UMWA) encouraged the opening of new mines. Then demand shrank as natural gas, petroleum, and electricity ate into coal markets; new inventions permitted more economical use of coal; and consuming industries grew more slowly. Under these circumstances it became difficult to sell coal at a price that covered costs of production. Operators, faced with substantial fixed costs, sought to avoid bankruptcy by reducing wages or by using labor-saving machinery.[9] Miners, their families, the coal mining communities, and West Virginia suffered the consequences.

Coal operators organized into local associations and a state association primarily to prevent miners from organizing and to control the political environment. The postwar mine wars and treason trials had enfeebled the UMWA and left the union all but defunct in the state.[10] When, in the Jacksonville Agreement of 1924, the UMWA won a favorable contract from the coal operators of the Central Competitive Field (western Pennsylvania, Ohio, Illinois, Indiana), the wage differential between the northern mines and the nonunion mines became so large as to encourage the opening of additional mines in West Virginia and other nonunion states, thereby exacerbating the industry's fundamental dilemma of too many mines and too many miners. In the long run, this was disastrous for the industry and the union as profits fell and northern operators began to abandon the union.[11] The UMWA shrank from 450,000 members to 150,000 as bituminous mine owners in western Pennsylvania, Ohio, and elsewhere rejected union contracts and harshly squelched union strikes. Only in Illinois and the anthracite fields of eastern Pennsylvania did the once-proud UMWA survive.[12]

Most businessmen, editors, and public officials of both parties saw it as something of a patriotic obligation to support the West Virginia operators' determined efforts to keep organized labor out of the state. They accepted the idea, as expressed by Clarence Edwin "Ned" Smith, editor of the Democratic Fairmont *Times*, that the UMWA "pressed down upon the brow of our honest laborers . . . a crown of thorns and crucified our industry upon the cross of conspiracy."[13]

Friendly courts provided the first line of defense against the alleged conspiracy. Cases arising in West Virginia defined the broad limits of injunctive relief in labor disputes and provided judicial blessing for yellow-dog contracts, personal service agreements that as a condition of employment prohibited union membership. In 1912, in what labor historian Irving Bernstein calls the "famous and transcendently important case of *Hitchman Coal and Coke Co. vs Mitchell*," a federal district judge, Alston G. Dayton, issued a sweeping and "perpetual injunction" that enjoined the UMWA from ever approaching Hitchman employees or the Hitchman company premises along the Ohio River in northern West Virginia. The union had violated the Sherman Antitrust Act and sought to induce breach of contract, Dayton held, through a "foul and injurious" common law conspiracy. Reversed in circuit court, the case went before the U.S. Supreme Court, and on December 10, 1917, the Court upheld Dayton's original finding that by seeking to organize the Hitchman miners, the UMWA induced breach of contract. In effect the Court in the Hitchman case endorsed a powerful double-barreled weapon against unionism—the yellow-dog contract and the sweeping injunction.[14]

In the postwar period, southern West Virginia coal operators embraced the *Hitchman* formula with enthusiasm, leading to the notorious case of *United Mine Workers v. Red Jacket Consolidated Coal and Coke.* Red Jacket, one of the largest mining firms in Mingo County, filed a complaint against the UMWA on September 20, 1920, charging the union with inducing Red Jacket employees to violate their personal-services contracts. The Red Jacket case was consolidated with others involving 316 West Virginia mines, representing the bulk of the state's output. Eventually, in 1927, the case reached the U.S. Fourth Circuit Court of Appeals, and Judge John J. Parker, citing the Hitchman case and other precedents, upheld injunctions against the UMWA based on charges that the union, by seeking to interfere with personal-service contracts, had violated the Sherman Act. The Supreme Court refused to hear the case, thereby making antiunion injunctions and yellow-dog contracts the law of the land.[15]

When the UMWA mounted a feeble effort to organize southern West Virginia in 1929, a newspaper editor wrote that the state was "knee deep in protective injunctions against labor agitators."[16] Some operators, in violation of a toothless 1913 law against the practice, continued to use deputized mine guards. They also hired Pinkertons, maintained arsenals, and used searchlights to guard against organizers. The adverse legal atmosphere and the determined efforts of coal operators and their associations succeeded in virtually wiping out the UMWA in West Virginia.[17]

In defending West Virginia against those who would "crucify the coal industry on the cross of conspiracy," coal operators also kept a watchful eye on politics and dominated their county governments and to a large extent the state government as well. Howard B. Lee, who served as the Republican attorney general in both the Gore and Conley administrations, recorded in his memoirs examples of the power of what he called the coal operators' "oligarchy." In coalfield counties the operators had company-paid deputy sheriffs hand out slates at the polls, and they expected miners simply to hand the slate to the company-paid election officials.

In 1927, according to Lee, Governor Gore sought to reform the state workmen's compensation commission by replacing the commissioner, a coal-industry man, with an expert from the insurance industry. The new commissioner, finding the fund insolvent, increased assessments against the coal companies and brought suit against one firm that was $300,000 delinquent. With the election of Conley in November 1928, however, coal operators insisted on reversing the reform. The new legislature in January 1929 did the coal industry's bidding, passing a law eliminating the compensation commission and its offending commissioner. The legislature then passed another law reestablishing the commission, and when Conley took office, he named the former coal operator commissioner to head the "new" commission. The Gore-appointed commissioner refused to vacate his office, but state police troopers under Conley's orders forcibly ejected the recalcitrant commissioner and installed the coal industry's man. Thus, in 1929 the coal industry wielded virtually a veto power over the government.[18]

Coal was only part of the equation. In 1929 more West Virginians were farmers than miners (increasingly some were both), and like coal miners, farmers did not generally share in the prosperity of the twenties. Although the idea of some historians that the advance of industrialism into the mountains during the late nineteenth century had destroyed a static, democratic, and benevolent mountain agrarianism may be somewhat overdrawn, it is certain that the era of the captains of industry profoundly affected mountain farming and left thousands of acres of rich mineral and timber lands in the hands of absentee owners.[19] In 1929, however, farmers still owned about 60 percent of the total acreage in the state. Moreover, West Virginia had less sharecropping and tenantry than elsewhere as most farmers owned the lands they worked. Of the owner-operated farms, 60 percent were free from debt in 1930, more than in any other state.[20]

The lack of debt reflected in part the relatively low purchase price of mountain farms, their small size (averaging only 106 acres, a fraction of which was likely arable, versus the 157-acre national average), and the relative lack of investment in expensive equipment. Because of the rugged topography, mountain farms produced few cash crops, and the U.S. Department of Agriculture classified many as self-sufficing, meaning the farm family consumed as much of their product as they sold or traded. During the twenties more and more farmers supplemented their meager farm income with outside work in the timber industry, coal mining, or elsewhere. In Pendleton County, for example, two-thirds of the county's farmers supplemented their farming with logging, county road work, grist milling, or teaching in the more than one hundred one-room schools in the county.[21]

Census data indicate that the average self-sufficing farm in West Virginia in 1929 earned about $563. From that, farmers had to pay $133 for feed, fertilizer, and labor. Average family expenses were $360. This left only $70 to pay taxes and other expenses.[22]

The typical West Virginia small farm of the twenties had no electricity and so lacked radios (unless battery-operated), refrigerators, electric stoves, and other amenities that town and city dwellers enjoyed. Most farm families had fruit cellars for storage of dried or canned fruits and vegetables, ice houses, and smokehouses for salting and curing meats. They used wood-burning stoves for cooking and heating. By 1929, many farm families had replaced their old kerosene wick lamps with the newer, brighter-burning mantel lamps. Some used gasoline-powered washing machines. Few had piped-in water, and most relied on outdoor privies.[23]

The West Virginia Agricultural Extension Service, led from 1919 to 1933 by a Cornell-educated New Yorker, Nat Terry Frame, was probably the most effective state agency in addressing human needs and seeking to modernize West Virginia agriculture, although it exhibited some bias toward the more commercially oriented farmers of the Farm Bureau organization. Frame, who was active in the national Country Life Movement, probably did more than anyone else during the twenties to promote rural uplift in West Virginia. He and his Extension coworkers were moved to action by data from the 1920 census and a 1922 study of rural child labor, which portrayed living conditions in rural West Virginia in a most unfavorable light. Conducted by the National Child Labor Committee with the assistance of the Agricultural Extension Service and illustrated with the photographs of Lewis Hines, the 1922 study was based on a survey of 657 families in eleven rural West Virginia communities. Among these, net income averaged less than $1,000 per year. Fewer than half the houses had screened windows, and more than 20 percent had no toilets or privies of any kind. The majority of the homesteads lacked lawns, flowers, or shrubbery, and, in the judgment of the surveyors, few provided children much in the way of cultural or intellectual stimulation. Because a large percentage of the men worked away from the farm, women and children did much of the routine farm work.[24]

Although the judgmental tone of the child-labor report reflected in part the urban, middle-class background of its sponsors, Frame and the Extension Service embraced the study as a touchstone and a clarion for change. To improve the conditions of life for rural West Virginians, the Extension Service sought programs to increase the cash income, to improve housing and homestead landscaping, and to offer educational opportunities for rural families, including mining families engaged in gardening. In addition to encouraging rural handicrafts, tourist homes, and state parks and forests as ways to supplement the income of subsistence farm families, the Extension Service also served as a unifying force among state farmers and rural families, leading the way in the organization of boys' and girls' 4-H clubs, women's clubs and annual camps and Country Life conferences. Extension workers organized annual summer camps for boys and girls in most counties of the state, and beginning in 1921 the Extension Service held annual statewide 4-H camps at Jackson's Mill, a 523-acre conference facility in Lewis County paid for by state appropriations and operated by the Extension Service. Jackson's Mill became a major gathering point for many state organizations.[25]

The Agricultural Extension Service cooperated closely with the West Virginia Farm Bureau, which was formed in 1919 by the joining of many county farm bureaus and agricultural societies. In the early twenties, the Farm Bureau promoted cooperatives for purchasing fertilizer and feed. It also sought to help the livestock industry by creating county livestock marketing associations. In 1924 it formed the West Virginia Livestock Marketing Association. Similarly it helped to organize the West Virginia Wool Marketing Association and marketing cooperatives in the poultry and potato industries. The Farm Bureau also helped to bring state farmers together and to promote the rural-life program through the publication of a monthly newspaper, the *West Virginia Farm News*.[26]

Through the lobbying efforts of the Farm Bureau, the agricultural interests of the state put together a bipartisan farm bloc in the legislature in the early twenties, which supported the efforts of the Farm Bureau by enacting legislation supplementing federal legislation in support of cooperatives. The key state measure was the Cooperative

Marketing Act of 1923. County agents helped educate farmers in the operation of cooperatives. The legislature also established the Bureau of Agriculture in 1923, giving both the commissioner of Agriculture and the director of the university Agricultural Extension Service key roles in the state agricultural bureaucracy. In 1924 the agricultural interests helped to elect Republican Howard Mason Gore, a Harrison County farmer, as governor. Gore had experience in the U.S. Department of Agriculture and served briefly in 1924 and 1925 as secretary of agriculture.[27]

The chief agricultural income in the state came from the sale of the livestock and livestock products of the north-central and western parts of the state. In the Monongahela, Kanawha, South Branch, and Greenbrier valleys, cattle grazed fields of bluegrass in bottomlands and on rolling hillsides. Cattle, hogs, sheep, and poultry were produced throughout the state. Hay and corn raising supplemented livestock production. Commercially significant apple production took place in the eastern and northern panhandles and in Clay County, in the central part of the state.[28]

Many rural counties in the western part of the state had declining populations after 1910. Long use of the land with few efforts to maintain fertility had reduced the natural productivity of the soil, and as improved roads reached areas once remote, farm families found that the competition with other agricultural areas made it difficult to earn a satisfactory living. In the absence of information as to their fate, it might be assumed that farmers who left the land in the rural counties during the twenties found work in the mining industry, but, given the decline in mining jobs after 1923, it is more likely that they left the state altogether, blazing the trails from rural Appalachia to midwestern urban centers, which would be condescendingly labeled "hillbilly highways" by the urban media of a later era.[29] This early movement out of marginal agricultural areas was reversed during the Depression, when fewer jobs were available in urban areas, but would resume under the influence of an economic upsurge in the late thirties and forties, stimulated by defense spending and World War II.[30]

Another blow to self-sufficient mountain agriculture was the epidemic of chestnut blight, which by 1929 had destroyed virtually all chestnut trees in West Virginia. Many small farmers had relied on chestnuts for food and for livestock feed, especially for hogs, which had been allowed to forage freely in the forest. The chestnut blight denied to the mountain farmers an item that might have helped them to weather the Depression.[31]

With cash income limited, one of the major problems faced by subsistence farmers as the decade wore on was the increase in the property tax. Principally a real-estate tax, the property tax provided the major source of revenue for local government, which in West Virginia was responsible for most road building and maintenance as well as schools, law enforcement, and care of indigents. From 1913 to 1929, the average tax per $100 of real estate rose from $0.44 to $1.26 in West Virginia while the national average went from $0.55 to $1.19.[32] Increases in taxes helped push many farmers to seek more cash-producing work off the farms, sell their land or livestock, or surrender their lands to the sheriff to sell at auction for nonpayment of taxes.

The timber industry, one of the chief sources of earnings supplements for self-sufficing farmers seeking cash, also fell on hard times after having reached its peak in the years before World War I, leaving farmers and timbermen unemployed and the magnificent forests that had covered the state only memories. The timber resources of the state had been exploited with little concern for the future. The cost to the environment in loss of topsoil through erosion, siltation of streams, and consequent flooding was immeasurable. Moreover, employees of failed timber companies remained in rural West Virginia, swelling the numbers of stranded industrial workers and increasing the pressure on mountain farmland.[33] By the end of the twenties, historian Jack Temple Kirby has written, many of the rural areas of Appalachia were "ripped up overpopulated mountain slums, their people abandoned by the sick timber and coal industries, their land inadequate for a return to subsistence farming."[34]

Despite the problems, Nat T. Frame, the state Extension director, later remembered 1928 as a year of growing confidence among West Virginia farmers. "There was an awareness," Frame wrote in his memoirs, "of the increasing impact of the outside world on rural life in West Virginia." Though job opportunities in the booming industries of America steadily reduced the farm population, those who remained believed that a better life on the farm was possible. In 1929, the Farm Women's Bureau set $1,200 as the goal for a minimum annual income. As hard roads shifted the centers of trade and community activities, legislation and organization changed the farmers' marketing opportunities and practices. "Financial motivation, extension education, and religious duty," Frame wrote, "were giving farmers confidence in their ability to maintain the $1200 minimum level of living that women were talking about."[35] Of course subsistence farmers had little hope of reaching the $1,200 goal. Ironically, many of the Extension activities as well as the new roads unintentionally encouraged youth not to dedicate themselves to a life of subsistence mountain farming, but to seek cash-earning opportunities in towns and cities.[36] Although the lure of modernization beckoned, for some, particularly for those who had committed their lives to a piece of hillside or bottomland ground, it was difficult to leave.[37]

Given the troubles in mining and agriculture, banks also struggled. Their total number fell from 349 in 1921 to 310 in 1929. Though consolidation accounted for some of the decline, most of it reflected bank failures.[38] The total assessed valuation of all categories of property declined annually after 1925, exacerbating the growing fiscal crisis of local government.[39]

Although West Virginians did not fully share in the national prosperity and the state's socioeconomic system faced grave challenges, the twenties nevertheless brought substantial change, and some of it helped to obscure the darker sides of West Virginia's society and economy and to give a sense of lift and movement that encouraged the boosters to believe their own propaganda.

With the Nineteenth Amendment, West Virginia's political parties opened their doors to women, and several became active politicians, serving on state and local party committees and running for political offices. In 1922 Anna Johnson Gates, a Democrat of Charleston, became the first woman elected to the state's House of Delegates, and in 1924 two other women were elected to the House, Mrs. T.J. Davis, a Republican from Fayette County, and Dr. Harriet B. Jones, a Republican from Marshall County. In 1926, Governor Gore appointed three women to serve out their husbands' terms: Hannah Washington Alexander Cooke, a Democrat of Jefferson County; Fannie Auschutz Hall, a Democrat of New Martinsville; and Minnie Buckingham Harper, a Republican of Keystone, McDowell County. Although the appointment was largely honorific, Harper had the distinction of being the first black woman state legislator in the United States.[40]

One of the most remarkable women politicians in the state was Izetta Jewel Brown, who came to West Virginia in 1914, when she married William Gay Brown, Jr., of Kingwood. When her husband died in 1916, Brown took over management of his farm. After studying agriculture and animal husbandry at West Virginia University, she established a modern dairy operation and became active in state agricultural activities, working closely with Nat T. Frame. At the Democratic National Convention of 1920, she seconded the nomination of John W. Davis for vice-president. In 1922 she ran in the state Democratic primary for the U.S. Senate and lost narrowly to Matthew Mansfield Neely. In 1924 she again sought the Senate nomination and, in another close race, lost to a former senator, William E. Chilton. At the national convention in 1924, she seconded Davis for the presidential nomination, and her name was among those placed before the convention for the vice presidential nomination. In 1927 she married Hugh Miller and, no doubt to the great relief of male leaders of the state party, moved to New York. She ran unsuccessfully for Congress in 1930 in Franklin D. Roosevelt's home district and later became a regional supervisor for New Deal agencies.[41]

The most prominent Republican woman was Lenna Lowe Yost of Huntington. A member of the state board of education throughout the twenties, she actively promoted women's suffrage and prohibition and organized the Republican women of West Virginia immediately following the adoption of the Nineteenth Amendment. In 1929 she sat on the executive committee of the Republican National Committee.[42]

In spite of the selections to legislative seats, appointment to committees, and the political prominence of a few, most women remained on the sidelines of state political power. In 1929, only one woman remained in the House of Delegates, Frances Irvine Radenbaugh, a Republican attorney from Parkersburg elected in 1928, and no woman had yet served in the West Virginia Senate.[43] The only state agencies in which women had substantial influence were the Board of Children's Guardians, a predecessor agency of the Department of Welfare, and the Extension Service. In 1929 Sue A. Staunton of Charleston presided over the bipartisan nonsalaried board, Mary L. Yager administered the work as executive secretary, and the nine field agents were all women.[44] The Extension Service hired women as home demonstration agents in many counties across the state.[45]

Lobbying by the new voters contributed to a spate of welfare laws including a law that enabled counties to provide pensions for mothers with dependent children. By 1927 thirty-five of the fifty-five counties had mothers pension funds. In 1923 the legislature authorized counties to establish welfare boards or to appoint a county welfare secretary, and in 1925 the legislature established a Crippled Children's Council, which relied heavily upon funding by civic organizations.[46]

Women also played leading roles in religious and private charitable organizations. In 1922 at Osage on Scotts Run, a mining district near Morgantown in Monongalia County, two Methodist women, Edna Muir and Mrs. Frank C. Shriver, rented space for a settlement house where they could work with the immigrant women and children. After their original building burned, Methodist women's home missionary societies in the state helped them to raise $20,000 for a substantial new brick structure, which included a chapel, gymnasium, classrooms, and an apartment for two resident deaconesses. Dedicated in September, 1927, the settlement house continued to receive support from Methodist women throughout the state.[47]

In 1928 the Presbyterian Board of Home Missions hired a young graduate of Wooster College, Mary Behner, to start a mission in Scotts Run. In October 1929, after just a year on the job, Behner's mobilization of student volunteers from nearby West Virginia University was attracting attention in the home-missions field.[48]

Most West Virginia women, of course, were neither politicians nor settlement-house workers. In boosting West Virginia as "the Nation's Treasure Chest," Jesse V. Sullivan of the West Virginia Coal Association pointed out the low number of women in the labor force and asserted that because of the state's wealth, fewer women had to work in West Virginia than in other states.[49] It was true, according to a report of the state Bureau of Labor in 1926, that while women made up 21 percent of the national industrial labor force, only 13 percent of the state industrial labor force was made up of women.

But the scarcity of women on payrolls did not reflect unusual wealth. Actually, outside of school teaching, there were few paying jobs available for women, and those available were primarily in the needle trades or laundries, two industries that employed more women than men. Ironically these industries also required the longest work days, and West Virginia was one of four states that neither placed limits on women's hours nor provided any protective legislation for working women.[50]

Though their names appeared infrequently on payrolls, most West Virginia women worked long and difficult hours, because many were either farmers' wives or coal miners' wives, laboring at onerous tasks unlisted in any official accounting. One of the characteristics of West

Virginia's self-sufficing farms noted by the 1922 study of rural life was that more than one-third of the men worked elsewhere for wages and left their wives and children to do most of the farm work, which consisted of physically demanding manual labor such as feeding and watering stock, carrying wood or coal, carrying water from the spring, and hoeing and raking, as well as the customary house chores such as cooking, washing, and child care. The number of men who worked off the farm surely increased as the decade wore on.[51] Miners' wives bore heavy burdens not only literally but psychologically. They faced the insecurities of life in the coal country, where the threat of death or serious injury to the male breadwinner loomed over the family. Between 1897 and 1928, more than ten thousand men died in West Virginia's coal mines, a rate of more than 330 per year, and in 1928 alone 475 died. [52]

West Virginia women, like women elsewhere, sought balm for their souls and order for their lives and society by creating and joining a myriad of religious, civic, business, and professional organizations. In 1920 the West Virginia Farm Bureau organized a state farm women's organization, which promoted Country Life conferences, organized many local home demonstration clubs, raised money to fund college educations for 4-H girls, and held an annual meeting at Jackson's Mill. By 1929 the farm women's organization had four thousand members in two hundred local organizations.[53] In 1929 the West Virginia Federation of Women's Clubs encompassed 117 local clubs, the West Virginia Federation of Business and Professional Women had nine clubs in eight cities, and nine cities had Quota clubs.[54]

Despite concentrations of blacks and immigrants in mining districts, by 1930 West Virginia was 90 percent American-born white and overwhelmingly Protestant. The foreign-born element in the population actually declined over the decade. Towns and cities continued to grow although at a slower pace than during the previous decade. By 1930 the state was 28 percent urban, and ten cities had populations of ten thousand or more. The largest were Huntington (75,572), Wheeling (61,559) and Charleston (60,408). The smaller cities were Parkersburg, Clarksburg, Fairmont, Bluefield, Morgantown, Martinsburg, and Moundsville.[55]

The political influence of the relatively small African American population in West Virginia was heightened because it was concentrated in the southern mining regions. Though segregated in schools and welfare institutions, blacks experienced fewer incidents of mob violence and endured fewer debilitating forms of labor exploitation in West Virginia than in the Deep South. The state legislature never disenfranchised black voters or passed Jim Crow laws to segregate blacks on common carriers.[56] Indeed, the arrival of black voters in southern mining counties in the late nineteenth century helped Republicans capture political control of the state from the Democrats, and in 1924 a black Charleston politician proclaimed that "the Negro is the balance of power in the State." Because they did have the vote and supported the prevailing party, black politicians had sufficient leverage to exact patronage and favors from the white political bosses of the Republican party.[57]

In 1921 the state legislature established the Bureau of Negro Welfare and Statistics, which in its biennial reports gave circumspect voice to African American concerns. Black appointees ran the segregated black school system, and black teachers worked under the same qualifications-based salary scale as white teachers.[58]

Blacks also organized for political purposes, largely in adjunct Republican groups such as the McDowell County Colored Republican Organization, the most powerful black Republican organization in the state. Also useful in mobilizing blacks for social and political purposes were the West Virginia chapters of the National Association for the Advancement of Colored People (NAACP). Founded in 1909, the NAACP had no chapters in West Virginia until 1918, when the Kanawha County chapter began, but by 1932 there were nearly a dozen in southern West Virginia.[59]

In McDowell County, blacks often served as justices of the peace, constables, and members of town councils. During the twenties blacks gained representation on Republican committees in most southern West Virginia counties, and over the decade, several blacks were elected from southern counties to the House of Delegates, though in 1929 only one remained, Tyler Edward Hill of McDowell County, who had served as director of the Bureau of Negro Welfare and Statistics from 1921 to 1927. Black politicians enjoyed some success in garnering support for black institutions such as West Virginia State College and Bluefield Collegiate Institute as well as establishing new institutions such as the Denmar Tuberculosis Sanitarium, the West Virginia Colored Insane Asylum, the West Virginia Colored Deaf and Blind School, the State Industrial School for Colored Boys, the State Industrial School for Colored Girls, and the State Home for Aged and Infirm Colored Men and Women.[60]

The increase of the black population in the southern mining counties also led to the growth of small black-owned businesses such as barber shops, grocery stores, lunch rooms, and cleaning and pressing shops. C.H. James and Son wholesale house of Charleston was one of the leading black-owned businesses of its kind in the state, perhaps in the country.[61]

Changes in transportation and communications did much to break down the tendency toward insularity and isolation in rural West Virginia and to promote the growth of a more cash-oriented economy. The rise of the automobile led to a "Good Roads Movement," which sought "to lift West Virginia out of the mud." Voters approved some $85 million in road improvement bond issues from 1919 to 1929, and state appropriations and federal aid added some $15 million. When the state road system began in 1921, none of the larger cities of the state were connected by an improved road of any type. By 1930, West Virginians were driving 230,000 automobiles over the 4,311 miles of state roads constructed by the bond money and some 32,000 miles of county roads. All but one of the state's counties had at least one hard-surfaced outlet to improved roads connecting with the rest of the state. The arrival of roads, automobiles, and trucks was a powerful inducement to subsistence farmers to produce more cash.[62]

Road building stimulated many new enterprises as automobiles, trucks, and buses competed for space on the growing network. In 1923 the legislature authorized the issuance of bus licenses, and within the next five years the state became honeycombed with bus lines. By 1929, eighty-six bus companies and five hundred buses provided intrastate transportation, and in cities like Charleston, Wheeling, and Morgantown, the buses began to take the place of electric railway or streetcar companies. Road building as well as the spread of dealerships, service stations, bus stations, garages, and other automobile-related enterprises added new dimensions to the state's economy and society. Automobiles and buses relieved West Virginians from their dependence on railroads for intrastate transportation, making it easier for farmers or rural people to travel to towns or mines to market farm products, to seek work that would put cash in their hands, or to take advantage of commercial or entertainment opportunities in the towns and cities. The expansion of bus lines enabled salesmen to peddle their wares in rural towns previously inaccessible. Vendors could market agricultural and other products from outside the state, creating deadly competition for local farmers, many of whom found the new roads useful as escape routes to brighter opportunities in cities and towns in West Virginia or beyond.[63]

The new roads and growing numbers of cars, trucks, and buses brought changes in the lives of rural West Virginians. The poet Louise McNeill, remembering the arrival of the road in the southern West Virginia farm community of her youth, writes poignant lines that could serve as an epitaph of a dying way of life:

When the new road was finished, it was hard, smooth, and gray-colored, and the Model T's came chugging along it, and the fancy Chevrolets, Maxwells, and Jewetts. When you went in by horse or foot, you could live almost anywhere, and the whole Swago Mountain country had been scattered with wilderness farms, houses, and old one-room schools. But after the road was finished, new houses and new school-houses were built alongside it, and then the barns came down too. Then the gas stations and the Dew Drop Inns. Back in the hills, the old houses and schoolhouses rotted down, blackberry vines crept over the broken porches, and the eyeless windows stared out at the encroaching wilderness.[64]

Another sign of rural transformation was the decline of churches, once an integral part of rural mountain life. A survey made by the state ministers conference in 1930 found most rural churches faced declining congregations and incomes. The state Extension official concerned with rural churches blamed the decline on several things including the good roads, which enticed some rural folks to leave the country for the city and others to go traveling on Sundays; poor agricultural methods, which contributed to lower farm incomes; and the decline of incomes from coal, oil, and gas.[65]

Though no poet has described it, the new technology also transformed the state's towns and cities. In modest imitation of their counterparts in larger and more affluent urban centers, real estate promoters now developed land more distant from downtown, and previously inaccessible hillsides became the new residential areas of an automobile-driving middle class. In 1929, sixty-three building and loan associations offered support to the builders, real-estate agents, and their customers.[66]

The emphasis on organization affected West Virginia's cultural life as entertainment, once largely provided by family and friends, became a business carried out by large organizations.[67] Motion pictures and radio helped create a greater sense of cultural community as West Virginians could see and hear the same entertainment as people in all parts of the country. Many cities, towns, and coal camps had movie houses, and the rise of "talkies" put some musicians (who had provided musical background to the silent movies) out of work. Radio came slowly to the state after Wheeling's WWVA first went on the air on December 13, 1926. By the 1930 census, only about one in four West Virginia families had radio sets.[68]

Most rural West Virginians still had no electricity. In 1929 there were forty-eight electric companies, but most were small. The largest, and one of the largest public utilities in the state, was Appalachian Electric Power Company, assessed by the Public Service Commission at $37 million.[69] In 1929 the Monongahela West Penn Public Service Company, another of the larger utilities, held a conference of Northern West Virginia extension workers to begin planning for a rural electrification project, but the coming of the Depression would delay the electrification of rural West Virginia for many years.[70]

An increased interest in sports such as baseball and boxing and the spread of movies and streetlights helped to enliven the cities and towns even at night and on Sundays. In 1929 Clarence Edwin "Ned" Smith, editor of the Fairmont *Times*, inquired of J.H. Long, a fellow journalist, concerning reported "liberal tendencies" as to Sunday activities in Huntington. Long reported that Sunday baseball had been enjoyed by large crowds for several years. At first police interfered, and opponents undertook court action to stop Sunday baseball, but after a while "no one cared." More recently the city had been the scene of a battle over Sunday movies. The ministerial association had gone to the city board of commissioners and persuaded them to enact an ordinance prohibiting Sunday movies. The citizens board, however, unanimously vetoed the ordinance. The ministers appealed to the prosecuting attorney, but he concluded that a state law prohibiting Sunday labor was too vague to halt the showing of movies. Long reported further that in addition to baseball and movies, Huntingtonians were "now staging boxing in an open air arena." Smith, who had an interest in a local hotel, hoped that similar activities could be promoted in Fairmont, where things tended to be slow on weekends as many people left town.[71]

Another industry that flourished nationally and in West Virginia was the manufacture of chemicals. American reliance on Germany for chemicals ended when World War I came, and during the war, the federal government built plants in the Kanawha Valley near Charleston at Nitro and Belle to manufacture explosives and mustard gas. Private firms such as Union Carbide and Du Pont also opened chemical plants. After the war, the Kanawha Valley chemical industry turned to the production of synthetic chemicals. In 1930 five chemical plants were producing some sixty chemicals in the valley.[72] A needed source of jobs and economic diversity, the chemical industry, like other major state industries, unfortunately contributed to air and water pollution.

Construction constituted a major component of the national prosperity of the twenties, and echoes of this are seen in West Virginia in the building of roads, public buildings, homes, and commercial buildings. Several counties built new courthouses, and the state erected a new capitol, selling bonds to finance the project. One of the largest banks in the state, the Kanawha Valley Bank of Charleston, dedicated a new twenty-story building in 1929. Historian John Alexander Williams has noted the clubby confluence of power that gathered under the roof of the new structure, including the Chesapeake and Potomac Telephone Company, the influential law firm Brown, Jackson, and Knight, and more than twenty coal companies.[73]

Completed in 1928, the Kanawha Valley Bank building epitomized a twenties building boom in Charleston that included several schools and churches, the first and second units of the capitol, the Daniel Boone Hotel, and the Diamond department store. In 1927, construction in Charleston fell to its lowest level since 1921, but the builders were busy again in 1928. In 1929, the downward trends of 1927 resumed.[74]

At the eastern end of the state, in the small agricultural county of Jefferson, editor John S. Alfriend noted a similar pattern of public construction in 1929. During the year an "architecturally magnificent" new district high school had been completed, and on Harewood Avenue in Charles Town, there was a new "colored" school "equal if not superior to any colored school in a town of this size in the South." Charles Town was also erecting a "White Way" and improving its streets. Shepherdstown had a new high school, and Harpers Ferry would soon begin work on a new school. Alfriend believed it "the most notable single year in the town's and county's history."[75]

The evidences of growth and change supported the boosters' contentions and helped to obscure the vulnerability of the state's economy. The Republican party derived the chief political benefits from the prevailing myopia. Over the decade, a majority of West Virginians voted for both state and national Republicans, and the Democratic party faced an uphill struggle. Even when John W. Davis, a native son, headed the national Democratic ticket in 1924, a majority of West Virginians voted for the Republicans Calvin Coolidge for president and Howard M. Gore for governor.[76]

In 1928, Republicans continued their mastery as a majority carried the state for Herbert Hoover over Alfred E. Smith. William Gustavus Conley defeated J. Afred Taylor for governor, and former governor Henry Drury Hatfield defeated the incumbent Democrat, Matthew Mansfield Neely, for a seat in the U.S. Senate. The two seats up for election on the state Supreme Court of Appeals went to Republicans, preserving the Republican monopoly of the five seats on the high court. In the state legislature, Republicans also continued to dominate with substantial majorities in both the Senate and the House of Delegates.[77]

After the 1928 election, Franklin Delano Roosevelt, who had campaigned in West Virginia as the vice-presidential candidate in 1920, asked leading Democrats in each state why the Democrats continued to lose. Twenty-six West Virginians who had been delegates to the national convention jotted replies to Roosevelt's query. Most focused on the issue that was peculiar to the 1928 election—religion. They believed that Republicans had avoided the important issues by successfully exploiting the Catholicism of the Democratic presidential candidate, Alfred E. Smith, before the heavily Protestant West Virginia electorate. Another major theme of the West Virginia delegates was that the Republican-controlled press of West Virginia had sold the electorate on prosperity "although many walk the streets jobless." "If it were not for the Baltimore *Sun* and the New York *World*," wrote Mrs. Percy Byrd of Clarksburg, "one would perish in this state for liberal political food."[78]

Although it is by no means clear that Democratic control of the state would have made any real difference given the bipartisan commitment of political leaders to the coal industry's conspiracy thesis, Mrs. Byrd was right about Republican control of the state's press. Of twenty-nine daily newspapers, only eleven were nominally Democrat, and in Bluefield, Beckley, and Clarksburg, Republican owners published both Republican and Democratic dailies. Of some 125 weeklies, fifty were Democratic. The Democratic Charleston *Gazette* enjoyed the highest daily circulation, with twenty-eight thousand. The *Gazette's* afternoon Republican rival, the *Daily Mail*, was a close second with twenty-five thousand. The Republican Huntington *Herald-Dispatch* had a circulation of nearly twenty-one thousand. Most of the dailies had circulations under five thousand. The largest chain, controlling some fifteen newspapers nominally both Democratic and Republican, was owned by Herschel C. Ogden of Wheeling, a maverick Republican who often campaigned for tax reform and against "the interests," much to the consternation of the dominant conservative wing of the Republican party and even to the dismay of conservative Democrats.[79]

Despite its strong grip on the state's political institutions, the election of 1928 proved to be the Republican party's last hurrah, and the newly elected governor, William G. Conley, would soon find himself and the state facing a crisis of unprecedented proportions. The Great Depression grew from circumstances beyond the borders of West Virginia, but the nature of the state's economy and society made it especially vulnerable to the wrenching changes of the Depression decade. The further advance of a cash-oriented economy during the twenties had undermined the viability of the traditional self-sufficient mountain agriculture. At the same time, the lumber and coal industries, after having heedlessly denuded mountains and polluted the streams, passed their peaks as employers, leaving stranded families the choice of using the new roads as escape routes to jobs in industrial centers or struggling to make a living from their mountain farms. The Depression for a time foreclosed the escape option, and during the early thirties, many unemployed workers had little choice but try to coax a living from the land.

2

Drought and Depression

On Thursday, October 24, 1929, responding to the news of rapidly declining stock prices on the New York Stock Exchange, throngs of Charleston businessmen and stock speculators rushed to the capital city's two main trading centers—Harris Winthrop and Company, and Stein Brothers and Boyce—to watch the ticker tape recite its disheartening news. At noon the ticker announcements escalated from sales of thousands of shares to sales of millions. The market closed at three o'clock, but running more than four hours behind, the ticker did not stop until seven thirty. By the end of the day, many local fortunes had disappeared.[1]

Economists and historians point out that the stock market crash was not a cause of the Depression but a symptom of the troubles that plagued the national and world economy. For much of the generation that lived through the Depression and certainly for those who were immediately hurt by the crash, Black Thursday served as a historic bench mark and symbol for the beginning of the Depression, but hard times had arrived earlier and in less dramatic fashion in West Virginia's coal camps and small towns and in its rural and agricultural districts.[2]

As the Depression deepened in West Virginia, it produced conditions that were among the worst in the country. Coal production fell from 146 million tons in 1927 to 83.3 million in 1932, and some thirty-three thousand coal industry jobs disappeared, leaving many coal miners and their families trapped in futility and hopelessness. From 1929 to 1932, one hundred banks collapsed, accelerating the rate of bank failure that had already been high in the twenties. Deposits dwindled from $328 million to $213 million. Farmers were devastated not only by the collapse of farm prices but also by adverse weather conditions, including widespread severe drought in the summers of 1930 and 1932 and severe flooding of the Kanawha River in July 1932. Farmers also suffered from the consequences of long-term misuse and abuse of the land. Manufacturing weathered the early months well, and the value of product actually increased in 1930 by more than $60 million and the average wage also rose slightly. But in 1931, manufacturing also collapsed, as value of product fell some $250 million and wages tumbled.[3]

The state, county, and municipal governments in West Virginia, like governments everywhere, were stunned by the collapse and ill-prepared by either philosophy or experience to deal with the crisis that began in 1927, grew in intensity at the end of 1929, and then persisted through months and years. Conventional belief had it that economic downturns were simply necessary and even beneficial characteristics of business cycles. From time to time, "readjustments" were necessary, and experience demonstrated that indeed recovery and resurgence eventually followed downturns. Although the classical economic theory of conventional wisdom did not closely approximate the real world, it had a compelling logic and simplicity that its followers were loath to abandon. Despite the Depression's persistence in the face of the painful readjustments, businessmen and government officials tended to insist on unrealistic policies. The prime example was the nearly universal adherence to the idea of the balanced budget and strict economy in expenditures. In summarizing the vagaries of theories and follies of policies followed at the time, the historian John A. Garraty has expressed what is essentially the view of the Depression-era British economist John Maynard Keynes: "With prices falling, unemployment high, and economic activity stagnating, deliberate deficit financing would have provided salutary stimulation," but it was the conventional wisdom to maintain rigid economies in order to balance budgets.[4]

Not only did the practice of "rigid economies" reinforce the deflationary forces in the economy, it supplied governments unwilling to undertake the task of unemployment relief a rationale with which to justify governmental parsimony. The need for relief, however, soon reached proportions beyond the ken of local governments and private charities. Should governments fly in the face of classical theory and attend to the problem with government programs? Did state governments have the knowledge, administrative experience, and competence (what in another context has been called "state capacity")[5] to address the issues? If statesmen the world over were baffled by the Depression and often followed wrong-headed policies, it should be no surprise that state and local officials in West Virginia, who faced some of the worst conditions in the country from 1929 to 1933, were also perplexed and often ineffective.[6] What is surprising, because it is an untold and largely forgotten story, is that West Virginia's leaders responded to the initial crisis as well as leaders in most other states.

William Gustavus Conley, the eighteenth governor of West Virginia, took the oath of office on March 4, 1929, in the state armory on Capitol Street after plans for an open-air ceremony succumbed to an unexpected rainstorm. Born in Kingwood, Preston County, in 1866, Conley had worked briefly in agriculture, coal, and lumber as a young man. He taught school, studied at West Virginia University, was elected Preston County superintendent of schools while still a student at the university, and became an attorney. During his career he served as a councilman and mayor in both Kingwood and Parsons and as prosecuting attorney of Tucker County. Appointed to fill an unexpired term as attorney general by Governor William M. O. Dawson in 1908, he was subsequently elected to a full term, which ended in 1913. Conley remained in Charleston, active in Republican politics, the coal industry, and the practice of law (representing corporate clients such as the Baltimore and Ohio Railroad and the Pennsylvania Railroad system) until he was elected governor, defeating Democrat J. Alfred Taylor of Fayetteville by 49,236 votes.[7]

Nothing in Conley's long career in state politics and government prepared him for the crisis-laden governorship, but in some respects he responded to the Depression with more willingness to adopt new ways than his Democratic successors. In his inaugural address, he emphasized the typical "good government" themes of the era: economy in administration, conservation, the need for new business and industry, good roads, and good schools.[8] Before his term ended, however, he faced many desperate problems, which drove him to advocate two propositions that were heretical for a conservative Republican or any political leader in times when the conventional wisdom called for slashing budgets and cutting taxes: that the state should impose new taxes to raise money for relief and that the state should seek direct federal aid for relief.[9]

The state constitution and political realities made Conley a virtual lame duck from the beginning of his term, and the early realization that he had no political future perhaps freed him from conventional political considerations. The biennial meeting of the legislature began in January 1929, before the inauguration of the governor, operating under the budget of the outgoing Gore administration. Conley had no opportunity to put a program before the legislature until January 1931, after the midterm election in which his party lost control of the House of Delegates, and his administration had to face a new generation of Democrats eager to uncover evidence of Republican wrongdoing. Moreover, the governor shared control of the budget preparation process with the other six elective state officers. From the beginning of his administration, Conley decried the weaknesses of his office and advocated constitutional amendments to change the date of inauguration and to make the governor the chief budget officer.[10]

During his first year, Conley pushed for completion of the new capitol building, and at the behest of the state coal operators, reorganized the workmen's compensation department. He also named a constitutional revision committee, reorganized the state road commission, and commissioned a study of the state road system. Conducted by Floyd E. Cunnyngham, who later became a member of the road commission, the study addressed criticisms of the system by calling for greater centralization of administration and urging the establishment of construction priorities which would lead to a "blue network" or arterial system of roads.[11]

Conley called an extraordinary session of the legislature in 1929, but he limited its mandate to approving a revised legal code. As the economic crisis deepened, he could have called another special session, and members of both parties urged him to do so from time to time, but like most governors during this time, he temporized, perhaps fearing to unleash partisan political squabbling and hoping that somehow things would right themselves. Finally, desperate budget problems and the need for a relief program moved him to call a special session in July 1932.[12]

After the stock market crash, Conley followed the lead of President Hoover in emphasizing confidence in business conditions. He joined with eight prominent businessmen in the *West Virginia Review*'s New Year issue to consider the question "What of West Virginia in 1930?" Conley reported that a survey of business conditions he had made at the request of President Hoover gave "every reason to be proud and happy for general business conditions in West Virginia." All of the businessmen except Justus Collins, a leading coal operator of southern West Virginia, expressed similar optimism. Rejecting the conventional boosterism, Collins warned: "Business has been sorely wounded, and the condition of the patient is not definitely known."[13]

As it turned out, 1930 was a dismal year marked by a devastating drought, continuing business decline, and the beginning of the end of the long Republican dominion in West Virginia. Not only did the collapse of the coal industry put a severe strain on relief resources, the drought of 1930 devastated agriculture and left many mountain farmers in desperate straits. While coal miners suffered from growing unemployment, farmers faced a nightmare summer of parched fields, dried-up streams, and ruined crops. Farm income in the state plummeted a startling $30 million. Farmers' purchasing power fell by half, and because they needed cash or lacked sufficient water to carry the livestock through the drought, they were forced to sell foundation stocks. Farmers needed help to obtain seed, feed, and fertilizer as well as food and clothes for themselves and their families. Governor Conley told the legislature that "no such blow has ever been experienced by the farmers of this state, and even with the most favorable conditions it will take years for West Virginia agriculture to heal its wounds."[14]

The drought was also costly to state forests. Some 2,622 forest fires damaged 350,000 acres of woodland. Thousands of acres were destroyed in the Monongahela National Forest. A state forester conservatively estimated the cost to woodlands at $500,000 and noted that counties, already financially pinched, had to find money to fight the fires.[15]

The suffering of the farmers produced reverberations throughout the state's economy. Bankers had loaned money for spring seed and stock, and with little or no harvest, farmers could not repay the loans. Merchants in rural towns could not sell their merchandise. Counties and school districts encountered growing agitation from farmers to cut the school year, to stop adding mothers to local pension rolls, and to halt local public improvements or road building and repair. These activities depended on local levies, and farmers wanted the levies cut. In some counties farmers called for a four-month school term, so that the levy could be cut in half. Some local officials argued against cutting local spending and activities, because spending cuts would also mean increased unemployment as road workers, construction and maintenance workers, and school teachers were thrown out of work.[16]

Families suffered tremendous strains under the impact of the drought and unemployment. Desperate and harassed parents sometimes even deserted their spouses and children. Some unemployed fathers left their families in the hope that their wives and children could then be cared for by some county or state agency. Though desertion by fathers was more frequent, Mary Yager, executive secretary of the state Board of Children's Guardians, reported that more mothers had deserted their children in 1930 than in any year on record. Miss Yager also noted that the state homes for white children at Elkins and for black children at Huntington were filled to capacity, and more homeless children were being placed under the guardianship of the board every week. Part of the reason for the overburdening of the children's homes was that farm families, who customarily took into their homes a great many children who were wards of the state, were no longer willing to take on the responsibility. Indeed many farm families who had been caring for child wards of the state now appealed to the board to take back the children, fearing that they could no longer feed and clothe them.[17]

The agents of the Board of Children's Guardians reported numerous grim stories. A farmer cremated his dead infant, because he could not afford a funeral; a mother driven mad by hunger and worry drowned her two children; and a ten-year-old girl who had been left home alone for five days after her father had been arrested was found nearly blind from cataracts, barefoot in winter, and suffering from frostbitten toes.[18] The counties still had poorhouses, and one of the worst consequences of the growing child-care disaster was that many children ended up living in dormitories of the county poorhouses, sharing beds with the elderly poor.[19] Health statistics also marked the state as one of the unhealthiest for children. In 1931 the state had the highest infant mortality rate in the country. The typhoid death rate was four times the national average of 3.1 per 100,000. As a consequence of statewide vaccination programs, the rates of death from diphtheria and smallpox were falling, but deaths from tuberculosis, though falling, remained high.[20]

President Hoover responded to the drought by calling a conference of the governors of the affected states in mid August 1930. Before his departure for Washington to attend the conference, Governor Conley received a message from the West Virginia Farm Bureau and county agents assembled in Jackson's Mill for their annual meeting. The gathering focused on the problems of the drought and heard detailed reports from farm agents on the conditions in different counties. The message to Conley was that "thousands of families are now in want and will need help." As the first rains in weeks fell across the state on August 14, Conley reported to the White House governors conference that West Virginia was sound "economically, industrially and financially," but that every county in the state had suffered to some extent from the drought. He urged that farmers be given additional credit and longer payment terms.[21]

The conference agreed to a plan of drought relief that called for the establishment of state committees to oversee relief operations; aid to farmers in obtaining loans; assistance from the Red Cross; reduced railway rates for food, feed, and livestock; and expedition of federal road spending to give employment to drought-stricken farmers. President Hoover told reporters that the conference had agreed that the burden of meeting the crisis rested upon the affected states and counties themselves.[22]

Upon his return, Governor Conley met with state officials and named a drought-relief committee, appointing former governor Howard Mason Gore as chairman. Gore's committee met several times and heard suggestions as to what might be done to help farmers through the crisis. A major problem was credit. Typical was the report of R.F. Forth of Putnam County, who told the committee that the most immediate need was for small loans that would provide money enough "to buy feed, keep chickens, horses and cows until next summer." Many also needed money for food and clothing.[23]

With state banks in desperate circumstances, finding adequate credit to meet the need proved impossible. Former governor John J. Cornwell, a member of the committee, said that the money needed "to tide these people over the hard period ahead" must be furnished by the businessmen of the towns and cities and the wealthy farmers. Gray Silver, a prominent Martinsburg farmer who had helped the Farm Bureau lobby Congress for cooperative legislation, urged a more organized effort to secure credit for farmers through the federal government. Suggesting that Congress might have to appropriate federal money to help farmers meet their tax bills, he estimated that the amount to help those in need would not exceed the cost of one battleship. Silver's idea that the federal government should play a role in relief fell on deaf ears in the Hoover administration, where the prevailing philosophy was that the burden rested with county committees that were to be organized by county farm agents. These committees were told to make it clear to farmers and local authorities that neither the state nor federal governments had money to give away.[24]

In the end the drought-relief program proved inadequate, because conditions were so bad that heroic local efforts could not meet the needs for relief and credit. The Red Cross provided some assistance but was unwilling even to attempt to address all relief needs. Railroads offered some rate relief to hard-hit counties, but only for a brief time. The key issue, credit, baffled most local committees. President Hoover, who moved with considerable dispatch to address the problem but resisted modifying his plan when it did not work, answered congressional critics by insisting that charity, mutual self-help, voluntary giving and local government leadership were the only ways to deal with the matter consistently with "American ideals and American institutions." "To open the doors of the federal treasury," he argued, would do more damage than good.[25]

The drought of 1930 and the growing Depression made West Virginia voters desperate for a change, and the election of 1930 turned out to be the harbinger of a political revolution in the state. On April 23, Republican U.S. Senator Guy Goff withdrew his candidacy for reelection, giving illness as the reason. Although Goff was indeed seriously ill, speculation at the time suggested that the Republicans sought a stronger candidate to face the likely Democrat nominee, Matthew Mansfield Neely, an attorney of Fairmont. Neely, the champion Democrat campaigner of the period, had already served four terms in the U.S. House of Representatives and one term in the U.S. Senate. He lost his Senate seat to Henry Drury Hatfield in a close election in 1928.[26]

A number of prominent Republicans showed interest in the Senate nomination including former governors Ephriam F. Morgan, Albert Blakeslee White, and Howard Mason Gore, and prominent Wheeling publisher Herschel C. Ogden. Any of these might have fared better than the eventual nominee, McDowell County coal operator and political boss James Elwood Jones. Conley, moved by the deep war chest that the McDowell millionaire could provide, committed a grievous political blunder by giving his blessing to Jones, thereby making it difficult for the others to mount serious campaigns.[27] Jones perhaps had help from Washington. According to Senator Hatfield, who was no friend of Jones, President Hoover met privately with Ogden and offered him a choice: appointment as ambassador to Egypt or as U.S. commissioner to the International Exhibition in Paris. Ogden turned down the offers but stayed out of the senatorial race, as did Morgan and Gore, neither of whom could raise enough money to face Jones.[28] In the end the primary turned out to be "one of the quietest in the political history of the state" as the temperature soared to over 100 degrees for days at a time during July and early August. Jones prevailed over former governor White and Benjamin Rosenbloom of Wheeling, a former congressman. Neely faced no opposition in the Democratic primary.[29]

Many Republican editors and political leaders thought Jones's nomination a disaster. Jones, who epitomized the growing Republican popular image as the party of rich businessmen and headed a county machine notorious in its methods (called "Jonesism" by the Republican Grafton *Sentinel*), made an excellent target for Neely, who pilloried the Hoover administration for unleashing the "great monster of depression which has murdered American prosperity in cold blood." Neely also made much of the tax system, alleging the forced sales of hundreds of farms and the financial suffering of many West Virginians. Jones offered shopworn formulations of conservative Republicanism with little regard for the sensitivities of voters. He defended the yellow-dog contract as a necessary response to the violence of organized labor and as "a bulwark of protection for thousands of law abiding and peaceful laboring men who were happy and contented in being permitted to earn their living without molestation."[30] In a radio address on election eve, Jones offered as solutions to the Depression higher protective tariffs and greater immigration restriction "to keep out of the United States the hungry hordes of cheap European laborers."[31]

On election day Neely swamped Jones by a margin of almost 140,000 votes, and a huge Republican majority in the House of Delegates vanished, to be replaced by a forty-two seat Democratic majority. A Republican majority of eighteen in the Senate was narrowed to four (seventeen to thirteen). Democrats picked up one congressional seat when Lynn S. Horner defeated a Republican incumbent in the Third District, and four Republican seats were retained by narrow margins. Incumbent Democrat Joe L. Smith won handily in the Sixth District. Young Jennings Randolph, at the beginning of a long political career, almost upset the Republican incumbent in the Second District, losing only by about eleven hundred votes.[32]

The 1930 vote left state Republican leaders fearful of their political futures. Republican congressman Hugh Ike Shott, publisher of the Bluefield *Daily Telegraph*, narrowly survived what he called the "slaughterhouse," which Republican candidates across the state had to march through. Because so many Republicans voted Democratic, he told a neighboring county chairman, the future "looks a little bit bad for us."[33] One of the victims, state senator and Republican national committeeman Walter S. Hallanan of Charleston, congratulated Shott for having survived the "revolution." "What they have been doing in other countries with bullets they did in the United States with the ballot box," he lamented. Decrying the "most unfortunate" candidacy of James Elwood Jones, which "gave the Democrats an opportunity to run roughshod over all of us," Hallanan insisted that West Virginia Republicans could have maintained a legislative majority "with any other candidate at the head of the ticket." Citing President Hoover's unpopularity, Prohibition, and the Depression, Hallanan believed Republicans faced "rather a dismal prospect for 1932."[34]

When the legislature met in January 1931, the Democrats controlled a majority in a house of the legislature for the first time since 1923. Taking advantage of this new-found power, the House Democrats launched investigations of many state offices. House committees scrutinized the road commission, state police, workers compensation commission, auditor, and public service commission. Committee reports charged that both the state road commission and state police had been turned into political machines and had engaged in corrupt activities. The road commission activities could be defended as typical patronage, but the charges against the state police aroused more serious concern. The House report alleged that state policemen in Logan County conspired with local authorities to protect slot-machine gambling and speakeasies. The report cited testimony that former sheriff Tennis Hatfield had held a party for his department, local politicians, and the state police at the old Hatfield homestead. The gathering had christened "the unholy alliance between the Hatfield regime in Logan County and the state police department." "A reign of terror" against opponents in the county followed the creation of this alliance. Testimony of state troopers before the committee alleged that the murder of the chief of police in Logan on December 2, 1930, resulted from his efforts to shut down the gambling parlors and slot machines. In early March 1931, the House committee demanded that state police superintendent Harry L. Brooks be dismissed.[35]

In the first and only meeting of the special commission, U.S. Senator Henry D. Hatfield "waved the bloody shirt" by recalling the rebel past of Logan Democrats and called the special prosecutor W.E.R. Byrne a "dirty hag." The prosecutor responded in kind, calling Hatfield " a consummate liar." Governor Conley struck a deal to stop the hearings on April 30. On June 6, Superintendent Brooks resigned.[36]

Meanwhile, in January 1931, the circuit judge of Logan county, Naaman Jackson, had privately appealed to Governor Conley to intervene in Logan County to help restore the rule of law. Jackson feared that the murderer of the Logan police chief would be acquitted by a Logan County jury because of the intimidating tactics of the sheriff's department and the willingness of the army of "special constables" to testify to anything. Attorney General Howard Lee agreed to prosecute the case, and a jury brought in from Monroe County and guarded by a large contingent of state police found the accused, Emmett Scaggs, guilty of the murder. After the trial, Attorney General Lee took charge of the sheriff's department in Logan County, dismissing Tennis Hatfield's deputies and closing the gambling parlors and speakeasies. The slot machines were destroyed or shipped out of state. Lee appointed a bipartisan board to advise on the rehiring of deputies for sheriff Joe D. Hatfield, who cooperated and was allowed to remain in office. Lee fired all mine guards, deputies hired by coal companies and special constables.[37]

While Governor Conley had to deal with these embarrassing scandals and the investigations of the increasingly confident Democratic opposition, he also had to try to work with the legislature to produce a budget and legislation to address the economic crisis. As the winter of 1930-1931 loomed, relief needs demanded attention. In addition to the destitution of the farming districts brought on by the drought, it now became clear that industrial unemployment posed an even greater problem. In December, the state commissioner of labor, Howard Jarrett, estimated that 43,140 workers could find no employment. Calvert Estill, the governor's chief administrative aide, pulled no punches in a frank assessment of the problem in a speech to the American Legion. The situation was "as serious in effect as would be an invasion of this country by an enemy," and thousands of men, women, and children, he said, were in such want that some could starve to death over the winter "unless those of us who are a little more fortunate help them."[38]

President Hoover strongly believed in the necessity of private and voluntary relief. He thought federal relief would do permanent harm to local government. As relief needs grew, particularly with the 1930 drought, Hoover encouraged efforts of the Red Cross and other private organizations but remained opposed to direct federal relief. In October 1930, Hoover set up the President's Emergency Committee on Employment. The committee, headed by Col. Arthur Woods, consulted with governors by telephone concerning conditions in their states and relief plans for the winter. The committee members found "desperate distress" in Kentucky and West Virginia, where they reported "deserving men, women, and children actually . . . suffering from hunger, exposure, and cold." Despite these findings, Colonel Woods reported that there was a widespread desire to handle the emergency without federal interference. The task of unemployment relief, Woods insisted, was the responsibility of state and local governments.[39]

Just as in the drought crisis, Hoover's Emergency Employment Committee called for the organization of state committees. On December 6, 1930, Governor Conley named a statewide committee of one hundred to deal with the unemployment problem. Commissioner of Agriculture John W. Smith headed the committee that sought to draft a relief plan to present to the legislature. On December 16 some seventy-five of the one hundred committee members braved wintry weather to meet in Charleston. Smith appointed an executive committee of nine, and it listened to several suggestions, some mundane and some imaginative, as committee members struggled to understand the predicament into which the country had fallen. Some thought the state unemployment figure of forty-three thousand exaggerated, but Reese Blizzard of Parkersburg argued that the unemployment figure underestimated the problem, because it included no farmers, most of whom were destitute. One solution proposed was the perennial Republican panacea, higher protective tariffs. Several suggested the need for more help from the federal government. In an assessment of the situation that could only be called visionary, T.C. McKinley, an official of the Libby-Owens Corporation of Charleston and chairman of the Charleston Area Community Chest said that because machinery was replacing labor, government should generate employment through public works projects. He proposed that the federal government build four national highways, two running east-west and two running north-south. Airports and tourist camps would be located at periodic intervals. The roadway would be one-hundred feet wide, and beneath it could be provided shelters to protect military forces from air attack. The committee heard another suggestion from Commissioner of Labor Howard Jarrett who recommended that persons regularly employed be asked to give a certain amount of their wage or salary over the next three months to provide a fund for relief of the unemployed.[40] The labor representative on the committee, John Easton of the West Virginia Federation of Labor, recommended that the eight-hour day be required, thereby providing work for more people and that there be a fifty-cent-per-hour minimum wage for all state and county work.[41]

In February 1931, Commissioner Smith died unexpectedly while in Morgantown for Farm Week. Governor Conley named former governor Gore as both agriculture commissioner and chairman of the unemployment committee. Gore, from Clarksburg, had briefly served as secretary of agriculture in the Coolidge cabinet before being elected governor in 1924. He had chaired the drought relief committee and had been a key member of the unemployment committee. Under Gore's leadership, the unemployment committee weeded through the various proposals and came up with several practical recommendations, which Governor Conley presented to the biennial meeting of the legislature. [42]

By the time the governor addressed the legislature at the opening of the biennial session in January 1931, he had abandoned boosterism and offered a more realistic assessment of the conditions facing the state. He pointed out that the coal industry had faced depression for a decade, and that "more recently certain other lines of business have felt the Depression that has prevailed . . . in every state of the union, and in fact, throughout the world." He also reminded legislators that the state suffered from "the most devastating drought of which we have any record." Farmers, he asserted, would have to have assistance from some source.[43]

The 1931 legislature, although politically divided between a Republican Senate and a Democratic House of Delegates, passed several acts recommended by the Gore committee and Conley to ameliorate the situation. Although not measures that had a great impact, compared to the actions of other legislatures during these confusing times, these were relatively forward looking. The legislative record in most states during this period was rather dismal. In early 1931, no state had a centralized unemployment relief commission, and none provided state funds for relief.[44]

Local governments traditionally provided for relief, but the conditions in West Virginia quickly absorbed whatever monies were available at municipal and county levels. To help provide drought and unemployment relief funds for these local jurisdictions, Conley recommended and the legislature authorized transfer of monies from county road funds to relief and authorized counties and municipalities to borrow money. The legislature also provided extensions for redemptions of delinquent lands seized by the state dating back to 1927. Following through on another Conley reform recommendation presented as an economy measure, leaders of both parties supported the creation of the department of public welfare by the merging of the Board of Children's Guardians, the Crippled Children's Council, and the Veterans Service Officer. West Virginia also joined twelve other states authorizing counties to give pensions to the aged poor rather than putting them in poorhouses.[45]

Conley persuaded the legislature to extend the state road building program as a means of providing jobs and relief. During the 1920s the state had spent nearly $100 million on "the Good Roads Movement." In 1930, road building had employed some eight thousand workers, some specifically for relief purposes. Among them were seven hundred prisoners, for whom there was no space in the prison at Moundsville. Available funds from the proceeds of bond sales assured the continuation of the construction program through 1931. The legislature agreed to Conley's proposal to reissue $10 million in state road bonds to finance road building into 1932 and also to allow the state road commission to undertake construction without advertising for bids in order to speed up the work and make jobs available.[46] During the fall of 1930 the state road commission employed several hundred men in seventeen drought-affected counties and also purchased twenty-two thousand guardrail posts to give some farmers work in the winter months. In January 1931 the commission rushed highway building projects forward "to provide employment at once."[47]

Although the legislature passed several of the governor's relief measures, the 1931 meeting was far from a love feast. The Democratic majority in the House of Delegates investigated state departments, and House and Senate clashed over different versions of the budget. Governor Conley vetoed ten different Democratic bills seeking to increase salaries of county officers or to increase levies. He extended the session seven times as Democrats fought to cut departmental budgets and salaries, and Republicans sought cuts in institutional budgets. The bitter three-month session finally ended on April 14, 1931, as the legislature reached sullen agreement on a budget and sent it to the governor.[48]

Drought and Depression   41

In 1930 and 1931, while the state suffered from the twin disasters of drought and depression, another calamity, perhaps the worst industrial disaster in the history of the country, took place virtually unnoticed by the press in Fayette County, where hundreds of men died building the Hawks Nest Tunnel. An engineering marvel, the tunnel was drilled through solid rock three miles long and up to forty-two feet in diameter to supply water to a Union Carbide and Chemical Corporation metallurgical complex. Drawing heavily upon black workers from the South and some white workers from the mountain farms of Appalachia, the tunnel offered work to thousands, but breathing the silica-laden air produced by the drilling put the workers at risk of silicosis, a deadly disease that destroys the lungs. The calamitous consequences of the Hawks Nest project were scarcely mentioned in the state press until an investigation by a U.S. Senate subcommittee concluded that 476 workers died, and some two thousand became seriously ill. The story was still largely suppressed in West Virginia, and as late as 1941, the construction companies involved succeeded in halting the distribution of a novel about the incident by West Virginia author Hubert Skidmore. A recent careful account by a medical scholar estimates that "over 700 men may have died in all—183 whites and 581 blacks."[49]

During the months between the stock market crash in October 1929 and the end of the legislative session in April 1931, West Virginians faced a succession of calamities. The double blows of drought and depression devastated farmers and miners as well as coal operators, manufacturers, merchants, and bankers. Conventional means of providing relief proved inadequate. An embattled Governor Conley and his unemployment committee offered innovative ideas to fight the Depression and found grudging support from the legislature, but the enormity of the economic collapse exceeded the capacity of the state government to respond. The election of 1930 represented something of a ballot box revolution as voters turned sharply against the Republican party in the hope that the Democrats could provide new solutions. Meanwhile the worst industrial disaster in the history of the country was in the making at Hawks Nest.

3
A Search for Order

From spring 1931 to the end of the Conley and Hoover administrations in spring 1933, the state and the nation slipped ever deeper into depression. Charleston *Gazette* publisher and former U.S. senator William E. Chilton complained to a friend in New York that "nobody away from here can understand how damnable hard the general situation is."[1] In the midst of growing disaster, a remarkable outpouring of local and private energies sought to help the victims of the Depression, but the efforts never met the need.

Individuals and families faced difficult choices about basic matters such as where to live, and where to find work and food. Some families abandoned cities and towns to seek sustenance from the land, intensifying the pressure on mountain lands of limited productivity. In the face of growing signs of disintegration, different groups in society seized upon diverse stratagems to cope with the predicaments they faced and to seek a sense of order through organization.

As in other states, local governments and private charities in all sections of West Virginia found themselves overwhelmed by spiraling costs and falling revenues. School districts curtailed the academic year by several months, cut teachers' salaries, and in some cases simply failed to pay salaries. Property owners, especially farmers, faced the threat of losing their lands for nonpayment of taxes.[2]

Local governments and private agencies tried to deal with the problem of relief, but they were all but helpless before the magnitude of need. Some tended to have a moralistic attitude toward the unemployed. In McDowell County, a southern county heavily dependent on the coal industry, the members of the county court met in early November 1930, after the election, to consider how they could deal with the burgeoning relief problem in the face of the coming winter. The court asked that coal operators divide the available work among their men so that every family head would be given some work each week. It also sought the assistance of the superintendent of schools and the coal operators in identifying those worthy of assistance "as it is felt that many of the cases are not worthy." The commissioners believed that a thorough investigation of each case should be made so that "loafers" would be denied aid that might help the "truly worthy." The county medical officer also reported an increase of cases. The commissioners agreed that "it should be the responsibility of the large coal companies to prevent suffering in their camps whenever possible," and they urged companies to cooperate with county officials in charge of charity work, the Salvation Army, Red Cross, and other private organizations.[3] At the beginning of 1931, the McDowell County Court slashed salaries of all county employees except teachers.[4]

In neighboring Mercer County, churches and schoolteachers collected food and clothes, a coal operator donated a carload of coal for the destitute (though freight would have to be paid for its delivery), and a committee planned a football game to benefit the needy, but county welfare agent Nellie Poff warned that with winter coming on, none of this was enough. She appealed through the local newspaper for more help.[5]

In Monongalia County in northern West Virginia, conditions in the coal industry had become desperate sooner than in southern West Virginia, because marketing the high-volatile coal of the northern fields had become more difficult. During the twenties, however, Monongalia County had developed a stronger network of private welfare organizations than the southern counties, and they were united in a Council of Social Agencies. The council struggled valiantly, but local contributions fell short of the need.[6] In neighboring Marion County, editor Clarence Edwin "Ned" Smith of the Fairmont *Times* worried privately about "growing unrest in this field due to starvation" and wrote to a friend that "a new effort should be made in the Fairmont field to get the operators together."[7]

Some fifteen miles from the beautiful new gold-domed capitol nearing completion in Charleston, coal miners and their families of Cabin Creek lived "on the point of starvation." In early March 1931, Kanawha County Welfare Secretary D.E. Shaffer issued an appeal to the public for food, money, and clothing saying that conditions there "cannot be exaggerated."[8]

Representatives of President Hoover's federal bureaucracy also found words inadequate to express what they observed in West Virginia. In the spring of 1931, a survey of conditions among children in the bituminous coalfields by the U.S. Children's Bureau found much malnourishment. The district representative of the president's emergency committee for employment, Fred C. Croxton, toured Monongalia, Marion, Harrison, Kanawha, Logan, and Boone Counties and found conditions so bad they were "almost unbelievable." Thousands of miners and their families existed on county relief, with most families getting about ten dollars a month. He was shocked to find people surviving on cornmeal, flour, and beans. "The situation I found," Croxton said, "was so bad I did not want anyone to have to take my word for it, so I asked two other men to make a survey." The two, Porter Lee and Walker Street, both members of the president's emergency committee, confirmed Croxton's findings. Croxton pointed out that the Red Cross chapters in the area lacked resources, and the counties had nearly exhausted their meager relief funds.[9]

President Hoover and his emergency committee looked to the Red Cross as the primary relief agency for both the drought and the unemployment in the hard-hit coalfields, but the Red Cross leaders insisted that their proper role was to assist only the victims of natural disaster not those who suffered the consequences of downward turns of the business cycle. When Croxton's survey of West Virginia's coal counties revealed the desperate conditions of coal miners and their families, Croxton and Arthur Woods of the president's committee urged the Red Cross to undertake unemployment relief in the mining counties. Croxton and Howard M. Gore, chairman of the West Virginia unemployment committee, discussed how the Red Cross might "edge over" from drought relief and without public announcement help hungry mining families. President Hoover himself called the Red Cross director, John Barton Payne, asking that the Red Cross "quietly and unobtrusively" go to the relief of unemployed coal miners.[10] Payne agreed to help, but the Red Cross continued to drag its feet. Some agency officials were sensitive to the charge that helping miners might make the agency appear to be pro-union in unorganized West Virginia.[11]

Hard times were not good times for trying to organize a union, but the conditions in the coalfields offered opportunity to the West Virginia Mine Workers Union, a breakaway group from the United Mine Workers of America led by a former hero of the UMWA, Frank Keeney. Keeney, a native West Virginian born in a Cabin Creek coal camp in 1884, had helped build the United Mine Workers in West Virginia before and during World War I. After the collapse of the UMWA in West Virginia following the mine wars and treason trials of the early twenties, Keeney, disagreeing with the strategy of trying to hold the line on wages during a time of business setbacks, drifted away from the union. He ran an orange drink stand for a while and then speculated in oil and gas. When UMWA dissidents held a national convention to set up a reorganized miners union in March 1930, Keeney attended and afterward returned to West Virginia to organize for the new union. The Reorganized United Mine Workers enjoyed some success in organizing West Virginia miners, but when a judge in Springfield, Illinois, ruled John L. Lewis's union as the legitimate United Mine Workers, all support for the West Virginia effort ended. Keeney then turned to the organization of the independent West Virginia Mine Workers Union (WVMWU). Northeastern socialists sent Keeney $100,000 and four trained organizers from A.J. Muste's Brookwood Labor College of New York. Now Keeney's group competed with the old UMWA and Communists of the National Miners Union for the loyalty of West Virginia miners.[12]

Just outside the coal town of Ward, some twenty-eight miles from Charleston, the Brookwood College organizers held Sunday rallies or "speakin's" and taught classes during the week in the African American schoolhouse. The writer Edmund Wilson visited Ward and was impressed by the racial cooperation: "In Ward, the blacks and whites do not mix, but they live in neighboring houses, bathe side by side in the same creek, hold offices together in the union and are now taking lessons in economics together." The night Wilson visited, a Jewish girl from Vassar taught the miners "Solidarity Forever" to the tune of the "Battle Hymn of the Republic." Wilson characterized the conditions of the workers at Ward as "near serfdom."[13]

On May 19, 1931, the miners of Ward, stirred by Keeney and his Brookwood aides, held a mass rally and decided to dramatize their plight with a hunger march on the capitol. Their company, the Kelley's Creek Colliery Company, had been working on and off, but had no orders, and the coal was simply piling up. Miners complained that they were in debt to the company store and could get no food. Several hundred men, women, and children marched the twenty-eight miles to Charleston and camped outside the city. They carried banners reading: "Yesterday in the Trenches," "Today Starvation," "Awake, the New Day Is Here." Governor Conley received a committee of miners led by Frank Keeney and then went to the miners' camp. Conley told the marchers that he regretted having neither "the power nor the means" to help them. He offered ten dollars of his own money for a relief fund and promised that better times were coming. He asserted his confidence that "whatever conditions may be now, we have the best government on earth." The marchers then paraded to the courthouse to hear speeches by their leaders and adopted a resolution asking the Red Cross to come to the relief of miners and their families.[14]

In July 1931, the West Virginia Mine Workers struck Kanawha Valley mines. Concerned about successes of the UMWA in the Morgantown-Fairmont field and reacting to the dismissal and blacklisting of WVMWU members in the Kanawha Valley, the union took a desperate chance even though, as Brookwood organizer Tom Tippett said in summing up reasons for the strike's failure, "conditions in the industry being what they were, the strike was doomed to failure before it commenced." After six weeks, the strikers were, in effect, starved into submission. Keeney, who had never lost a strike, held out until there was no hope of victory, but at the end evicted families dotted the valley, and Tippett admitted, the union was "unable to purchase a rag or board to shelter many of them." Unable to give the strikers anything but speeches, Keeney admitted defeat in mid August 1931.[15]

Pundits at the time wrote the union's obituary, and some historians have written that the WVMWU expired in 1931.[16] In fact Keeney tried to keep the union alive by making it the advocate of hungry miners and their families. In August 1931, after the strike ended, Keeney and John Harlow, a minister from the Kanawha coal town of Gallagher, led a hunger march on Charleston, demanding relief from the governor. Mayor R.P. Devan refused the marchers permission to enter the city, and armed city and state policemen stood at the Kanawha City bridge to stop them. Governor Conley again went out to the miners' camp and told them he had no authority to help. Again he offered ten dollars for their treasury.[17]

In the summer of 1932, Keeney labored on in Kanawha, Boone, Putnam, and Logan Counties, still getting support from the Brookwood labor college organizers and the League for Industrial Democracy. Though many miners probably believed that some form of organization would help bring order and security to their lives, under the circumstances more basic needs came first. Symptomatic of the problems of Depression unionism was an incident that occurred in Boone County

A Search for Order 47

in the summer of 1932. Keeney and his lieutenant, Brant A. Scott, were speaking to a large group of miners at a coal camp when relief trucks sent by the Boone County Court arrived. The miners immediately deserted the speakers to line up for their relief rations.[18]

In June 1932, Kenney and Harlow led another, larger hunger march to Charleston. When they were refused entrance to the city, they camped at Splash Beach, just at the entrance to the Kanawha City bridge. The numbers swelled at Splash Beach as miners came not only from Kanawha mines but also from Boone, Logan, Putnam, and Raleigh Counties. A committee visited Governor Conley, and he told them the state had no funds to help. Citing a 1931 law empowering county courts to divert other funds to relief, he urged them to return home. The committee then went to the Kanawha County Courthouse but were told that the county had exhausted all relief funds.[19]

At the end of the first week of June, about two hundred people were encamped at Splash Beach and six hundred more were reported en route from Boone and Logan Counties. Governor Conley agreed to meet the miners committee again, and though he reiterated the state's inability to provide relief, he did take action on some of the miners' grievances. On the complaint that families of unemployed miners had been evicted from their homes by the Wacomah Fuel Company on Paint Creek, Attorney General Howard Lee reported that he had ordered the company to halt all evictions and would instruct the receiver to take over operations of the company as it had paid no taxes. Governor Conley also told the committee that he had sent the director of the Department of Welfare, Calvert Estill, to investigate conditions in Boone County, where the miners reported widespread hunger. Urging the marchers again to return home, he also warned them not to disobey the law. After a few more days at Splash Beach, with supplies and hopes dwindling, the miners broke camp and headed home.[20]

Fate was unkind to Keeney and the WVMWU. Out of work and sometimes out of a place to live, a rag-tag band of loyalists hung on, some living in ragged tents during the winter of 1932-1933, until the UMWA would seize the day after the passage of the National Industrial Recovery Act in the spring of 1933. By the time the reporter Lorena Hickok visited West Virginia in August 1933 to report on conditions for Eleanor Roosevelt and Harry Hopkins, the conventional wisdom of those she talked to was that the WVMWU was an outlaw union that had been responsible for all the trouble in the past. She visited a tent colony a mile from the Ward mine, near Charleston, made up of some forty blacklisted WVMWU miners and their families who had been living in their tents since the fall of 1931. Hickok described sanitary conditions in the camp "unspeakable" and the people as "the most miserable looking crowd I ever saw in my life." Although most of the men were able-bodied, they had no chance at jobs because they were members of the "outlaw union."[21]

Although Keeney urged his men to join the UMWA in 1933, he was, as historian David Alan Corbin has written, "ostracized by the UMW as a false prophet." Unable to work either as an organizer or miner under the UMWA regime, he accepted a call from the American Federation of Labor in 1937 to organize a rival union to the UMWA, but that effort also failed. Keeney ended up as a parking-lot attendant in Charleston.[22]

Although the WVMWU quickly faded from the scene, its brief and poignant career did much to attract the attention of the metropolitan press and to dramatize the plight of the West Virginia coal miners. The *New Republic*, the *Nation*, and the *New York Times*, among others, gave much sympathetic attention to the WVMWU.[23] Moreover, Governor Conley's experiences facing the unemployed hunger marchers of the WVMWU no doubt encouraged him to break with tradition and to seek both new taxes and federal aid for unemployment relief. The experiences with the more radical WVMWU perhaps encouraged coal operators to be more receptive to the UMWA in 1933.

The WVMWU also inspired labor troubadours who wrote new songs and revised many of the old mountain ballads and religious hymns with new verses telling the story of the strike. The classic labor song "We Shall Not Be Moved" originally centered on the events of 1931 in southern West Virginia and included the line "Frank Keeney is our captain, we shall not be moved." One of the Brookwood organizers, Tom Tippet, was interested in folk music and met Walter Secrist, a coal miner and lay preacher at Holly Grove, near the junction of the Kanawha River and Paint Creek. Secrist composed "The Striker's Orphaned Child," based on the death of a miner in an attack on a miners' tent colony at Holly Grove in 1913 and a militant labor version of the song "West Virginia Hills." In 1932 Secrist went to a private studio in Charleston and recorded "West Virginia Hills" and another song he had learned from Tippet, "The Death of Mother Jones." According to Archie Green, the historian of coal mining songs, Secrist's recording "may have been the first record specifically made for and used in a union organizational campaign." Tom Tippet took Walter Secrist and other miner folk singers to Brookwood to inspire the students and staff there.[24]

The restiveness of labor created something of a "red scare." Some local authorities believed communists inspired all labor activism. The danger of the "red menace" preoccupied early discussions of the state relief committee.[25] In a talk to the Charleston Rotary Club, former state police superintendent R.E. O'Conner claimed that the Soviet Union financed the activities of local communists who were led by Frank Keeney and Thomas Tippet and who also worked through the American Federation of Labor (AFL). Keeney and Tippet, he said, sought new party members by distributing food and clothing to the county poor. O'Conner said the communists claimed eighteen thousand members in the county but that an accurate count would be more like five thousand. Although there might have been communists among Keeney's followers and within the AFL and United Mine Workers, the authentic communist organization was the National Miners Union, and unlike in "Bloody Harlan" Kentucky, it had little support in West Virginia. William Z. Foster came to Charleston with officials of the National Miners Union on June 14, 1931, but when he tried to speak from the courthouse steps, he was escorted out of town by local police, who perhaps were unusually concerned with security on the eve of a visit to Charleston by President Hoover.[26]

Meanwhile the United Mine Workers sought to gain a toehold in northern West Virginia at Scotts Run, in Monongalia County. In May 1931, miners there walked out on their own because of wage cuts, and Van Amberg Bittner, the UMWA organizer in the area, persuaded the miners to join the UMWA. He proceeded to negotiate a broad-based agreement with some forty operators, which provided for a checkweighman, the eight-hour day, pay for "dead work," and a grievance procedure, but this UMWA beachhead did not survive, because nonunion mines actually paid higher wages than the thirty cents a ton in Bittner's agreement.[27]

Because of the bitterly hostile political and legal climate, union-building in the West Virginia coalfields was nearly impossible even in relatively prosperous times. With the coal industry collapsing, Keeney's West Virginia Mine Workers, Foster's National Miners Union, and Bittner's UMWA all faced long odds.

Conley's sympathetic efforts in dealing with coal miners provided little real help or comfort. He followed the lead of President Hoover in trying to persuade the business community to hold the line on wages and encouraged efforts to modify the antitrust laws in order to control production and to stabilize wages in the coal industry. In October 1931, he invited coal operators to a conference to broach these matters and told those who assembled, "It is wrong to cut the wages of miners below a living and reasonable surplus wage in order to meet cut-throat competition." He urged the West Virginia operators to cooperate with operators in other states to stabilize the industry.[28]

The idea of industrial cooperation or some sort of sanctioned cartelization of coal had long been discussed as a way of managing the excess capacity in the industry. Even Herbert Hoover, as secretary of commerce in 1922, had recommended an industrial stabilization plan featuring operator associations, unemployment insurance, and systematized distribution and transportation of coal, but when Congressmen James Davis and Clyde Kelly of Pennsylvania introduced a bill with similar characteristics during his presidential term, Hoover did not support it.[29]

West Virginia operators generally opposed stabilization bills, because most schemes included union recognition. Clarence E. "Ned" Smith, editor of the Fairmont *Times* (who would later become a member of the U.S. Coal Commission), made this clear in an editorial widely reprinted in state newspapers in April 1932. Conceding that the coal industry was in desperate shape, that fifty thousand men, women, and children were at the point of starvation in the Fairmont field, and that the only solution seemed to be some sort of government takeover of the industry, he nevertheless resolutely opposed the Davis-Kelly bill, because it would grant recognition to the United Mine Workers. He blamed the UMWA not only for past sins of conspiracy and violence, but also charged that the UMWA efforts in Scotts Run in 1931 had resulted in a collapse of the industry there.[30] Recalling the 1921 armed miners' march, Judge Clarence L. Estep of Logan testified in Senate hearings that the bill's passage would throw the bituminous industry into "utter chaos" and would result in the "devastation" of southern West Virginia.[31]

Whether Conley's pleas or fear of the Davis-Kelly bill had anything to do with it is unclear, but in late 1931, 137 coal operators in West Virginia, Virginia, Kentucky, and Tennessee incorporated into a regional sales agency, Appalachian Coals, Inc. James Draper Francis of the Island Creek Coal Company and Charles C. Dickinson of Charleston played leading roles in organizing Appalachian Coals, which soon faced legal troubles as the Justice Department charged the combine with violation of the Sherman Act. In January 1933, however, the Supreme Court overruled the Justice Department, giving the green light to cooperative marketing arrangements in the coal industry.[32]

While coal operators and miners sought in their different and antithetical ways to bring order through organization, unemployed veterans also organized to push for political solutions. Demanding immediate payment of bonuses for their service in World War I, some twenty thousand veterans from around the country joined what was called the Bonus Expeditionary Force (BEF) and trekked to the national capitol. Unemployed West Virginia veterans from across the state joined the march, including 250 men from Charleston, and though most who went soon returned, a small group of West Virginians joined forces to elect officers and to construct more permanent dwellings than the tents they had first used. They dragged driftwood from the Potomac and materials from the city dump to construct their "barracks." They made beds from dried grass and tried to catch fish from the Potomac to go with the potatoes given them by a sympathetic donor. William Riffner of Point Pleasant, elected commander, told reporters he intended to stay until the bonus was paid.[33]

In early June the West Virginia BEF contingent moved into an abandoned government building. The army engineers condemned the building as unsafe and ordered the men out, but they refused to leave. Having won the vote on the bonus bill in the House of Representatives, the men were now lobbying the Senate. Senator Neely supported the effort, but Senator Hatfield was "out of town." A reporter found the West Virginia bonus marchers becoming pessimistic and suffering from food shortages.[34]

A new state commander of the BEF, Herbert Brown, publicly condemned Governor Conley for saying he "opposed mass assemblages gathered for the purpose of intimidating legislative bodies or other officials." Brown also claimed that Conley refused to let hunger marchers on the lawn of the capitol and ridiculed the governor's "generous hearted" gift of ten dollars. Brown said Conley made a "mockery of democracy" and that the BEF would work to "turn West Virginia into a state where mountaineers are really free."[35]

In July a "contact car" from the Bonus Army in Washington went to Martinsburg in the eastern panhandle and sought help from local veterans' groups. The bonus marchers also invited an audience to come hear the song of the Bonus Expeditionary Force at the Apollo Theater in Martinsburg and to buy the music as a way of helping their cause.[36]

The BEF men who visited Martinsburg insisted that they would never honor an eviction order, but just three days later, on July 28, President Hoover ordered the Army chief of staff, Douglas MacArthur, to evict the BEF. General MacArthur, calling the veterans "a mob . . . animated by the essence of revolution" executed the order with élan, driving the men from town and burning their billets.[37]

Some of the West Virginians went to Johnstown, Pennsylvania, where the BEF sought to regroup after the debacle in Washington. When the mayor of Johnstown ordered the BEF to leave, the national commander, Walter W. Waters, issued an order to disband. A dissident group, headed by Waters's chief of staff, Kentuckian Doak Carter, and encouraged by the West Virginia state commander, sought to keep the organization going and proposed to move to Huntington. The city fathers of Huntington were shocked and rushed telegrams to Carter, warning him that Huntington, hard pressed to feed its own unemployed, could not feed the marchers and would not welcome them. West Virginia mobilized extra state police and road commission trucks to cooperate with the local police in escorting the marchers quickly out of town and across the river into Ohio should they arrive. It was reported that some four hundred men would decamp to Huntington, but by August 5 only about seventy-five veterans, traveling in dilapidated automobiles or trucks or hitchhiking had reached Huntington.[38]

Carter established his headquarters at the Park Tower Hotel, and when the city police chief and commander of the state police detachment went to his room to order him to move his men out of the city, Carter readily complied. He had planned to set up camp temporarily outside the city until he could see how many men wanted to continue the BEF organization, but after talking with the police officials he abandoned the plan. He told reporters, "We are accustomed by this time to being run out of places."[39] For the next few days, Carter tried to find someplace to establish a refuge for the routed BEF, and when officials of Walter Waters's organization complained that Carter did not speak for the BEF, he adopted a new name for his venture, the American Emergency Force (AEF). When the governors of both Ohio and Kentucky made it clear that the marchers would not be welcome in their states, Carter turned to a scheme to establish a colony on a fifteen-thousand-acre tract in the state of Chihuahua, Mexico, but

President Ortiz Rubio refused to grant permission for the AEF to enter Mexico. Carter left Huntington in mid-August with plans to make a personal appeal to the Mexican president, but because his organization was broke, he tried to raise money by traveling about in West Virginia and Ohio lecturing on "The History of the Bonus March."[40]

In Charleston, meanwhile, the BEF set up its headquarters on Capitol Street, equipped a "barracks" in the west end, which could accommodate ten to twenty homeless veterans each night, ran an employment service, crusaded against panhandling, and distributed food to needy veterans. It also campaigned openly for probonus candidates and held meetings with local legislative candidates of both parties.[41]

The former state commander of the BEF, Herbert C. Brown, who had assisted Doak Carter in the abortive effort to establish the BEF in Huntington, became the state commander of another, more militant veterans organization called the Khaki Shirts of America (KSA), in ominous imitation of European fascist groups like Hitler's Brown Shirts and Mussolini's Black Shirts. Brown said his organization was "the beginning of a folk movement such as this country has never seen." Appealing not only to veterans but also to "the industrial worker, the farmer, and other common people of America," the KSA sought not a new party, but to clean out "the crooked politicians in the old parties."[42]

Meanwhile, government and private efforts to fight the Depression continued on several fronts in 1931 and 1932. The state Extension Service, the state Farm Bureau and the Farm Women's Bureau organized a special campaign in 1931 to encourage the production and preservation of surplus food for winter relief in the depressed mining areas. Recalling the help from farmers in other states that West Virginians had received during the drought, these agencies called upon West Virginia farmers to repay the debt by providing food relief in the needy industrial regions of West Virginia. After the terrible drought of 1930, state gardeners enjoyed a bumper crop of fruits and vegetables in 1931. In a number of counties, farm groups organized unemployed workers to collect and store the surplus. They were given time tickets that they could later cash in for food. In Cabell County, churches, civic organizations, and theaters donated money to buy jars and sugar for canning. The automobile dealers association donated twenty used cars and trucks that farmers could obtain by using fruits and vegetables as partial payment. The Council of Social Agencies in

Monongalia and other groups in Mercer, Lewis, Wayne, and Taylor Counties also promoted food preservation for relief.[43]

As part of the 1931 campaign, the Extension Service and Farm Bureau cooperated to send a home demonstration agent into Logan and Mingo Counties on an emergency basis to teach canning to miners' wives. President Everett S. Humphrey of the Farm Bureau persuaded the coal operators of the two counties to allow the agent into their camps, and Mabel Sutherland, the county welfare secretary, introduced the young woman, Esther Brucklacher, to the leaders and miners' families in the different camps. The goal was "to can every bit of food in the county which could not be used at their tables fresh."[44]

Though many miners kept gardens, knowledge of how to can was surprisingly rare. Miners wives had pickled corn and beans, because that was the only way they knew to preserve food. Despite temperatures that soared to above one hundred degrees, the women attended Miss Brucklacher's demonstrations in the summer of 1931 with great interest and went home to can as much food as they could. Finding "no feeling of social strata" she held her demonstrations with native white, black, and foreign women together.[45]

President Hoover's committee received a new name in August, 1931—the President's Office for Unemployment Relief (POUR)—but it still had only sympathy and advice to offer. Clinging to his commitment to private charity, and moved by reports of starvation in the mining counties of Appalachia, President Hoover, through POUR, asked the American Friends Service Committee (AFSC) to carry out a program to feed children in the coal mining areas. Money would be provided by the American Relief Administration, an agency set up to help Europeans after World War I, and by the Rockefeller Foundation. Altogether the program would have $400,000 for its first year of operation.[46]

From the beginning the AFSC looked for long-term solutions for the plight of mining families and not just short-run relief. The AFSC board of directors discussed the idea of resettlement of miners on small farms, but one of the members, Dr. Mary Smity of Bryn Mawr, said that "send them to the farms" was too simple. She maintained that much planning would be necessary to make resettlement successful. The AFSC never had the time nor resources to carry through on a resettlement program, but their ideas certainly influenced Eleanor Roosevelt and led directly to the New Deal's resettlement schemes and the Arthurdale project.[47]

In September 1931, the AFSC launched the program that undertook the feeding of miners' children in forty-one counties in six Appalachian states. Within five months fifty-five workers, mostly volunteers, had fanned out across the region in second-hand cars and were at work feeding some forty-thousand children. While the money lasted, the project was a lifesaver for many children in the coalfields, and in retrospect, it would appear to have been a training ground for relief workers and a seed bed for ideas that would shape federal relief and rehabilitation ideas in the New Deal era. Homer Morris, an economist and the field director of the project, with the help of the AFSC field workers carried out a study of miners that concluded that there was a surplus of two hundred thousand coal miners in the bituminous industry. These men were "stranded in isolated coal camps" and could not escape without outside help. He presented the plight of the miners as "a challenge to social engineering."[48]

In early April 1932, representatives of the President's Office for Unemployment Relief and the AFSC workers held a conference in Williamson, West Virginia, to discuss the situation in the coal camps where the Friends were working. The Friends told ghost stories at night to entertain themselves, but their daytime discussions were more frightening. Reports of the ten district directors of the project left no doubt that large numbers of unemployed miners and their families would need help for a long time to come. Most of the unemployed miners could not expect to return to mining, but few were prepared to do anything else. The director in Mingo and McDowell Counties, Mary Kelsey, warned that "No informed person gives any hope for any improvement of importance in 10 years on account of the large surplus of labor in the mining camps." Some people had suggested to her that the miners be moved to small farms and the camp houses be dynamited "as a kindness to both operators and men."[49]

One of the concerns expressed by those at the conference was the possibility that employers might try slicing their payrolls drastically so that a smaller number of men might be more fully employed instead of spreading employment thinly. Fred Croxton of POUR feared that if employers should force thousands of underemployed men out of the mining camps it could have serious consequences "and might even undermine the entire structure."[50]

Another of the ideas the AFSC explored was the development of ways for unemployed or underemployed miners to supplement their primary livelihood. In the lumbering camp of Duty, Mingo County, the Quakers provided food that the school teacher prepared for the undernourished children. An elderly chair maker named Hopkins from across the mountain was persuaded to leave home for the first time at the age of seventy-five to come to Duty to teach the local men how to make chairs of the native hardwoods with woven hickory bark seats. In sewing classes, women of Duty learned to make quilts of attractive design, such as the "Hominy Bird." The chairs and quilts provided items to sell to supplement inadequate incomes.[51]

Finding a cooperative superintendent at the closed Crown Mine in Monongalia County, the AFSC sought to make it a pilot project to see what might be done to help the fifty-five stranded families there. As was true in most Appalachian mining communities, the terrain at Crown Mine did not lend itself to gardening, so the AFSC sought to promote various handicrafts including carpentry, furniture making, shoemaking and repair, and sewing.[52]

In the spring of 1932, two Brooklyn schoolteachers, William and Ruth Simkin, moved into a company house at Crown to work more closely with the community than could be done from a central office. The Simkins attended the conference in Williamson and perhaps were inspired by the example of the furniture-making project at Duty. In any case they believed furniture making might be a way for some of the Crown miners to escape dependence on mining and sought help through the university Extension Service. There they met Tom Skuce, state Extension forester, who had many useful ideas about furniture-making as a rehabilitation project. Skuce believed the man to lead the furniture-making project was Bud Godlove, a traditional mountaineer craftsman who lived 150 miles from Morgantown in the Monongahela National Forest. A fifth-generation furniture maker, Godlove, who had never been more than fifty miles from his home, was persuaded by Homer Morris to come to Crown to teach miners to make furniture. The project flourished, and soon the Godlove chair makers joined cabinet makers from Bertha Hill mine and others who did metalwork, needle work, and weaving to form Mountaineer Craftsmen's Cooperative Association. Located for a time in a former junk shop near the Monongahela River in Morgantown, the MCCA was one of the most successful enterprises to emerge from the Friends' efforts. This cooperative endured for several years producing and marketing handcrafted wooden furniture and other items and marketing the products of garden clubs in the Monongahela Valley.[53]

Another result of the AFSC project, which lasted about two years, was that it provided a cadre of trained and dedicated personnel who stepped in and played a leading role in setting up and operating the West Virginia relief organization in a number of West Virginia counties in the winter of 1932-1933. The director of the West Virginia Unemployment Relief Administration, Calvert Estill, praised the work of the AFSC, noting that it "has carried on supplementary child feeding programs in four counties, has furnished administrative personnel in a number of counties, and has taken complete charge, with its own workers, of the administration of relief in the County of Lincoln, where the county court refused to cooperate with the State Administration in the relief of destitution."[54]

The Friends were generally well received by all elements of the community including local officials, coal operators, and mining families, but they encountered occasional problems with uncooperative local officials and unfriendly operators or miners. The worst incident took place when two young relief workers were threatened in a school south of Charleston because of a rumor that they were feeding only Republicans. As they drove back to Charleston, shots rang out from a hillside, and a bullet ripped through the windshield and out the top of their car. Neither was hurt, and the AFSC rejected Governor Conley's offer to call out the state militia to protect the relief workers.[55]

A reporter from *Christian Century*, James Myers, visited Monongalia County in the summer of 1932 and found the Friends working closely with the county court and the Council of Social Agencies in seeking ways to rehabilitate families and communities in the coalfields. Myers called these projects "the most extensive program of voluntary community effort" he had ever seen. Sewing, dressmaking, and shoe-repair classes in the coal camps produced clothing for the families and a surplus for sale in a shop provided by the Hotel Morgan. The state Agricultural Extension Service, the Red Cross, Fred Croxton of POUR, and the Friends worked to bring about a large increase in subsistence gardening.[56]

Dr. William E. Brooks, pastor of the Presbyterian Church in Morgantown and president of the county welfare board, worked day and night on relief and rehabilitation, but he told Myers the task was impossible:

He pointed out to me [Myers] very forcefully the fallacy and the unfairness of expecting a local community . . . like Morgantown to bear the entire burden of relief for thousands of miners who were brought here into this county by the coal companies, which are in turn owned almost entirely by outside capital. "These wounded men are left lying by our roadside," he said. "We are doing our best to play the Good Samaritan, but it is a national problem, and it is only fair that national resources help to fund relief."[57]

The president of the Monongalia Council of Social Agencies, Mrs. Friend E. Clark, also worked extensively, coordinating a volunteer group of eighty women doing social case work in mining camps. She told Myers that their efforts to provide relief barely scratched the surface.[58]

In many cities and towns, Community Chest served as the chief vehicle for raising funds for local charities, and the burden of helping the growing numbers of destitute fell heavily upon Community Chest and its member organizations. In 1932 Community Chest raised its largest fund ever, but nationally this amounted to only $35 million, a sum far short of need.[59] In Charleston, for example, Community Chest sought to raise $145,000, which would be shared by numerous charitable and social service organizations such as the Salvation Army, Red Cross, Hillcrest Sanatorium (for children), Federated Jewish Charities, Public Health Nursing Association, Colored Day Nursery, the Family Welfare Society, YMCA, Boy Scouts, Girl Scouts, milk and shoe funds for children, and the Social Service Exchange, a clearing center for exchange of information among the various social service organizations.[60] From 1929 to 1933, the Charleston Community Chest never met its fund-raising goal, falling short nearly $50,000 in 1932, and it is clear that the amount sought was inadequate to meet the needs of all these organizations under the difficult circumstances of the times. The executive secretary of the Charleston Community Chest, Belle Greve, resigned in frustration in 1933 to take a position with a charitable organization in Cleveland.[61]

The experience of the Social Services Union of Martinsburg, a private welfare agency funded by Community Chest and the principal relief agency in Berkeley County, was probably typical of charitable organizations in West Virginia's smaller cities. During the first four months of 1932, it spent almost all of its $9,000 annual allocation from Community Chest. In May, it announced that it was suspending operations during the summer months in order to save its meager resources for winter. By late summer Community Chest in Martinsburg had exhausted its resources as well and was unable to raise additional funds.[62]

The American Legion launched one of the most ambitious private efforts to deal with unemployment early in 1932. Calvert Estill, the director of the new state department of welfare, also chaired the Legion's state welfare committee. As part of a national effort, the American Legion in West Virginia tried to mobilize all major industries and labor organizations to fight unemployment. Responding to a call from Governor Conley, on February 8, a group broadly representative of major economic interests gathered in the Public Service Commission room of the capitol for a meeting presided over by welfare director Estill. The Legion plan to stimulate employment called for one million people across the country to pledge to spend three dollars a day. Legionnaires also would go door to door encouraging citizens to undertake improvements to their properties to put the idle to work.[63]

The plan was launched in West Virginia with a great deal of fanfare. On February 17, a full-page advertisement in the Charleston *Gazette* proclaimed "Bring Idle Men, Idle Dollars Together!" The director of the Legion's campaign in Charleston told volunteers for a door-to-door campaign: "You are in the army against depression and you must fight to save the country." The Charleston campaign generated $150,000 in employment pledges.[64]

Other cities in the state participated in the American Legion campaign. In Bluefield the Legion and other private organizations sought to raise money through door-to-door solicitation to put two hundred men to work on improving the city park. The unemployed would be given two days work a week at $1.50 per day. The canvassers found it difficult to meet their goal of $10,000. After a week they had only $5,200. Frustrated in their efforts to raise relief funds to employ workers, the Bluefield unemployment fighters turned to the idea of finding a half acre of land for each unemployed worker to garden. The city agreed to furnish equipment and seed if landowners would contribute the land.[65] In Princeton a mass meeting in the Mercer County Courthouse planned a door-to-door canvass to raise funds for relief of the estimated one hundred families in destitute circumstances.[66]

Whether Community Chest or American Legion or simply organized groups of concerned citizens, the private efforts fell short of needs. State-funded road construction projects during the spring and summer of 1932 gave work to some of the unemployed, but there were not enough road jobs to go around. When in early June Berkeley County relief authorities announced that road work would be available for the unemployed, four hundred applicants appeared for the eighty to one hundred jobs available. By the time the work started in mid-June, 650 men sought the work. The available work, which paid a meager $2 per day, was staggered on a weekly basis, presumably affording the workers some $20 per month.[67]

The collapse of mining and urban jobs encouraged movement back to the countryside of some who had moved to the coal camps or to a city for work. In the spring of 1932, a traveler in southern West Virginia observed many gardens prepared on the steep hillsides and wondered how it was possible to plant on such precipitous slopes. He also noticed much new fencing and new log cabins on small plots of ground, indicating that some unemployed miners were trying to make homes on the angular mountainsides of Logan and Mingo Counties generally considered too steep for agriculture.[68]

In Martinsburg, an observant reporter noted the increase in the number of empty houses and the downward spiral of rents in the town and ascribed it to two parallel movements. Because of reduced earnings, many young couples just starting families had been compelled to give up independent housekeeping and move in with their parents or other relatives. At the same time, many people were abandoning the city to return to farms or places in the country where they could grow food. Indeed people who owned houses in the city were trying to trade them for country property. One real-estate agent predicted that there would be 125 to 175 empty houses by April 1, 1933, when many leases would expire.[69]

In early 1933, Kanawha county agent T.Y. McGovran tried to encourage former farmers to return to the land in order to escape welfare dependence. McGovran and a group of interested citizens organized a two-pronged approach that sought to make available both subsistence gardens and farms, where, they envisioned, unemployed urban dwellers would move "back to the country." If no dwelling was available on the land, they hoped to persuade the federal government to provide surplus army tents. By April 1933 McGovran reported that more than fifty families had been resettled on a portion of 1,100 acres provided by a coal company on the Poca River. These families had moved in, and in pioneer fashion they had cleared the land, built log cabins, and started homesteads.[70]

Another way some West Virginians sought to mitigate the effects of the economic collapse was through establishment of barter systems. Kanawha county agent McGovran set up a simple system in which the county agent's office served as a clearing house for barterers, who could call at the office offering items for trade and listing needs. Among the listings one day in December 1932, for example, were proposals of one William Cobb to trade a house and lot in town for a farm, of a woman who wished to exchange a fur coat for vegetables, and of someone who offered a thirty-five pound pig for a twelve-gauge shotgun. County agents elsewhere expressed interest in copying the idea, and when the American legislators association held a regional meeting in Charleston, Dr. Roy Blakey, an economist of the University of Minnesota in town to talk to the legislators about taxation, advocated large-scale trade and barter as one of the solutions to the Depression. He proclaimed the Kanawha County barter system as "a step in the right direction."[71]

In March 1933, the city of Morgantown organized a large-scale cooperative barter and trade market to handle noncash exchanges of food, furniture, hardware, implements, and labor. Former businessmen skilled in the various lines headed the sundry departments. Proponents of the exchange saw it as a forerunner of similar exchanges throughout the state with the possibility of developing interregional exchanges.[72]

No doubt with tongue in cheek, Jarvis Currence, a justice of the peace in Clarksburg, entered into the spirit of the growing barter economy by setting a list of barter fees, including one pig for issuing a summons, one bushel of apples for trying a case, and one good heifer or bull calf for taking an inquest on a dead body.[73]

One activity that boomed during the Depression was reading. On a March day in 1932, the Martinsburg Public Library loaned 655 books, the most in a single day in the library's history up to that point. Mary Stribling, the librarian, suggested two reasons for the reading boom. Many people were unemployed and had nothing else to do, but they read not simply to escape. Most passed over fiction and read history and economics in an attempt to understand what was happening.[74]

Meanwhile the downward spiral of state revenues continued, and the state government made drastic spending cuts. On January 7 Governor Conley urged further retrenchment in all agencies, and on January 21 the state board of control ordered institutions to operate on current receipts rather than general revenue.[75] In February the state treasurer, noting the continuing shortfalls in revenue, urged that all state agency expenditures be reduced by 20 percent.[76] In June, the state board of education reduced the salaries of all state college faculty by 10 to 20 percent.[77] Despite a 19 percent reduction in appropriations by the 1931 legislature and an additional $600,000 retrenchment by the executive department, on July 1, 1932, the general revenue fund of the state had a deficit of $2.5 million.[78]

Facing a growing deficit and rising unemployment, as well as the possibility that pending federal legislation might offer opportunities for federal relief loans, Governor Conley called for a special session to meet on July 12, 1932, and the general approval that met the call raised hopes that the session could be conducted in a spirit of cooperation in spite of the approaching election.[79] On the eve of the special session, only thirty miles from the capitol, another disaster struck, adding to the woes of the legislators and to the misery of West Virginians. Torrential rains sent Paint Creek and Armstrong Creek over their banks, and they swept through the area, destroying almost a hundred homes, leaving a thousand homeless, and killing at least eighteen.[80]

As it turned out, the temptations of politics in a crucial election year overwhelmed any inclinations toward bipartisanship. When the legislature met, it faced the heavy irony of meeting for the first time in the plush new capitol while it deliberated over the collapse of the state's finances and economy. Conley set before the legislature an eleven-point program designed to deal with the deficit, give tax relief, and provide unemployment relief. As he had in 1931, Conley recommended that the time for redemption of lands delinquent for taxes in 1929, 1930, and 1931 be extended. He also called for the reduction of salaries for all public officials, the reduction of fees paid to county sheriffs for keeping of prisoners, the passage of a bill providing for the semi-annual payment of taxes, and a prohibition against using county relief funds for direct payments to the able-bodied unemployed. Conley also sought enabling legislation that would allow municipalities, counties and the state to obtain the benefit of federal unemployment relief legislation being contemplated by Congress. On the matter of tax limitation, Conley recommended that the legislature enact a statute limiting the taxes levied by local tax-levying bodies and submit to the voters a constitutional amendment to limit tax rates.[81]

In the most controversial part of his program, Conley requested new revenues to meet the deficit and to establish a $500,000 fund for unemployment relief. Perhaps having in mind the hunger marchers he had faced only recently, Conley said the state should not be impotent in the future as it had been in the past to help those in difficult circumstances. He said it was important not only to be able to help meet extraordinary circumstances wherever they might arise but also to preserve confidence "on the part of a needy public in the state itself." To raise the emergency budget-balancing revenue and the relief fund, Conley proposed taxes on cigarettes and other luxuries.[82]

The Democratic House of Delegates, following the theme of the political campaign, attacked profligate spending and taxation and emphasized economy and retrenchment rather than relief. Approving neither new revenues nor borrowing from the federal government, the House sought to eliminate the deficit by further drastic cuts. Some Republicans joined the Democrats in their attacks on spending and bureaucracy. U.S. Senator Henry D. Hatfield wrote his cousin McGinnis, a member of the legislature, urging him to fight against the big spending, bureaucracy, and paternalism of the Conley administration, trends that, the senator lamented, he observed in both Charleston and Washington.[83]

Although not specifically part of the call for the special session, the legislature passed bills eliminating the state bridge commission and the state prohibition department and requiring that all state legal duties be carried out by the attorney general's office, thereby eliminating departmental lawyers. Conley vetoed all these measures, but the legislature passed most items over his veto. Only one, which halted a measure that would have cut personnel in all state-supported institutions by 20 percent, was sustained. The legislature refused to approve borrowing. Neither would it approve the establishment of a state relief administration or a relief fund, the general argument being that the Republican administration could not be trusted to use borrowed money responsibly. Indeed the House of Delegates proposed to investigate the governor and other state officials, and Delegate Shirley Ross of Kanawha, to the cheers of his colleagues, even talked of impeaching the governor. "If we can get rid of him, we'll have some prosperity in West Virginia," Ross asserted.[84]

The tumultuous special session ended July 27. Its chief result, the Tax Limitation Amendment, would haunt the state throughout the Depression years and beyond. Tax reform had been an issue for nearly a decade. During the war years and immediately afterward, world markets eagerly sought the raw resources that the state's mountains yielded, and West Virginia had enjoyed something of an industrial boom. Business income soared, towns and cities grew, and the state, in neo-mercantilist fashion, provided expanded public services. The state and its subdivisions issued bonds to finance such things as new roads, schools, and government buildings. When the boom faded, and personal and corporate incomes declined, the public debt—with its interest and sinking fund payments—and the cost of maintaining the new services remained. Because of lax administration and the lack of scientific assessment, the property tax, the main source of state revenue, became "a slough of inequality" and, combined with the sense that taxes were "too high," drove taxpayers toward revolt. John Fairfield Sly, a West Virginia University political science professor who became one of Kump's chief early advisers, believed that the cost of government in West Virginia was not high compared to such costs elsewhere but only seemed high in comparison to declining incomes.[85]

As early as 1925, the legislature had approved a tax-reform amendment calling for the limitation of taxes on intangible property only, but voters rejected this "narrow classification" proposal. Governor Conley's Constitutional Commission in 1930 called for a similar tax-limitation amendment that would cover personal property employed in agriculture as well as all intangible personal property. Tax Commissioner Thomas C. Townsend, eager to build a platform on which to run for governor, called for a broader plan of tax limitation that would classify all forms of real and personal property and place different tax limits on each category. Townsend's plan was rejected by the legislature in 1931, but the House of Delegates in the special session of 1932 resurrected the broad classification plan, although they revised the language so that Democrats could deny Townsend credit for the measure. According to Sly, at the end of the bitter and contentious special session, "a tired and irritated" Senate finally accepted the House bill, although it was poorly drafted, largely because "we had to get something to vote on." In just this way, the legislature passed one of the most consequential measures in the state's history and sent it before the voters for their approval in the 1932 election.[86]

The gubernatorial candidates of both parties, Herman Guy Kump the Democrat and Thomas C. Townsend, the incumbent Republican state tax commissioner, supported the amendment, although Kump personally believed it to be an economically unsound idea. Organized labor favored the amendment, believing that it would lead to more equitable taxation.[87]

Meanwhile on July 15, Congress passed and President Hoover signed the Emergency Relief and Construction Act, a relief measure making some $300 million available for loans to states. The loans would be repaid by reductions in allotments of federal road funds.[88] As the legislature would not act on his relief proposals, Conley, saying "thousands are literally in want as we face another winter," defied the solons. Acting unilaterally, he named a bipartisan state relief board and applied for federal loans from the Reconstruction Finance Corporation (RFC). The board met promptly and elected a chairman, Charles K. Payne, a Charleston banker and a Democrat. Other members of the four-man board were John B. Easton, president of the state Federation of Labor; A.W Laing, a Charleston coal operator; and the Rev. John Gass of Charleston, former president of the state conference of social work. The board chose the Department of Public Welfare as its administrative agency, and the welfare director, Calvert Estill, as administrative officer. Two federal employees loaned by the U.S. Children's Bureau, Mary Skinner, a nationally recognized figure in the social services field, and Katharine Lenroot, helped to organize and carry out the relief program.[89]

As the special legislative session ended on July 27, the state road commission announced the beginning of emergency highway construction with funds provided by the federal emergency relief legislation. Employment for some fifteen hundred men would be provided by projects to build some fifty-six miles of new roads. Intended primarily to provide work relief for the unemployed, the projects required the maximum use of hand labor and the employment of local residents. The jobs paid thirty to forty cents an hour, and each worker could work no more than thirty hours per week.[90]

The relief administration worked through the structure of county welfare boards, which had been created by legislation of 1923. In most cases these boards had been moribund, but now they were revived and became the focus of local relief efforts in the fall and winter of 1932-1933. The federal legislation required local surveys before any application for aid, and the process was rather cumbersome. Probably typical was the case of Berkeley County, where the Community Chest, which had handled relief work for several years, had collapsed under the burden of the Depression and no longer functioned. On September 22, 1932, the county court and local leaders in relief work met with Mary Skinner of the state unemployment relief administration. The local welfare workers explained the plight of local families, six hundred of whom now needed relief. Many existed on the verge of starvation and went without food for days, except for apples and flour, which was still available from the Red Cross. The relief workers believed they would need at least $35,000 to ward off malnutrition during the coming winter. The county court could provide only $8,000, and the Community Chest could no longer raise private funds. Skinner explained that to obtain the federal relief funds they would have to have a county welfare board approved by the unemployment relief administration to administer the funds, provide for a strict accounting of all funds, and present a survey of needs and resources, showing that local resources were exhausted. The federal monies could be used only for work relief.[91]

After the Berkeley County welfare board was named, it took over the work of the former Social Services Union of Martinsburg and announced a drive for local funds, saying the RFC funds would not be sufficient and that some necessary relief activities were not covered by the RFC money. The welfare board set up shop in a failed bank. A local reporter noted the irony and pathos:

> Where once under the high vaulted ceiling and before elaborate cages well-dressed, prosperous people waited, impatient to deposit their money, there now stands another line of waiting people. But the picture is now of tragedy. All the plump, shining, hurrying prosperity is gone. The ones who wait so patiently now in front of the gilded cages have nothing to deposit.... Their faces are pinched, sallow, and their eyes tell of experiences of which most of them have drained the cup of misfortune to the bitter dregs.

Hundreds of people were coming into the former bank to pick up the elaborate eligibility forms or to obtain blue slips enabling them immediately to draw on meager local relief funds to obtain food or clothing at local stores.[92] Maude Mason, the executive secretary of the welfare board, reported in December that the distress, destitution, and suffering were the worst ever in Berkeley County. She arranged with a shoe repair company to repair the shoes of the destitute free of charge and hoped to persuade barbers to make a similar offer.[93]

Kanawha County and Charleston also proposed to put people to work repairing streets and roads with Reconstruction Finance Corporation money, setting aside local funds to help those unable to work. Local relief workers set up a central labor bureau in the court house and were taking hundreds of applications for work from people of all classes.[94]

In Huntington, a committee seeking RFC aid said 15,000 citizens were in immediate need of food, shelter, and clothing, and city facilities such as streets and sewers needed extensive repairs. Sewing machines and equipment used during World War I to make garments for soldiers were being put back into use to make clothes for the needy as the Red Cross supplied cotton and women volunteered labor.[95]

As early as July 23, 1932, just one week after passage of the emergency relief bill, Governor Conley inquired about RFC loans and by early September submitted the first application. During the next six months, he submitted twenty-five separate applications to the RFC, and eventually fifty-three of the fifty-five counties received funds. Also during this period, a team of RFC social workers toured the state to determine relief needs of the different parts of the state.[96]

Governor Conley's director of relief and welfare activities, Calvert Estill, became an outspoken advocate of a carefully coordinated national relief program. Testifying before Congress in hearings on relief legislation in January 1933, he said that the current "haphazard, patched-up" relief program was destroying the health and morals of the unemployed by requiring that they be destitute before they could get help. Moreover, he noted, "it has not been possible thus far to give adequate relief to the needy and distressed people of West Virginia" where the average allowance had been seventy to eighty-nine cents per week per person, an amount "dangerously far below minimum standards." He advocated the establishment of national standards and federal grants as well as loans.[97]

Estill argued that West Virginia's experience proved the necessity of a government-financed public welfare program. He pointed out the failure of Community Chest and other private efforts in West Virginia's cities and concluded, "The day has passed when a few generous citizens . . . can be expected to dig down into their private purses and contribute funds sufficient to finance all the local welfare work." Now government at all levels "must make provision to finance adequately its welfare program . . . distributing the burden of cost for such a program equally upon all taxpayers."[98]

After the Democratic sweep in November, the state government, like the national government, faced five months with a lame-duck chief executive. Governor Conley still had the constitutional obligation of preparing a budget for the biennium and presenting it to the new legislature, which convened in January. The new governor would not be inaugurated until March. With both houses of the legislature overwhelmingly controlled by the Democrats, Conley's efforts clearly were an exercise in futility.[99]

Like President Hoover, Conley, although not a candidate in 1932, endured considerable vilification in the opposition press and in the legislature. The Charleston *Gazette* occasionally complimented

Conley during his term, approving of his actions in cleaning up Logan County, applauding his resistance to intense political pressures on important appointments, and even commending him for acting out of a sense of public duty in calling the special session of 1932, but when Conley fought to keep the special session focused on relief rather than further cost cutting, the *Gazette* called him "inept, futile, and almost non-existent" and said that "his incessant timidity and fright would be ludicrous were the situation not so dangerous." Denouncing his proposal to tax cigarettes and other luxuries, the *Gazette* said: "In the light of want and misery, with unemployed thousands clamoring for bread, with a vast horde of office-holders lapping away at the public trough, our great statesman and Governor, William G. Conley, perceives the flicker of a cigarette in the dark. . . . So with the zeal of a jelly-like crusader he calls for more taxes and threatens to veto the good work of the legislature." The Parkersburg *Sentinel* condemned his administration as "profligate" and "wantonly extravagant"—all in addition to the threat by the legislature to impeach him.[100] The Buckhannon *Record* condemned Conley as the worst of a long line of inept and sometimes corrupt governors who had led the people of West Virginia into "the most tangled and impossible governmental mess that the latter day history of the state has recorded."[101] Conley's successor blamed his administration for the deficit crisis of 1933, charging it with "venality" and excesses.[102]

On a cold Sunday morning in late November, after the political explosion that had destroyed the Republican dominance in West Virginia, Conley endured another explosion that added injury to insult. With the staff of the governor's mansion enjoying the day off, the governor endeavored to start the furnace on his own. When he ignited a match, a gas explosion knocked him down and burned his face and arms. Only after a week in bed ordered by his doctor could Conley join in the preparation of his lame-duck budget.[103]

The new legislature that met in January was the first one since 1893 in which Democrats controlled both houses. Forty-six percent of the Senate and 73 percent of the House of Delegates were new and inexperienced legislators and looked to governor-elect Kump for leadership. Conley went through the motions, reiterating previous recommendations and noting that draconian cuts had already been made in state expenditures. He again asked for a state relief fund, doubling the previous request to $1 million.[104] The legislature ignored Conley's budget and recommendations and marked time until Franklin D. Roosevelt and Herman Guy Kump could be inaugurated.

The long Republican rule of West Virginia was rejected by the voters in 1932, and if Conley had been a candidate, he would certainly have suffered the fate of most Republicans in this Democratic landslide. Conley has received slight attention from historians and the period of his governorship has fallen into the dark hole of obscurity into which West Virginians have consigned much of their twentieth-century history. Although his portrait hangs in the state capitol today, he is scarcely remembered. He came into office as the candidate of corporate interests and coalfield "oligarchs," but he tried to steer the state through the most difficult crisis of its history with some sense of concern for those who suffered most. Compared to other state governors during the early Depression, Conley responded more readily than most to the distress of farmers and workers. With his call for state and federal unemployment relief, he proved more willing to advocate such measures than his Democratic successors. Like President Hoover, Conley appears to have lacked political skill and made little effort to rally popular support for his efforts. Of course, the stunning collapse of the state's economy and the consequent rise of unemployment and debt and the slashing of government spending created an untenable situation for any incumbent.

The hard times of 1931 to 1933 saw much impressive private effort to organize against the Depression, but from many quarters the realization grew that the complexity of relief needs generated by the economic collapse outran the traditional means of response. Those on the front lines of the fight saw the need for a farther-reaching organization encompassing private efforts, local and state governments, and the federal government.

Both concerns for the unemployed themselves and fears for "the whole structure," as Fred Croxton put it,[105] drove the search for broader efforts. Unfortunately, the legislature and the voters of West Virginia unnecessarily impaired the ability of the state government to respond to the crisis with the passage of the Tax Limitation Amendment, which John Sly called "a most hazardous jump in the dark."[106]

4
A "Jump in the Dark"

The popular solution to West Virginia's Depression crisis—the Tax Limitation Amendment of 1932—turned out to be untimely, ill-advised, and poorly crafted, adding a mind-numbing constitutional conundrum to the desperate economic situation. The amendment virtually paralyzed the new and largely inexperienced state government, presided over by Herman Guy Kump, the first Democrat in the Governor's Mansion since 1921, and it inhibited the efforts of the state, counties, and municipalities to deal with the Depression and to cooperate with the New Deal.

While Franklin D. Roosevelt and his lieutenants pushed an emergency program of relief and recovery through Congress, the Tax Limitation Amendment, more by accident than design, required that Kump, by instinct a conservative, lead the way in a substantial restructuring of government in the state at the expense of courthouse, school-district, and municipal politicians. The amendment also required a substantial change in sources of public finance in the state, offering a historic opportunity to devise resource depletion taxes that would help the state to retain more benefit from its natural resources. After a bitter struggle, the legislature, following the conservative path proposed by Kump, shifted the burden from the regressive property tax to various forms of indirect and also largely regressive taxation, such as a consumer sales tax. The new order in West Virginia would put a high premium on organization of interest groups to seek the legislature's favor. Preoccupied with virtually reinventing the state's system of public finance and governance, Kump resented the efforts of Harry Hopkins and the Federal Emergency Relief Administration (FERA) to push the state toward more support for the unemployed. Though eager to bask in the reflected glow of Roosevelt's popularity, he lacked enthusiasm for the New Deal and what he came to see as its constant intrusions into state sovereignty.[1]

As the desperation of the Hoover-Conley years reached high tide in the summer and fall of 1932, voters in West Virginia, like voters elsewhere, were ready for a "New Deal." Ironically, the Republican gubernatorial candidate of 1932, Thomas C. Townsend, was probably more attuned to the need for change than Kump. Townsend, a native of Fayette County who had gone to work in the coal mines at age ten, was much more sympathetic to organized labor than Kump. A graduate of the West Virginia University law school, Townsend had often supported tax reform efforts as far back as 1905, when he had been chief clerk of the tax commission. He had served as tax commissioner from 1909 to 1911 and had advocated a minerals-depletion tax, a heretical violation of the prevailing conspiracy thesis, which held that nothing must be done that would cripple West Virginia's coal industry in its fight against its northern rivals and the United Mine Workers. He served as prosecuting attorney in Kanawha County from 1913 to 1917, receiving much attention for sending several legislators to prison for accepting bribes. He then became an attorney for the United Mine Workers and successfully defended union officials in the treason trials of the early twenties. As tax commissioner in the Conley administration, he proposed a tax classification and limitation amendment in 1929, and as something of a tax-revolt mood grew, Townsend, with the support of the Ogden newspapers, used his call for tax reform to defeat his conservative rivals for the Republican gubernatorial nomination in 1932. The West Virginia Federation of Labor supported him, and the United Mine Workers leader in the state, Van Bittner, called Townsend "a man of the common people." Corporate interests who usually supported the Republican party felt uncomfortable with Townsend.[2]

The voters wanted change, and Townsend, with long experience in state government and a record of advocating reform and working with the labor movement, offered the best hope. But Townsend struggled under several ultimately unbearable burdens. In a year in which big business suffered credibility with voters, Townsend might have survived the abandonment of his candidacy by that important element, but, with an overwhelming "turn the rascals out" mood prevailing, his long experience in state government became a disadvantage. If the big-spending Republican regime of the twenties was responsible for the voters' woes in West Virginia, Democrats argued, did it make sense to reward one who had been part of the regime? Moreover, after the Republican debacle in the election of 1930, and the worsening of the Depression in the succeeding months, a defeatist mood stalked Republicans. Newspaper publisher and congressman Hugh Ike Shott of Bluefield decried the "defeatist complex" in a letter to a friend and said, "The Republicans themselves seem to be putting over the idea . . . that the party is to be beaten this year."[3] The unpopularity of President Hoover also hurt Townsend's chances, and whistlestop visits to the state by a tired Hoover, who kept his swollen right hand in his pocket and mumbled speeches about the need for protective tariffs, did little to help.[4]

If Townsend frightened some conservative Republicans, Kump, on the other hand, seemed the least threatening of the Democratic candidates to conservative business interests. Born on October 31, 1877, the son of a Confederate veteran in the Hampshire County town of Capon Springs, Kump grew up in comfortable if modest circumstances on a five-hundred-acre farm devoted to stock raising. Educated at home and in local schools through the eighth grade, he then briefly attended Shenandoah Normal School in Winchester, Virginia. After teaching two terms and working as a deputy county clerk in Hampshire County and as paymaster of the Consolidation Coal Company's Monongah mine, Kump returned to Virginia in 1903 to study law at the University of Virginia. In 1905 he began practicing law in Elkins, and in 1908 launched his political career by successfully running for prosecuting attorney in Randolph County. After two terms he suffered his first political defeat in the 1916 primary, and then he served briefly in the army, spending all his enlistment in Washington. After the war, he was elected mayor of Elkins and in 1928 was elected judge of the Twentieth Judicial Circuit. In addition to his legal practice, Kump invested in banking, real estate, and farming.[5] Nothing in Kump's career suggested anything but a competent, safe, rural conservatism, not unlike the Democratic conservatism that had governed West Virginia from 1872 to 1897, and offering no real departure from the stolid Democratic opposition of the Republican era. Kump called himself Wilsonian, but his views really more closely approximated the last Democratic president before Woodrow Wilson, Grover Cleveland.[6]

Some of the roots of the bitter factionalism that plagued the West Virginia Democratic party throughout the New Deal years can be discerned even in the moments of triumph in 1932. Senator Matthew Mansfield Neely, eager to establish himself as the state party leader, successfully organized West Virginia for the nomination of Franklin D. Roosevelt, but he could never settle on a choice for the gubernatorial nomination.[7] This critical political mistake by the leading Democratic politician of the state contributed to the dilemma of the West Virginia Democrats, because Neely's failure to see to the election of a pro-Roosevelt governor resulted in the election of a conservative Democrat. Neely begged his friend William E. Chilton, former U.S. senator and publisher of the Charleston *Gazette*, "in heavens name, to put your finger on the man," but Chilton could think of none with sufficient "absence of political corns and bunions."[8] Observing the primary lineup, Neely complained that there were "two and three-fourths candidates for every one and one-third locust in the state."[9]

Kump prevailed in the primary over several Democratic hopefuls who might have been more comfortable with Franklin D. Roosevelt and the New Deal and with Neely and the more liberal wing of the state Democratic party. Because his rivals for the nomination divided the liberal vote, Kump, with strong support in the agricultural counties of the east, won the nomination with only 28 percent of the total.[10]

After Kump won the nomination in early June, the state party chairman—Robert G. Kelly, a member of the prominent Charleston legal firm Brown, Knight, and Jackson—presided over a meeting of the Democratic state executive committee at Parkersburg to lay plans for the general election campaign. Although the defeated candidates and other party functionaries pledged support, the unity displayed at Parkersburg quickly dissipated as Kump and Senator Neely argued over patronage, and Kump accused party rivals of conspiring with the Ogden newspaper chain. Some Democrats felt Kump displayed little enthusiasm for Roosevelt.[11]

His Democratic rivals, United Mine Workers leader Van Bittner, and the Ogden newspapers all branded Kump early on as the candidate of the "interests" or "utilities." It was certainly true that he was more solicitous of the business interests than the other candidates. During the legislative session of 1931, Kump wrote to former governor Cornwell expressing fear that "our fellows are going to be too extreme" and might retard recovery. He believed that tax reform might be necessary, but "we must have the greatest care lest we destroy certain industries."[12] When Van Bittner called him the candidate of the public utilities, he called the charge "absurd," but privately, he confided to the state Democratic party chairman, Robert Kelly, that a similar charge by the Ogden press "is a two-edged sword and may wound the hand that wields it."[13]

Although Governor Conley and his welfare director, Calvert Estill, tried to make unemployment relief the central issue in the fight against the Depression, both Townsend and Kump and the legislative majority, reflecting the interests of businesses with substantial real estate and property-owning voters, focused on tax relief. Kump, however, harbored serious doubts about constitutional revision as a solution. In 1930, even before he had announced for governor, Kump labeled Townsend's reform plan "economically unsound." The best way to bring about tax relief, he believed, was by cutting spending. He agreed with former governor Cornwell, who now observed West Virginia's political wars from Baltimore, where he was chief legal counsel for the Baltimore and Ohio Railroad, that the first thing to do was to cut all public expenditures "to the bone."[14] Political reality dictated, however, that Kump support the Tax Limitation Amendment, which had become in the minds of many who yearned for a simple solution the panacea for all that was wrong with West Virginia. Democrats in the 1932 special session of the legislature were able to substitute for Townsend's proposal one of their own so that the amendment that went before the voters would bear a Democratic label. Kump preferred, however, that constitutional tax limits be placed only on agricultural property. He believed it "unwise to imbed inflexible provisions in our constitution that would make it impossible to give relief to any business or industry that may be in distress." Even before the legislature adopted a specific amendment, Kump presciently warned that a classification amendment "will probably make it impossible for certain sparsely settled agricultural counties to support their necessary institutions without State aid." Of course, part of the problem, from Kump's perspective, was that the amendment would place in the constitution the requirement that business and industrial property would be taxed at a higher rate than homes or farms. He agreed on the need to provide relief to the farmer and homeowner, and he believed railroads, power companies, and other public utilities would have to pay higher taxes, but he feared the inflexibility of setting high limits on business and industry.[15] Rather than constitutional tax reform, Kump emphasized reducing spending, calling for a return to the spending levels of 1920, and a reduction of the public payroll in the state by at least 25 percent.[16]

On the campaign hustings, Kump proved an articulate, extemporaneous campaigner, putting together catchy lines and colorful phrases such as "axe reform" to dramatize his call for cutting the budget and public payroll.[17] Speaking before a crowd of some seven thousand at the Morgan's Grove Fair near Shepherdstown in early September, Kump said, "The only tax reform that will relieve the people of West Virginia from the cruel burden they bear is to clean house in Charleston and everywhere that political henchmen cling to the public payroll." He urged voters to "turn out the chronic officeholders and economize in public expenditures as we have been compelled to do in our private affairs."[18] At the Wayne County Fair at Ceredo two weeks later, he asserted that the "pillage, peculation, plunder and predatory practices of office holders of this state must end now."[19] Before the Kanawha County Democratic Women's Club the next day, he promised that as governor "my first act will be to hurl from the State House all those malefactors whose pillage, peculation, and predatory practices are ruining our state."[20]

Kump took state chairman Kelly's advice and concentrated on the southern coal mining counties where the Republican party had large numbers of registered voters. Although he had little sympathy with organized labor and slight experience in dealing with industrial workers, Kump campaigned doggedly through the southern counties, where Kelly feared Townsend might prevail with margins that would offset Democratic strength elsewhere. In the end, Kump won by nearly sixty thousand votes, polling slightly fewer than Roosevelt in the state. Townsend ran ahead of Hoover, but the wide margins that Townsend hoped for in the coal counties did not materialize. The Republican disaster was too massive for Townsend to overcome.[21]

The election swept away the remnants of the old Republican regime in West Virginia leaving only seven Republicans in the Senate and fifteen in the House of Delegates. All elective positions of the state executive branch and all congressional seats went to Democrats.[22] Hugh Ike Shott lost his congressional seat in the Democratic deluge, but he was philosophical: he had not enjoyed it much anyway. During his two terms in Congress, business and industry and everything else had gone to smash, "so my experience hasn't been one of sweet dreams on beds of peace and roses."[23]

The victors of 1932 faced no bed of roses either. Because the new legislature and Congress took office in January, and neither Kump nor Roosevelt would be inaugurated until March, the state had to endure not only the spectacle of the discredited Conley presenting a budget to an overwhelmingly Democratic legislature, an exercise in futility, but also the fruitless last months of Herbert Hoover's presidency. Meanwhile the banking situation grew increasingly grim.

The unfortunate lame-duck interregnum was awkward, but Kump used the time to prepare. A friend of former governor Harry Flood Byrd of Virginia, he traveled to Richmond as the guest of Byrd and Governor John Garland Pollard and spent ten days in the Old Dominion studying Virginia's system of public finance.[24] William E. Hughes, editor of the Morgantown *Dominion News*, persuaded Kump also to seek advice from experts at West Virginia University. Although not keen on the idea at first, Kump invited Dr. John Fairfield Sly of the university political science department to Elkins, and Sly convinced him that university scholars could help. Thus was born Kump's "little brain trust." Sly and his associates provided substantial help in wading through the complexities of the legislative and constitutional morass that the Tax Limitation Amendment generated.[25]

In the last week of January, with the new legislature in session but more than a month before his inauguration, Kump began a series of meetings in the Senate president's office with key figures of the new legislature and members of the university advisory group in what became an unofficial joint legislative committee on efficiency and economy. With the governor-elect leading the way, the group devised a program and began drafting statutes, but many interruptions occurred. Legislators and incoming administration members were plagued with an army of "deserving Democrats" crowding the capitol corridors seeking jobs. Meetings had to be conducted behind guarded doors to prevent interruptions by determined job-seekers. The joint legislative committee, an extra-legal body, became the driving force of the regular session in the waning days of the Conley administration. Working far into every night, the group came up with a six-point legislative program: a balanced budget, bills to put the Tax Limitation Amendment into effect, emergency reorganization of schools and local roads to prevent the disruption of essential services that could result from the loss of local revenue, emergency state relief for local budgets to pay the salaries of school teachers, new revenues through a general sales tax to replace in part revenue lost under the amendment, and a long-term agenda for constitutional amendments creating such things as the short ballot, executive budget, and a permanent committee on efficiency and economy for long-term planning. Distracted by the imperatives of the Tax Limitation Amendment and the fiscal crisis, the planning group failed directly to address the most serious problems, such as the condition of the banking system, the plight of the unemployed, and the impoverishment of the state's rural counties.[26]

In the week before the inauguration, the snowballing national and local banking crisis required the governor-elect's participation in a series of meetings with bankers and Conley administration officials. On March 1 Conley and Kump appeared together before a joint meeting of the legislature to recommend emergency banking legislation that would enable the governor and banking commissioner to follow the example of surrounding states and call a bank holiday if necessary or to modify banking rules. On March 2 Governor Conley used the emergency powers to impose banking restrictions, providing that depositors could withdraw only 5 percent of their deposits.[27]

On March 4, 1933, Democratic administrations were inaugurated in both Washington and Charleston. In Charleston the inaugural parade—made up of politicians and dignitaries in cars and several marching bands braving the cold, wind, and snow—made its way from downtown up Quarrier Street to the capitol. There, after a brief farewell by Governor Conley, Judge Haymond Maxwell of the Supreme Court of Appeals administered the oath to Kump.[28] In his inaugural address, Kump pointed out that the Tax Limitation Amendment, by reducing the yield of the general property tax by some $17 million would require new taxes as well as a new role for the state in school and road administration and finance. Although the Tax Limitation Amendment would also immediately affect the counties' abilities to provide relief for the destitute as they had done in the past, Kump made no mention of the need for the state to deal with unemployment relief other than a vague reference to the welfare of "those thousands of my fellow citizens who live far from the splendor and elegance of this State Capitol." Whatever was done must give business "no just cause for alarm." He repeated his campaign promise to carry out "a complete change of personnel in the public service of this State" and requested the resignation of "all officers and employees whose tenure is subject to executive action."[29]

One of the problems of the Tax Limitation Amendment was that while it limited taxes on farms and residences, it also cut taxes on corporate real estate, thereby denying the state a major source of tax revenue. Kump and his advisers believed that these revenues should be recaptured through some other form of taxation. To reassure the business interests of the state, however, Kump and his "brain trust" began hearings immediately after the inauguration to consult with various industries as to how the corporate property taxes lost under the amendment might be recaptured. First came the electric light and power group, then the railroad corporations, then separate delegations from the coal, oil, and gas interests, wholesale and retail dealers, telephone and telegraph companies, and others. John Sly and his team of university professors believed that these hearings helped to educate the business interests to the necessity of paying new indirect taxes, but the sessions also enabled the lobbies for the various interests to "educate" the governor's advisers and to lobby for the least painful taxes.[30]

The banking crisis continued after the inaugural. On Sunday evening, March 5, President Roosevelt proclaimed a national bank holiday. Emergency federal legislation soon followed, which provided for reopening of banks with liquid assets and the reorganization of the rest.[31] As the Treasury Department worked to place national banks and federal reserve banks on a sound basis, the federal treasury urged states to see to the soundness of state banks. Kump learned of the regulations on March 15. Writing to his brother Kerr, he said, "I am more anxious about the banking situation than I can express, and I really have no one to whom I can turn." The legislature had just adjourned leaving a large number of bills for his consideration, and the transition was incomplete, with hostile members of the Conley administration and new appointees jostling for his attention and creating confusion. Kump devised a plan that sought to assure the soundness of banks allowed to reopen. He left it to the incumbent commissioner of banking to supervise the reopening of the banks and was shocked to learn that the commissioner permitted all state banks to reopen. Federal authorities required some federal reserve member banks in the state to remain closed, but even weak state banks were permitted to reopen. Concluding that there was hopeless incompetence in the banking department, on March 24 he appointed Bluefield banker Waitman C. Given as commissioner of banking and ordered him to cooperate with federal authorities and to hold anyone found to have been engaged in wrongdoing to a strict accounting.[32] In the meantime, President Roosevelt's quick action in the banking crisis and his reassuring "fireside chat" of March 12 ended the immediate crisis for the nation's banks, and soon thereafter in every city deposits far exceeded withdrawals.[33]

Although the banking crisis was the most pressing immediate matter, almost everything the Kump administration did resulted from the far-reaching impact of the Tax Limitation Amendment, which severely reduced the basis for local government revenues.[34] With a loss of revenue resulting from the amendment estimated to be $17 million to $20 million, in order to maintain the existing level of government services, not to mention meet debt payments or special needs occasioned by the Depression, new sources of revenue would have to be found.[35] Legislators and voters had seized upon the amendment without anticipating its untimely consequences. Had voters known the full impact of the amendment at the time of the election, it is unlikely that they would have approved it, because it ended some traditional local institutions and substantially limited the autonomy of local levying bodies, compelling the more distant authorities in Charleston to engross more taxing power and authority over county and municipal governments. Kump's leading brain truster, John Sly, believed that only after the furor of the election had died down did people begin to ask just what had been done—"the citizen was accordingly slow to accept the fact that he had made a most hazardous jump in the dark."[36]

On four separate occasions in 1933—during the regular session from January to March and the two extraordinary sessions—West Virginia's state government tried to deal with the consequences of both the Tax Limitation Amendment and adverse judicial reactions to implementing legislation. The amendment was itself something of a riddle—obscurely written, sweeping in scope, and of uncertain legality. Legislators and Kump's team of draftsmen tried to guess what it meant and what the scope of appropriate legislation should be, but the legislature and the Supreme Court of Appeals read the amendment differently. In a series of decisions, the court quashed efforts to put the amendment into operation and threw Kump's program and local finances into turmoil.[37]

Preoccupied with the banking crisis, the tax-limitation muddle, and the confusion of the transition, Kump allowed the legislature to adjourn on March 13 with the intention of calling it back into session within a few weeks for a more deliberate consideration of the six-point program he and his brain trust had devised. On April 10, the first extraordinary session of 1933 convened, and it remained in session until June, enacting most of Kump's program, including enabling acts for the Tax Limitation Amendment, increases in gross sales taxes to make up for revenue losses under the amendment, establishment of the county-unit system in education, state takeover of some thirty thousand miles of county roads under a single state road commissioner, and a balanced state budget.[38]

Throughout the crisis of 1933, Democratic job seekers plagued Kump. He could not name Democrats to government positions quickly enough to satisfy the faithful. The problem loomed larger for Kump than for his Republican predecessors or for his friends Byrd and Pollard in Virginia because of the long period that the West Virginia Democrats had been out of power and also because the Depression made state government jobs more attractive. Some key jobs remained in Republican hands for months, and this angered applicants and their sponsors who remembered Kump's promise to "hurl from the statehouse the malefactors of peculation and privilege." After six months of Democratic control, "Osker," a letter writer in the Nicholas *Chronicle*, warned "Kumpie" that the men and women of Nicholas County who worked day and night for a Democratic victory grew impatient for "a little piece of sow belly."[39]

Robert G. Kelly, the state party chairman, handled appointments for the new administration. Thousands of applications flooded his office in downtown Charleston. Kelly, described in the press as "debonair and dapper," personally interviewed up to fifty applicants a day from all over the state. Despite the demands on his time, Kump continued to be personally besieged by the job seekers. The bulk of his incoming correspondence came from those seeking positions. Reporter Sam Mallison wrote that the greatest strain on the governor was listening to "heart-rending stories" of hundreds of men who had once commanded large salaries in private industry now begging for minor appointments.[40]

Another dimension of the patronage problem was the question of federal political appointments and the bitter rivalry between Governor Kump and Senator Neely. The rift between the Democratic leaders came quickly and widened throughout 1933. In January governor-elect Kump had suggested to the Democrats in the legislature that the primary election be eliminated as an economy measure, but Neely wrote to delegate Rush D. Holt opposing the suggestion, and Holt read the letter to the Democratic caucus to the discomfiture of Kump's supporters. Federal appointees named by Neely openly spoke out against Kump's program, and those who opposed administration bills in the legislature, such as Holt and Abram J. Lubliner of Mercer County, seemed to be closely associated with Neely. Kump denied any rift and hoped when Neely addressed the legislature in a joint session on May 9 that he would give a ringing endorsement of the Kump program, but when Neely spoke he lavished praise on President Roosevelt, Congress, and the legislature—but he never mentioned the governor.[41]

Kump believed that Neely opposed his friends who sought federal appointments. Claiming that West Virginia suffered patronage losses because of the "lack of attention to her interest in these large federal appropriations," Kump tried to arrange a meeting of the congressional delegation in Washington on June 28 to discuss the matter, but only one of the congressmen agreed to meet. Summarizing the situation for former governor Cornwell, Kump said he was too busy to try to build a personal political machine, "but I am not going to throw down my guard to snipers, nor do I propose to hand a club to someone to bludgeon me."[42] Rescheduled for July 6 in Washington, the meeting was canceled when Senator Neely was "unable" to attend, even though Kump had made the trip to Washington.[43]

After the abortive meeting in Washington, the breach between Kump and Neely became irreconcilable, and soon Democratic politicians in West Virginia aligned themselves with one or the other. The party split into two factions which, with occasional amoeba-like additional dividing, engaged in byzantine intrigue and sometimes near hand-to-hand combat throughout the New Deal years. Although personal enmity and petty resentments played a part in the factionalism, the factions did have recognizable ideological differences. On the whole Kump represented a throwback to the nineteenth-century Bourbon Democrats, who allied themselves with advancing industrial capitalism while voicing an old-fashioned rural conservatism. Kump saw government's proper role as limited, distrusted federal intrusions into state matters, looked to "wise observance of the inexorable laws of supply and demand" as the solution to economic problems, was unsympathetic to organized labor, and feared that relief would pauperize the population and destroy individual initiative. He readily joined forces with the railroad, mining, and power interests represented by Robert G. Kelly and his law firm in Charleston, Brown, Jackson, and

Knight. His conservatism was not unlike that of the last Democratic governor, John J. Cornwell, who had become chief counsel of the Baltimore and Ohio Railroad and a Kump ally.[44]

Neely, on the other hand, strongly supported federal initiatives, courted organized labor, and supported New Deal liberalism. The main issue, however, was patronage. Kump controlled the state's patronage, and Neely generally controlled federal patronage. Both used it as a political weapon in the bitter internecine strife. Democrats could engage in their factional fights while consolidating their control of what was once a solidly Republican state, because the Depression had virtually destroyed the Republican party, and it could offer little effective opposition.[45]

Despite the growing rift in the Democratic party, Kump and his statehouse faction managed to push the Kump reforms of 1933 through the legislature. Like President Roosevelt in his first hundred days, Kump benefitted from the sense of crisis and the idea that "something must be done." Although there was a vociferous band of liberals in the legislature, the legislative majority supported Kump, who wielded state patronage effectively by holding it hostage to the successful passage of his program.[46]

The loudest resistance came from schoolteachers who bitterly fought the county-unit bill. School reformers and the West Virginia Education Association had advocated the county unit or some version of educational centralization in the state for a decade, but reform efforts had failed, according to a report of the state Department of Education, because of the "withering blasts of local selfish interests."[47] William Cassius Cook, superintendent of schools in the Conley administration, had advocated state financing of the schools to increase spending per pupil and to equalize educational opportunity throughout the state.[48] Calvert Estill, Conley's director of public welfare, advocated the county-unit system as a means of saving money to put into unemployment relief.[49] Kump's county-unit plan, however, seeking nothing more than to respond to the dictates of the Tax Limitation Amendment, unintentionally made the old system of school districts inoperable. As Superintendent William Woodson Trent said at the meeting of the state education association at Wheeling in 1933, by passing the Tax Limitation Amendment, "we took away one method of support before supplying another."[50]

When the county-unit bill came up for debate in the first extraordinary session, a tremendous demonstration of a kind previously unseen in Charleston took place against it in what was the first effort of an organized education lobby to directly influence legislation. In addition to inundating the legislature with letters and telegrams, teachers, administrators, and board members from all corners of the state, taking advantage of the recently built roads and perhaps also eager to see the new capitol, descended upon Charleston. Before the House of Delegates convened each day, hordes of opponents of the bill swarmed onto the floor to buttonhole members, and then they filled the galleries to overflowing and loudly cheered opponents of the bill. Many educators sincerely believed that the county-unit system would injure their schools. Teachers employed by the larger and better funded systems feared that the poorer rural districts would benefit at their expense. Some worried that local pride and initiative would be lost. As for board members and administrators, they faced the loss of their positions, because the county-unit system would substitute fifty-five county boards for the 398 district boards.[51]

Kump did not easily abide opposition, and he reacted sharply to what he called the "school lobby." Speaking before the Young Democratic Clubs of West Virginia at its annual convention at Clarksburg on May 13, Kump said he had met all the lobbies—the gas lobby, the oil lobby, the coal lobby, the railroad lobby—but the school lobby was "the most disappointing, most unyielding, most unrelenting of them all." He said education "should not be subjected to the device of the ward politician."[52] The governor's harsh language shocked teachers, who insisted that such remarks were unjustified. Many in the capitol, however, unaccustomed to the demonstrative methods employed by the teachers, applauded Kump, and the county-unit bill passed with relative ease on May 22.[53] Kump's blunt denunciation of the teachers lobby helped him win a legislative battle, but it cost him the long-run support of school teachers.

When the first extraordinary session of the legislature concluded in June, it had enacted most of the bills that the governor had called for. West Virginia now had property-tax relief, a balanced budget, centralized control of education and roads, and reformed local government. Kump, his advisers, and the majority in the legislature believed that they had done all that they needed to do. The new functions undertaken by the state were to be financed largely by a gross sales tax (basically a business and occupation tax), a consumer sales tax, an income tax, and a series of other indirect taxes including levies on production and privilege taxes.[54]

Meanwhile, county assessors worked out their valuations under the tax-limitation enabling act, and tax bills went out with October 1 as the due date. On September 1 an unexpected disaster fell: the Supreme Court of Appeals struck down the enabling act in a series of decisions. The court held that all taxes must fall within the constitutional limits, and taxes for debt service must come first. Whatever remained after debt service might be devoted to current expenses. If the limitations could be ignored in levying taxes for current expenses, as provided by the enabling act, the court asserted, the purpose of the amendment would be defeated.[55] Estimates by the tax commissioner's office showed that under the court's ruling, many counties and municipalities with heavy bonded debt would be unable to raise money under the property tax for current expenses. Meanwhile, with no legal authority to collect taxes, local jurisdictions had no funds to pay workers. Fearful that some jurisdictions would lack suitable police protection, Governor Kump ordered the state police to be prepared to take over law enforcement wherever necessary. Most policemen and other officials, however, worked without pay, uncertain that they would ever be paid.[56]

Governor Kump desperately wanted to avoid calling another extraordinary session, because he feared it might be unmanageable. After having loyally accepted Kump's program and the advice of the committee on efficiency and economy during the first regular session and the first extraordinary session, the members of the legislature were beginning to have ideas of their own and to resent the braintrusters. Members of the House of Delegates, particularly, began to feel that the governor had encroached upon legislative prerogatives. House members wanted to hear no more of brain trusts or programs or the committee on efficiency and economy.[57] Led by Rush Dew Holt, a bespectacled and energetic twenty-eight-year-old from Weston, the "liberal" faction in the House became openly hostile to Kump. Holt opposed most of Kump's program and led the fight against the consumer sales tax, which he called ruinous to the poor man. He also identified Kump as a creature of the utility corporations and led a vigorous House investigation of the utilities.[58] Kump believed Senator Neely and his ally, Charleston *Gazette* publisher William E. Chilton, encouraged the opposition and that Neely and Chilton sought a second extraordinary session to embarrass him and to push their own political and patronage agendas.[59]

Another reason Kump wanted to avoid reconvening the legislature was that he was under direct pressure from Harry Hopkins, the federal relief administrator, and the White House to come up with relief money to supplement federal relief funds, and he did not want to ask for relief funds while the legislature faced the uncertain tax-limitation dilemma.[60] He told presidential aide Marvin McIntyre that a special session of the legislature could cause the "seething cauldron" of the coalfields to boil over. It could also prevent the party from prevailing in a special election for a congressional seat.[61] Writing to his friend William E. Hughes at the Morgantown *Dominion-News*, Kump said emergencies arising in both Washington and Charleston forced him to ignore carefully made plans in order to "combat social disaster." "This is war in every way," he wrote, "except that we do not hear the rattle of musketry and roar of artillery."[62]

Despite Kump's strong desire to avoid another extraordinary session, the refusal of the Supreme Court of Appeals to rehear the tax-limitation cases on October 27, 1933, left him with no choice. He had to recall the legislature to try again for a suitable enabling act so that county and municipal governments could be rescued from their dilemma. With great reluctance, he also told the legislators, without comment, that the "Federal Emergency Relief Administration calls upon West Virginia to provide . . . $500,000 per month for human relief."[63]

In a first attempt to solve the tax-limitation puzzle, in November 1933 legislators of the second extraordinary session enacted a measure providing that the state assume all outstanding school and road bonds in local subdivisions, thereby making all monies collected under the tax limits available for current expenses. This measure, however, flew in the face of a clear constitutional prohibition against the state assuming county or municipal debts, and on December 29, 1933, in the case *Berry v. Fox*, the court held the law unconstitutional.[64]

For the fourth time the legislature revisited the issue of implementing tax limitation. In desperation a group of delegates led by Wilbert Henry Norton of Cabell County arranged a meeting with Judge Joseph N. Kenna, the most recently elected member of the Supreme Court of Appeals and a former member of the House of Delegates. Although Kenna would not give an advisory opinion, he made suggestions on how the legislature might write a statute that would be upheld by the court. Finally, based on Kenna's suggestions, the solons turned to a solution earlier discussed but discarded. The levies available under the limits would be divided—up to 30 percent would be devoted to debt service with the remaining 70 percent to be available for current expenses. The new enabling bill soon faced a challenge in the state supreme court, and to the great relief of many, survived the test.[65] Meanwhile, Kump's fears about the consequences of another extraordinary session proved unfounded. Democrat Andrew Edmiston handily defeated former governor Howard M. Gore in the special election for the Third District congressional seat on November 21, 1933, and the "seething caldron" in the coalfields did not boil over.[66]

The second extraordinary session had to tackle the unpleasant task of making up for revenue shortfalls of some $11 million, which resulted from the final solution of the tax amendment muddle. Three approaches came before the legislators. The governor proposed a program that would recover the shortfall through three revenue measures: a surtax of 60 percent on all utility and corporation rates in the general revenue act of 1933, a luxury tax on tobacco, cigarettes, candy, bottled drinks, and amusements, and a consumer sales tax of 2 percent on retail sales of all but "essential food stuffs." The Senate proposed to reduce the surtax to 20 percent, drop the luxury tax, raise the consumer sales tax to 3 percent and drop the exemption on "essential food stuffs." The House of Delegates bitterly opposed the consumer sales tax and proposed a completely different mix of revenue measures: depletion taxes on gas and oil, a franchise tax on corporations, and a one-cent increase in the gasoline tax. In the end a conference committee worked out a compromise that became the Supplemental Emergency Relief Act. It provided for a 50 percent surtax and a general consumer sales tax of 2 percent with no exemption for essential food stuffs. The luxury tax was dropped, as the Senate had proposed. In the end the House surrendered, worn down by the long and grueling struggle to enact implementation legislation for the Tax Limitation Amendment.[67] The Charleston *Gazette* lamented that the triumph of an "unholy alliance" of reactionary Democrats and Republicans in the Senate had frustrated the "progressive" program of House Democrats and foisted upon the people of the state a tax program that placed the burden upon the people rather than upon the favored industries.[68]

When all was done, West Virginia's leap in the dark left the state with a substantially different system of taxation, the economic and social consequences of which had scarcely been considered. Responding to the cry of "tax relief," the politicians had framed and the voters had approved a constitutional reform that severely limited the tax base of local government and made it impossible for cities and counties to continue being primarily responsible for education, roads, and relief of the destitute. To replace the lost revenues from property taxes, the state relied on a complicated mix of indirect taxes. No longer would it simply be a matter of the state board of public works setting rates for the public utilities and locally elected assessors setting rates for businesses, homeowners, and farmers. The new system involved the interests of many economic groups, some of which were well-organized and better-prepared to defend themselves in the new arena, as the corporate lobbies demonstrated in the crisis of 1933, arranging to hold their taxes relatively steady in spite of the antibusiness sentiment of the time, while consumers, unprepared and indeed uninvited to present their cases, had to shoulder much of the burden of replacing the revenue lost through the Tax Limitation Amendment. Kump believed the consumer sales tax appropriate because it would obtain needed revenue from "a large class of our citizens who, though enjoying every benefit of residence have paid practically no taxes, because they were non-property owners."[69] The non–property owners were, of course, the least able to pay taxes.

The new system made the state primarily responsible for schools, roads, and care of the indigent, but the state could not match the overall funding formerly available to school districts, municipalities, and counties. The attempt to do so, combined with the other obligations of the state, had ill-fated consequences. The road system constructed during the twenties disintegrated because of lack of maintenance, county schools suffered a severe drop in funding, higher education withered, plans for graduate education at the university were postponed, and state institutions generally decayed.

Although the consolidation of schools into county systems resulted in some savings of administrative costs, these were not enough to offset the overall loss of revenue to education under the new system, and the schools struggled throughout the decade to maintain a nine-month term and reasonably decent standards. Superintendent William Woodson Trent often found himself at odds with both Kump and Kump's successor, Homer Adams Holt, as he continually attacked the underfunding of schools. Meanwhile the average salary of teachers and principals, already low, was cut by 12 percent in 1933, and funds for new buildings and maintenance dwindled to almost nothing. In 1935 Governor Kump called for further teacher-salary reductions, arousing many organizations such as the American Legion, the Congress of Colored Parents and Teachers, the Federation of Women's

Clubs, and the State Federation of Labor to fight for education reforms. Although legislators rejected reform, they did stop Kump's efforts to reduce teacher salaries even further.[70]

Municipalities also lost their basic revenue source and had to devise various new taxes, such as municipal gross sales levies, public utility taxes, parking fees, amusement taxes, and special fees for garbage collection, sewerage, and water. In 1940 the West Virginia Chamber of Commerce noted that state cities collectively had $700,000 less revenue than in 1930.[71]

If farmers and homeowners paid less in property taxes, they paid more indirect taxes, and in the end there was little real tax relief for state citizens. Resident taxpayers also incurred losses in services out of proportion to any tax savings as the state, municipalities, and counties curtailed maintenance and construction of streets and roads, police and fire protection, public medical buildings, and schools. Those in greatest need of relief, the unemployed, were subject to the consumer sales tax for food and other necessities. Indeed, if the real purpose was to save the poor subsistence farmer or the small family farmer, the results clearly fell short of intentions as the number of small farmers, after rising sharply early in the Depression, began a steady and irreversible decline in 1935. Retail businesses also suffered from the burdensome responsibility of becoming, through the collection of sales taxes, the state's tax collector. The greatest savings under the amendment accrued to large owners of real estate and absentee owners of property who enjoyed the tax reductions but avoided the new indirect taxes and generally suffered no loss or inconvenience from the reduction of government services.[72]

An unplanned result of the Tax Limitation Amendment that proved useful to the conservative statehouse politicians was the fact that state control of secondary roads gave them a political tool, as the state road commission now controlled many jobs that were previously under the control of county courts. This was at the same time a severe blow to county courts and local courthouse machines, because it stripped them of their chief function as well as the source of their patronage and political power. One thoughtful but inaccurate observer saw this as "a move toward the final disposal of this antiquated institution."[73]

For many years state road jobs would provide a plentiful supply of patronage for statehouse Democrats, who organized state road Democrats into the Old Hickory Club, a fitting memorial to Andrew Jackson, an early promotor of spoils politics. The end of prohibition with the repeal of federal and state laws led to the creation of a state-operated system of liquor stores, which, as John A. Williams has noted, "provided not only payrolls but purchasing contracts, leasing arrangements, insurance and banking requirements, plus other plums not yet dreamed of in these comparatively innocent early years." Expansion of state welfare and conservation programs provided additional jobs for the statehouse patronage machine.[74]

Despite its many shortcomings, the Tax Limitation Amendment became sacrosanct. The statehouse Democrats held up the amendment and its implementation as great achievements, pointing to the improved financial health of the state treasury and the high rating achieved by its bonds and contrasting the financial condition of the treasury in the mid to late thirties to 1933, when the state had teetered on the brink of default.[75] Governor Kump especially defended the amendment and the consumer sales tax despite the recommendation of his chief braintruster, Dr. John Sly, that the amendment, which Sly called "a jump in the dark," be rewritten and resubmitted at the next election.[76] Although Kump had been privately lukewarm about the amendment during the 1932 campaign (favoring "axe reform" instead), he found the amendment useful as a rationale for opposing state appropriations for relief or for matching funds under New Deal programs like the Federal Emergency Relief Administration and its successor the Works Progress Administration or the Public Works Administration. Kump contended that the prohibition on debt in the state constitution and the various restrictions of the Tax Limitation Amendment made it impossible for the state or its jurisdictions to participate in matching-fund programs. The state could participate in federal programs, Kump insisted, on a grant basis only.[77]

Reflecting on the amendment and its consequences at the beginning of 1936, Kump's Commissioner of Banking, Fred L. Fox, also thought the amendment had been adopted by the voters with little understanding of the consequences. He pointed out that the middle of a depression was not a good time to adopt a new taxation system. Despite these views, Fox opposed any attempt to change the system.[78] Even Kump's successor, Homer Adams Holt, admitted in 1937 that "any mention of the amendment with any attitude other than that of reverent approach was considered a hostile act towards it." Holt, nevertheless, upheld the sacred text and, seeking to condemn his successor, told a farewell banquet in 1940 that Senator Matthew M. Neely had once had the temerity to suggest that the amendment "be abandoned in order that the State might be enabled to increase taxes to raise money to match Public Works Administration funds."[79]

As governor, Holt sought federal legislation to exempt the state from matching requirements, but when that strategy failed, he found ways for the state to obtain limited amounts of federal matching funds for state institutions through self-liquidating funding. Fees for college dormitories, for example, could be dedicated to retiring bonds used for matching Public Works Administration grants, leaving the state government unobligated.[80]

Anticipating the self-liquidating or "pay as you go" solution to the tax limitation dilemma in 1934, John Sly and his associate George Shipman argued that basing government services on the ability of different groups in society to pay "is foreign both to the democratic idea of government, and to the American theory of the place of social service in the life of the state." Such a policy, they suggested, would provide many services for the wealthy but few for the poor. They believed such was not the intent of the Tax Limitation Amendment.[81]

As the decade went on, municipalities and counties found ways to participate in matching programs despite the constitutional restrictions and the rhetoric of the governors. Ironically, Charleston, under a Republican mayor, Daniel Boone Dawson, displayed no qualms about seeking federal matching funds and was able to modernize its infrastructure with such federally assisted projects as the Kanawha Boulevard, a new Southside Bridge, a municipal auditorium, new schools, four new fire stations, a sewer system, slum clearance, and public housing. Huntington, Wheeling, and the smaller cities also accepted long-term, low-interest debt under New Deal matching programs in order to undertake similar badly needed improvements.[82]

Clearly, though, the Tax Limitation Amendment and its enabling legislation placed a straitjacket on the state's fiscal possibilities, inhibited the state's ability to participate fully in New Deal recovery programs, and prevented counties and municipalities from taking full advantage of federal matching programs. Historian John Alexander Williams has suggested that the regressive system of taxation and the chronically underfinanced, patronage-ridden public services had more than economic consequences: they also contributed to the growth of an "inferiority complex" that reinforced a defensive mentality among West Virginians.[83]

This view of typical rolling pasture and grazing land in Appalachia was taken between Morgantown and Elkins in September 1938. Farm Security Administration photo by Marion Post Wolcott. Library of Congress.

Farm Security Administration photographers took many pictures of West Virginia mining towns, like this 1938 photo of Davy, in southern West Virginia. Like many mining towns, Davy had a railroad running through it. Farm Security Administration photo by Marion Post Wolcott. Library of Congress.

Pursglove mine, on Scotts Run, near Morgantown, ca. 1938. This was in the area frequently visited by Eleanor Roosevelt. Mary Behner Christopher Collection, West Virginia State Archives.

Civilian Conservation Corps tents and barracks, constructed in 1935 at East Dailey, near Tygart Valley Homesteads. West Virginia State Archives.

Arthurdale, the Preston County subsistence homestead advocated by Eleanor Roosevelt. West Virginia and Regional History Collection, West Virginia University Libraries.

Women on relief make mattresses in Monongalia County under the aegis of the West Virginia Employment Relief Administration, ca. 1934. West Virginia and Regional History Collection, West Virginia University Libraries.

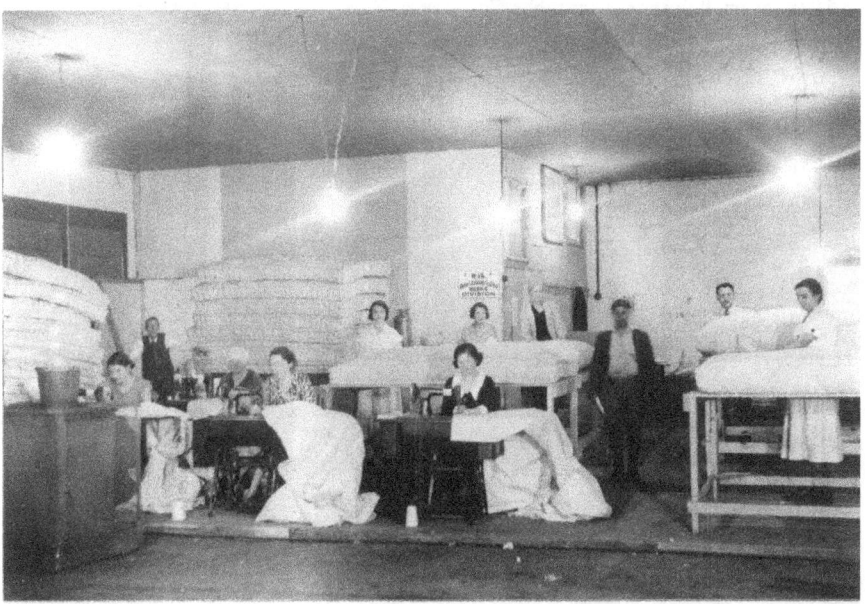

Nursery care for children was one of the programs of the Monongalia County Relief Administration, ca. 1934. West Virginia and Regional History Collection, West Virginia University Libraries.

The Shack, the Presbyterian settlement house on Scotts Run, was established in 1928. Mary Behner Christopher Collection, West Virginia State Archives.

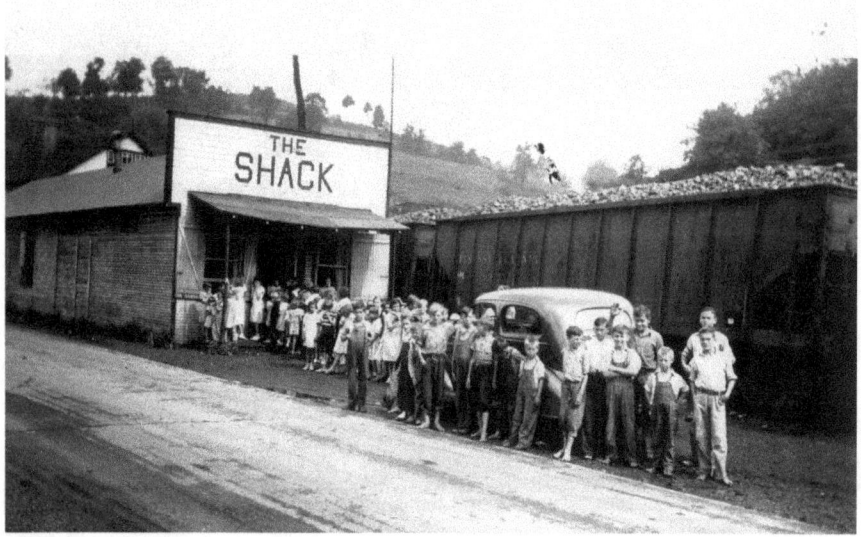

A scene illustrating the American Friends Service Committee's feeding program for Appalachian children, 1932 or 1933, in Monongalia County. Mary Behner Christopher Collection, West Virginia State Archives.

Walter Donaldson of Orlando, Gilmer County, reads to his children in 1938. The Works Progress Administration identified him as the millionth man to learn to read and write through the WPA Adult Education Program. West Virginia State Archives.

Among the largest capital improvement projects undertaken in West Virginia by the WPA were the Southside Bridge (1937) in Charleston and the upgrading of Kanawha Boulevard to a five-lane thoroughfare (1941). In this 1936 view, the new bridge approaches take shape prior to the dropping of the center span from the old bridge. West Virginia State Archives.

Roadbuilding and landscaping at the Tygart Valley Homesteads in East Dailey, 1935. West Virginia State Archives.

William Gustavus Conley, Republican governor from 1929 to 1933, was an early advocate of both federal and state aid for the relief of the unemployed. Gravely-Moore Collection, West Virginia State Archives.

Herman Guy Kump led the statehouse faction of conservative Democrats during his term as governor, 1933-1937. West Virginia State Archives.

Homer Adams Holt, attorney general from 1933 to 1937, governor from 1937 to 1941, was a reluctant New Dealer who battled the CIO, John L. Lewis, the West Virginia WPA Writers Program, and Democratic liberals. West Virginia State Archives.

Rush Dew Holt raised money for his successful 1934 campaign for the United States Senate by selling "Holt bonds" to union members. The maverick "Boy Senator" soon disappointed his labor supporters. West Virginia and Regional History Collection, West Virginia University Libraries.

President Franklin D. Roosevelt with Governor Homer Adams Holt and Senator Matthew Mansfield Neely, rival leaders of the West Virginia Democratic Party, at Reedsville, on a trip to Arthurdale, May 5, 1938. West Virginia and Regional History Collection, West Virginia University Library

5
The Blue Eagle

While Governor Kump and the legislature struggled through the financial, legal, and constitutional quagmire brought about by the Tax Limitation Amendment, Congress passed numerous measures during the hectic first hundred days of the New Deal that would directly affect West Virginians. Proposed by President Roosevelt and his advisers, many of these measures were passed with slight debate by an overwhelmingly Democratic Congress eager to move quickly in the emergency. Among them were banking reforms and legislation to deal with agriculture, industry, unemployment relief, and social welfare. Committed to capitalism but unsure how to stop the Depression, Roosevelt was willing to try new ideas. Responding to critics, he asserted, "The country needs, and unless I mistake its temper, the country demands, bold, persistent experimentation."[1]

Members of Roosevelt's cabinet who spoke in West Virginia in the early days of the New Deal made no secret of the experimental nature of their programs. Secretary of the Interior Harold Ickes visited Shepherdstown in October and declared that the election of 1932 had been a "social revolution" that marked the passing of the old order of "rugged individualism" and the rise of a new order more committed to the common destiny. In the new venture, he said, "we will all go up or down together."[2] Secretary of Agriculture Henry Wallace told a meeting of the West Virginia Dairymen's Association in Martinsburg that the nation could solve its economic problems if "we are willing to pass through a period of social experimentation." With disarming candor, Wallace added: "There is no kidding ourselves. We do not know how the things we are trying to do will turn out."[3]

The key legislation for business and industrial recovery in the early New Deal was the National Industrial Recovery Act (NIRA), which, though short-lived, had far-reaching economic, social, and political consequences for West Virginia. The result of substantial debate within the administration, the industrial recovery legislation exemplified New Deal experimentation and a tendency toward what historian Ellis Hawley has called "economic ambivalence." Some advisers believed the solution was to protect business from too much competition and antitrust laws. Others wanted to promote competition. Some adhered to the classical notion of rigid government economy, and others wanted a massive government spending program. Friends of organized labor wanted to promote labor's interests. In the end, the National Industrial Recovery Act failed because it tried to accommodate too many of these contradictory interests.[4]

The act established the National Recovery Administration (NRA), provided for suspension of the antitrust laws for businesses that accepted industrial code agreements, stipulated that the codes would contain minimum wages and maximum hours for labor, guaranteed collective bargaining for organized labor, and established a pump-priming public works program under the Public Works Administration (PWA). At the presidents's urging, funds were provided for experimental resettlement communities. Roosevelt entrusted overall supervision of the National Recovery Administration to Gen. Hugh S. Johnson, an emotional, hard-working administrator given to strong drink and colorful language. Donald Richberg, one of the main authors of the act, was chief counsel. Interior Secretary Harold Ickes headed the PWA and the resettlement projects.[5]

One of the most immediate consequences of the NIRA in West Virginia was a stunningly successful organization drive by the United Mine Workers of America (UMWA). As 1933 opened the UMWA languished near extinction in West Virginia and dispiritedly faced the rivalry of the independent West Virginia Mine Workers Union and the communist National Miners Union. Yet even before Roosevelt signed the act on June 16, 1933, John L. Lewis, the UMWA leader, seized the opportunity offered by section 7a, the NIRA clause guaranteeing labor the right to collective bargaining. He sent a hundred UMWA organizers to West Virginia, and they fanned out across the coalfields, ready to sign up new union members.[6] Van Amberg Bittner, president of the UMWA's District 17, coordinated the drive from the union's Charleston headquarters. For a leader of mine workers, Van Bittner was atypically mild-mannered, soft-spoken, and well-groomed. He talked like a college economics professor and ran his organization with cool efficiency.[7] The success of the UMWA's organizing drive would make him one of the most influential figures in the state.

Organizers told the miners: "The President wants you to join a union." If pressed to explain, they would say that they meant the president of the union. Within one week after the bill was signed, Bittner reported, "The entire Northern field as well as the New River, Winding Gulf, Kanawha field, Mingo, and Logan are all completely organized. We will finish up McDowell, Mercer and Wyoming counties this week."[8] On June 23, 1933, Bittner celebrated West Virginia Day and the union's victory with a rally (which he later called "the greatest meeting of my life") in the Charleston Armory. He told the assembled miners of southern West Virginia, "You are now free citizens of the United States and you enjoy every right the constitution and the laws give to the citizens of the United States."[9] In little more than a month, the union recruited 160,000 members and became the strongest union in America with a total enrollment of 500,000. In southern West Virginia, long one of the most difficult areas for the UMWA, membership rose from seven in 1933 to 85,764 in June 1935. Membership in the state rose from about 16,000 in May 1933 to 107,000 in June 1935.[10]

The remarkable turnabout in southern West Virginia surprised many observers who had expected determined resistance to the union by coal operators and their political allies in both parties, who had long seen the UMWA as an unspeakable conspiracy. In Kentucky the UMWA had a much more difficult time as local authorities in counties such as Harlan, Clay, Whitley, and Bell joined with operators to stop union activities. Substantial bloodshed and property destruction resulted,[11] but in West Virginia, which had its bloody struggles in the past, the unionization campaign proceeded with little conflict. From the relatively objective perspective of the eastern panhandle, which produced no coal, an editorial writer in the Martinsburg *Journal* reviewed the long and bitter history of the effort to stamp out unions in the southern coalfields. "It is hard to tell how many men have been killed; how many crimes of one kind or another have come out of the fight for and against unions in the Norfolk and Western region from Bluefield to Kenova." But now, the editorialist noted, a simple act of Congress and the edict of the president had ended that conflict which had been so much a part of life and politics in the state.[12]

Some, however, still expected the worst. Lorena Hickok, writing to Eleanor Roosevelt from southern West Virginia in August, warned of an extremely dangerous situation, which she believed would require extreme measures. After talking to UMWA organizers in Logan County, she reported that the UMWA failed to understand the situation. Under an NRA code, she believed, the whole industry would have to be reorganized, and many miners would never work in the mines again. The organizers were telling the miners all would go back to work at high wages. Hickok also doubted that many operators were reconciled to working with the union. She saw both sides as irresponsible gangs needing "someone to stand right over them with a whip and make them behave." Without a strong hand, without "a Big Boss," she believed, a very violent situation would ensue. "There's bound to be trouble," she wrote to the first lady, "and only the President, by assuming the powers of a dictator, can prevent it." Hickok also believed that a personal appearance by the secretary of labor, Frances Perkins, might help prevent a violent confrontation.[13]

Hickok's concerns about operator-miner violence were justified given the history of southern West Virginia labor-management relations, but unionization under the NRA proceeded with few hitches. Operators, however reluctantly, acquiesced to the new order. The common difficulties for all involved in the industry had brought about a conciliatory feeling in many camps and a desire to do whatever was necessary to bring order and stability to the industry. Both the union and operators had for a long time discussed some kind of stabilization plan. Coal miners who had never belonged to the union became convinced that only through the union could they bring about improvements in wages and working conditions.[14]

The UMWA seized upon section 7a as a guarantee of collective bargaining and moved quickly to exploit the opportunity, but in other industries there were doubts about the meaning of the NIRA provision.[15] Conflicts arising in West Virginia's textile and steel industries raised questions about section 7a and the promise of collective bargaining under the NRA. With the wave of organizing campaigns after passage of the recovery act, some anti-union employers responded by establishing company unions or "employee representation plans" as a way of fulfilling the letter of the law without allowing employees access to a full-fledged bargaining agent. Employer efforts to deny employees an independent bargaining agent led to a wave of strikes in the summer and fall of 1933.[16]

Did the guarantee of collective bargaining mean that workers could choose their own representatives? Or could a company meet the bargaining requirement by providing a company organization for workers? Organized labor generally believed that the NIRA's section 7a required that the workers be represented by a single independent union chosen by a majority of the workers. NRA administrators Johnson and Richberg, however, contended that neither did section 7a exclude a company-sponsored union nor did it require that a single union representing a majority be the bargaining agent. They foresaw a kind of proportional representation in which several unions might represent workers in a firm. In August 1933 President Roosevelt adopted a recommendation of the NRA advisory boards that a National Labor Board be established to oversee disputes arising under section 7a. This board under the chairmanship of Senator Robert Wagner of New York took the position, different from that of the NRA administrators, that the democratic tradition of American politics—that the majority rules—should prevail in labor matters as well.[17]

One of the early cases to come before the National Labor Board involved the Berkeley Woolen Mills in Martinsburg. Employees of the mills went on strike on August 15 because management refused to accept the United Textile Workers as the bargaining agent. Management asserted that they had no obligation to deal with worker representatives who were not employees of the mill. A unanimous National Labor Board ruled that Berkeley Woolens Company was in violation of section 7a, which granted the right to collective bargaining to workers by "representatives of their own choosing," whether or not they were fellow employees. Senator Wagner said the decision in the Berkeley Woolens case would be widely recognized and would "help clean up the atmosphere." The lesson seemed to be that the employer was obligated to recognize the union chosen by the employees.[18]

Another case arising in West Virginia, however, marked a major setback for collective bargaining under the NRA and underlined the weak enforcement position of the National Labor Board (NLB). Workers at Weirton Steel plants in Wheeling and Clarksburg, West Virginia, and Steubenville, Ohio, went on strike when the paternalistic owner, Ernest T. Weir, refused to deal with representatives of the Amalgamated Association of Iron, Steel, and Tin Workers. Weir, a long-time foe of unions, had established a company union in response to section 7a and insisted that the company union represented his workers. In October, following a procedure called "the Reading formula" it had adopted to deal with similar situations, the NLB called a halt to the strike and provided for an election in which workers could choose their own representatives. At first Weir cooperated with the NLB, but once the men were back at work he repudiated the agreement. He would allow workers to vote only for the company's employee representation plan, and he would not allow the NLB to supervise the election. Despite protests from General Johnson and Senator Wagner, the company-sponsored election was held on December 15. The NLB asked the NRA to rescind Weirton Steel's right to display the NRA blue eagle and turned the case over to the Justice Department. The Weirton case, which remained bottled up in the courts until the Supreme Court declared NRA unconstitutional in a separate case, unmasked the essential toothlessness of the National Labor Board and opened the door for others to defy both the NRA and NLB. It also helped set the stage for stronger labor legislation, as Senator Wagner drafted a bill reiterating, clarifying, and strengthening collective bargaining.[19]

Through the summer of 1933, the NRA helped major industries to create and agree upon codes of fair competition. When this work began to bog down and business recovery wavered in July, General Johnson organized a new initiative to help rekindle the hopes of recovery. What he proposed was to go beyond big business and conduct a nationwide campaign to persuade all employers to uphold NRA standards on wages and hours. Johnson chose the blue eagle as the symbol of the campaign and WE DO OUR PART as the motto. These helped create something of a national crusade as towns and cities all over the country joined the effort.[20]

In West Virginia, as elsewhere, newspapers compared the NRA campaign to the outpouring of wartime enthusiasm in 1917. In Charleston four hundred businesses immediately applied for the blue eagle compliance symbols to post in their stores and shops. Volunteers combed the city and Kanawha County to sign up more businesses and to enlist housewives in a commitment to buy only from participating firms.[21] A reporter in Martinsburg described the city's campaign beginning "with a flourish, fanfare and excitement distinctly reminiscent of war time." Flags decked the streets and store after store displayed the blue eagle and motto on a red, white, and blue poster. Barbers, mechanics, and shoe repairmen organized their own associations to set prices.[22] A house-to-house canvas by 160 volunteers got half of Martinsburg's housewives to support businesses displaying the blue eagle.[23]

Despite the excitement and ballyhoo of parades, speeches, and canvasses, the most important work for the National Recovery Administration in the summer and fall of 1933 was the negotiating of the industrial codes for fair competition. In no industry was the task more difficult than in coal. Coal production took place in some thirty-three states under a wide variety of mining conditions. Moreover, the coals produced varied widely in chemical composition, uses and value. Some coal was best used as a steam fuel, some as a metallurgical industry fuel, and some as a home heating fuel. Freight rates varied widely and, of course, so did wages. Not the least of the divisive factors in the industry was the heritage of bitter conflict between the UMWA and the nonunion operators and the conviction of southern nonunion operators that their unionized northern competitors had conspired with the union against them.[24]

Over a long, hot Washington summer, General Johnson tried personally to lead coal industry representatives to agreement on a code of fair competition, but he lacked conciliatory skills and knowledge of the industry. His efforts prolonged the debates rather than moving them toward resolution. In September, while other industries completed their codes, a committee of coal industry leaders debated. Duncan Kennedy of the Kanawha Valley Coal Operators Association chaired the committee, and Tom Kennedy of the UMWA was secretary. Other members were Lewis, Percy Tetlow, Van Bittner, and Philip Murray for the union and J.D.A. Morrow of the Pittsburgh Coal Company, Charles O'Neil of the Peale, Peacock, and Kerr Coal Company, James Francis of the Island Creek Coal Company, and Ralph E. Taggart of the Stonega Coal and Coke Company.[25] Many issues divided the committee, but one critical factor was the determination of the former nonunion fields of West Virginia to maintain a favorable wage differential. When it appeared in early September that the wage differential might be lost, Governor Kump rushed to Washington to argue in a conference with NRA administrator Johnson and Harry Hopkins, relief administrator, that the loss of the differential would lead to increased unemployment and a rise in the amount of delinquent taxes on land in West Virginia.[26]

The coal miners, whose hopes had risen with Roosevelt's election and the passage of the NIRA, grew restive as the debates dragged on and the prospect loomed of a damaging national strike. John L.

Lewis, who believed he could negotiate a favorable agreement, spent long hours on the telephone urging his agents in the field to keep the lid on and to calm strike fever.[27]

On September 14, President Roosevelt summoned representatives of operators and miners to the White House and told them that if they did not agree on a code within twenty-four hours, he would impose one. One hour beyond the deadline, the coal committee finally reached agreement. On September 18 the president signed the bituminous coal code, which the *New York Times* called the "keystone to the arch of the recovery program."[28]

Once the code was completed, an accord on a contract covering some 70 percent of the industry followed quickly. Called the Appalachian Agreement, it covered Pennsylvania, Ohio, West Virginia, Virginia, eastern Kentucky, and Tennessee. Taking into account the cost variables in each region, the agreement did allow wage differentials, but not as broad as they had been before, and the practical result was to blunt the southern wage advantage.

Incorporating the code requirements, the agreement also provided for an eight-hour day and forty hour week, a checkoff of union dues, the miners' right to select checkweighmen, prohibition of payment in scrip, prohibition of any requirement that miners buy at the company store or live in a company house, and a minimum age of seventeen for employment in the mines.[29] The agreement also provided for a four-step grievance procedure. A jubilant *United Mine Workers Journal* called it "the greatest victory ever won by organized labor."[30]

Both miners and operators in the Northern regions—the former Central Competitive Field—saw the agreement as promoting the kind of "competitive equality" that they had been seeking since before World War I. Unionization and "competitive equality," however, embodied the rhetorical Frankenstein monster of those who fought so long and bitterly against the organization of miners in West Virginia.[31] Production and employment figures for West Virginia in the two decades following organization and national agreements, however, did not justify the angst coal operators and their political allies had suffered in the era of the conspiracy theory.

Given the desperate straits of the coal industry and coal miners in West Virginia in 1932, the NRA provided the stimulus for a fairly robust recovery. Nationally some eighty-five thousand more miners were at work in 1935 than in 1932, and twenty-four thousand of these new jobs were in West Virginia. Coal production in West Virginia rose from 86.1 million tons in 1932 to 99.8 million tons in 1935. Total wages in 1935 were 75 percent over 1932 as two agreements under the NRA code moved the average annual wage from $677 to $1,096. Moreover, although some operators cooperated reluctantly, labor-management relations in the industry improved markedly as labor boards in each district helped keep the peace between the UMWA and management.[32] Bigger pay envelopes for the miners helped to stimulate general business activity. Retail sales in 1935 were 35 percent over 1933, led by a 41 percent increase at food stores. General merchandisers and motor vehicle dealers followed closely behind.[33]

The short-run successes of the NRA, however, tended to create new problems or reactivate old ones. The NRA never addressed the basic dilemma of the industry—overcapacity. The price increases allowed by the NRA code inadvertently intensified the problem by providing incentive for small operators to open new marginal operations—the Depression era version of the traditional "snowbird" mine. Though the snowbirds provided additional employment, the industry did not need the additional production, and the undercapitalized small operations lacked safety precautions. Another consequence of NRA was to increase the cost of labor and thereby to encourage both strip mining—which minimized labor costs—and the mechanization of loading. Both of these developments threatened to lead to the resumption of a trend already seen as a critical problem before NRA—the long-term reduction in mining jobs. Strip-mining would also add to the growing environmental disaster in West Virginia's mountains. The increase in production costs also meant an increase in prices, threatening coal's competitive position relative to other energy sources. It was something of a tightrope walk for the industry to increase wages and prices but to remain competitive against other energy sources.[34]

As historian Keith Dix points out, New Deal industrial policies alone do not explain the spread of coal mine mechanization in the late thirties. Interest rates and capital costs were at historically low levels, and the mine supply industry offered a larger selection of well-tested machinery than ever before. Faced with the trend, the UMWA generally and reluctantly accepted mechanization. At the union's 1934 convention, a delegate proposed, to the cheers of many, that the union oppose all mechanized mining, but when John L. Lewis shouted, "You can't turn back the clock," the audience roared its assent.[35] Still, some locals resisted. When the first mechanical loaders arrived at Scotts

Run in Monongalia county in 1936, it took some fast talking by local union officials to convince miners that a strike would be unjustified and unsupported by the union. It was a painful dilemma for miners, but John L. Lewis, eager to establish the union as a responsible organization willing to cooperate with management in a businesslike way, consistently supported mechanization as a necessary step to bring order and rationalization to the coal industry. As Keith Dix has shown, the mechanization of loading did not necessarily mean the loss of jobs, but it did mean a change in the nature of coal mining, and some coal loaders, accustomed to the traditional piecework system, could not adjust to the new order, which increased the amount of supervision and moved to an hourly-wage system.[36]

The NRA also had problems overseeing the complex rules and variations of the coal code. An admirable wish to decentralize enforcement of regional price conflicts resulted in a weak enforcement of the code. There were jurisdictional conflicts and long delays in resolving price disputes and getting action on violations. Although the legislation provided for labor and consumer advisory groups, the administrative staff tended to sympathize with the business view and to ignore the advisory groups.[37]

Despite the shortcomings of the NRA regime in coal, West Virginia miners and operators and editorial opinion across the state strongly supported the NRA in the belief that it brought substantial and beneficial change. Even with their concerns about mechanization, miners felt more secure and enjoyed their fatter pay envelopes, and operators welcomed stability and the opportunity for more profitable bottom lines.[38]

The defenders of the old order were not completely silenced. In a speech to the West Virginia Mining Institute in December 1933, William Beury, son of coalfield pioneer Joseph Lawton Beury and vice president of the Algoma Coal Company in McDowell County, defended practices outlawed by the NRA code and the Appalachian Agreement and lashed out at the "young students party and the professors bund" who criticized coal-field society. It had been necessary for the coal operators to be patriarchs, he argued, and the company houses and company stores had been necessary to keep workers. Requiring workers to receive part of their payment in scrip had been a means of protecting women and children, because lump-sum payments would result in wages going for "liquor or labor racketeers." Beury also insisted that the "professional police" (better known as mine guards) hired and paid for by the coal operators were superior to elected officers in other towns.[39]

On the last day of October 1934, Governor Kump struck a blow at this remaining bastion of the old order in the coalfields—the mine guard system—when he ordered Sheriff Maginnis Hatfield of McDowell County to "disarm and disband" the 195 so-called "courtesy" deputies who were cloaked in the privilege of public authority but paid and controlled by the coal operators. In addition to the 195 courtesy deputies, the county had forty-three regular deputies paid by the county.[40] Kump issued the order, based on a legal opinion by Attorney General Homer Holt, because, he said, many citizens of the county had expressed fear that with so many armed deputies there was a strong possibility of violence. What applied to McDowell would apply to others, and in December, Attorney General Holt issued warnings to prosecuting attorneys in other mining counties to see to it that the employment of all special deputies be dispensed with immediately. It was estimated that Holt's order would end the jobs of several hundred men who had worked for the coal companies to keep order in the camps, keep labor organizers away, and to keep political control in the hands of the mine operators. The Huntington *Herald-Dispatch* expressed the general view when it applauded the demise of the system: "It is happily true that conditions which brought it into existence no longer prevail."[41] In 1935 the legislature enacted a law formally abolishing the mine-guard system.[42]

In March 1934 the NRA responded to growing criticisms by setting up a national recovery review board under the chairmanship of the renowned defense attorney Clarence Darrow. The Darrow board spent four months studying the codes and issuing reports. The first report, in early May, harshly criticized the NRA as a tool of monopoly.[43] In West Virginia, both business and labor leaders condemned the Darrow report, and editors across the state strongly defended the NRA. The Huntington *Herald-Dispatch* said, "Chairman Darrow and his colleagues may think it would be a fine thing to return to the 'savage,' 'wolfish,' competition of other days, but they certainly are not speaking for and do no know the temper of those engaged in the production of coal." The Morgantown *Dominion News* commented: "The dominant feeling here, both among operators and the general public, has been one of gratefulness that the industry upon which principal dependence must be placed is again able to operate with profit to the owners and miners alike."[44]

Because the coal industry was something of an NRA success story, particularly in West Virginia, General Johnson accepted an invitation by F. Witcher McCullough, the state chairman of the national emergency committee, to celebrate the NRA's first birthday with a visit to Charleston. On June 16, 1934, the longest parade in Charleston's history greeted Johnson and Donald R. Richberg, one of the chief authors of the recovery legislation and the chief counsel of the NRA. Some two-thirds of the marchers were coal miners representing UMWA locals from West Virginia, Virginia, and Kentucky. The parade's numerous floats included a Miss NRA float featuring a live eagle in a cage. Eleven bands representing high schools, colleges, American Legion posts, and the miners local of Hartwell, McDowell County, provided music and color. An estimated ten thousand miners were in town for the event, and many of them attended the ceremonies at Laidley Field and listened to remarks of Governor Kump, who also read a letter from President Roosevelt; Van Bittner, the UMWA leader in West Virginia; Edward F. McGrady, assistant secretary of labor; Donald Richberg; and Johnson. McCullough served as the general chairman of the celebration.[45]

In welcoming Johnson, Bittner said the NRA had saved the coal industry and that coal miners "thank God for Franklin D. Roosevelt." Richberg reiterated the administration's commitment to collective bargaining, and Johnson, whose speech was broadcast over a national network, used the occasion to denounce the opponents of the NRA, such as the "communistic" Darrow board, the opposition press, and "partisan politicians." The Darrow board, he asserted, "announced a doctrine of pure Soviet communism straight from the book of Red Russia." Those who opposed the NRA were "like the scribes and pharisees of Biblical times who had only one answer to any advocate of human improvement—'crucify him.'"[46]

Despite the enthusiasm for the NRA demonstrated at the birthday party in Charleston, the agency and its chief administrator came under increasing fire from a broad range of critics, not just the Darrow Board, reporters, and Republicans. Progressives, trustbusters, social-welfare reformers, and consumer spokesmen had opposed the NRA from the beginning, charging that it was too much under the control of big business, and they felt that events had confirmed their fears.[47] Johnson, who drank heavily, began to act bizarrely and unpredictably, and many of his associates came to believe he should be dismissed.

The Blue Eagle

Gradually eased out of power by Roosevelt during the summer of 1934, he finally resigned in September.[48]

The most important long-term consequence of the National Industrial Recovery Act in West Virginia might have been political rather than economic. The success of the organizing drive in 1933 made the UMWA almost overnight one of the most important forces in state politics, and the power would grow and endure for many decades after the blue eagle's flight had ended. Though the union failed to elect its choice for governor in 1932, the Republican Thomas Townsend, by 1934, with more than one hundred thousand miners on its rolls, it was ready to serve notice on the conservative politicians of both parties that it was now a political force.

In 1934 the Republican senator Henry Drury Hatfield had to face reelection. The near-certain prospect of a Democratic victory in the senatorial election encouraged many leading Democrats to seek the nomination. Among those running were Clem Shaver, former chairman of the Democratic National Committee and a friend of Postmaster General Jim Farley; Louis A. Johnson, former national commander of the American Legion, who later served as assistant secretary of war under Roosevelt and secretary of defense in the Truman cabinet; Graham Sale of McDowell County (whose campaign bumper sticker read: "My vote is for Sale"); William E. Chilton, publisher of the Charleston *Gazette*, who had served in the U.S. Senate during the Wilson administration; Arthur B. Koontz, a Democratic national committeeman and gubernatorial candidate in 1920; and J. Alfred Taylor, former congressman and one-time speaker of the House of Delegates. The conservative faction of the party led by Governor Kump bestowed its blessing upon Shaver, and several of the others sought the endorsement of Senator Matthew M. Neely, leader of the "liberal" faction of the party. Neely, however, in a move he would regret, turned to a twenty-nine-year-old leader of the liberals in the House of Delegates, Rush Dew Holt. Holt, elected to the house in the Democratic sweep of 1930, had, with Neely's encouragement, led Democratic critics of Governor Kump and had conducted a noisy investigation of the utilities industries. When the question arose as to whom labor and the liberals should support, Neely persuaded Van Bittner, the UMWA leader, to throw his support to Holt rather than to any of the conventional candidates.[49]

As reporter Sam Mallison would later tell the story, Holt was as surprised as anybody by the UMWA's decision to support him for the U.S. Senate. During the early summer of 1934, he was considering whether to run for reelection to the House of Delegates or to take a big gamble and run for Congress. Mallinson advised him to consult Van Bittner who, as head of UMWA, "carried more votes in his vest pocket that any man in West Virginia." To Holt's surprise, Bittner said he would not support him for Congress but urged him instead to run for Hatfield's Senate seat.[50]

With the UMWA, American Federation of Labor, and Neely supporting him, the young Holt shocked his better-known opponents in the Democratic primary, running fifty thousand votes ahead of his nearest rival, the administration-backed Clem Shaver. Party tradition held that the leader of the ticket in an election should name the state chairman, but when the state committee met at the Waldo Hotel in Clarksburg in August, Robert Kelly, who was Kump's handpicked chairman, raised the specter that to turn the choice of a chairman over to nominee Holt would be the same as turning the party over to Van Bittner, the UMWA boss. State committee members, who generally represented the conservative wing of the party, and many of whom held state appointments, voted forty-nine to four to retain Kelly as the chair.[51]

When the party leaders including Holt, Neely, and Kump met later the same day to lay plans for the fall campaign, Holt denounced the leadership, calling Kelly a "rattlesnake" and "political racketeer" and detailing the utility connections of Kelly's father's law firm, Brown, Jackson, and Knight. Kump warned Holt to "keep his unholy hands off the legislature." Neely and Kump also exchanged verbal blows and revived old insults. The meeting disbanded with the party in disarray.[52] Holt ignored the statehouse political organization and named Huntington publisher Joseph H. Long chairman of his campaign.[53]

In spite of this uncivil war within the Democratic party, the party's candidates prevailed in 1934 with Rush D. Holt leading the ticket. Senators Hugo Black of Alabama, Alben Barkley of Kentucky, and Neely spoke in the state for Holt, but his greatest support came from the UMWA as he wrapped himself in the cloak of organized labor and the New Deal.[54]

Senator Hatfield, who was supported by the coal and utility companies, denounced the New Deal and all its works. He strongly condemned the NRA and declared that Holt was no Democrat but a Socialist. When it was over, Holt had prevailed by almost seventy-thousand votes, and all six of West Virginia's Democratic congressmen had retained their seats.[55]

Holt's victory demonstrated both the popularity of the New Deal and the rising power of organized labor in West Virginia in the aftermath of section 7a. Despite all that the conservative wing of the party could do to prevent it, the UMWA raised a young member of the House of Delegates from relative obscurity to win a seat in the U.S. Senate. Dubbed by the press "the boy senator," Holt was still six months shy of his thirtieth birthday and had to wait until then to be formally sworn in as senator. In the meantime he occupied an office in the Senate Office Building and received his salary as a senator.[56]

The NRA came to a sudden end on May 27, 1935, when the Supreme Court struck down the National Industrial Recovery Act in the *Schecter Poultry* or "sick chicken" case. The court ruled that the act improperly granted sweeping legislative power to the NRA and that, in any case, the Schecters' poultry business was in intrastate commerce and not properly subject to regulation by Congress.[57]

Although the critics of the NRA considered it a failure, both management and labor in the coal industry generally felt that the NRA approach to stabilizing the industry had been successful enough to pursue further. Even before the *Schecter* decision, the UMWA and many operators had advocated a separate and stronger law for the coal industry. Henry Warrum of the UMWA staff proposed establishment of a coal commission that would oversee a system that would guarantee minimum prices and establish market agreements and production quotas. Miners would be protected with guarantees of collective bargaining, minimum labor standards, and a rehabilitation program for displaced miners. The problem of excess capacity would be addressed with a special program that would allow the secretary of the treasury to buy up coal properties and place them in a national coal reserve. In January 1935 Senator Joseph Guffey and Representative J. Buell Snyder of Pennsylvania agreed to introduce Warrum's proposal.[58]

West Virginia operators were suspicious of the Guffey bill, as it came to be called, because of its provenance. They had long accused the Pennsylvanians of conspiring with the UMWA against them, and they feared the Guffey bill could be yet another manifestation of that conspiracy. West Virginia operators maintained that Pennsylvania had a large freight-rate advantage over the southern districts and that the wage advantage of the southern mines had recently narrowed or, as in the case of the Fairmont field, disappeared altogether.[59] Another argument of the West Virginians against the Guffey bill was that production quotas based on previous tonnage would be like giving "an old age pension to a coal mine" and would discriminate against them and in favor of the older regions.[60]

After the demise of the NRA, and after removing production quotas and the notion of a coal reserve from the bill, Congress passed the Guffey bill as the Guffey-Snyder Act of 1935, even though supporters of the bill, including President Roosevelt, believed the legislation would not pass the test of constitutionality. They hoped to buy more time for the industry to continue its recovery.[61] When the Supreme Court found Guffey-Snyder unconstitutional in 1936, Congress removed the offending provisions on wages and hours and sought quick passage of a similar measure, but Senator Holt, in part of a broad range of activities that scandalized his labor and liberal patrons, filibustered against the bill and prevented its passage in 1936. (Van Bittner wired him: "Your action on Guffey Bill is a demonstration of ingratitude that will never be forgiven.") Senator Neely, furious at his prodigal protégé, helped steer the bill through the Senate to enactment in 1937 as the Guffey-Vinson Act.[62]

Some West Virginia coal operators, fearing domination of the coal commission by Pennsylvanians, opposed the bill, but editorial opinion generally favored it. The Beckley *Post-Herald*, a Republican newspaper in the heart of the southern coalfields, agreed with critics of the price-fixing provision of the bill but said that "the coal industry is sick unto death, and emergency measures are justified on that basis, for the patient must either get better or die." Other newspapers took a similar position, seeing government regulation as necessary to stop cutthroat competition and raise wages. The Wheeling *Intelligencer* opposed the measure because of its price-fixing feature and argued that the government would now be forced to regulate oil and gas.[63]

Meanwhile, in the summer of 1935, Senator Wagner succeeded in his efforts to strengthen the government's guarantee of the right to collective bargaining with the passage of the National Labor Relations Act, which resurrected section 7a of the National Industrial Recovery Act. The Wagner Act, as it came to be known, established a permanent independent agency, the National Labor Relations Board, that would oversee employee elections and restrain employers from unfair labor practices. The legislation also outlawed employer-dominated company unions. The Wagner Act protected the gains the UMWA had made in West Virginia under the NRA.[64]

The Guffey-Vinson Act of 1937 set up the National Bituminous Coal Commission, a regulatory body comparable to the Interstate Commerce Commission, Federal Trade Commission, National Labor Relations Board, and the Securities and Exchange Commission. The coal commission, however, was originally limited to an existence of only four years, and in 1939, it expired two years earlier than originally planned, when Congress transferred its functions to the Department of the Interior.[65]

The National Bituminous Coal Commission as set up under the 1937 measure contemplated bringing stability to the industry by fixing prices. The president appointed Clarence Edwin Smith, editor of the Fairmont *Times* (and a close Neely ally) as a member of the commission. The membership was supposed to be broadly representative of the industry and the public, but Smith joined the chairman, Charles S. Hosford, a former Pennsylvania coal operator; Walter Maloney, a lawyer from Missouri; and Thomas Haymond, a former coal operator from Kentucky to form a pro-operator majority.[66] Congressional critics of the commission charged that the appointees received their posts as political payoffs. Columnist Drew Pearson in his "Washington Merry-Go-Round" claimed that Hosford, Smith, and Maloney dominated the commission and spent most of their time arguing over patronage and office furniture. The appointment of another Neely confederate, F. Witcher McCullough, as secretary of the commission appeared to be another political payoff. McCullough had headed both the NRA and WPA in West Virginia.[67]

The coal commission found setting prices and devising marketing rules to be difficult tasks. When it announced the minimum prices in November 1937, a storm of protest arose from large-scale coal users such as the railroads and municipalities. After a federal appeals court in the District of Columbia ruled that the failure of the commission to hold public hearings provided the basis for injunctive relief, the commission suspended its price schedule and started over again. Other legal problems delayed a new price list until October 1940.[68]

In the absence of government price controls, the industry moved rapidly to head off price cutting by setting prices through regional sales agencies. Appalachian Coals, Inc., led the way by persuading producers of high volatile coal in West Virginia, Kentucky, Tennessee, and Virginia to abide by prices as set by the regional agency. Producers in the low volatile fields met at White Sulphur Springs and in New York to form a similar plan, and in Northern West Virginia operators planned a Fairmont field sales agency.[69]

The National Industrial Recovery Act and its "little NRA" imitators in the Guffey legislation have generally been adjudged failures by economists and historians. Historian William E. Leuchtenburg has written: "The large corporations which dominated the code authorities used their powers to stifle competition, cut back production, and reap profits from price-raising rather than business expansion."[70] Brookings Institution economists concluded that the NRA had retarded recovery, injured the wage earner, and diminished the volume of production. In effect the NRA, with the blessings of Johnson and Richberg, its chief administrators, became too much the tool of the business corporations at the expense of the public interest. The NRA did provide a brief psychological boost to the economy in its early stage, but after the honeymoon was over, enthusiasm faded.[71] A more recent perspective by political scientists Theda Skocpol and Kenneth Finegold suggests that the United States in the early 1930s lacked the "state capacity" to administer industrial planning. As a consequence, the NRA was condemned to be "at first, a charismatic mobilization effort, and then an arena of bitterly criticized and inconclusive efforts."[72]

Historian Paul Salstrom is an especially harsh critic of the NRA, blaming it for a long list of Appalachian problems that he believes grew from the policy of encouraging higher and more uniform wages through the unionization of the Appalachian coalfields. Higher wages and NRA codes, he maintains, brought pressures for higher prices and mechanization, sabotaged employment, and denied to Appalachian producers the competitive edge over northern producers that they had enjoyed with low wages. The new loading machines not only displaced hand loaders but also created more dust—the source of black lung disease—and thereby endangered the health of the miners who remained.[73]

Despite the flaws of the National Industrial Recovery Act and related legislation of the early New Deal, these measures had important economic, social, and political consequences for West Virginia. During the period between the enactment and demise of the NIRA, the West Virginia coal mining industry stopped its slide and began to recover. Coal production, employment, and wages increased. Mining companies earned profits. Labor-management relations improved, and northern and southern producers put aside ancient hostilities to seek industrial stability. Differences now were more likely to be settled at a bargaining table than by violence. The codes helped to establish a pattern of maximum hours and minimum wages. These short-term gains, however, did not address other long-term problems of the coal industry or of West Virginia. There were still too many mines and too many miners, and when operators turned increasingly to mechanization, miners reasonably feared the consequences. In 1938, largely because of a severe business recession, more than eleven thousand miners lost their jobs, but mining employment rebounded in 1939.[74]

Nationally, the improvements in wages, employment, and working time during the NRA era represent a small upturn in what was a general downward movement in the coal industry and the national economy from 1929 to 1939. The decade saw the loss of almost one hundred thousand jobs in coal mining nationally.[75]

During the early days of the Depression, those who were concerned about the fate of the coal miners believed that the trends toward mechanization and reorganization of the industry would result in a vastly reduced mine worker force and that many of the miners who were unemployed would never work in the mines again. What happened in West Virginia from 1933 to 1952, however, exceeded the expectations of the most optimistic. By 1939 there were only three thousand fewer miners than in 1929, and there were seventeen thousand more than in 1932, when employment had fallen to only 86,829. With the exception of the 1938 recession, wages, employment, mechanization, and production all increased, though at different rates. Wartime demand and a postwar boom led to employment levels of between 100,000 and 126,000 every year (except 1945) until 1953.[76]

The significant and permanent declines in coal-mining employment came in the fifties as a consequence of changes in coal consumption patterns, competition from other energy sources, and the introduction of a new generation of labor-saving mining methods such as strip mining, auger mining, and continuous mining. International crises such as the Korean War and the Cold War and a turn toward more conservative national industrial policies also affected the climate that transformed the coal industry. It is a moot point, but mining corporations likely would have adopted the new technologies even had there been no New Deal.[77]

The NIRA failed to bring about national economic recovery, but the Blue Eagle gave emergency resuscitation to a moribund coal industry in West Virginia and set in motion important reforms with long-term social and political consequences. By ending abuses of the coalfield oligarchs in the management of their domains, by ending child labor, and by opening the door to the triumph of collective bargaining and thus of the United Mine Workers of America, the legislation achieved reform goals that had seemed impossible at the beginning of the decade. These reforms transformed life in the coalfields, bringing closer to reality the constitutional promises of free speech, freedom of association, and freedom of the press. The ending of the mine-guard system by the state contributed to the new order. The idea of national labor-management agreements within the industry would survive the NRA and help end intersectional bitterness.

The rise of the United Mine Workers as a political power transformed the political paradigm in West Virginia more than the election of 1932 had done and made possible further legislative advances for the organized labor movement and the working man. In 1932 conservative Democrats had replaced conservative Republicans. In 1934 organized labor established new expectations for Democratic politicians. Now they would have to consult union leaders as they had once looked to coal operators, bankers, and utility and railroad executives.

Although statehouse Democrats retained control of the legislature in their factional battle with the federal Democrats, the rise of organized labor forced Kump, his successor Homer Holt, and their allies to address labor's concerns. Also, some New Deal initiatives required the adjustment of state laws. As a consequence of these converging forces, the thirties produced a plethora of state legislation aimed at giving the working man a greater sense of security. In the coal industry, the end of the mine-guard system led a list of reforms, which included a requirement that all coal be weighed before it is passed over screens to insure that a miner received full pay for all the coal he mined, a miner's certificate law to assure that miners had a basic understanding of proper mining procedures, safety requirements for motors and explosives used underground, and (largely as a consequence of the Hawks Nest disaster) establishment of a silicosis fund to provide compensation for death or disability resulting from the disease. The legislature also prohibited child labor, required the regular inspection of steam boilers, established a comprehensive unemployment compensation system in conjunction with the federal Social Security Act, and strengthened and made more accessible to workers provisions of the workmen's compensation law.[78]

Some of the reforms were more impressive on paper than in reality. Martin Cherniak, author of *The Hawk's Nest Incident*, calls the 1935 silicosis law "an unmitigated disgrace," because it was designed to make successful claims nearly impossible.[79]

The coal industry still had found no magic formula for long-term stability, the national and state economies remained troubled, workers continued to face great dangers in the mines, and the blue-collar life throughout the decade retained a large measure of uncertainty and insecurity. Measured against the desperate conditions of the early thirties, however, when people talked of dynamiting coal company housing and unemployed miners joined hunger marches, results of the New Deal industrial recovery legislation did prove positive, breathing new life into West Virginia's coalfields and making organized labor a powerful economic and political force.

6
A Failed Experiment in Federal Relief

The NRA brought some recovery to the coal industry, stimulated business activities in the many communities dependent upon coal, and lowered the state's high unemployment figures. Even so, unemployment remained a severe problem in West Virginia as in the country, and the question of what should be done to help the unemployed demanded the New Dealers' attention. One of the enduring consequences of the New Deal was a nationwide move away from reliance on private and local care of the indigent and unemployed toward a more public, centralized, bureaucratic, and professional approach to relief. It was a difficult task and proceeded with mixed results across the country.

Convinced that only federal help could save the unemployed, President Roosevelt took a more positive attitude toward federal relief than Herbert Hoover. He enlisted his New York director of relief, Harry Hopkins, for a similar role in the federal government. On May 12, 1933, Congress passed legislation setting up the Federal Emergency Relief Administration (FERA) to take over emergency relief from the Reconstruction Finance Corporation. New Deal efforts to provide relief for the unemployed and the establishment of Social Security in 1936 set the nature of American social welfare for at least half a century.[1]

FERA represented something of an experiment in federal-state cooperation in providing relief for both the unemployed and the unemployable. Congress appropriated $500 million to FERA for distribution to the states through grants (rather than loans), half of which required matching funds from the states. The power to give or withhold the grants gave the federal government a means of persuading states to contribute to the relief efforts. By requiring that the states set up centralized relief agencies, the legislation helped to eliminate the archaic local administration of relief, which prevailed in most states. Federal requirements and the development of state agencies led to much wider participation in relief activities. FERA and other federal agencies often required broadly representative boards on both the state and local levels, but the carrying out of federal programs by largely untrained, unprepared, and sometimes uncommitted state administrations tended to frustrate New Deal relief and reform goals.[2]

The Conley administration had set up a state relief agency during its waning months, and its machinery became the basic conduit for federal relief funds in the early days of the New Deal. In time the West Virginia Unemployment Relief Administration—later called the West Virginia Relief Administration (WVRA)—would be the focus of much political contretemps, but, preoccupied with the Tax Limitation Amendment and its ramifications, Governor Kump gave almost no attention to unemployment relief in the early months of his administration. He accepted the bipartisan board of the West Virginia Unemployment Relief Administration that had been appointed by Governor Conley. Conley had appointed Maj. Francis Turner, a Democrat, acting director of the Department of Public Welfare when Calvert Estill resigned as director with just a few weeks remaining of the Conley administration, and Turner continued in the position with the Kump administration. An insurance man from St. Albans, Turner had served as the chairman of child welfare for the American Legion before accepting the position as acting director. The Department of Public Welfare served as the administrative arm of the Relief Administration until November 1933, when the West Virginia Civil Works Administration took over.[3]

The Federal Emergency Relief Act of 1933 provided for direct payments to the unemployed, but Hopkins encouraged the states to follow the New York example and to use the federal money for work relief rather than for welfare handouts. West Virginia was one of the states that most closely followed Hopkins's advice. Hopkins strongly believed that the dole was demoralizing. If the private sector could not provide enough employment, he believed, the government should step in and provide a living wage for government-generated work projects. Hopkins and his staff also stressed the need to use the money for women and white collar unemployed as well as for the traditional blue-collar unemployed. When FERA proved unable to meet the burgeoning need with the winter of 1933-1934 on the way, Hopkins went to the White House and persuaded Roosevelt to support a federal work-relief program, the Civil Works Administration (CWA). The experiences with FERA and CWA provided the background for the larger program of federal work relief, the Works Progress Administration, established by Congress in April 1935.[4]

Although the states theoretically administered the federal relief money granted under FERA, Hopkins and his staff kept a tight reign on the state relief organizations, particularly those that responded slowly to the crisis. Bitter conflict broke out between the FERA administrators and some state officials who resented federal interference. West Virginia, whose scenes of poverty came to symbolize the worst of the Depression, became one of the states that drew Hopkins's personal attention. The hard-working, chain-smoking Hopkins could be blunt with recalcitrant governors like Kump who did not share his commitment to the unemployed. When West Virginia and neighboring Kentucky and Virginia failed to appropriate relief money, Hopkins threatened to cut off federal funds, but of the three, only in Kentucky were federal payments halted. With a much smaller relief population, and with two powerful U.S. senators, Harry Byrd and Carter Glass, Virginia ignored the federal threats and suffered no disadvantages.[5]

Because they believed West Virginia's problems to be particularly severe, FERA field agents urged continued funding of the West Virginia relief program, but Kump and Hopkins fought a running battle over the appropriate role the state should play. The federal legislation provided that the state should match the federal grant 3 to 1, but Hopkins sought only a "reasonable" commitment from the state. Kump argued that the Tax Limitation Amendment and the ensuing litigation made it impossible for the state to appropriate any funds for relief. On August 14, 1933, noting the serious relief needs in West Virginia, Hopkins informed the president that a financial expert had studied the situation and had found the state quite able to pay a reasonable share of the cost of relief. Nevertheless, Hopkins said, governor Kump "has shown no inclination to do anything." Hopkins, clearly hoping to move the governor to action, told President Roosevelt of Kump's foot dragging and proposed to cancel all further federal relief grants to West Virginia. Roosevelt forwarded Hopkins's memorandum to Kump and asked the governor to "do something about it." Kump immediately arranged a trip to Washington to personally present his case to Hopkins and Roosevelt. The president met with Kump and agreed that West Virginia could have more time to sort out its constitutional crisis. Upon his return to Charleston, Kump thanked the president for his "sympathetic understanding" but insisted that "grave consequences" would attend an extraordinary session of the legislature to ask for relief funds.[6]

Arguing that the Tax Limitation Amendment seriously reduced the ability of local jurisdictions to provide relief, Kump sought to cut relief costs by reducing rolls and cutting payments. Echoing a claim of New Deal opponents that many relief clients refused to accept private employment, he ordered the director of public welfare to cut the work relief rate from 30 to 22.5 cents per hour and to drop from the rolls all able-bodied relief recipients who had refused to accept private employment.[7] This policy, he told former governor Cornwell, had had "a salutary effect," although it did generate complaints that "helpless women and children suffer."[8]

While Kump procrastinated over the matter of a special session and state payments for relief, FERA continued to pay 95 percent of the state's relief bill. In October 1933, the FERA field agent estimated that 110,000 families in the state needed relief. Reports from relief administrators and residents in many parts of the state reflected desperate and worsening conditions. In Kanawha, the state's largest county, 20 percent of the families were on relief. From the beginning of federal relief in October 1932 to June 1933, families received a grant of $16.20 per month. By September 1933 the monthly grant in Kanawha County—an amount that was supposed to cover all food, rent, clothing, utilities, and medical expenses—had fallen to $11.00 per family. The county relief administrator reported that under these circumstances, families on relief could scarcely obtain enough food and could pay no rent. He feared a growing tide of evictions and noted that "even now the county truck is working almost continuously moving evicted people." The administrator also reported serious medical problems among the relief population, especially undernourishment among children and widespread tuberculosis.[9] In spite of the rather desperate conditions, the relief administrator noted that no suicides had been recorded and concluded that this was evidence of the "courage and dogged perseverance of the American people."[10]

The relief administrator in McDowell County, the largest coal producing county in the state, asked the state relief administration for additional funds to cover growing relief needs as coal mining employment continued to decline. Some six thousand children in the county could not attend school, because they lacked clothing and books. A drive for used books and clothing failed, because many of the families who usually contributed were now on the relief rolls. Some were reduced to using gunny sacks and flour bags to clothe themselves, and many were barefooted. The county administrator also reported an alarming growth in the number of cases of typhoid, diphtheria, and dysentery, especially in the coal camps.[11]

Small agricultural counties, where many families depended on subsistence farms and seasonal work in forest-related or mining industries, also reported severe problems. For example, in southern Wayne County, subsistence farmers along the narrow bottom lands and rough hillsides had made some cash in the past by working in the mines of Mingo and Logan Counties or making railroad ties in the winter, but now the mines were closed, and the Norfolk and Western had abandoned its line in the county, ending the local market for railroad ties. In July 1933, 70 percent of the county's population was on the relief rolls. Direct relief of $2 per month per person was granted to those families with no means of support and with no able-bodied males over eighteen in the family. The able-bodied unemployed were to sign up for work on county roads. A local resident, noting the widespread suffering in the county, implored Governor Kump to supplement work relief with more direct relief.[12]

In Monongalia County the relief director—Alice Davis, a social worker who had worked with the American Friends Service Committee's Appalachian relief program and in Russia in efforts to relieve the Russian famine in the twenties—urged the state relief administration to make a special effort to bring families who had by now been on relief rolls for two or more years back to normal ways of living:

There is a limit to human endurance, and people that have been living on a family budget of $8 or $10 *for all their needs* over a period of years are on the road to becoming permanent unemployables. I sometimes think that it would be kinder to let them all starve quickly rather than to keep them barely alive for years and then turn them loose with permanent disabilities due to malnutrition. Perhaps the physical end of it is not so bad as the mental and spiritual. I wonder how many of us would bear up under the conditions that we impose on our clients in the coal camps? A diet of beans and salt side, supplemented by Red Cross flour and what vegetables they can raise on hill-sides that are fit only for goat pasture. Furniture consisting of old powder boxes, a table, and one bed for five or six persons. Filthy privies with vaults running over and draining down into the houses below.

She compared conditions in Monongalia County to those she had seen in Russian villages during the famine.[13]

In July twelve counties had at least 45 percent unemployed, and most of those hardest hit were counties that relied heavily on subsistence agriculture—such as Lincoln, with a startling 84 percent, and Wayne, with 70 percent. The coal mining counties Raleigh, Mercer, Marion, and Mingo all had more than 50 percent unemployed.[14]

In August, Hopkins sent FERA investigator Lorena Hickok to West Virginia "to observe not only the status of relief work . . . , but its effect on people and [to] try to get a picture of how the ordinary citizen feels about relief."[15] Noting the bitter relations between owners and miners and the desperate economic situation in the coalfields, Hickok felt great troubles were inevitable and proposed a startling solution. She told Mrs. Roosevelt that "the only way out of the mess I can see" was for the president to become an "absolute dictator." She noted the frustration of relief workers who blamed Governor Kump for the decline in relief available in the state. Welfare director Francis Turner, who impressed her more than most politicians she talked to in the state, told her: "Here we are with our entire civilization built on a rotten foundation and tottering, and you've got a lot of damned fool capitalists and petty politicians fiddling while the whole thing collapses." Turner feared that if the federal relief program failed, by 1936 it could be just "Roosevelt against the Reds."[16]

In October Hopkins again demanded that Kump do something about relief. Having reviewed Hickok's letters as well as reports of FERA field agents and the West Virginia county relief administrators, Hopkins concluded that the relief being given was "woefully inadequate." Because this problem was "by far the most important in West Virginia," it was perfectly clear, Hopkins insisted, "that West Virginia is not doing its part." He urged upon Kump the necessity of throwing other things aside to address the desperate situation of the unemployed. The federal government would again provide money for October, but Hopkins asked Kump to come to Washington to discuss the future of relief in West Virginia.[17]

On October 20 Kump and other state officials met in Washington with Hopkins and Howard O. Hunter, the field agent responsible for West Virginia. Hopkins pointed out that FERA had granted West Virginia almost $6 million, but the state had done absolutely nothing to provide funds for relief. According to Hunter's account of the meeting, "The Governor whined and cried and beat his chest vigorously, explaining how hard it would be to get the West Virginia Legislature to do much about this situation, and told us his sob story about the present tax jam they are in." Hopkins finally insisted that the governor give definite assurances that he would call the legislature into special session before November 25 to seek relief funds, or FERA would take over the administration of relief in West Virginia and tell the world that the state refused to do anything.[18]

After meeting with Hopkins and Hunt, Kump again appealed to the White House and talked to the assistant secretary to the president, Marvin H. McIntyre. McIntyre, probably seeking to cool the governor off, suggested that Kump present his case in writing. The next day, Kump wrote to angrily deny any shirking of duty or disloyalty to the president and expressed resentment that Hopkins would not count the state's road building as a relief program and that Hopkins threatened to cut off all grants to West Virginia or to take over the state's relief program. He reviewed for the White House the state's constitutional dilemma and listed reasons why he should not call a special session to ask for relief appropriations. He also reminded the White House of the president's "sympathetic understanding of our problems over here as expressed to me last August." He said he was relying on the president's assurances that West Virginia would be taken care of until "we could do more for ourselves."[19]

There was no formal federal takeover of the relief program, but because Kump had failed to respond to the need for state relief monies, leaving the federal government to pay the whole bill, Hopkins and Hunter assumed greater control over the administration of relief in West Virginia. Major Turner had become seriously ill, and Hunter proposed that a new administrator or deputy administrator be appointed. Kump recommended a candidate for the position and was to have him meet with Howard Hunter, but when Kump's candidate dropped out, Hunter decided to name a professional administrator from outside West Virginia. Having FERA's own man in the position would, Hunter reported, "fit right in with the possible necessity of our taking over the whole situation if the Governor falls down on his job." In early November, Hunter took William N. Beehler to Charleston, and with the approval of the state relief administration board, installed him as deputy administrator, Turner retaining the title of administrator.[20] Beehler, the president of the Kentucky Conference of Social Work, was a graduate of the University of Richmond and the New York School of Social Work and had served for six years as the executive secretary of the Family Welfare Society of Lexington, Kentucky, and as a part-time instructor in social work at the University of Kentucky.[21]

During the nearly two years Beehler administered West Virginia relief, he served as a lightning rod for political bolts thrust by all manner of politicians. When it seemed in the spring of 1935 that Hopkins would dump him to satisfy the politicians as an election year approached (Beehler would survive until mid-summer), Ogden press columnist Charles Brooks Smith wrote that Beehler would find a place in the history of the state—"the chapters devoted to political annals, sagas, and legends." According to Smith, "his was a most remarkable adventure, replete with thrills, hairbreadth escapes, intrigues, conspiracies, double crossing, victories, condemnation, praise, heckling, and hell in horrendous quantities."[22]

Beehler fought doggedly to build a modern, professional, and politically neutral relief delivery system in the state, but just as FERA and CWA ultimately failed to build the kind of federally directed relief program that many social work professionals wanted, Beehler failed in West Virginia. In spite of Smith's predictions, Beehler and his efforts were soon forgotten, and the West Virginia welfare system succumbed to the pressures of politicians and turned away from the strong professional social work orientation that Beehler sought to promulgate.

Beehler's arrival coincided with the beginning of the new federal relief program, the Civil Works Administration. Hopkins—worried in the fall of 1933 about the coming of winter and the demoralizing effects of idleness on the unemployed, and also frustrated with the slowness of Interior Secretary Harold Ickes to push forward federal public works projects under the Public Works Administration—persuaded the president to switch almost $1 billion from the Public Works Administration to finance an experiment in federal work relief. The PWA, headed by the cautious secretary of the interior, Harold Ickes, had been slow to put the idle to work, and Hopkins promised to put 4 million unemployed to work by December 15.[23]

On a Saturday morning in December 1933, just a month after his arrival in West Virginia, and as wary state policemen stood by, Beehler met with more than four hundred members of the Unemployed League under the dome of the capitol and assured them that the seventy-five thousand jobs allotted to West Virginia under the CWA would be filled within the week. The lack of tools would be no excuse. All red tape would be cut. "Is there a man among you," Beehler asked, "who, if he hasn't a shovel, isn't willing to pick up stones and carry them to where they belong?" The statehouse corridors rang with the shouts of "No!" During his speech, women in the crowd interrupted him to tell of sending children to bed without food and of having no shoes or clothes for their children. They shouted their approval when Beehler promised that local administrators would push the work through at any cost so that the jobs would begin within a week. He said, "If they go to jail, I'll go with them." Only when the rattlesnake banner of the American Revolution with its motto DON'T TREAD ON ME was unfurled did the state police become nervous. They allowed the banner, flanked on each side by the Stars and Stripes, to remain for several minutes and then ordered that it be folded. The leaders of the group complied without protest.[24]

True to his word, Beehler filled most of the job quota for West Virginia within a week. In Kanawha County, the CWA jobs took persons off local work relief jobs that paid an average of $5 per week and gave them jobs that paid $13.50 per week.[25] Governor Kump appeared with Beehler at a meeting of county relief workers in which Beehler announced the distribution of CWA jobs to the counties. To the cheers of some two hundred relief workers, Kump for the first time made a public commitment to ask the legislature "to do everything possible for the relief of the needy."[26]

At the end of 1933 and in early 1934, FERA field agent Howard O. Hunter reported to Hopkins that he was "a little proud" of the administrative changes they had made in West Virginia relief and that Beehler had "taken hold of his job splendidly."[27] Describing Beehler as "a sawed-off, insignificant-looking little runt," Hunter said he had nonetheless won the respect and confidence of the people he worked with.[28] On December 15, 1933, Hunter himself addressed a joint session of the legislature, summarizing the federal role in West Virginia relief and calling on the legislators to appropriate matching funds.[29]

In his reports to Hopkins, Hunter still despaired of the governor and legislature, but because so many West Virginians were unemployed, he urged continued federal funding. The number registered for work relief ran three to four times the number of jobs available. This created pressure to further limit work hours to spread the available CWA jobs. Many West Virginia counties, Hunter suggested, did not have simply an unemployment problem. Instead, he said, "they are in a permanent state of collapse due to abandoned industries and a lack of any present resources to support their present population." He urged that a study be made to determine what was needed to rehabilitate economically bankrupt counties and to improve child welfare in the state.[30]

What Hunter had observed about West Virginia was something that many New Dealers sensed about other states with collapsed industries. Hopkins himself challenged his FERA staff with the problem, saying it was something new and not particularly FERA's problem. The Appalachian relief workers of the American Friends had already identified the problem of stranded populations. The question, Hopkins asserted, was "what are we going to do about coal miners of coal mines that are never going to open and with steel workers of steel mills that are never going to open?" Hopkins said it was the subject of at least twenty dinners and conferences he had attended since arriving in Washington. "Everybody says: 'What are we going to do about it,' and no one does anything." He proposed that FERA should take over the job immediately while it had money enough, because "one year from now we may not have any." "If we are ever going to do anything about this problem," Hopkins told his staff, "the time is now."[31]

Hopkins hoped FERA and CWA might turn to the question of rehabilitation, but for the CWA time was even shorter than Hopkins predicted. Alarmed at the costs, Roosevelt ordered the CWA to close down in the spring of 1934, and Hopkins dutifully carried out the order. FERA continued, however, to adapt work relief to all skills and backgrounds and to seek ways of going beyond mere relief and toward rehabilitation, but FERA too would not survive long enough to do more than tentative explorations of rehabilitation.[32]

Despite Hunter's endorsements of his leadership, Beehler quickly came under attack by both organized relief recipients and politicians. Cuts in the number of CWA jobs led the Unemployed League to promote a strike of CWA workers. Hopkins received a telegram from the league complaining that Beehler had not responded to their complaints and asking that he be investigated in order to forestall drastic action "which we are trying to hold down."[33] Rallying in Charleston on January 24, 1934, scores of men and women listened as a chunky black man with a battered guitar shouted, "Are we together?" and plunked out haunting mountain melodies. Walter Seacrist, head of the league, said members wanted reinstatement of dismissed workers, increased pay, and investigation of political discrimination.[34]

Beehler reported to Washington that the strike was limited to Charleston, where five hundred of five thousand workers stopped work briefly. Friendly members of the league told Beehler that the strikers were inspired by "paid agitators" from the Committee for Progressive Labor Action in New York.[35] On another occasion, some one thousand members of the Unemployment League marched on the relief headquarters in Charleston demanding more jobs. Relief administrators met with them and explained the shortage of relief funds, but the demonstrators demanded that a wire be sent to Harry Hopkins informing him that CWA was unable to take care of actual distress."[36]

At the same time that the Unemployed League called for an investigation and strike, the West Virginia Senate voted to investigate Beehler's alleged mismanagement and political favoritism. Because the Democrats had just come to power after so many years in the minority, they were determined to control all important positions, and the jobs available under the Civil Works Administration made politicians realize the importance of local welfare boards. These boards, bipartisan in membership, were appointed by county courts from lists approved by the Department of Public Welfare and had been set up during the Conley administration. Although the boards were nominally made up of six Democrats and six Republicans, many Democratic politicians complained that Beehler was a Republican (he wasn't) who was trying to create a political machine. In many counties, disgruntled local Democrats sought to purge county administrators who refused to make political affiliation a factor in determining eligibility for work relief. The ultimate source of much anger and misunderstanding was that Civil Works could give jobs to less than half of those who wanted them. The half who did not get jobs blamed political influence, and indeed relief administrators across the state faced tremendous pressure from boards who wanted jobs for deserving Democrats of one or the other party factions and in some cases for deserving Republicans.[37]

In many cases the fight was between county relief administrators, often women with social work backgrounds trying to follow a nonpartisan policy, and local politicians who wished to use the new bounty to reward the faithful. In Logan, to cite an example, Democratic partisans sought the removal of county welfare secretary and relief administrator, Mabel Sutherland, apparently in the hope that someone more amenable to rewarding the party faithful could be appointed. At one point, according to an account in the Logan *Banner*, "agitators" urged a crowd of unemployed outside the unemployment office to break the doors and "go in and get that woman secretary."

A Failed Experiment

The arrival of state police officers brought the situation under control.[38] Beehler defended Sutherland, who had social work training and had been county welfare secretary since 1927. He investigated the Logan County situation and found that the demands for her removal grew from a fight between Democratic factions with the Democratic sheriff leading a vendetta against Sutherland.[39]

In Kump's home county of Randolph, a similar factional fight led to demands for the removal of the county administrator, Mrs. B. M. Hoover. Governor Kump called Washington to tell Aubrey Williams, Hopkins's chief aide, that he had a strong personal interest in keeping Mrs. Hoover in office, and Beehler also supported her. Williams, however, insisting that Hoover was guilty of being involved in political activity, demanded that she be fired. The governor's wishes prevailed in this case.[40]

Beehler's efforts to maintain a completely nonpartisan relief administration infuriated Democratic politicians. A Logan County constituent complained to Senator Matthew M. Neely that "Beehler would no more appoint a Democrat to a position of trust or even give employment to one than you or I would pick up a viper." The writer called for Beehler's removal.[41] At different times Senator Neely, the state legislature, the governor, a FERA field representative, the state congressional delegation, and in 1935 the newly elected Senator Rush Dew Holt, as well as many county politicians and newspaper editors, sought Beehler's removal.[42] Beehler, who had hoped to carry out his work in a nonpartisan manner, felt compelled to publicly announce that he was a registered Democrat.[43]

Two major problems plagued the relief administrator. One was the profound resentment that some West Virginia politicians, including the governor, expressed toward Beehler and other social workers whom they considered to be "outsiders." Another was his nonpartisan political stance, a notion completely unacceptable to politicians. The *Coal Valley News*, published by Democratic state senator Luther R. Jones, praised Beehler's administrative skills but noted that "the man holds politics and anyone mixed in politics in utter contempt." The *News* argued that such an attitude "disqualifies him for the high position of responsibility he holds."[44] In testimony before the state senate committee investigating CWA, Beehler said that the reason for an attempt to oust Mary Amend, the CWA director in Barbour County, was simply the desire for Democratic patronage. The committee chairman, Anderson C. Herold, responded, "What of it?" Herold acknowledged that patronage was indeed the point and that the Democratic party should control the administrators of the relief program. Herold charged that the relief machinery in West Virginia was controlled by "Republicans of the old school who are leading so-called social welfare workers around by the noses" while they build up the Republican party.[45]

Governor Kump held a similar opinion of Beehler's efforts at political neutrality. By December 1933, the governor had awakened to the political importance of the county welfare and relief boards. He told Beehler that these bipartisan boards, because they were appointed by the Conley administration, should be dismissed. "No right thinking person will wish to capitalize human relief for political advancement," he assured Beehler, "but a wholesome administration of these organizations requires that they be in the hands, not only of competent people, but those who are in sympathy with the administration and its humane aims and purposes."[46]

Despite the views of the Democratic majority in the legislature and of Governor Kump, Beehler and the WVRA persisted in efforts to achieve a relatively nonpartisan relief system. In cases where it judged that county welfare boards were excessively political, the WVRA removed relief from the care of the county welfare boards and created new, six-person bipartisan relief boards. The Kanawha relief board was among those reorganized. The new board sought to avoid efforts of both the Democratic county court and the Republican city administration of Charleston to influence relief.[47] The WVRA also fired some county administrators and other personnel, which also disturbed local politicians, but Beehler told Aubrey Williams, Hopkins's deputy, "This is a far different thing from the charges of Senator Neely that I am deliberately building up a Republican machine."[48] Beehler assured Harry Hopkins that Neely was just playing to the galleries.[49] For nearly two years, Hopkins defended Beehler against the demands of Neely, Kump, Holt, the entire state congressional delegation, and the state legislature that he be removed.[50]

Complicating the effort to maintain a nonpolitical relief administration was the growing split within the West Virginia Democratic party. Not only did Beehler have to contend with efforts of Republicans to hold on in some counties where they had controlled the welfare boards, he also had to deal with the bitter factional split within the Democratic party in which Kump and the statehouse faction battled Senator Neely and the federal faction for patronage and influence. Neither Kump nor Neely could control the WVRA nor CWA, which made the relief agencies and Beehler the targets of both factions. After the West Virginia legislature finally passed legislation providing $250,000 per month in relief funds in March 1934, Kump sought to reassert control over relief. He renamed the agency the West Virginia Relief Administration (WVRA) and added three members to the existing four-member board, assuring a conservative Democrat majority.[51]

Kump complained frequently and bitterly that despite the fact that he was expected to sign grant requests and that the state was expected to turn over substantial funds to the WVRA, he had no control over the personnel and policies of the relief administration. When the West Virginia legislature finally passed a relief appropriation in March 1934, FERA field agent Howard Hunter reported to Hopkins that "we should give Kump a little credit for this as he tremendously helped in getting it through."[52] For Harry Hopkins and his staff, however, it was a case of too little and too late. They held the governor in something near contempt, because Kump appeared to be insensitive to the desperate need for unemployment relief in West Virginia and had supported an appeal to the legislature only under intense pressure from the White House. Moreover, because the state had been so slow to appropriate relief funds, FERA and CWA, rather than cutting West Virginia off without federal relief funds, had essentially taken over the job in West Virginia. From a constitutional perspective, Kump had good reason to complain, because Hopkins and his deputies treated Kump arrogantly and accorded him little respect as a governor. On the other hand, the president had made clear in signing the Federal Emergency Relief Act that the responsibility to act rested first with the state and local governments and that the federal government would make funds available only after local jurisdictions had done their utmost to relieve the needy. Because Kump would not or could not do what the law required, Hopkins, driven by a sense of urgency, chose to ignore him and to get on with the work of providing relief for West Virginians.[53]

During their brief existences and despite the incredibly cacophonous uproar that accompanied them in West Virginia, FERA, its state arm (the WVRA), and the Civil Works Administration accomplished a great deal, especially in providing relief for large numbers of unemployed West Virginians and in engaging the efforts of others in supporting the effort through voluntary, uncompensated work on county welfare committees, case committees, local relief boards, and on the state relief administration board. From its inception in 1932 to November 10, 1936, the West Virginia Relief Administration spent $74 million for relief. Of this sum the federal government contributed all but $8.5 million. Unlike most other states, much of the relief provided was through work relief. This was in keeping with Hopkins's and Roosevelt's inclination toward work relief instead of the dole. William E. Beehler, like his FERA superiors, believed that work relief contributed to a healthier outlook on the recipient's part as work allowed no time for brooding. Moreover, Beehler noted, work relief preserved the worker's skills and brought about improvements in public property.[54] According to Beehler, West Virginia was one of less than half a dozen states where every able-bodied relief recipient had earned relief on a work project.[55] In neighboring Kentucky, jobs consumed only 25 percent of FERA relief funds.[56]

The WVRA engaged in numerous innovative activities to put men and women to work and sought to aid a wide spectrum of unemployed workers. The CWA alone during the fall and winter of 1933-1934 spent almost $14 million putting some eighty thousand employees to work on road, street, bridge, and airport improvements; sidewalk building; pest control; improvements to public lands, cemeteries, parks, athletic fields, schools, colleges, and the university. The CWA also did much to improve water supplies and sewer systems and built 35,400 fly-proof sanitary privies in a statewide campaign under the auspices of the state health department to improve sanitation.[57] In 1934 in Kanawha County alone, WVRA employed 170 men in the building of some twenty-one hundred new outhouses, largely in small coal camps where bad sanitary conditions had prevailed.[58]

The WVRA employed nurses in a wide variety of public health projects. Other relief workers sealed closed coal mines, repaired books for schools and libraries, improved parks, or worked in community garden, canning, and meat-processing projects to produce commodities for distribution to relief recipients.[59] In November 1934, some five hundred unemployed teachers were at work in adult education, nursery school, and recreation projects. During 1934, two camps and ten treatment centers provided assistance to more than 40,000 transients, part of the vast army of the unemployed that wandered the nation's roads and rails.[60]

The rush to provide emergency employment for the destitute unemployed made it difficult to address the problems of rehabilitation that Hopkins had called to the attention of his staff, but FERA and CWA did lay groundwork for later efforts with such activities as the Red House resettlement project for stranded families and programs that sought to help farm families to become self-supporting and independent of relief.[61]

FERA monies continued to pay for the bulk of West Virginia's relief burden after the demise of the CWA in the spring of 1934, and the emphasis continued to be upon work, with 66 percent of cases remaining on work relief in the fall of 1934. The difference was that the CWA had provided employment to the able-bodied with wages that offered more than the barest subsistence. While the CWA had afforded unskilled workers the opportunity to earn up to $13.50 per week, the average relief per case in West Virginia in November of 1934 was $17.67 per *month*. Later it would fall below $10 per month. With this amount the recipient and his family were expected to meet the cost of food, shelter, fuel, medical care, clothing, school supplies, transportation and household necessities. Commodity allocations from the Federal Surplus Relief Corporation provided some supplement for the family food budget.[62] The West Virginia figure was usually less than half the national average for FERA, which was $25-29 per month, a figure equivalent to the average *weekly* wage of industrial workers in the pre-Depression era. Clearly, as Harry Hopkins admitted in 1936, FERA relief was never adequate. Even if a family got $25 a month, it would still get $900 less per year than the $1,200 then regarded as the minimum necessary for subsistence.[63] Nevertheless, there were those who feared the effect of the dole at any level. A FERA study of relief in Logan County in 1934 noted that some people opposed relief and demanded that benefits be small enough that people would seek work rather than becoming fond of relief. The study pointed out, however, that there was no work to be found at any wage in Logan County and that benefits remained so small that in many cases even a minimum standard of health and decency was not possible.[64]

In his reassessment of Appalachian economic history, historian Paul Salstrom reflects the conventional wisdom of contemporary critics of New Deal relief. He maintains that "high" relief payments kept workers from continuing to follow the traditional subsistence agriculture of the pre-Depression era and made them increasingly dependent on money income.[65] It is possible that some subsistence farmers in the most remote areas who lived in chronic poverty obtained a higher standard of relief from the WPA than they could get from their farms, but given the low relief payments in West Virginia, that is unlikely. Only from the perspective of cashlessness could direct relief or work-relief payments in West Virginia be called high.[66]

Mountain farmers, many of whom were simply refugees from failed industries, sought relief not to escape work but because they needed it. Alarmed at the high number of families seeking relief in rural West Virginia counties in 1935, Aubrey Williams asked FERA field agent C. C. Stillman to investigate four rural counties to determine the cause of the high number of relief recipients. Stillman reported that the relief load was high in Lincoln, because many who had left to work in the lumber mills and coal mines had returned in "destitute circumstances." From 1930 to 1935, more than a thousand families from the mines and mills crowded into Calhoun County, where post office listings showed three or four families living on farms that had supported only one family before 1930. Wayne County was also deluged with refugees from the coalfields of both West Virginia and Kentucky. The Webster County relief rolls were made up largely of workers stranded by "the cessation of the lumber industry many years ago." The mountainous and rugged terrain of the county contained "no farms of any size to which these people might turn for sustenance."[67] As Jack Temple Kirby has pointed out in *Rural Worlds Lost*, the subsistence way had already been wrecked by 1930, and the rush back to the land of the early thirties put more people on the land than the land could sustain.[68]

By almost any standard, the amount of relief provided was small in West Virginia, but it was more than the niggardly local or private relief that had prevailed until 1932, and the creation of a centrally-directed state relief organization represented an improvement over the antiquated system of county poorhouses and private charity. The shift of responsibility for public welfare from the local level to the state and federal governments resulted in the establishment of local boards and committees and generated more and broader citizen involvement than had prevailed in the days of strictly local or private relief. The economic conditions rendered private charity temporarily ineffective, and the entrance of government into areas formerly dominated by private charity no doubt inhibited recovery of private charity; but the emergency relief efforts of 1933-1935 involved a larger number of private citizens in efforts to relieve unemployment and

A Failed Experiment

distress than ever before, and by 1937, as the federal government sought to move away from direct relief, private charity rebounded. The Charleston community fund set a new record in its 1937 campaign.[69]

William N. Beehler believed that one of FERA's most serious problems in setting up a relief program in West Virginia was the lack of trained social workers. He wanted to attack this problem in two directions. For the short term, he wanted to hire social workers from outside the state to help in both the state and county offices, but because West Virginia politicians strongly resisted hiring "outsiders," he believed the long-term solution was to train West Virginians. In the summer of 1934, WVRA arranged for Marshall College and West Virginia University to conduct social-work training sessions for 120 students. To provide more intensive training, in the autumn of 1934, FERA gave sixteen students scholarships to attend various universities, including Western Reserve, the University of Chicago, the University of Minnesota, the Carnegie Institute of Technology, the University of Pittsburgh, and the Atlanta School of Social Work.[70] In April 1935, the board of the WVRA resolved to urge West Virginia University to organize a permanent school of social service to train West Virginians for social work "so we in the future can look after our own social needs." Board member Rabbi Ariel Goldberg said trained professional social workers were essential to the work and had saved hundreds of thousands of dollars in relief funds in the state. "Relief conditions in West Virginia are very good," Goldberg said, "despite criticisms of the politicians and would be better still if the politicians would adopt a hands off policy."[71]

Meanwhile, the problem of retaining the few trained social workers in the service of WVRA became more difficult because of the swirl of political charges and countercharges and because state politicians particularly targeted non–West Virginians. In the fall of 1934, a WVRA official reported an exodus of the few professionally trained social workers and a growing difficulty in interesting social workers to work for WVRA.[72]

In the end, the effectiveness of FERA-CWA programs depended heavily upon how they were carried out on the local level. What President Roosevelt, Congress, federal administrators like Harry Hopkins, or state officials like Kump intended was not necessarily what took place at the most critical point—where the program met the relief recipient. Because the WVRA depended heavily upon personnel recruited within the counties to serve on boards and to carry out its work, the quality of administration, the level of expertise and the depth of commitment to the program varied widely.

How local relief administrators interpreted their purpose also determined the nature of local execution of federal programs. Was FERA simply a stopgap program to prevent the unemployed from becoming violent revolutionaries? Or was it to seek the rehabilitation of the relief recipient and his family? Two West Virginia counties provide examples of each response. The Kanahwa County Relief Administration definitely leaned toward concern about radicalism, and the Monongalia County relief operation took the broader view.

In instructions and guidelines for its investigators or "visitors," who were largely untrained for the work, the Kanawha relief board asserted that the purpose of the government's program was to maintain morale in a time of crisis. Determining who should receive relief was a trying task, and the Kanawha board, acknowledging its own lack of knowledge of "professional welfare work," tried to establish the "fundamental humane principles that should prevail" in relief work as a guide for its untrained "investigators." The policy established by the board required courtesy and promptness in carrying out interviews and quick, definite decisions, noting that "empty stomachs will not wait on red tape." Investigators were also urged to restrict their interviews to the facts concerning relief and to refrain from basing decisions on rumors or gossip, politics, or personal animosity. The board warned that "an unsympathetic interview can make a red."[73]

In Kanawha County at the outset of relief work in 1932, two relief boards were established—one the Republican-dominated board appointed by the city administration of Charleston and one the Democrat-dominated board appointed by the county court. When the city ran out of relief money, it asked the county court to assume control of relief, and the boards merged, with the city administrator of relief, a Republican, becoming administrator. Tension between the old county board and the Republican administrator led to mutual charges of political discrimination and mismanagement. The state administrator, William N. Beehler, and the WVRA applied to Kanawha County a solution used in several counties where political conflict paralyzed relief efforts—they appointed a new bipartisan relief administration for the county. This action contributed to the charges of Democratic politicians that Beehler favored Republicans, but the new Kanawha board, chaired by Charleston insurance man Frank R. Bell, itself came

A Failed Experiment

to the defense of Beehler, telling a state senate investigating committee that Beehler was "a very capable, honest and energetic executive" and that attacks on him "were not fair, just, or warranted." The board insisted that it had "in every possible way endeavored to run the Kanawha County Administration free from politics." The investigating committee concluded nonetheless that Kanawha County relief continued to be dominated by "former Republican office holders."[74]

Relations between Beehler and the Kanawha board deteriorated in 1934 as the board took increasingly skeptical positions toward initiatives of the state relief administration, calling them "impractical, un-American, uneconomical, and half-baked." The Kanawha board refused to support community-garden projects, which the WVRA promoted across the state as a means of utilizing the unemployed to produce food for the needy during the winter. Rejecting offers of free use of land for gardening projects, the Kanawha board argued that putting the unemployed to work growing and canning vegetables competed unfairly with commercial canning companies. The board also resisted a project to put people to work making mattresses for the relief recipients, because they believed this competed with private enterprise and because there was no evidence "that a lot of people need mattresses." The board asked the state board to

> instruct us definitely as to whether we have the privilege and authority to operate for them in Kanawha County using our best judgement or whether we are simply to be a Board of automatons directed to carry out all the hairbrained schemes of all of the theoretical dreamers. If such a program continues, private industry, which pays the taxes that support this relief work, will be forced out of business.[75]

Eventually Governor Kump, who apparently shared this skepticism, appointed Frank Bell, the chairman of the Kanawha board, to the board of the state relief administration. Bell resigned from the state board when a FERA field agent accused him of using his position to sell insurance to the state. Bell then became a bitter and determined enemy of both Beehler and Hopkins. In a letter to the governor, which was released to the press, Bell said Beehler was "drunk with power" and would not listen to reason, and "the relief rolls are filled with people who have never worked and who never intend to work."[76]

The Kanawha County relief administration provided an example of a local board motivated more by anticommunism than commitment to

New Deal reform goals. In contrast, the Monongalia County relief organization exemplified an effort to cooperate closely with state and federal authorities. It produced a program strongly committed to democratic procedures, local initiative, and rehabilitative goals. It benefitted from the fact that during the twenties the county had built up a network of public and private social welfare organizations to deal with the growing problems generated by the county's mining industry, which imported great numbers of workers without providing adequate facilities to support the larger population. The presence of the state university in Morgantown gave local welfare organizations a useful resource not available elsewhere in the state. Monongalia was also one of the counties in which the Quaker Appalachian relief program had operated, and the county director of FERA was a former Quaker worker, Alice Davis.

Davis believed that relief had to go beyond trying to fill the physical needs of recipients, who, she suggested, after months of unemployment and poor food, tended to fall into a state of mental lethargy. She also noted the duplication of relief efforts by well-meaning civic and religious organizations, and the tendency for local communities to become dependent upon outsiders. To try to encourage local initiative and the involvement of the depressed communities in planning and decision-making in relief programs, the Monongalia FERA organized fifteen community councils. The first met at the Shack, the Presbyterian mission in Pursglove and included presidents of the Parent-Teachers Association and representatives from the United Mine Workers, garden clubs, and all religious and social groups.[77]

The community councils became sounding boards for all relief and welfare activities in the communities and furnished much volunteer labor. Each council also had a community case committee, which met regularly with case workers. Local initiative largely accounted for the forty-two garden clubs in the county, which involved some two thousand members. Garden clubs cared for nine hundred acres of community gardens in the summer of 1934 and operated fifteen canning kitchens. They also sponsored canning clubs, mothers clubs, recreation, nutrition work, and adult education.[78]

Each of the fourteen communities also had a community center, usually established in a house provided rent free by a local coal company, and the various activities of the community councils and garden clubs operated out of the community centers. The community centers served as feeding centers for the schools, providing daily hot lunches for more than a thousand children. The centers also provided visiting housekeepers, women who earned work-relief money by helping teach others home management, and some of the centers ran nursery schools, sewing classes, and public health nursing programs.[79]

Eleanor Roosevelt became especially interested in Monongalia County's coal camps and relief activities early in the Roosevelt administration. She visited the area regularly and frequently corresponded with Alice Davis. It was Davis and her Russian companion Nadia Danilevsky who showed Mrs. Roosevelt the Scotts Run mining community, which reinforced the first lady's determination to obtain a subsistence homestead project for the area.[80]

The Monongalia County approach of encouraging voluntarism, community action and local initiative held much promise as a model for building an effective and democratic relief and rehabilitation system, but in 1935, the "anti-outsider" mood rampant among state politicians pressured the county court into forcing the resignation of Alice Davis as administrator of the local FERA program. Davis, an experienced social worker who had arrived with the Friends' child-feeding program in 1932, was forced out on the charge that she was holding a job that should go to a West Virginian and on the absurd suggestion by some that she was "an agent of Soviet Communism." Although the Monongalia program did not depend on the work of Davis alone, her dismissal boded ill for the future, as it reflected the growing politicization of the relief system. The chairman of the county relief board, William E. Brooks, protested her resignation, as did the WVRA, which declared that she "had made Monongalia County the outstanding county in the State in the handling of the whole matter of relief." Brooks said the real reason for the county court's action was that some members wanted to make relief a political matter, and Davis stood in the way. He urged that the university hire Davis to organize a social-work curriculum.[81]

Eleanor Roosevelt expressed sympathy and invited Davis and her companion Nadia Danilevsky to "spend a day or two here at the White House."[82] Davis was philosophical about the situation and told Mrs. Roosevelt that although she really did not "know quite what happened to us," it was a good time to leave as "the air has been cleared of a lot of malice and hatred that seems to grow like a nasty boil in these little communities." She took comfort in the news that the local Democratic party committee had risen up to demand that the relief board remain intact.[83]

The uprising of conservatives against Alice Davis and the Monongalia County relief operation reflected in part the growing frustration of ordinary citizens with the persistence of large relief rolls. President Roosevelt himself grew alarmed at the burgeoning relief rolls as the Depression persisted. In his State of the Union Message in January 1935, Roosevelt decried the dole as "a narcotic, a subtle destroyer of the human spirit," and he insisted, "The Federal Government must and shall quit this business of relief."[84] He called for a gigantic federal program of emergency public employment that would give work to three and a half million jobless at a cost of nearly $5 billion dollars. He drew a distinction between relief recipients who for reasons of age or physical or mental incapacity were unable to maintain themselves independently and "employables" on relief because of a continuing nationwide depression. Roosevelt said that care of the unemployables had been and should remain a local problem. Under the new arrangement, the states would be responsible for the care of unemployables and the federal government would operate a work-relief program only for the duration of the Depression.[85]

In March, perhaps taking his cue from the president, Governor Kump released to the press a letter addressed to state relief administrator Beehler urging relief officials to promote subsistence gardening among relief recipients to prepare for the day when "the public bounty must end." Citing the appalling federal and state expenditures for relief, he urged every breadwinner to "turn to his own resources and diligently find a way to become self-supporting." Otherwise, he darkly warned, it might become the task of the government to force employables to work and "to sequester their earnings for dependents."[86] The state press responded positively to Kump's jeremiad, indicating a rising frustration and anxiety about the persistence of unemployment relief.[87]

The transition to the new system of divided responsibilities between the state and the federal government went forward during the summer and fall of 1935. In West Virginia "outsiders" like Alice Davis and state administrator Beehler would not survive under a strictly state administration of relief. Kump had never been happy with Beehler and the coterie of social workers he brought into the state. He told Harry Hopkins, "There is no occasion to have outside people in West Virginia to arbitrarily administer relief. We have honest, competent devoted citizens of the state who can adequately and efficiently perform these duties."[88] Kump believed he had an agreement with

Hopkins in late 1934 to replace Beehler with a West Virginian, and state newspapers had proclaimed Beehler's imminent departure. Months passed with no word from Washington. Aubrey Williams told Beehler that Hopkins was suspending judgment on the matter. Kump telephoned, wrote letters, and sent telegrams, but Hopkins, to the governor's great exasperation, refused to respond. Finally, Hopkins sent word through a subordinate that, since the federal government no longer had anything to do with the state relief administration, Kump could do as he pleased. On July 25, 1935, Kump dismissed Beehler and named a West Virginian, C. L. Allen, as administrator of the WVRA.[89] Thus ended Beehler's tempestuous tenure as West Virginia relief administrator. Kump refused him a reference, and his federal sponsors offered him no position. Eventually he found a job with the Jacksonville, Florida, department of public welfare.[90]

For Kump, the firing of Beehler was a Pyrrhic victory. The governor could control the state relief administration, but the WPA soon became the main arena of action and patronage, and Kump was to have even less influence in the WPA, which was strictly a federal operation, than he had with FERA.

The period from 1933 to 1935 saw the search for a way to organize and finance a modern relief-delivery system to replace the failed system of private charity and local public relief. The effort to accomplish this through a combined state-federal process advanced over extremely rugged terrain in West Virginia. Politicians fought over the spoils and resisted the efforts of West Virginians like Francis Turner and William Brooks and "outsiders" and social workers like Alice Davis and William N. Beehler to create a professional, nonpolitical system. Despite the many shortcomings of the evolving system, it provided desperately needed relief in West Virginia. In emphasizing work relief instead of direct relief in the FERA program, West Virginia's system, unlike that of most states, presaged the work relief emphasis of WPA.

7
Reshaping the Welfare System

When President Roosevelt said in January 1935, "We must quit this business of relief," he meant the dole—giving money to people because they were unemployed or unable to seek work. He sought to divide the relief burden into two general classifications: the unemployed and the unemployable, and he proposed to return care of the unemployable to the states and local governments who had cared for the destitute in the past. The able-bodied unemployed, who were without work because of the Depression, he believed should be put to work by the federal government at wages higher than the dole but lower than the prevailing wage so as not to encourage the rejection of opportunities for private employment "until economic recovery would make work relief unnecessary." Roosevelt and Harry Hopkins also wanted a work-relief program that would be a federal operation from top to bottom in order to avoid the bitter conflict that had characterized FERA's relationship with the states. To complement work relief and to assist the states in providing a more permanent system of caring for the unemployable, Roosevelt proposed Social Security.[1]

The Emergency Relief Appropriation Act of 1935 put the president's work relief ideas into effect by authorizing the expenditure of nearly $5 billion for work projects. Harold Ickes hoped to get the lion's share for the Public Works Administration (PWA), which sought to "prime the pump" with large capital-intensive public works projects, but Hopkins persuaded the president to put most of the money into labor-intensive projects through the Works Progress Administration (WPA). The WPA option had the advantage of being able to put more people to work more quickly, thus putting more money into the pockets of workers. It also had the disadvantage of generating many projects of slight lasting value, the notorious "boondoggles" of depression lore.[2]

In West Virginia, FERA had operated primarily as a work-relief rather than as a direct-relief agency. It would have made sense to convert the West Virginia FERA into the WPA, as was done in most states, but the constant struggle for control among political factions, the bitter relations between Governor Kump and Harry Hopkins on the one hand and Kump and administrator Beehler on the other, and the antisocial worker, anti-outsider themes of its opponents, made WVRA an agency too much distracted by activities unrelated to its mission. Rather than turning the WPA program over to the state FERA agency, Hopkins decided to create an entirely new organization in West Virginia. Far from resolving the problems, the creation of a new organization resulted in delays in putting the unemployed to work; strained relations between the WVRA organization, a remnant of which soon became the statehouse-controlled Department of Public Assistance, and the incoming WPA organization; and initiated a fight between the contending Democratic factions for control of WPA that was, if possible, even more acrimonious than the political battles over FERA.

As the WPA swung into action in the fall and winter of 1935-1936, Republicans and conservatives constantly complained, with some justification, that the WPA was a political vehicle for the Democratic party. Harry Hopkins had insisted that FERA be completely nonpolitical, but he found it difficult to stick to that when he became administrator of the WPA and discovered he had to clear state administrative appointments with Democratic senators and congressmen. Robert E. Sherwood in *Roosevelt and Hopkins* says Hopkins almost resigned at that point but was talked out of it by Roosevelt, who persuaded him "that he could square his conscience with the realities of the two-party system of government."[3] Later Hopkins said, "I thought at first I could be completely non-political. I found that was impossible. Then they told me I had to be part non-political and part political. I found that was impossible, at least for me. I finally realized there was nothing for it but to be all-political."[4]

Despite the obvious patronage possibilities presented by the WPA, serious charges of politics on a large scale occurred in only a few states, but West Virginia rated high on this select list, which included neighbors Kentucky and Pennsylvania as well as Missouri, Tennessee, Mississippi, and Illinois.[5] In West Virginia the most serious charges of political abuse came from Democrats. Decimated by Depression-era setbacks, the once-powerful Republican party could mount no serious attack. Nevertheless, the party still controlled a substantial part of the state press, particularly through the Ogden chain, and Ogden columnists such as Charles Brooks Smith, Sam Mallison, and Calvert Estill kept up a drumbeat of criticism of the WPA and other New Deal agencies.[6] Governor Kump, his successor Homer Holt, other disgruntled conservative Democrats, and the maverick junior senator, Rush Dew Holt, all raised serious questions about WPA as did radical organizations of the unemployed themselves.

On June 8, 1935, without consulting governor Kump, Hopkins appointed a West Virginian, Frank Witcher McCullough, as state administrator of the WPA.[7] McCullough, who had sought the Democratic nomination for governor in 1932, had also been the state director of the National Recovery Administration and the National Emergency Council and had already clashed with Kump. Furious that Hopkins would name a political rival to the post, Kump tried to block McCullough's confirmation. Though it proved unnecessary, the entire congressional delegation threatened to march to the White House to enlist President Roosevelt's support for the appointment.[8] Confirmed as state director, McCullough set up his headquarters in the two top floors of the twenty-story Kanawha Valley Bank Building in Charleston. Before the end of 1935, he presided over an organization of fourteen separate bureaus and divisions and 149 administrators.[9] Unlike William N. Beehler and the Civil Works Administration, who had put more than seventy-thousand to work in short order in the fall of 1933, McCullough's WPA took several months to fulfill its more modest goal of forty-eight thousand jobs.

When he saw he would not control WPA appointments, Governor Kump fought the WPA as he had FERA. He insisted that West Virginia projects must be based on federal funding only, because, he maintained, neither the state nor its local governments could afford matching funds under the state's Tax Limitation Amendment. His state road commission drew up applications for some $30 million worth of WPA rural road projects, but Kump withdrew the projects, saying they committed the state to spend money it did not have. He also accused McCullough of raiding state offices for personnel, and on July 19, 1935, when several state road commission engineers took jobs with the WPA, Kump held an emotional press conference and fired the state road commissioner, Ernest L. Bailey. Bailey, suggesting that the summer heat must have gotten to Kump, then took a job directing the WPA roads projects.[10]

On the same day he fired his road commissioner, Kump also wired the president charging federal authorities with a long list of outrageous activities in the state, such as ignoring and affronting "duly constituted state officials," carrying out "large intrastate activities through and by non-residents without consulting state officials, demanding that state officials assume responsibility for huge sums of relief and public works funds without corresponding authority to control" the spending. He also charged, without providing specifics, that federal "subordinates have conducted clandestine investigations into state affairs."[11] A week later Kump again wired President Roosevelt, saying he had never sought to interfere with federal patronage in the state and only wanted "to proceed with my constitutional duties as governor of this state without interference by federal subordinates and to be protected against flagrant invasion of the rights of a sovereign state."[12]

Kump also sent letters to the secretary of the interior, Harold Ickes, and the agriculture secretary, Henry Wallace, complaining of federal interference and federal investigations in West Virginia and informing them that it had become necessary to fire his road commissioner because of these activities.[13] Five days after firing Bailey, having been given the green light by Aubrey Williams, Harry Hopkins's assistant, Kump fired relief administrator William N. Beehler and replaced him with a West Virginian, C.L. Allen.[14]

Meanwhile, the withdrawal of the road projects slowed down the drive to put the unemployed to work on WPA jobs. Kump insisted that the projects be rewritten in such a way that it would be clear that the state had no financial obligation. He wrote lengthy letters to all members of the state congressional delegation urging them to see to it that all WPA projects in West Virginia be on a grant basis only. The congressmen responded inviting Kump to come to Washington to make a joint plea to "proper authorities."[15]

On August 20 the congressional delegation, Governor Kump and his attorney general, Homer Holt, met with Harry Hopkins in Washington, and afterward Kump claimed Hopkins had assured him that grants would be made "where contributions are impossible." He also said Hopkins pledged to spend $30,000,000 in two years on roads. Forwarding West Virginia press clippings about the meeting to Hopkins, McCullough said that the governor quoted him "maliciously, surreptitiously, and incorrectly" and that this was but one example of the "reckless and careless statements Governor H.G. Kump has been making." McCullough suggested that "one or the other of us should take a well-timed 'crack' at him."[16]

On August 28, the former road commissioner, Ernest L. Bailey, carried the attack to the governor. He told the Associated Press that he had drawn up the road projects with the governor's approval and fulfilled the state's matching obligations with no commitments beyond in kind contributions or supervisory costs that were already being incurred. He said the governor agreed at the time and particularly was interested in maintaining control of the supervisory positions. Bailey maintained that on road projects the difference between contribution and noncontribution meant the difference between a reasonably serviceable and durable all-year road and a mere grade and drain job employing largely hand labor. He implied that the governor's grants-only approach undermined the roads program.[17]

Clearly the lure of patronage helped ignite the political jousting over WPA, but in addition to the baser emotions, deep-seated convictions also came into play on both sides. Kump claimed only the best intentions and accused his opponents of playing politics with relief, but underlying his reaction ran a deep conservatism and a feeling, reinforced by political allies and friends, that the New Deal was out of hand. Fayette County coal operator William McKell warned him of the growth of "One Big State," and Kump agreed: "We all wonder where we are going, but I know of nothing to do except try to keep in step."[18] The governor's brother Kerr reported that their friend Governor Cornwell was discouraged and worried that "union labor" was running both Congress and the White House. Kerr Kump added, "The difficulty that I really find is the character of the present federal officeholder and the tendency of the times to put the ground pole on top of the fence." The governor counseled his brother that "we can only stand by just now in the hope that we may exercise some steadying influence."[19] In the midst of his fight over the WPA, Kump made an emotional extemporaneous speech at Marshall College in Huntington in which he asserted that he was unafraid of his critics; assailed the national "spending orgy," saying that "we may borrow but payday will come"; and lamented in a trembling voice that these were "unhappy days" at the capitol.[20]

Kump's opponents had concerns about both patronage and political philosophy. They feared that the governor, who already controlled a substantial amount of patronage in the state government, might gain control of the WPA patronage and use it to run against Senator Neely in the 1936 primary. They also saw him as an obstructionist who, determined to "rule or ruin," stood in the way of the beneficent goals of President Roosevelt and Congress.[21] State administrator McCullough told Hopkins that "the Governor does not fully comprehend the spirit and intention of WPA."[22] Lorena Hickok, Hopkins's traveling reporter, spent two hours with Kump and told Hopkins that the governor seemed to have bad advice and simply did not understand what was going on with the relief situation. "He's just dumb," she said.[23] An editorial by Walter Hart in the Morgantown *Dominion-News* fixed the responsibility for the delay in starting up WPA projects squarely on Kump and, mincing no words, said the innocent farmers who had long prayed for roads were the ones who were paying the penalty for "a political viciousness on the part of the state administration probably without parallel in the history of this nation."[24]

Hickok called the West Virginia situation "just one awful political mess. A Kump-controlled relief administration out to wreck a Neeley [sic]-Holt controlled works progress administration." Hickok had low opinions of both McCullough and C.L. Allen, the Kump-appointed head of the relief administration. McCullough had not yet had a chance to prove himself, she said, but he had told her he was "terribly-ridden by politicians." Allen, on the other hand, "has had a chance to do more damage—and has." She said that the state relief administration had "sold WPA short all over the state," and while attacking the WPA for being political was even more political. She charged that relief in Charleston was in control of Republican politicians who were "out to ruin Roosevelt" by expanding the relief rolls. In both Charleston and Huntington, Hickok reported, staffs of incompetent investigators and the lack of case work supervisors resulted in relief rolls twice what they should be. She claimed the state relief administration was still carrying on work projects "including 10 or 15 airports on leased private property . . . while piously begging Aubrey for more money because they weren't able to feed the people."[25]

In early November Aubrey Williams called Kump to Washington to discuss the end of FERA and the restructuring of the state relief operation, explaining, "We require a set-up over there in which we can have confidence." Kump took it as another in a long series of affronts he believed he had suffered at the hands of federal officials. On November 7, he wrote to the president to protest "the implication of wrong-doing" in Aubrey William's statement and "the charges of certain designing individuals in this state to the effect that I have been guilty of 'treachery' to you." Kump denied any disloyalty to the president "notwithstanding the fact that I have encountered nothing but obstruction and opposition from Federal office-holders in the course of my administration." Kump insisted to the president that "I have sturdily maintained that you have no part in it, nor knowledge of it."[26]

Two weeks later Kump again wrote to suggest that the president had not been fully informed of "the full import of conditions existing in our state." Kump said that the work relief program was "engulfed in the savage ambitions of politicians," but in a classic frying-pan-into-the-fire alternative, he suggested that it was not too late to turn the work relief program over to the West Virginia State Road Commission and the state relief administration, both of which the governor now controlled.[27]

In addition to the effort to prevent his enemies from controlling the substantial patronage of the WPA, Kump's anxiety also grew from concern about the burden of caring for unemployables as the time approached in which the state would have exclusive care of those unable to work. Moreover, the state would continue to be responsible for employables until such time as the WPA could employ them, and the WPA appeared unprepared to put many to work on November 15, 1935, when the transition was to take place. To ease the burden, Aubrey Williams informed Kump that FERA would make a final grant of $650,000 to West Virginia for December.[28] Kump told reporters that the end of federal relief created an impossible situation: "Whether properly or improperly, a relief load has been created in our state that we cannot carry."[29]

By the beginning of 1936, West Virginia's Democratic factions were attempting to paper over the serious differences within the party. At Jackson Day dinners in ten West Virginia cities on January 8, speakers avoided discord. Senator Neely's dinner at Fairmont drew members of Governor Kump's cabinet, and the senator insisted: "I am at peace with everyone in the state." Though Senator Holt spoke elsewhere, he sent best wishes to his Senate colleague. Governor Kump spoke in Parkersburg, where several members of the other factions appeared. The show of harmony was more shadow than substance, a quadrennial ritual of crocodile smiles.[30]

The efforts to put aside at least the appearance of division extended to the heads of the state relief administration and the WPA, C.L. Allen and F. Witcher McCullough. In early 1936, McCullough invited all involved state and federal agencies and political officials to a discussion of the recovery program, and Allen agreed that the program was worthwhile. Governor Kump, who had at first agreed to come, said he was unable to attend.[31]

Even as Democrats tried to paper over their differences, demands for an investigation of the WPA arose from a different source, the unemployed themselves, or at least from groups claiming to represent the unemployed. Meeting in joint convention in the Kanawha County Courthouse in Charleston, the Unemployed League of West Virginia and the Townsend Revolving Old Age Pension Club issued a resolution charging director McCullough and the state WPA with "callousness to human distress; the politicalization of relief, and the bickering of factions over power and patronage while thousands go jobless and hungry." They pointed out that while an army of political jobholders had held administrative jobs since June, "thousands of men and women receive no relief and have no jobs." They asked federal administrator Hopkins to conduct a sweeping investigation.[32]

Meanwhile Senator Rush Dew Holt grew increasingly estranged from the liberal faction of the party that had plucked him from the House of Delegates in 1934 to make him a senator before his thirty-fifth birthday. The Ogden newspapers' Charles Brooks Smith reported that the WPA had fallen under the control of Senators Neely and Holt and that Holt had the upper hand, "insisting on being high card in the distribution of patronage and threatening to be a bad actor if blocked."[33] When McCullough issued an order that anyone holding elective office must step down from the WPA administrative payroll, Holt protested that it was an attempt to get his friends. On January 16 he warned McCullough: "You have consistently taken the attitude that you can get around me by nice words, but it will take more than nice words to cover this up."[34]

Although the United Mine Workers had backed Holt enthusiastically in 1934, state mine worker leader Van Amberg Bittner grew disturbed at his protege's independent ways. Bittner assured Holt that "McCullough is cooperating with us 100%."[35] He also warned Holt pointedly that Ogden and his papers were bitter foes of the New Deal and the UMWA and that it was "not a practical proposition for men and statesmen who favor President Roosevelt and his New Deal to play with opposition newspapers who are doing everything possible to destroy our great humanitarian program."[36]

In February 1936, WPA field representative Wayne Coy raised a number of questions about the Parkersburg region, where Senator Holt's brother Matthew was employed as district engineer. Coy noted that the district used money for approved projects to spend on unapproved projects, and that the projects tended to be overloaded with administrative personnel. Coy recommended that the administrative personnel be replaced, but McCullough persuaded Coy to put them on temporary status until an investigation could be pursued.[37]

On February 17, 1936, in the first of four speeches in which he would lambast the West Virginia WPA, Senator Holt charged on the Senate floor that McCullough was using the WPA to make himself governor and that the agency was "not only a failure but a disgrace to West Virginia." He claimed that McCullough was president of a loan-shark company charging 42 percent interest and was actively involved in lobbying the legislature for a small-loans bill and for a bill to make silicosis a compensable disease. The WPA in West Virginia stood for "Witcher's Political Army," he said.[38]

Aubrey Williams, assistant WPA administrator, reacted immediately to Holt's charge, saying WPA would tolerate no one using an administrative position to run for office. McCullough would have to make "a public avowal" that he was not a candidate for governor if he were to retain his position with WPA. Upon hearing of Williams's statement, McCullough issued an announcement saying "I am not a candidate for governor or any political office in the state of West Virginia."[39]

On February 21, McCullough fired Matthew Holt, the senator's brother, and other Holt appointees in the Parkersburg office. Holt charged that the dismissals were in retaliation for the speech Holt had made attacking McCullough on the Senate floor. Aubrey Williams ordered Matthew Holt and the others reinstated pending an investigation.[40]

On February 24, responding to demands of Senator Holt on the floor of the Senate and Senator Neely in a letter to the administrator, Harry Hopkins ordered "a full and complete investigation" of the WPA in West Virginia. In organizing the WPA, Hopkins had set up a division to investigate and turn over to the Justice Department any charges of fraud, corruption, or other crimes by WPA personnel. The investigations division assigned Alan Johnstone to investigate the West Virginia WPA. During late February and early March, Johnstone and three associates spent eight days in the state.⁴¹

Johnstone refuted all of the charges Holt had made in Senate speeches on February 17, 24, 25, and 26. Holt charged that WPA workers could be assigned to projects only if approved by county political bosses. Of the fifty-five thousand workers on West Virginia projects, forty thousand had been assigned by the National Employment Service (NES). More recently, to speed up the process of getting the unemployed to work, the WPA itself had assigned workers to jobs using the same relief rolls as the NES. Johnstone said he and his associates had interviewed many officials and relief clients and concluded that political considerations were not a factor in the assignment of relief.⁴² Johnstone's investigation also found no basis for Holt's charge that McCullough was using the WPA to build a political machine or that administrative appointments reflected any improper political scheme. The report reproduced telegrams, however, which indicated that Holt had tried to obtain additional patronage on the WPA administrative rolls.⁴³ As for Senator Neely, the report noted that "from October to the middle of December which roughly represents the formative period of the Works Progress Administration in West Virginia, Senator Neely was on an official trip to the Orient."⁴⁴

Johnstone found nothing improper in the firing of Senator Holt's brother and other appointees in the Parkersburg office. The decision was based on recommendations of the field representative, Wayne Coy, and was reached before Holt made his first attack on the WPA in the Senate, not afterward, as Holt charged. Johnstone also found evidence that Matthew Holt had solicited money from employees of the Parkersburg regional office to pay for a political broadcast by his brother.⁴⁵

Senator Holt of course rejected the Johnstone report as a "whitewash" and accused Harry Hopkins of being "too damn dumb" (using a phrase Hopkins sometimes used) to understand what was going on in West Virginia.⁴⁶ In a statement to the press, he said "investigation by the WPA forces was like sending Baby Face Nelson to investigate Dillinger."⁴⁷ He charged in a Senate speech that a campaign of intimidation was waged against his friends. "Czar McCullough and his political cossacks are riding ruthlessly over the prostrate form of a helpless people," he asserted.⁴⁸ Holt repeated all his charges in an address on the CBS program "Public Opinion," insisting that the whole purpose of WPA in West Virginia was to make McCullough governor and to reelect Senator Neely and that it operated as "a thorough censorship and spy system."[49]

Some of what Senator Holt said rang true, but because his own house was in considerable disorder, Holt was not an effective critic. Clearly, as Johnstone's report noted, administrative positions were awarded through the patronage system. There was nothing new nor nefarious about this, but the scale of patronage possibilities presented by the WPA and other federal agencies exceeded anything West Virginia politicians had ever seen. The need for jobs enhanced the patronage value. Holt himself, however, was a major practitioner of spoils politics, and he may have believed that he could seize control of the federal patronage system in West Virginia. The *enfant terrible* of liberal Democrats, he sooner or later broke openly with nearly all his former political allies in the liberal wing of the state Democratic party, including Senator Neely, Van Bittner of the UMWA, and Witcher McCullough. The conservatives, Governor Kump and his successor Homer Holt (no relation to the senator), hated Holt from the early days of the Kump administration, when he had led noisy denunciations of both Kump and "the utilities." McCullough claimed that Holt returned from the funeral of Huey Long of Louisiana with the notion of making himself the Huey Long of West Virginia politics.[50] In any case, Holt's strident manner of political combat did not serve him well, and he was on his way to becoming a one-term senator. His attack on the WPA in West Virginia was easily deflected, and politicians soon simply ignored Holt as his political base of support dwindled.

The Johnstone report downplayed Holt's harangues and gave the state WPA a clean bill of health on the corruption charges. Other evidence, however, suggests that politics posed more of a problem than the report admitted. When Lorena Hickok reported to Harry Hopkins in November 1935 that Witcher McCullough was "terribly ridden by politicians," she added that "Holt was doing most of the riding."[51] One of the most damning bits of evidence is a consultant's report on the WPA recreation program. Signing his report simply as "Meyer," the consultant drove through snow and frigid temperatures to attend district recreation conferences in Morgantown, Beckley, and Huntington during January and February of 1937. He noted that he had not been in the state long before

I saw a situation that I had not confronted anywhere else—and I grew more disgusted as I journeyed on. The program is practically blocked by politics. The overwhelming majority of the appointments were, and are being, made through political pull and in many, many cases without the slightest consideration of fitness. There are dozens of people assigned to the project who haven't the slightest interest nor concern about recreation and without any ability. In many cases it is honestly pitiful. There are a dozen or more over fifty-five years of age who can not do the job. They do not hesitate to talk freely about the political angle of the set-up and, in one case, the man asked when he should start campaigning.

The state administrator of the recreation program told Meyer that he could carry on an intelligent recreation program only in about a dozen counties.[52]

Despite a sometimes paralyzing level of political influence, the WPA eventually generated numerous projects to put the unemployed to work in construction, rehabilitation, conservation, and various programs for writers, teachers, artists, and musicians. Although some projects were useful only as ways to offer work, other WPA projects had enduring value. It is easy to list and appreciate the physical and social results of WPA projects such as the Southside Bridge in Charleston, a therapeutic center for the Morris Memorial Hospital for Crippled Children in Huntington, the black high school in Morgantown and various other educational buildings around the state, the building and improvement of airports, or the writing of *West Virginia: A Guide to the Mountain State*, but the impact on the morale of workers and their families is more difficult to assess. Given the depth and durability of the economic collapse and the necessity of providing some kind of relief, it is difficult to imagine an alternative that would have met the needs as well.

Kump's obstructionism slowed the early efforts of the WPA, but the road projects were eventually approved, and a great many unemployed workers became involved in the building and improvement of farm-to-market and creek-and-hollow roads. In discussing such projects at a statewide meeting of WPA officials, Col. George D. Babcock, a regional WPA engineer, said that the key in selecting roads to be built should be "the forgotten man" far back in the hills. The farm-to-market roads were to be twenty-two feet wide with an eight inch stone base and covered with gravel, shale, or red dog (an ash product of the spontaneous combustion of coal mine slag piles). The creek-and-hollow road program would widen rural trails and paths to at least nine feet, using a stone base so horses and farm wagons could pass in all seasons. Particular attention would be given to portions of the roads that had become periodically unusable. For some rural communities, these improvements would provide year-round communication for the first time and an opportunity for the rural unemployed to work near home. The roads also provided escape routes for the rural young who would seek work in urban areas beyond the state's borders at the end of the decade.[53]

In addition to the rural road program, the WPA also helped the state's cities to repave worn out streets in business sections; build or replace water systems; improve and build city and county government buildings, parks, and swimming pools; and set up recreation programs. The WPA also continued some initiatives the FERA program had started in West Virginia in cooperation with the state health department, such as the building of sanitary privies and the sealing of abandoned coal mines to eliminate acid discharge into streams.[54]

Though most of the WPA projects were designed to employ blue-collar workers at construction projects, some of the more innovative projects generated work relief for women, artists, musicians, librarians, teachers, and writers. In West Virginia, the WPA efforts in these areas led to some of the first attempts to organize citizens groups to think systematically about state and regional cultural matters.[55]

Though there were no unemployed artists listed on West Virginia relief rolls in 1935, the federal art project (Federal Project Number 1) encouraged West Virginia's WPA to set up art centers to provide jobs for the unemployed and to encourage an interest in art. By 1942 there were WPA art centers at Parkersburg, Fairmont, Huntington, and Osage on Scotts Run in Monongalia County.[56] There was relatively slight interest in the federal art project, but every large town in the state requested music projects, and more than two hundred musicians sought WPA work in 1935. Among the unemployed musicians were many who had played in movie theaters in the era of the silent films and had been left stranded by the coming of the talkies.[57] The supervisor of the West Virginia music project, Verna C. Blackburn, had played piano in vaudeville and directed orchestras until she came to Huntington in 1915 to work in the Lyric, Orpheum, and Keith Albee theaters. She said she had "worked steadily in theaters until Talking Pictures replaced shows, and since have contracted orchestras."[58]

By September 1936 municipal bands in Wheeling, Huntington,

and Clarksburg provided WPA employment for local musicians. In 1938 a new municipal band was organized in Parkersburg.[59] Bands in Red House and Arthurdale also received support from the state music project. The Huntington WPA orchestra played its first concert on March 16, 1936, and in the next fifteen months it played 428 concerts before 145,154 people.[60] For National Music Week in May 1937, the WPA bands planned activities such as a music festival at Oglebay park in Wheeling, which was broadcast by local radio; a musical story of the life of Stephen Foster by the Clarksburg band; and an ambitious musical pageant in Huntington based on the history of Cabell County and using historical musical instruments such as the dulcimer, spinet, and melodian.[61] The WPA bands played music-appreciation concerts at Vacation Bible School classes at various churches and concerts on WPA playgrounds, at state hospitals and other state institutions, and over local radio stations.[62]

In some states, including neighboring Kentucky, where the state WPA sponsored a Folk Song Festival that led to the recording of important traditional music, the WPA encouraged folk music,[63] but Verna Blackburn, the state director in West Virginia, seems to have thought only in terms of brass bands and orchestras and did little to encourage local traditional music. At one point she reported that "colored people of Wheeling" wanted to have a project, but "I have not given it much thought as their instrumentation consisted of Banjo, Guitar, etc." Toward the end of the decade, the music project did undertake an important effort by sending workers with recorders into remote regions of the state to record the songs, voices, and music of the people living in the remotest sections of the state. At Arthurdale, the homestead subsistence community in Preston County, there was much interesting musical activity, such as square dancing, mountain balladry, and gospel singing. The interest in square dancing revitalized fiddling, and a mountain fiddle maker was found and brought in to teach young boys the art of fiddle making. In the surviving reports of the federal music project of West Virginia, there is no evidence of curiosity about the ethnic music of industrial communities, nor of labor music.[64] Despite this unfortunate shortcoming of the music program, the efforts made did encourage city-dwelling West Virginians to support municipal bands and orchestras and made such music more widely available to citizens of all economic and social levels than ever before. Some efforts were also made to encourage traditional mountain music.

The statewide library project began slowly but eventually led to efforts of citizens groups to promote state libraries. A federal library consultant visited the state in April 1938 and reported that "the agency which is legally enabled to sponsor such a project (the Public Library Commission) has no funds or headquarters."[65] The Federation of Women's Clubs took up sponsorship of the project, and during its first year, the library project placed workers in existing libraries, organized new public libraries (often by converting former club libraries), hired workers to keep school libraries open during the summer, encouraged principals to hire school librarians, and employed workers to repair damaged books.[66] At the end of 1940, the library project employed some 317 workers.[67]

On August 10 and 11, 1940, the WPA and the General Federation of Women's Clubs sponsored what they believed to be the first professional library conference on methods and standards ever held in the state. Librarians met in Huntington as a planning committee "studying the West Virginia library problem from every angle." One result of their work was a meeting at Jackson's Mill on September 28, 1940, which organized the West Virginia Better Library Movement.[68] The movement faced a tough challenge. The federal director of the WPA library projects suggested that such activities could gain attention for the West Virginia WPA, because "West Virginia is known as the State with the least library service."[69]

The state department of education sponsored a WPA program to put teachers to work providing adult education and literacy training for families on relief. In 1936, almost eight hundred unemployed teachers were teaching classes to some thirty-three thousand people.[70] WPA publicists dramatized the literacy and adult education programs by designating a West Virginian, Walter Donaldson of Orlando, as the one millionth person taught to read by the WPA. They told his story in the "Photo Story Series," showing him in Claude Heater's adult education class, practicing his reading in the kitchen of his rural home, and at work on a WPA job at a rock quarry.[71]

Some of the WPA's activities in West Virginia received attention from the agency's filmmakers. In 1936 moviegoers could see *A Better West Virginia*, which provided glimpses of projects both large and small. During the 1936 flood, a WPA film crew rushed to Wheeling to capture scenes of WPA men and women at work during the disaster rescuing victims, helping to feed the homeless, cleaning up in the aftermath, and working to rehabilitate the city. Masterpieces of public relations, these films stirred viewers with arresting scenes, stentorian commentary, and evocative music.[72]

One of the most controversial undertakings of the WPA was the national writers project, which provided work for unemployed writers. The West Virginia writers wrote some local histories and gathered material for a state encyclopedia, but the most important work was the writing of *West Virginia: A Guide to the Mountain State*, a pioneering effort to assess the state's social and cultural heritage and to provide a thorough guide to important and interesting places. Although some politicians, including Governor Homer Adams Holt, attacked the *Guide* and sought to censor its content, it turned out to be an excellent compendium of information about the state.[73]

The Public Works Administration (PWA) also carried out important activities in West Virginia but with less fanfare or political confrontation than FERA or the WPA. Considered to be a "pump priming" agency, the PWA focused on capital-intensive projects and sought to stimulate economic recovery by creating jobs in the bellwether construction industry. Created by the National Industrial Recovery Act of June 1933, PWA was administered by Secretary of the Interior Harold Ickes. Unlike Harry Hopkins, Ickes found it difficult to authorize expenditures without a thorough justification and a precise accounting. Ickes' scrupulousness won him the sobriquet "Honest Harold," but his methods frustrated any sense of urgency. Of course the nature of the projects undertaken by the PWA made haste difficult. Public works had to be carefully planned.[74]

In the case of West Virginia, the PWA found some resistance in the beginning because the Tax Limitation Amendment had left cities and counties with empty treasuries and limited revenues, and Governor Kump opposed the concept of matching funds. Compared to the directors of other federal agencies in the state, the state director of the PWA, M.L. O'Neale, maintained a very low profile. For many counties or cities, raising matching funds or undertaking debt to satisfy the PWA grant-loan mix was difficult. Most PWA projects provided a 45 percent grant and required a 55 percent contribution by the county, city, or town undertaking the construction. The 55 percent could be raised through voter-approved bond sales or loaned through the PWA. Despite the more stringent financing requirements than those of the WPA, the PWA projects totaled more than $15 million between 1933 and 1937 and included construction or improvement of water systems for forty-six communities, sewer systems for eleven communities, incinerators for three cities, thirteen hospitals, several state college buildings, forty-six county and state educational buildings, a county courthouse for Raleigh County, a toll bridge for St. Albans, and funds for state road construction. In January of 1937, PWA approved plans for building the Elk River bridge and Kanawha Boulevard in Charleston.[75]

After Kump left office, the state itself took advantage of PWA and WPA help to improve deteriorating state institutional facilities. The PWA helped modernize the School for the Deaf and Blind in Romney, expand the Pinecrest tuberculosis sanitarium in Beckley, and repair or construct buildings at West Virginia University and the state colleges.[76]

The PWA stimulated the growth of citizen involvement and organization. Many projects required community referendums to approve bond issues. Some communities established citizens advisory committees to plan for bond referendums and to establish priorities for public improvement projects. Citizens groups also campaigned to persuade their communities to vote for bond issues.[77]

Roosevelt and his advisers considered the WPA a temporary stopgap to provide work for unemployed victims of economic circumstance, and they regarded the PWA as a stimulus of private enterprise. New Dealers assumed that economic recovery was coming. When recovery arrived, private employment would soak up the sea of unemployed. They understood that some people were "unemployable," and these would remain the responsibility of state and local governments, as they had been before the Depression. The Social Security Act of 1935 provided federal matching funds to local jurisdictions for care of the blind, the disabled, and dependent children. To qualify for the matching funds, local governments first had to establish a suitable public welfare agency. The days of relying on private charity and poor houses for care of the indigent were to come to an end.[78]

West Virginia had been one of the first states to establish a department of public welfare, but with the federal domination of welfare activities under FERA and CWA, the state welfare department had largely confined itself to dealing with children's issues. With the reorganization of public welfare required by the WPA and in anticipation of the federal Social Security Act, Governor Kump asked that the House of Delegates and Senate to name a joint committee to prepare legislation to put West Virginia's laws in compliance with the requirements of forthcoming federal Social Security legislation.[79] He also again called upon Dr. John Fairfield Sly and West Virginia University professors to help draft a new welfare law. Since his work in the early days of the Kump administration, Sly had moved to Princeton University to head an institute studying local government, but in the spring of 1935 he agreed to help prepare a study entitled "Care of the Unemployable in West Virginia."[80] In November, Sly and Professor George Shipman of West Virginia University issued their report, which called for a revamping of state welfare services. The department of public welfare had been focusing on child welfare and the care of crippled children, but, the report noted, "child welfare is only one phase of the problem of social welfare." The report recommended that all welfare work be brought under one agency, and that the agency should also supervise county welfare institutions.[81]

Sly drafted legislation, and he and Dr. Stephen P. Burke of West Virginia University met with the joint legislative committee to work out details of what became the West Virginia Public Welfare Act of 1936. The legislation needed no substantial new revenues, the basic requirement laid down by Governor Kump. Monies the state had previously appropriated for the WVRA and the Department of Public Welfare would now support a new Department of Public Assistance.

Despite his general skepticism regarding relief programs, Kump called the legislature into special session to pass the public welfare law. Because the joint committee and its experts had done their work well, the legislature took only a week to agree on a final version, enacting it on June 20, 1936. West Virginia thus became one of the first states to have a social security law carefully patterned after the federal statute.[82]

The law set up a Department of Public Assistance (DPA) to be financed through federal grants-in-aid under social security, state appropriations, and county revenues. The DPA would administer the care of "unemployables" as classified under the federal Social Security law—old age assistance and aid to the blind and dependent children. General relief, that is the care of unemployables not classified under the federal law, would be the responsibility of the counties, with the state supplementing county funds when necessary. The legislation required counties to set aside fifteen percent of their levy for relief purposes. The old Department of Public Welfare became the Children's Bureau of the new department. The new law also provided for the widespread involvement of citizens by requiring a five member state advisory board and county welfare councils made up of uncompensated, appointed members. Kump appointed university professor Stephen P. Burke as chairman of the state board.[83]

About a week after the passage of the law by the special session of the legislature, Frank B. Bane, the executive secretary of the federal Social Security board and former head of the Virginia Welfare Department, addressed in a very frank fashion the question of the new law's prospects before an audience in Charleston. He noted that the law was well written, but added, "It is perfectly possible to make it just a glorified poor relief if you permit it. To make sure of this, have some of the appointments made on the basis of how the applicants for position voted in the last election." He also said that for it to work, it had to work "as well in your southern counties as in your northern counties."[84]

Bane reflected the concern of some New Dealers and social-work professionals about the ending of FERA. He also spoke from knowledge of what had happened to FERA in West Virginia and what was happening with the WPA. County welfare councils and relief boards had been subject to intense political pressure in the past, and the councils provided for under the new welfare law could face the same fate. The new councils would have five members including the president of the county court and four members appointed by the governor, a provision not likely to promote nonpartisanship. Indeed, the new law made certain that one party would have a majority, unlike the previous system of county boards, which had sought to promote bipartisanship by providing for parity between Democrats and Republicans on the boards. However, the legislation made a strong effort to insulate the new public welfare agency from political influences by requiring that no more than three members of the county council be of the same political party nor be political officeholders nor members of political committees. The county councils were to choose county directors from a list of persons approved by the state board as qualified by training and experience.[85]

Francis Turner, who had headed the Department of Public Welfare since the waning weeks of the Conley administration in 1933, had made something of a name for himself by energetically addressing child-care issues in the state while FERA had handled relief and was a favorite of New Dealers to head the new Department of Public Assistance. Lorena Hickok told Hopkins that he was "the only man in the state in whom I personally have much confidence" and the only one who spoke honestly and frankly with Governor Kump. She believed both factions of the Democratic party trusted him, and he could "straighten out the mess." She assumed he would be Kump's choice to set up a permanent welfare agency.[86] As early as April 1935, the Charleston *Gazette* reported that Turner was conducting a study of West Virginia's social needs to prepare for the possibility that he might be called upon to administer the new program.[87]

As soon as the new law became effective, however, Governor Kump defied the spirit of nonpartisanship and fulfilled part of Frank Bane's prescription for "glorified poor relief" by naming his secretary, Alfred Willis Garnett, as the director of the new agency. Garnett was a former prosecuting attorney and chairman of the Democratic party of Boone County, one of those southern counties Bane worried about. Garnett's only experience remotely connected to his new job was a stint as state pardon attorney in 1933. His chief qualification was that he was a political intimate of the governor.[88] Francis Turner headed the Children's Bureau in the new agency and continued to work with WPA to improve conditions of indigent children.

Frank Bane was not alone in worrying that the new system could just be a return to the old days of poor relief. Many professional social workers and liberal economists had hoped that the New Deal would create a national Department of Welfare to oversee national relief and health coverage, and they had seen FERA as a step in that direction. Now they worried that the return of general relief to the states and local governments would be a step backward.[89] Edith Abbott, president of the National Conference of Social Work, pleaded in *The Nation*, "Don't Do It Mr. Hopkins." "All who have recognized the miserable incompetence of the old system know that returning to local relief authorities means returning to everything that is reactionary in the field of social welfare," Abbott contended. The "local politicians temporarily banished by the resolute orders of the Federal Relief Administrator will return to welfare controls."[90] These views of social workers and welfare reformers did not reflect public attitudes, however, and Hopkins and Roosevelt, with a view to the 1936 election, responded to polls that showed that a majority favored returning the control of relief to state and local governments. Many people were unsympathetic with relief recipients and felt that poor people could get off relief if they tried.[91]

Governor Kump was among those who were skeptical about relief. While urging the legislature to do what was necessary to avoid being "lost in the backwash of progress," Kump also worried about dangers to self-reliance inherent in the new programs. He said, "I am amazed at the number of people who present their claims for public money to be obtained without effort upon their part and to be spent without restriction. This attitude must cease and citizen, city, county, school district and state must look to their own ability and their own resources before demanding assistance too often based on no more pressing 'emergencies' than their own inertia."[92]

The Department of Public Assistance took over from the West Virginia Relief Administration in November 1936. The DPA law sought to integrate all public care functions of the state. The new department administered relief grants for the categories of assistance set by the federal Social Security law. These included old-age assistance grants, aid to the blind, and aid to dependent children. The DPA also dispensed general relief grants for other indigents unable to work. In addition to awarding assistance grants, the DPA concerned itself with crippled children, foster care, and the licensing of child care facilities. It administered aid to veterans and emergency medical and dental care for indigents, distributed commodities, and certified workers for the WPA and youth for the Civilian Conservation Corps (CCC) and the National Youth Administration (NYA). It would also be responsible for the care of employables who received no work from WPA or PWA.[93]

By July 1937 the DPA case load had grown to 38,900, and spending was outrunning available funds. The department made a determined effort to reduce the case load and costs through reinvestigation and retrenchment. In 1937 the DPA reported that general relief grants averaged fourteen dollars per month.[94] In the winter of 1937-1938, the director of the Ohio County DPA reported that the average grant had fallen to ten dollars per month, an amount insufficient to "enable these families to live in . . . decency and health." He said this had been the worst winter of the Depression for Ohio County's unemployed and that the DPA was being severely criticized for falling short of the efforts of its predecessor. He applied to the WPA for help in starting a community gardening and canning project to try to provide food to supplement the meager cash grants of those on relief rolls.[95]

In 1939 the legislature, reflecting a growing disapproval of relief and concern about the cost, turned to somewhat draconian measures to bring the relief costs down. In his biennial message, Governor Holt noted the difficulty of estimating what relief would cost in the biennium. It depended heavily upon how much of the burden the WPA would continue to bear. Should business conditions worsen or should the WPA further cut back, Holt believed it might be necessary to call a special session to deal with relief. In the meantime, he asked the legislature to cut $500,000 per year from the Department of Public Assistance biennial budget.[96]

The legislature cut $300,000 from the department's $6.75 million budget and established the requirement that any able-bodied relief recipient must work for the state. The state road commission or any political subdivision of the state could requisition male relief recipients from county welfare councils. Workers would be credited with thirty-five cents per hour and could work no longer than an eight-hour day. The requirement extended to all able-bodied males over the age of sixteen in families receiving relief. The department estimated that only about five thousand persons would be physically able to participate.[97] "Weeding out the deadwood" became the chief goal for the summer of 1939 as the department sought to reduce the relief rolls in the face of the budget reduction.[98] Director Garnett announced in April that all thirty thousand relief recipients would be required to cultivate gardens with seed provided by the department. If they grew no garden, their relief grants would be denied. "It is hoped," Garnett said, "that the plan will enable the department to make substantial reductions in relief grants everywhere, especially in rural counties, where the percentage of persons on relief is above the state average."[99]

What happened in West Virginia when the state and counties resumed control of relief reflected a national pattern of harsher administrative practices, reduced relief grants, and lower personnel standards. Part of the problem was that although the economy continued to struggle and unemployment remained high, a more conservative Congress reduced WPA funding in the late thirties leaving to the states not only the care of unemployables but employables as well. Speakers at the 1940 National Conference of Social Workers bemoaned the results of putting the states in charge of general relief. Harry Greenstein, the former director of FERA in Maryland, said the unemployed had been abandoned to "a precarious existence dependent upon inadequate and often nonexistent local resources."[100] Edith Abbott said, "Things have gone steadily from bad to worse since that fatal decision about 'ending this business of relief' was made in 1935."[101] Few beyond the professional social-work community, however, supported the idea of the federal government returning to the relief business. When a committee under Senator James F. Byrnes held hearings on unemployment and relief policies in 1938, Harry Hopkins himself strongly rejected the idea that the federal government should ever again be involved in direct relief.[102]

In 1940 the liberal faction of the Democratic party defeated the statehouse Democrats, and Matthew M. Neely became governor. He appointed a new director of public assistance, Raymond Kenney, and the new director promised a more liberal public assistance program. An immediate change in policy was to extend assistance to families of coal miners out of work because of strikes. Kenney also promised to liberalize grants, eligibility requirements, and the general policies of the Department.[103] The coming of the war, however, would create a new set of problems.

The New Deal relief and social welfare legislation led to substantial and enduring changes in the way West Virginia dealt with its poor and unemployed. Programs like the WPA and PWA, and Civilian Conservation Corps, and NYA (which are discussed in a later chapter) provided emergency care for unemployed workers and youth and left behind substantial enhancements of the state's physical infrastructure in public roads, bridges, buildings, recreational facilities, state parks and forests, and schools. New Deal programs stimulated needed attention to public health programs, libraries, and cultural activities. Most importantly, when the emergency programs ended by 1942, the New Deal left behind a whole new network for public assistance and a new attitude toward the unfortunate, which rejected the antiquated philosophy that the poorhouse and private charity sufficed for their care. The new structure emphasized the responsibility of state and local governments, with the assistance of the federal government through Social Security, to care for the indigent. In 1937, to help fill the need for an estimated 1,200 social workers in the new assistance program and private social work, West Virginia University set up a new department of sociology and public welfare. In 1941 it became the social work department.[104]

Though governors like Kump and Holt accepted the new system grudgingly and too often turned it into a new patronage tool, or recommended inadequate funding, the new commitment to social welfare and the organization of state and county welfare agencies were permanent legacies of the New Deal. The new organization represented modernization, but modernization did not mean resolution or perfection. In the face of the state's persistent economic problems, enduring business indifference or opposition to the very idea of relief, and chronic social dilemmas, the danger of "glorified poor relief" persisted.

8
The New Deal and Mountain Agriculture

By the time Herman Guy Kump moved into the Governor's Mansion and Franklin D. Roosevelt took up residence in the White House, the ravages of the past fifty years of industrial abuse of the landscape as well as the lack of a scientific approach to mountain agriculture and forestry had left much of West Virginia's land exhausted. The West Virginia landscape presented, as Jack Temple Kirby writes of Appalachia in *Rural Worlds Lost*, "a tragic picture of post-industrial ruin and agricultural dislocation."[1]

Farmers everywhere faced hard times during the Depression. In the South more than half the tobacco and cotton farmers were sharecroppers or tenants and lived in desperate poverty, rarely seeing cash. Landlords operated commissaries, which charged usurious interest rates to advance money for necessities. A combination of New Deal programs, mechanization, land consolidation, and the introduction of new crops led to a profound transformation in the relationship of the people to the land. During the late thirties, much of the work force "tractored off the land," abandoned the cotton fields for the cities. Historians of southern agriculture have compared the developments of the era to the eighteenth-century enclosure movement in England.[2] In the Dust Bowl of the southern plains, New Deal policies also encouraged the advance of a more capital-intensive agriculture that required less labor and led to an exodus to California.[3]

West Virginia farmers faced an equally difficult but different situation. In contrast to the monocultural South, most West Virginia farmers owned their land, although rates of tenantry rose during the Depression. Few were burdened with mortgages. The 1932 Tax Limitation Amendment lowered property taxes, although farmers, like others, had to pay a broad range of indirect and largely regressive taxes. Many mountaineer farmers with the largest land holdings had earned most of their income from nonagricultural pursuits, collecting payments for coal, oil, and gas leases, and selling land to coal and timber companies. Smaller land owners had been part-time or subsistence farmers and had worked for timber or coal companies. The big timber companies had long since moved on, and by the mid twenties coal mining offered fewer opportunities for employment. Mountaineers who had become dependent on wages sought to return to the already overpopulated land. In some of the coal counties much of the land was owned by absentee agents of industrial capitalism.[4]

From 1930 to 1935, the farm population in West Virginia increased by 115,000 and the number of farms by 23,000. As the number of farms increased, the average size declined from 106 acres to 90. Almost half the farms had fewer than 50 acres. Even with the marked increase in the number of people dependent upon farms, gross farm income tumbled from $93 million in 1929 to $69 million in 1939.[5]

Despite the difficulties of farming mountain land, farmers owned 61 percent of the state's total acreage. Agriculture provided a livelihood for more than a quarter of the population; agricultural products ranked fourth in value in the annual production total.[6]

More than half of all West Virginia farms were of the self-sufficing or low-income category, struggling to make it on annual cash incomes of $500 or less. Of the roughly 105,000 farms in the state, only about 25,000 enjoyed reasonable commercial success, earning gross annual incomes of $1,900 or more.[7] Three northern panhandle counties, Brooke, Ohio, and Marshall, and two eastern panhandle counties, Jefferson and Berkeley, had the lowest percentage of poor farm families, but in all other counties more than 30 percent of farm families were cash poor. In Clay, Mingo, Logan, Calhoun, and McDowell Counties 80 percent or more of all farm families fell into the low-income category. The neighboring states of Kentucky and Virginia also had numerous self-sufficing and low-income farms, but they also had more crop variety and more commercially oriented farming than West Virginia.[8]

From the earliest days of the Depression, West Virginia farm families crowded the relief rolls.[9] In August 1933, information about the need for relief in the state's rural areas shocked Harry Hopkins. The collapse of coal-mining employment had produced extremely high relief rates in coal-mining counties, but the relief rates in some agricultural counties ran even higher. The highest percentages of families on relief in coal-mining counties were in Mingo (59) and Raleigh (63), but in agricultural Lincoln County, 89 percent of all families were on relief. Other agricultural counties also had high relief demands.[10]

After employment in the coal industry revived somewhat with the NRA, coal-county relief rolls declined from the desperately high rates of the early thirties, but agricultural-county rolls, although they also declined, remained higher than in the industrial areas. By January 1935, 27 percent of West Virginians remained on the relief rolls, and all five counties with the highest unemployment rates (more than 40 percent) were all primarily agricultural. The worst was Wayne with 49 percent. The coal counties all had rates under 20 percent.[11]

Why was the demand for relief so high in the agricultural counties? Many public officials believed that rural people needed no relief since they could produce their own food, but in fact, many mountain farmers needed help as badly as stranded industrial workers. In part the ballooning of relief rolls reflected the chronic poverty of postindustrial rural Appalachia, where many farmers had long depended on nonfarm work to raise cash. With the timber, coal, and other employment increasingly unavailable, the farmers became too dependent on farms that had not furnished their families a living for a long time. A back-to-the-land movement added to the pressure on scarce resources as thousands turned to the land to seek a living they could no longer find in failed mining and timber camps, towns, or cities. Finding the soil too poor and eroded and their knowledge of farming inadequate to make good farms out of bad land, they also turned to relief. Meanwhile, young men and women who might have left the farms for towns and cities remained with their parents, "dammed up" on the mountain farms of Appalachia. Yet another part of the rising rural relief load was made up of worn-out farmer-laborers left unable to work by lifetimes of hard work, disabling injuries, diseases, and poor diet.[12]

If things were so bad on these mountain farms, why did farmers and their families remain? In 1935 a survey by the WPA found that 75 percent of Appalachian farm owners and 71 percent of farm laborers lived in the counties in which they were born. The lack of mobility inhibited adjustment to the economic realities of inadequate resources. The WPA survey concluded: "The non-commercial, self-sufficing character of most of the farms and the remoteness of many of the mountain valleys have created an economic and social structure almost completely lacking in dynamic factors."[13] Mountaineers were reluctant to leave their homes, but even if they had been willing to leave, in a time of depression, there was no place to go. When, at the end of the decade, employment opportunities arose in defense industries, a substantial movement of peoples off the land began.

Despite the chronic poverty of the countryside, many who worried about industrial unemployment and its potentially explosive consequences believed that the only solution was to send workers back to the farms. The notion that stranded industrial workers could find salvation in the countryside contributed to the schemes for the establishment of subsistence communities for stranded workers. In the summer of 1933, Mabel Sutherland, the relief director in Logan County, told Lorena Hickok that the majority of miners in Mingo and Logan were farmers who came from other states after World War I. Now they wished to return to their farms. "Dozens of them came in here in the spring," Sutherland said, "and asked us to send them back to the farms."[14]

Hickok wrote about Logan County to Mrs. Roosevelt, who, after the two had visited Scotts Run, near Morgantown, was interested in resettling coal miners on farm land. Hickok warned, however, "There isn't much good farm land around here. Too many hills. Many of the gardens have been washed away this summer, and those that are left look damned pathetic."[15]

For the stranded miner or timber worker who sought to turn to the land for a living, the unsuitability of most areas of former high coal and timber employment to any kind of farming compounded their problems. Webster and Wyoming Counties, for example, both active in timbering and coal before the Depression, had so little arable land that they could well be labeled nonagricultural.[16]

Mingo, McDowell, and Logan, counties in the southwestern corner of the state with heavy coal-mining unemployment, also had steeply sloping mountainsides and high, hog-back ridges largely unsuitable for agriculture. Coal camps, rail lines, tipples and other accoutrements of the coal industry filled the narrow bottomlands where pioneers had once tended their gardens. To farm in these mountainous counties meant cropping steep slopes or foraging livestock in hillside forests where the vegetation played a crucial role in holding the top soil in place. Of course, in some spots in the mountains on nearly impassable dirt roads beyond the coal towns, a few large farm families lived in isolated coves and hollows, raising gardens and tending livestock and subsisting reasonably well with little cash. When wage-paying work faded, these isolated farmers could cook a barrel of corn mash, run off about three gallons and sell them for two dollars each in the coal towns. This would produce enough cash to pay for a nearly two-week supply of flour, coffee, baking powders, chewing tobacco, and salt. Everything else they needed, they raised on their farm. One of the best things about New Deal relief programs, a southern West Virginia preacher later recalled, was that they made it possible for God-fearing mountaineers to refrain from selling illegal moonshine.[17] This subsistence way of life was fading by the late thirties as the WPA roads and automobiles arrived, and older boys and then the men and whole families left for Ohio or elsewhere in search of jobs.[18]

Before President Roosevelt forced Harry Hopkins to close down the CWA in the spring of 1934, Hopkins had intended to throw the CWA into the task of rural relief and rehabilitation. To find out what conditions of rural housing were—and to give work to unemployed rural women—in 1934 CWA launched a nationwide survey of farm housing. In West Virginia, the work was carried out by the University College of Agriculture and the Extension Service through a committee chaired by Gertrude Humphreys, state home demonstration agent. Field workers trained and guided by the U.S. Department of Agriculture's Bureau of Home Economics asked three hundred questions of 9,425 homeowners in Grant, Mercer, Monongalia, Randolph, and Wood Counties, chosen as representative of different parts of the state. A comparison of the CWA survey with the similar 1922 survey of rural life conducted by the Extension Service and the National Child Labor Committee suggests that material conditions had not improved in the intervening twelve years. Two-thirds of the frame houses needed paint. About half of all houses needed structural repairs. Porches sagged, roofs leaked, and foundations were cracked. Only 12 percent had piped-in water, and water had to be carried in (usually by the farm wife) an average distance of 175 feet. Because few farm families had electricity, most could not use modern conveniences such as refrigerators, electric stoves, and washing machines. Seventy-one percent relied upon kerosene or gasoline lamps for lighting. Most cooked on coal or wood stoves. The survey found that fewer than one home in ten had sanitary toilet facilities. The findings suggested many possibilities for CWA and extension work in rural rehabilitation, but by the time the report was finished, the CWA had expired, and the state extension service had no personnel to deal with questions of housing, home water systems, home heating and lighting, and sanitary waste treatment.[19] FERA continued to address the issues of rural rehabilitation and to lay the foundation for later New Deal programs.[20]

Clearly West Virginia's rural areas needed help, but early New Deal agricultural programs addressed few of the difficulties of West Virginia's farmers. The Agricultural Adjustment Act of 1933, seeking to stimulate overall economic recovery, looked to the problems of commercial and wealthier middle-class farmers and gave little attention to the lower end of the scale—the sharecroppers, tenants, and subsistence farmers. In the effort to bring order to agriculture, it was the landlords and large farmers, organized in the national Farm Bureau Federation and often associated with the Extension Service, that gave voice to agriculture's needs and promoted the expansion of agribusiness.[21]

West Virginia's more commercially oriented farmers belonged to the West Virginia Farm Bureau. During the twenties, the state Farm Bureau had taken on a quasi-public role and had worked closely with the Extension Service.[22]

In May 1933, allegedly because the Extension Service had become too closely associated with the Farm Bureau, the West Virginia University Board of Governors fired Nat Terry Frame, who had directed the West Virginia Extension Service throughout the twenties. The real cause of his dismissal was that he had cooperated closely with the defeated Republican regime, but Democrats and Republicans alike protested. County farm bureaus passed resolutions of protest, the heads of the West Virginia Farm Bureau, Grange, and West Virginia Farm Women complained to the federal director of the Extension Service, the director of the Extension Service protested to the president of West Virginia University, and a delegation of farmers went to see Governor Kump. Behind these protests lay not only the esteem with which Frame was held in the state agricultural organizations but also a concern that his dismissal constituted an attack on the Extension Service. Ironically, though he seemed to have his problems with the statehouse Democrats in West Virginia, in early 1934 Frame was called to the White House to discuss problems of the Monongahela Valley with the Roosevelts and others planning the Arthurdale project. Shortly thereafter he went to work briefly for the Civilian Conservation Corps. Later he directed the Oglebay Institute in Wheeling.[23]

Frame and Everett S. Humphrey, the president of the West Virginia Farm Bureau, both criticized early New Deal measures such as the National Industrial Recovery Act and the Agricultural Adjustment Act (AAA), noting that one raised the prices of things the farmers had to buy and that the other was largely irrelevant to West Virginia farmers, who produced few of the targeted commodities and consumed most of what they produced. Frame, a victim of the changed political climate, had something of an axe to grind but also was one of the most experienced and most thoughtful agricultural professionals in the state. He urged that the small businessmen and organized farmers of West Virginia be "on the alert lest little businessmen and little farmers be caught between the great millstones of big business and big agriculture and ground into peasantry."[24]

Although West Virginia farmers produced few of the staples targeted under the AAA for crop reduction payments, a relative handful of West Virginians received benefits under AAA programs. Wheat farmers formed associations at Charles Town, Martinsburg, Moorefield, Lewisburg, and Point Pleasant, and 972 farmers signed contracts agreeing to take acreage out of wheat production. During thirty-two months of the wheat program, West Virginia farmers received only $235,600, an average of about $80.79 each per season. Under the corn-hog program, farmers in all fifty-five counties received payments, and in fifteen counties, farmers received payments for restricting tobacco acreage. Even with restricted planting, wheat, hog, and corn production rose slightly in West Virginia.[25] Later New Deal farm legislation would pay farmers for using conservationist practices and for applying lime and phosphate to pastures. In 1939 government payments of all kinds to West Virginia farmers under AAA programs amounted to only $1.8 million.[26] In 1940, J.O. Knapp, the director of the state Extension Service, estimated that fifty-seven thousand farms, about half of the total in West Virginia, received AAA payments averaging thirty dollars per year, including the costs of phosphate and lime furnished by the AAA.[27] Compared to its impact in states with larger and more commercial farms, the AAA in its various forms had a relatively small effect on West Virginia. When, in January 1936, the U.S. Supreme Court declared the original AAA unconstitutional in *United States v. Butler*, West Virginians took little note.

In many parts of the country the difficulties of small farmers came from technological changes that increased the output per worker and substituted capital for human labor. The U.S. Department of Agriculture, the land grant colleges, and the Extension Service long had sought to encourage farmers to produce enough income for a satisfactory standard of living. The Extension Service and county agents tended to focus on the better-managed farm and to ignore the low-income and part-time farmers. The agricultural establishment, in fact, found itself remarkably ill-informed about rural poverty and ill-equipped to deal with it at the beginning of the depression.[28]

In West Virginia, the Extension Service was probably more oriented to the small family farm than in any other state. County agents and home demonstration agents promoted many youth activities through nearly thirteen hundred 4-H clubs, summer camps in fifty of the fifty-five counties, and statewide camps at Jackson's Mill. The Extension Service also sought to interest farm wives in various activities and sponsored some 430 women's clubs. Despite all the opportunities, most of the poorest farmers showed little interest in organized activities or Extension programs. In 1940 J.O. Knapp, the state Extension director, lamented that the low income farmers "don't belong to our farm organizations. They don't read literature in the way of bulletins. They don't attend meetings. The only way to reach these folks is through personal contact."[29] It was probably also true that Extension workers preferred to work with those who were better educated and readily responsive to their efforts. In effect, those who needed Extension help the most were least likely to obtain it.

Some tenant farmers and sharecroppers in the South found their voice in the Southern Tenant Farmers Union and made their condition known,[30] but there was no similar voice for the low-income mountain farmer of West Virginia and Appalachia. While coal miners organized to become a powerful political force in the state, and even unemployed workers joined the Unemployed League to voice their concerns, the most destitute farmers were too inchoate and isolated to join in common cause. In a time when many groups in society organized to seek order for their lives, low-income farmers remained unorganized and voiceless.

Although the AAA was oriented to landlords and big agriculture, other New Deal programs sought to help poor farmers through resettlement, low-interest long-term mortgages for tenants, low-interest loans, help in debt management, electrification, and soil conservation and erosion control. The Federal Emergency Relief Administration offered work relief and started ambitious efforts in rural rehabilitation to help farmers and other rural people to become self-supporting and independent of relief. The Works Progress Administration provided work relief to farmers as well as to unemployed industrial workers.[31]

The most dramatic of these initiatives in West Virginia was the launching of three resettlement communities: Arthurdale in Preston County, Red House in Putnam County, and Tygart Valley in Randolph County. Because Eleanor Roosevelt took a personal interest in Arthurdale, it received much attention from both the government and the press.

Monongalia County in Northern West Virginia was one of the counties where the American Friends Service Committee's Appalachian feeding program had worked.[32] The Friends had concluded that the people of the area needed more than relief, because there were too many coal miners who would never go back to work. They believed the solution to the problem was to resettle coal miners outside of the coal region "on better farm land than can be found in the hills." They recommended that miners be encouraged to farm in combination with mining. If they lived on a farm, they would be assured of a food supply even if the mines provided irregular employment. They could also keep a wood lot, and they and their wives could engage in handicrafts to supplement their income.[33]

The Friends' ideas struck several responsive chords in Washington in 1933. As governor of New York, Franklin D. Roosevelt had supported experimental resettlement of the unemployed in rural areas, and Mrs. Roosevelt had taken a special interest in the idea. The most ardent advocate of the subsistence homestead idea within the federal bureaucracy was Agriculture Department official Milburn L. Wilson, a former economics professor at Montana State College. Wilson's mentors at the University of Wisconsin had interested him in the idea, and he believed that in Utah he had found a practical example of his professors' idea in the Mormon village. There he observed neat farmsteads with clean streets and urban conveniences of power and plumbing. Wilson promoted a compelling image of a new type of industrial city where people could remain close to the soil. Electricity, rapid communication, and the automobile, Wilson believed, made the dream a practical possibility.[34]

In the early days of the New Deal, Mrs. Roosevelt invited Wilson to the White House to discuss the idea with others including Clarence Pickett of the Friends, Mrs. Leonard Elmhirst (the former Dorothy Straight and the main financial backer of the *New Republic*), and Louis

The New Deal and Agriculture 169

Howe. After the meeting Mrs. Roosevelt and Howe talked to the president, and he heartily endorsed the plan.³⁵ He persuaded Congress to add $25 million to the National Industrial Recovery Act for promoting subsistence homesteads. After Congress passed the legislation during the Hundred Days, Harold Ickes appointed Wilson to head a Subsistence Homestead Division in the Interior Department. Wilson hired Clarence Pickett to serve as his assistant with special responsibility for coal mining communities.³⁶

With its limited funds, the Subsistence Homestead Division hoped to demonstrate the usefulness of the concept with pilot projects. The plan called for the government to buy land, build houses and roads, acquire the needed livestock and farm machinery, and attract employers for the homesteaders. The government would then arrange to sell to the homesteaders over thirty years. Homesteaders would come from the population of stranded industrial workers in rural areas as well as from low-income farmers trapped on unproductive lands.³⁷

Clarence Pickett called Mrs. Roosevelt's attention to Monongalia County as a place ripe for a subsistence homestead project. At Pickett's invitation, Lorena Hickok visited the area and saw Scotts Run, the notoriously depressed mining region just outside Morgantown. Hickok, who in her travels for Harry Hopkins saw some of the most depressed places in the country, said it was "the worst place I'd seen."³⁸ Historian Steven Haid describes Scotts Run as by far the most distressing and blighted part of Monongalia County:

> The run itself was a sulfurous, golden stream that snaked its way among the steep hillsides through a narrow valley floor to its juncture with the Monongahela River. Along its slopes ran some of the richest coal veins in the world, yet on the hillsides existed some of the most cruel and biting poverty imaginable. A world traveler visiting Scotts Run described it as 'the damnedest cesspool of human misery I have ever seen in America.' Sanitation conditions were at their primitive worst. Rickety houses sat precariously on the hillsides with their open sewers and privies draining into the stream. Huge smoldering slag piles dotted the valley, poisoning its air and screening the sunlight from the dismal valley crevice. To these conditions were added the facts that there were few paved roads and very little flat land for building, gardening, or playgrounds.³⁹

In late August, Eleanor Roosevelt, driving her own car over the mountain roads from Washington, went to see for herself. Clarence Pickett arranged for her and Hickok to stay with a mine superintendent and his wife in Arnettsville. Leaving her car the next morning, they traveled in a battered Friends' car with Alice Davis, who had worked with the Friends and was now director of relief for Monongalia County. Davis introduced Mrs. Roosevelt as "another Friend" as they visited miners' families in places like Crown mine, Jere, Bertha Hill, Osage, Guston Run, Cassville, and New Hill. As she made these rounds, she met heads of families who had been on relief for three to five years, many of them living in rickety shacks on the hillsides of Scotts Run. A working miner with six children showed her pay slips, which indicated that after deductions for rent, oil, and the company store, he had less than a dollar a week left.[40]

The conditions she observed in Scotts Run and Hickok's reports about southern West Virginia convinced Mrs. Roosevelt that something must be done about West Virginia's stranded coal mining families to prevent a violent revolutionary situation from developing. She was impressed with the efforts the Friends had made in Monongalia County and immediately did all she could to help by using her influence in Washington and also by making personal contributions and helping to find private funding for other Friends projects. The Friends had organized a self-help cooperative to try to resettle destitute miners on a farm in Preston County, and Mrs. Roosevelt set out to get the Subsistence Homestead Division's support.[41]

By mid October 1933—with Louis Howe and Mrs. Roosevelt leading the way—the Division of Subsistence Homesteads had purchased one thousand acres of land in Preston County known as the Arthur farm, and plans were hurriedly drawn up for what was officially called the Reedsville Experimental Community but which became commonly known as Arthurdale. In November, soon after the purchase had been made, Mrs. Roosevelt, Louis Howe, and Clarence Pickett took a train to Fairmont to confer with architects and builders. Hoping to move in the first homesteaders by Christmas, Howe immediately ordered fifty prefabricated Cape Cod cottages. The cottages turned out to be small, lightly-constructed summer beach houses, totally inadequate for the cold West Virginia winters. At considerable expense, a team of architects from New York redesigned and enlarged the structures. In the meantime, the schedule for moving in the first homesteaders was delayed by six months.[42]

Later houses at Arthurdale were built of native stone and at considerably less expense, but cost overruns characterized the Reedsville project. The belated discovery, for example, that a stratum of porous rock lay beneath the land caused great expense in making the water supply safe. Secretary Ickes, who was not fond of the subsistence homestead idea, confided to his diary that since Mrs. Roosevelt had made Arthurdale her pet project, "we have been spending money down there like drunken sailors."[43] Clarence Pickett, who was a strong advocate of the idea, later wrote of his concern "at seeing many prompt, if not hasty, actions being taken by people next to the President—actions which would have to be brought into some kind of order."[44] Even Mrs. Roosevelt would later admit that "much money was spent, perhaps some of it unwisely."[45] Ickes wanted to centralize control of the subsistence homestead projects; Wilson, Mrs. Roosevelt, and Howe wanted control in the hands of independent local corporations. In the spring of 1934, Ickes moved to centralize control in Washington. Wilson, believing centralized administration compromised his idea of "grassroots democracy," resigned as director of the Division of Subsistence Homesteads to become assistant secretary of agriculture.[46]

Meanwhile, under the local direction of Bushrod Grimes, the work went forward at Arthurdale. A community center, school, and homes were built, and homesteaders, many of them selected from the "best families" of Scotts Run, moved in, but problems continued to plague the project. Part of the idea was that industrial work would be available in the community, but getting suitable employers to locate at Arthurdale proved difficult. At Mrs. Roosevelt's urging, the Mountaineer Craftsmen's Cooperative Association (MCCA), which had enjoyed some success in furniture-making and other handicrafts, was moved from Morgantown, but when a commercial furniture maker tried to set up in Arthurdale, the cooperative collapsed, because the men could make more working for wages. The furniture company failed, but MCCA could not be revived. Another idea was that the community could make post-office boxes, but a congressman from Indiana, representing the district that had the factory with the monopoly on making post-office boxes, succeeded in persuading Congress to prohibit Arthurdale from competing with the private manufacturer, because it would lead to "sovietizing all industry." A shirt manufacturer and a maker of radio cabinets failed in succession. In fairly short order, experiments in progressive education in the community's school were abandoned, and after two years the school became a part of the regular West Virginia school system.[47]

The other West Virginia subsistence homestead projects received much less attention than Arthurdale, but they were similar in purpose, although the Red House project had a somewhat different beginning. Red House (later named Eleanor) started as a Federal Emergency Relief Administration project in the early New Deal, when Harry Hopkins sought ways for FERA to provide rehabilitation as well as relief for stranded coal miners and subsistence farmers.[48]

Like Arthurdale, the Tygart Valley community, about ten miles from Elkins, was one of the early projects of the Subsistence Homestead Division and sought to help stranded timber workers. In the spring of 1935, all resettlement and rural rehabilitation programs were transferred to a new agency, the Resettlement Administration.[49]

The Red House project also had ambitious beginnings. County agent Thomas H. McGovran, whose father had promoted back-to-the-land solutions for unemployed urban workers, sought federal help, and West Virginia relief administrator William N. Beehler convinced his superiors in FERA to undertake the project, which was to be the first of its type in the United States.[50] Officially called the Red House Garden Farms, Inc., the project sought to relocate 150 stranded industrial workers and their families in the community twenty-five miles northwest of Charleston along the Kanawha River in Putnam County. Each family, chosen from relief rolls, would have the opportunity to rent and eventually to purchase homesteads consisting of nearly an acre, a house, barn, hog pen, chicken coop, two hogs, and chickens. Milk cows would share community pasture land. Plans called for converting the colonial style home of pioneer Joseph Ruffner (the "Red House") into a community center and building a school. There would also be a canning plant, a woodworking shop, and twenty small shops where homesteaders could earn cash to supplement their subsistence gardening. The nearness of Charleston would provide a market for eggs and other farm products as well as a place where additional work might be found.[51]

The Red House homesteaders began to move in on April 1, 1935, and eventually some 150 families, including four hundred children, lived in the little white cinderblock houses.[52] Like Arthurdale, Red House was plagued with problems. The object of repeated attacks by opponents of the government's plan to rehabilitate stranded workers, the project had four different managers in its first four years. Many of the homesteaders found it difficult to obtain sufficient cash from surplus farm produce or from work in the community's shops. Efforts to attract an industrial employer to a site in the town failed. By the spring of 1938, the population was in decline, with only 115 of the 150 houses occupied.[53]

Each subsistence homestead project had its own problems, but some were common to all. It was difficult to attract industry to the sites, because many businessmen believed it inappropriate for government to promote industrial activities in competition with private enterprise. The remoteness of Arthurdale and Tygart Valley from suitable transportation and markets made them especially unattractive as manufacturing sites. Red House, located on the New York Central Railroad near Charleston and Huntington and not far from other cities, still had trouble attracting industrial employers. Some leading New Dealers always had seen the concept as wrongheaded. Secretary of Agriculture Wallace, who certainly was no enemy of experimentation, thought it a mistake to try to combine agricultural and industrial functions in a rural resettlement plan. Rexford Tugwell, who favored government planning and sympathized with the low-income farmers and unemployed workers, nevertheless saw the subsistence homesteads program as utopian and escapist. He preferred a plan for government to buy and retire from agricultural production submarginal land, and for resettlement of farm families on better land as the best solution to the problem of rural poverty. Harold Ickes, the administrator in charge of the program, saw it as "nothing but a headache from the beginning."[54]

No doubt for some of the subsistence homesteaders the experience improved their lives. The program allowed some of the original homesteaders to escape horrible conditions, to buy land and homes on attractive terms, and to make a better life for themselves and their families. Although some returned to the coal camps when they could again obtain work, those people who remained in Arthurdale, Red House, or Tygart Valley would regard subsistence homesteading as a success. As a public policy experiment, however, the subsistence homesteading program failed. The goal was to show that government could help people to escape poverty by establishing subsistence homesteads at a reasonable and largely recoverable cost. At Arthurdale, however, instead of setting up families for $2,000 or $3,000 each, as originally estimated, the cost was more than $10,000 each. At Arthurdale and most other subsistence homesteads, the homesteaders remained dependent on the government. Only general economic recovery could rescue them from that dependence, and the recovery did not come until World War II. By that time the government had lost interest in the subsistence homestead concept, and beginning in 1942, it began to liquidate its remaining holdings in the communities.⁵⁵

The whole business of resettlement, whether through subsistence communities or the moving of farm families from poor lands to better lands, aroused much congressional opposition and generated negative publicity for the Resettlement Administration (RA). Congressional conservatives successfully derailed the reform ideas of the agency's leaders. The administrator, Rexford Tugwell, who wanted to conduct an all-out war against rural poverty, resigned in 1936. In 1937, to satisfy congressional critics, the Farm Security Administration (FSA) replaced the RA, and the emphasis shifted from relocating farmers to better land to the improvement of existing family farms.⁵⁶

Russell G. Ellyson—a West Virginian, graduate of the West Virginia University College of Agriculture, and a former county agent—headed the rural rehabilitation efforts under the CWA, RA, and FSA in West Virginia. One of the goals of the FSA was to reduce farm tenancy, which, although not as high in West Virginia as in the South, grew during the Depression years and by 1939 reached about 25 percent of all farms. During the period 1937 to 1940, the FSA helped seventy-four tenants purchase farms at an average cost of $6,000. Tenants received loans at 3 percent interest over forty years. Obviously, the numbers helped barely scratched the surface of tenants who would have liked to buy the farms they worked, but Congress limited appropriations for the purchase program.⁵⁷

To help tenant farmers, the FSA also tried to improve tenant contracts and to lengthen the tenure of farm leases, especially in the eastern panhandle, where the rate of tenantry was highest in the state. In Jefferson and Berkeley Counties, the common practice was for tenants to move each year. If a tenant secured longer leases, he could save the annual cost of moving, estimated at fifty dollars by FSA, and he could make longer-term plans for his farming operations. The FSA sought to convince owners that longer term leases would also be to their advantage, because the tenant would have a greater interest in improving the fertility of the soil and enhancing the value of the property.⁵⁸

The FSA also tried to help low-income farm families to rehabilitate their farms through small, low-interest loans. Farm tenants, day laborers, or owners unable to obtain credit elsewhere could apply to the FSA for help in purchasing livestock, equipment, home furnishings, and various pieces of equipment for the home and farm. Farmers were required to have a home and farm management plan to help them pay their loans and to consult regularly with a FSA supervisor. Thousands of West Virginia low-income farmers became clients of the FSA through the loan program.[59]

As Director Ellyson explained to a conference on low-income farm families in 1940, the special circumstances of mountain farming made it very difficult for families to repay FSA loans, pay other debts, meet current obligations, and maintain satisfactory health conditions. Although these farmers could not obtain bank loans, they managed to open accounts with grocers, doctors, and hospitals and accumulated substantial debts. The FSA tried to help them reduce their debt burden by persuading creditors to reduce the debt or to extend the time for payment. Many of the FSA clients worked small acreages in rugged terrain and saw little cash. In Barbour County, for example, 41 percent of the families had farms averaging less than fifty acres, and much of the fifty acres was waste land. On such farms, rehabilitation efforts faced long odds.[60]

Although the FSA found it politically prudent to refrain from promoting communitarian or cooperative projects, the agency did offer small community loans for such things as canning machinery, tractors, or other equipment for which there was a need in the community and the cost was greater than one farmer could afford. Another notable FSA initiative was a medical-care plan. In 1940 farmers in seven West Virginia counties were able to obtain medical coverage for eight dollars per year for the head of family and two dollars for each additional family member. The FSA arranged with doctors to provide the service and hoped to expand the idea to other counties. It also made grants for environmental sanitation, persuading impoverished farmers to protect their water supply, screen their homes, and build sanitary privies.[61]

Ellyson told the 1940 low-income conference that the FSA sought to sell farmers on good farm and home management, but not all families took advantage of FSA advice. Some families had never really been anything but part-time farmers who had depended on coal or something else for part of their income. With no cash income and no training as farmers, they obtained small farms and tried to make a living. The smaller and poorer the farm, the more difficult was the task of management, but often, Ellyson suggested, the hill country people lacked education and management skills.[62]

The most enduring national impact of the FSA came from its efforts to call attention to the plight of the rural poor through photographs, films, and books. These materials now form a rich source of information about the era's social and economic history. Pare Lorentz, a West Virginian, directed two of the most powerful of the agency's documentary films, *The Plow that Broke the Plains* (1936), a vivid depiction of the dust-bowl conditions on the prairies, and *The River* (1937), which called attention to the consequences of poor land use. The agency contracted with several outstanding photographers to record the conditions of rural life throughout the country. Some of the photographs formed the basis for books such as Dorothea Lange and Paul Taylor's *An American Experience* (1939) and James Agee and Walker Evans's *Let Us Now Praise Famous Men* (1941).[63] Some of these photographers, including Ben Shahn, Walker Evans, Arthur Rothstein, and Marion Wolcott Post, traveled in West Virginia and captured many poignant and revealing scenes of everyday life in both coal towns and farming areas.[64]

The efforts of the FSA represented an historic pioneering attempt to attack the human suffering, social injustice, and economic waste of chronic rural poverty, but Congress never appropriated enough money for the agency to carry out its statutory mission. Congressional conservatives opposed the concept of the FSA as they had the Resettlement Administration and forced the agency to operate more like a bank loan officer seeking good risks than an agency carrying out a broad attack on rural poverty. In West Virginia the rehabilitation work among low income farm families with small and unproductive mountain farms now appears unrealistic and may have encouraged and prolonged dependency on government. Did it really make sense to encourage families who were not the best of farmers to try to make a living out of farms that even the best of farmers could not have made succeed? In the end, the FSA must be seen, like the subsistence homestead program with which it was saddled, as another New Deal experiment that failed. The agency passed away under the pressures of conservative opposition and the exigencies of war.[65]

Much more successful was the New Deal's effort to bring electrification to rural America. Even in this case, however, New Deal efforts faced substantial roadblocks in West Virginia, and to the extent that electrification was successful, it helped to hasten the demise of traditional mountain agriculture. President Roosevelt created the Rural

Electrification Administration (REA) by executive order in May 1935 and appointed one of the chief advocates of rural electrification, Morris L. Cooke, as administrator. Roosevelt established the REA largely because private utilities, judging returns on rural power to be inadequate to offset the costs, had proven unwilling to furnish power to rural areas. In 1935 only 10 percent of American farms had electricity, but when Cooke invited the utility companies to cooperate in providing rural areas with power, the power companies insisted that all farms that needed electricity were already served. Other conflicts, including a disagreement over rates for rural customers, led to open hostility between the power companies and the REA, and Cooke decided to work through rural cooperatives.[66]

In West Virginia, the first intimation of the coming of electricity to the countryside was a survey carried out by the state relief administration in cooperation with county extension agents in February 1935. Some fifty thousand rural residents were interviewed regarding their interest in electricity and willingness to pay for it.[67] When it became clear that REA had discovered a large market for electricity, private power companies moved to build "spite lines" to block REA cooperatives, which by law could not build lines where private companies had built. Barbour County was the first to organize a rural cooperative, the Barbour Power Company, and to apply for REA assistance, but a private company offered to carry out the project, and the REA application was withdrawn. Other counties followed the example of Barbour, and in all cases private power companies stepped in to keep REA out. A Hampshire County cooperative failed when power companies invaded its territory. In Hardy County, however, rural residents formed the Hardy County Light and Power Association, and despite a determined effort by Potomac Light and Power to discredit the REA, voted to stick with REA.[68]

As late as 1937 fewer than 10 percent of farm families in West Virginia enjoyed the benefits of electricity. The REA charged that the state public service commission (PSC) encouraged private companies to block REA cooperatives. REA administrator John M. Carmody asserted that "in no other state has the utility opposition been so consistently successful in breaking up rural power projects." Among legal roadblocks thrown in the way of the cooperatives was the PSC's insistence that they were utilities and must therefore apply to the commission for certificates of convenience. On the basis that it did not have a certificate, the state supreme court issued a temporary injunction against the Hardy County cooperative. In view of the difficulties faced by West Virginia cooperatives, which of course had no money to pay lawyers to fight legal battles with power companies, Carmody suggested to groups applying for REA loans in Jackson and Roane Counties that they reconsider, because under the circumstances in West Virginia, they would face difficulties paying for their loan.[69]

The utility companies, with the cooperation of the Extension Service and the state public service commission, managed to kill off most of the fledgling cooperatives. By 1940, only three REA cooperatives had managed to survive in West Virginia: the Hardy County Light and Power Association, serving 142 customers; the Harrison Rural Electrification Association, with 451 customers, and the Craig-Botetourt Electric Cooperative, serving 119 customers in Monroe County.[70] By comparison, in 1939 in Virginia, REA cooperatives serviced half of all farm customers, and a spirit of cooperation prevailed between the cooperatives and the private electric power companies. In 1941, of forty-four thousand Kentucky farms with electricity, thirty-six thousand were served by REA cooperatives.[71]

While the power companies in West Virginia blocked REA cooperatives, they moved ahead with plans to extend their own power lines into rural areas. In 1937 officials of the Monongahela West Penn Public Service Company met at Jackson's Mill with agricultural extension workers to seek the cooperation of the Extension Service in extending power lines to farmers in Northern West Virginia. In 1938, at another conference at Jackson's Mill, representatives of other private power companies and extension agents announced plans to promote rural electrification throughout the state. The power companies sponsored follow-up conferences in 1939 and 1940 and built five demonstration kitchens and a laundry at Jackson's Mill to illustrate the many uses of electricity. At the 1940 conference, power company officials claimed that West Virginia led adjacent southern states in the advance of rural electrification with 21.9 percent of farms wired, compared to 20.3 in Virginia, 16.9 in North Carolina, 15.2 in Tennessee, and 11.6 in Kentucky.[72] Clearly, although REA played but a small direct role in the electrification of rural West Virginia, the competitive threat of rural cooperatives pushed the electric companies to extend their power lines to rural customers.

The immediate benefits of electricity to the farm family were enormous. The farm wife escaped much drudgery with the coming of running water, indoor toilets, washing machines, electric stoves, and other electrical appliances. Clean and bright electric lights replaced the kerosene lantern. Electricity revolutionized many farm tasks and in West Virginia gave a particular boost to poultry raising. Refrigeration helped in food preservation and processing. The long term impact, however, like the impact of all modernizing technologies, was to hasten the decline of subsistence agriculture and indeed of farming as a way of life as electricity led to dramatic increases in productivity, making subsistence agriculture virtually obsolete.[73]

The most thorough attempt of a federal agency to seek a path to order through the economic disarray of Appalachia was a study of economic and social conditions by researchers and specialists on mountain life in the U.S. Department of Agriculture. Guided by historian Lewis Cecil Gray, the USDA study noted the abuse of the land that had resulted from the unregulated exploitation of a century by uncontrolled burning, destructive lumbering, and unwise clearing of land for farms. For the timber industry it was not just a question of Depression. The unwise actions of the past would take time to repair, and the USDA group believed that the antidote to the unregulated exploitation of the past would be a strong dose of government planning.[74]

The increase in population during the first three decades of the twentieth century combined with the abuse of natural resources meant that too many people were chasing too few resources in the region. The only way conditions of life could be fundamentally improved, the report maintained, would be "by removing some of the population." Some secondary problems could be alleviated by concentrating the population in "farm-forest communities," where residents could combine part-time farming with employment in forest industries or combine work in the mines with forestry or part-time farming. To carry out the necessary adjustments in mountain life, the USDA study recommended that a planning agency vested with adequate powers and resources be established. Successful planning would probably require public ownership of "a large proportion of the forest lands."[75]

Historian Ronald D Eller has suggested that the proposal for an Appalachian planning agency was partially fulfilled with the establishment of the Tennessee Valley Authority (TVA) in 1933. The TVA's authority, however, did not extend to West Virginia. Not until 1965 did the federal government establish a region-wide agency, the Appalachian Regional Commission, but it was not the kind of resource planning agency that Lewis Gray and his colleagues had in mind. Public ownership of forest lands did grow during the Depression as the TVA, the National Park Service, the state park system, and the U.S. Forest Service obtained lands. The amount of land in agriculture fell by some 661,000 acres over the decade, which represents 6,234 farms of average pre-Depression size.[76]

The ideas of statewide soil conservation and land use planning, which came into practice at the end of the decade, may have been influenced by the planning notions of the Gray report. On the whole, however, the Gray report had limited influence. Its statist and planning orientation, influential in the early New Deal (as exemplified by the subsistence community experiment), had fallen out of favor by the time the report appeared in 1935. Neither Congress nor the state governments of the region found the recommendations practical, so the report was shelved.

Toward the end of the decade, the Department of Agriculture, through its Bureau of Agricultural Economics (BAE) and the Extension Service, addressed the severe erosion and land abuse issues through the promotion of a community-based land-use planning program. The BAE sought to identify submarginal and unproductive lands and to withdraw them from production. It hoped to promote "grass roots democracy" at the same time by having farmers elect local land-use committees that, with the technical assistance of the BAE and the Extension Service, would shape local land-use plans and help to identify lands unsuitable for agriculture.[77]

One of the ways the BAE and the state Extension Service sought to deal with erosion and land abuse was by establishing general guidelines for proper use of sloping land. The government agronomists suggested that slopes up to 5 percent could be safely cultivated with proper management. Some slopes between 5 and 25 percent could also be cultivated under certain conditions depending on the nature of the soil and subsoil, the underlying geologic conditions, the amount of precipitation, the extent and degree of erosion, and the type of crops grown. The guidelines urged that cultivating slopes to avoid erosion and preserve soil fertility also required the use of legumes and other soil-building crops in rotation with close-growing rather than row-planted crops. In addition, slopes between 5 and 25 percent should be protected with winter cover crops, contour plowing, and strip-cropping—the width of both the plowed and unbroken strips narrowing with increases in the steepness of the land.[78]

The New Deal and Agriculture   181

The BAE guidelines also suggested that slopes of up to 35 percent could generally be used for pasturing, that slopes of between 35 and 40 percent might be used in certain circumstances, and that practically all slopes over 40 percent should be in forest trees. These guidelines had no mandatory force and were intended to be modified to fit community conditions,[79] but they called into question the viability of much of the state's farming. Less than one-fifth of the state's 15.3 million acres had slopes of less than 12 percent, and about one-fifth had slopes of 12 to 25 percent. Two-fifths of the acreage sloped 25 to 40 percent, and more than one fifth had slopes of 40 percent or more. The writers of *West Virginia: A Guide to the Mountain State* noted that West Virginia agriculture had been facetiously but aptly labeled "perpendicular farming."[80]

In early November 1939, the BAE sponsored an Appalachian land-use conference and tour through part of West Virginia to illustrate the physical, social, and economic problems that grew from the abuse of Appalachian land. A *Divine Comedy* of land-use, the tour demonstrated a full catalog of land use sins and their consequences along with a few redeeming examples of progressive and scientific agriculture. Starting on the western edge of the state at the Big Sandy River basin in Wayne County, one of the poorest counties in the state, the tour took note of the destructive clearing of hill-sides for part-time and subsistence agriculture and by timbering operations. The rugged watershed had lost its natural stability because of the destruction of the original forest cover. Because the slopes were too steep, the exposure of the land surface caused deep erosion and accelerated run-off of surface waters. Many of the streams filled with sand and gravel, and infertile subsoils washed down from the hills over once rich bottom lands. Moreover, lack of proper rural sanitation polluted ground water. Such scenes helped to explain why so many of Wayne's farmers sought relief.[81]

After passing through Huntington, the tour examined the problems of the West Virginia portion of the Ohio River basin and the lower Kanawha River basin between Huntington and Point Pleasant. Along the Ohio and up the Kanawha as far as Nitro, the wide bottom lands offered an excellent topography for agriculture, but constant cropping without fertilization had depleted the soil. Annual growing of the same crops without rotation and proper tillage had led to disease infestation in corn, potatoes, and melons. At one time the area had been one of greatest inland melon-producing areas in the United

States, but the decline of soil fertility and the problem of wilt had ruined melon production. Moving inward from the bottoms, the slopes quickly rise, and minimal pasture quickly gives way to land, which, though rather densely-settled, was judged submarginal for agriculture.[82]

The tour also stopped at several farms to illustrate some of the problems of Appalachian farmers and efforts of various agencies to help. At Lesage, for example, FSA provided loans to a farmer struggling to make a living for his family of six with a five-year lease on a farm that had forty-five tillable acres. The FSA also made a community loan to the Lesage Community Tractor Service to buy a tractor to serve seven farms.[83]

In Mason County, the tour visited a land-use adjustment project where the FSA worked to help rehabilitate family farms. The problems faced by these farmers typified the situation in much of the state. Although once a fairly prosperous agricultural region, a century of heedless exploitation of the land through extensive clearing and intensive farming had led to severe erosion and the loss of practically all top soil. Even if the soil had not been ruined, many of the farms in the area were too small for profitable operation. Crop yields were low, pasture lands were so poor they had unusually low livestock carrying capacities, and the good timber had long since been annihilated. The farm families lived in poor housing still bereft at the end of 1939 of the amenities that came with electricity. Already densely settled, the area's population became increasingly "dammed up" on the little subsistence farms of Mason County. Little supplemental off-farm income was available, and many residents relied upon WPA or other forms of relief. No prospects of emigration for industrial employment elsewhere appeared on the immediate horizon.[84]

Along with the decline of agricultural productivity associated with the reckless depletion of the soil came serious social problems. The more enterprising families sold or abandoned their worn-out lands and left the area. Those who purchased or squatted on the land were less likely than the previous owners to manage it properly. With a declining tax base, roads and schools suffered. Most schools were of the one- or two-room variety. No doctors were available. Health care consisted of a public health nurse in the county seat at Point Pleasant. The FSA sought to help with small loans and management advice.[85]

Further stops on the land-use tour were at Red House Farms and

The New Deal and Agriculture 183

Charleston. The tour then moved through Kanawha, Fayette, and Greenbrier Counties, noting prominent scenic and industrial sites, including Hawks Nest State Park and the Electro-Metallurgical Company power plant.[86]

In Greenbrier County the tour demonstrated some positive efforts in West Virginia agriculture, such as the Ross Tuckwiller farm, where beef experimental work sponsored by the USDA and the West Virginia Agricultural Experiment Station had been carried out since 1914, and where the Soil Conservation Service (SCS) and the Civilian Conservation Corps had worked on soil conservation since 1935. The Greenbrier County program included efforts to fence all woodland to protect it from grazing, and the planting of a million trees to protect soil in steep and badly eroded areas. The project encouraged better pasture management including treatment with lime and superphosphate and regular mowing and pasture rotation. The CCC built stock ponds for use in drought and constructed diversion terraces. The SCS encouraged contour strip cropping, the establishment of sod water ways in croplands, and the planting of more alfalfa.[87]

At the Greenbrier River, the tour reached the entrance to the Monongahela National Forest. Also along the Greenbrier was the site of a former saw mill town abandoned in 1914. Typical of the more than one hundred such towns left in the wake of the timber industry and scattered through the area, some remnants of the former population remained, having bought former company houses and a patch of ground for farming. The depleted and tax-delinquent land of the former timber company came under the control of the national forest.[88]

The 1939 land-use tour helped set the stage for the BAE to promote land-use planning to avoid recurrence of past disasters. BAE land use specialists and the state Extension Service chose Lewis County, in the north central part of the state, as a demonstration area in the shaping of a community-based state land use program, because it provided something of a microcosm of the purely agricultural Appalachian county of the state. With a topography ranging from level to rugged, it typified the terrain of many Appalachian counties and severely tested the land-use guidelines. In 1935 about 93 percent of the land in Lewis County was in farms, despite the fact that some 20 percent of the land had slopes exceeding 40 percent. About 25 percent of the farms averaged only $480 income per year. As was typical for the state, about 70 percent of the land was classified as pasture land

and only 15 percent as crop land. The largest farms were devoted to stock ranching and had annual incomes around $2,000. Farm tenancy had risen over the decade from 12 to 20 percent.[89]

By the end of 1940, Lewis County had elected community land-use planning committees composed of local men, older boys, women, and older girls. Representatives of these communities and of educational and relevant government agencies met as a county committee. With the help of the guidelines developed by technical advisers in the Extension Service and BAE land-use specialists, the committees studied, mapped, and described the soils, topography, erosion, and climate in each of the communities. In the process they identified their major land-use problems and recommended corrective actions. As Lewis County began to address the problems at the end of 1940, twelve other counties had elected committees and were at various stages in the process, and a state advisory committee began to look to the development of a state land-use plan.[90]

Compared to some West Virginia counties, Lewis County's gently rolling hills provided relatively good agricultural conditions, but in the southern part of the county, circumstances more typical of the most rugged counties prevailed. There, in a narrow nine-square-mile area abutting similar land in Braxton, Upshur, and Webster counties, almost half of the land had slopes of 40 percent or more. A dozen streams or "runs" cut the area into a series of steep valleys and narrow ridges, with only occasional narrow strips of level bottomland providing land suitable for crops. Before World War I, the land was heavily timbered, and logging and some coal mining had afforded employment to those who lived in the area, but sometime shortly before 1930, the narrow-gauge railroad, which had hauled the coal and timber from the region, was removed. The sixty-three families that remained, a typical case of a "stranded" population, sought to scratch a living from the hillsides, even though about half of the population owned no land. Some rented, some worked land on sufferance of relatives, and a few simply squatted.[91] Most of them had been part-time farmers who had combined farming with lumbering, mining, and road work. Some had been carpenters, others had worked in the oil and gas fields, and others had found employment on the narrow-gauge railroad. Wages from these various occupations had been necessary supplements to the meager cash returns of their farms.[92]

People living in this area had an average annual income of only $369. Half of the households had a total gross cash income of less than $200 for the year. The Lewis County land use planning committee had concluded that "an average farm family of good farming ability" would need about ninety aces of almost completely cleared land on the better farm land of the county to make it possible for them to pay for the farm and still live reasonably well. In the southern area, however, most of the farms were under 50 acres, and because of the steep slopes, a large amount of the land could not be considered agricultural.[93]

Most houses in the area were of board and batten or unpainted frame construction in varying states of disrepair. Over half of the heads of families reported chronic physical disabilities, which impaired their abilities to do the kind of hard work demanded by farming. Adequate medical care would have been difficult to obtain even if these families could pay for it, because the nearest doctors were twenty-five miles away in Buckhannon, Webster Springs, or Weston. Young men, unable to find work elsewhere, generally remained in the area. Young women were more likely to marry someone outside the area and move away.[94]

The public policy dilemma of dealing with populations such as those in the Big Sandy basin, the Mason County area, and the mountainous southern tip of Lewis County reflected the more general question of what, if anything, should be done about the half or more of West Virginia's agricultural population that fell into the same low-income category and shared many of the same characteristics. The question of southern Lewis County also provided a test of whether a recommendation from the "grass roots," a local land-use committee, could lead to the actual removal of land from production. In 1939, the Ireland Community land-use planning committee classified the nine square miles of rugged country as "land now in farms in which farming should be discontinued, and the land put to some other use." The area, labeled on maps simply as "C Area" was part of the Ireland Community but had no representative on the land-use committee. The Lewis County land-use planning committee endorsed the recommendation. A survey conducted by BAE sociologist C.R. Draper concluded that even the people of the area agreed that it was unsuited to agriculture.[95]

Draper foresaw several possibilities for the area. If WPA and other relief agencies continued at their current levels of operation, they could maintain the population at its prevailing low level of subsistence with no prospect of any long-term improvement. A second possibility would be for the state or federal government to buy out the land for public use, an approach, Draper noted, likely to be opposed by the residents of the area, who although they understood that the land was ill-suited to agriculture, were reluctant to consider moving. Assuming that the recompensation for the land would provide the only funds for relocation, Draper pointed out that only half the population actually owned the lands they lived on, and that the compensation for the land would not likely afford even the owners enough to permit them to relocate on good land. They would probably end up in similar circumstances in another part of Lewis County or nearby.[96]

Another possibility, Draper suggested, was to discourage further migration into the area while offering incentives to the current population to leave. Because of the low average age of the population, the effect of such a policy might not be felt for a long time, but eventually a balance between population and resources might be reached. In the meantime, residents could be encouraged to make their home gardens and livestock yield a larger, more varied and better balanced food supply. If families continued to live in the area, Draper added, "Inasmuch as the principal export of this area appears to be children, it is of utmost importance that their health and education should be one of the principal aims of any adjustment program."[97]

The state land-use planning committee also considered what should be done about southern Lewis County. Recognizing that the question of "land now in farms in which farming should be discontinued" presented one of the most complex problems in West Virginia agriculture, the committee agonized over the issue and considered whether relocation or rehabilitation was the appropriate long-term solution.[98] Dodging a definitive answer, the committee endorsed instead a short-term "unified program" approach for area C and suggested that it serve as a model for the state's low income agricultural areas. In Lewis County, the various agencies involved promised to cooperate to help the families get the most possible out of their marginal farms. The FSA agreed to give families grants as well as loans to help them carry out farm management plans and to allow workers there to combine part-time WPA work with FSA loans. The county home demonstration agent would work closely with homemakers, helping them carry out the FSA management plan while emphasizing the Extension Service's "Feed the Family First" food program and teaching local homemakers better food preservation techniques. The county agent agreed to emphasize the need for raising livestock for meat and growing feed. He also would encourage farmers to grow nuts, berries and fruits for supplemental cash. The county agent and the FSA would together help local farmers to set up marketing cooperatives.[99]

The idea of moving people off of unproductive land or land with slopes too steep for cropping or pasturing was a common one during the thirties, but often mountain families were attached to their land in ways BAE experts found difficult to understand. Historian Jack Temple Kirby quotes a West Virginia woman at the end of the twenties describing her devotion to her mountain acres: "It is almost sinful how I love these old acres here . . . how I lay store by every inch of the land, each blade of grass or grain it grows, how I believe there is no spot in the universe so perfect, so dear, and so sweet as the West Virginia mountains."[100]

Less poetically, the mimeographed guide for the 1939 land-use tour said of the low income area in Mason County: "The percentage of land owners is surprisingly high, it being an accepted fact that, due to sentimental attachment or other reasons which are difficult to explain or understand, the people in the area hold to their land and pay their taxes even though necessities are lacking and the land is depleted."[101]

Despite the attachment of people to their mountain lands, the sad reality is that the traditional subsistence-oriented mountain agriculture was no longer viable by the time the Great Depression arrived. The advance of industrial capitalism into the mountains in the nineteenth century had resulted in much alienation of the land as out-of-state land and industrial corporations purchased or leased thousands of acres. Mining, timbering, and destructive, unscientific agriculture damaged the environment, undermining the semisubsistence economy. Open ranging of hogs and cattle ended, and livestock production plummeted. Mountain farmers, in the meantime, became accustomed to wages and cash and either abandoned their farms or left them to be operated by their wives and children while they worked in the mines and mills. When the mines laid off their workers and the timber camps and saw mills closed down, many returned to their mountain farms "to overcrowding, to eroding ridges and spoiled creeks where the hogs no longer roamed."[102]

New Deal policy toward Appalachian agriculture had two contradictory tendencies reflecting both New Deal economic ambivalence and changes in thinking between the early New Deal, which tended toward centrist and planning ideas, and the later New Deal, which was more oriented toward the idea of the government providing a suitable setting for capitalistic enterprise to flourish. During the early days of the Depression, resettlement ideas proliferated, but experiments like Arthurdale aroused much conservative opposition. Beginning about 1937 with the Farm Security Administration, the focus shifted to rehabilitating poor farmers where they were, but the costs of rehabilitation also aroused conservative opposition. The planning concept reemerged in the later New Deal years in combination with the idea of "grass roots" organization of farmers and citizens to plan for appropriate use of the land and the removal of unsuitable land from agricultural uses. New Deal policies in West Virginia did much to provide relief for struggling farmers, to improve soil treatment and conservation, and to seek ways to reverse the mistreatment of the land,[103] but none of these efforts had any long-term success in preserving West Virginia small farmers or restoring the semisubsistence agriculture of the preindustrial past. As was true almost everywhere in the country, farm population peaked in 1935 and declined steadily thereafter as young people especially abandoned West Virginia farms for factories or entered the military services during World War II.[104]

9

The New Deal and Families in Distress

When the impact of the Great Crash hit Huntington in 1929, Milton Levine was in the sixth year of ownership of a men's clothing store, the Togery, which catered to the students of Marshall College. He witnessed the failure of the Huntington Bank and Trust Company, the Union Bank and Trust Company, and the Coal Exchange. By 1933 Levine, married and the father of three young children, had lost his business, a fate shared by his father, whose women's clothing store failed, and many of the small businessmen of Huntington. For Levine, the Depression became a nightmare succession of temporary jobs, a rejected attempt to obtain a job as a WPA timekeeper (he claimed he lacked the right political connections) and failed efforts to get back into business. In 1974, then working as a credit manager, Levine told an interviewer that he never really recovered from the Depression: "Whatever I lost, I lost myself, and maybe I should have got up, but I didn't.... Boy, it was really something!"[1]

Levine's story no doubt could be repeated by many small businessmen who struggled to survive in the cities and towns of West Virginia. When small businesses failed, proprietors and their families, like the many unemployed blue-collar workers and the struggling farmers, also faced daunting prospects. Some hung on by engaging in trade and barter operations. In Philippi, Blaine Nestor lost his teaching job in the Depression cutbacks and took over his uncle's small grocery store, where he could clear about fifteen dollars a week, although much of the trade was on a noncash basis. People came to the store with baskets of eggs, homemade butter, cottage cheese, and dressed and live chickens. In the summertime customers brought produce from their gardens to trade for flour, sugar, and coffee, and Nestor sold the bartered goods. His wife, also a former teacher, supplemented their store earnings with money earned as a WPA caseworker.[2]

An important measure of the New Deal is how it helped families like the Levines, the Nestors, and the thousands of others whose lives the Depression disrupted. As Levine's self-deprecating statement suggests, the psychological impact of unemployment was especially difficult for men, who were conditioned by cultural and social expectations to be breadwinners. Women also carried a heavy burden, because as housewives they often had to figure out how to make do with what was never enough. Children in families struggling to survive precipitous declines in income experienced unwholesome stresses, and in the poorest or broken families, children were sometimes abandoned to public care. Young people coming of age during the Depression faced disheartening prospects. For minority families, racial and ethnic discrimination amplified economic problems.[3]

Despite the increase in female employment outside the home during the twenties, many still considered home and hearth to be the proper sphere of women's work, and this was especially so in West Virginia. In 1938 the editor of the *West Virginia Review*, Lawrence E. Rollins, offered a panacea for the Depression often articulated by conservatives and traditionalists. He argued that the heavy unemployment of the Depression resulted from the entrance of so many women into the work force during World War I. When the war ended, "tens of thousands" of married women remained on the job in shops and offices, taking jobs that traditionally went to men. These women, Rollins argued, could do better jobs as homemakers. Their husbands would be happier, future generations would profit, and unemployment would be less of a problem if women would just return home to the work "that really belongs to them."[4]

Whatever women thought about "their proper sphere," in West Virginia as elsewhere, as historian Susan Ware notes, "the Depression propelled many women into new patterns of behavior that might not have occurred otherwise," and many of these new activities took place outside the home.[5] Women in working-class families with unemployed men desperately needed to earn money to help sustain their families, and even middle-class families needed the earnings of the wife to maintain accustomed consumption levels.[6]

Despite the pressures on women to seek work outside the home, strong prejudices against the employment of women, especially married women, persisted and indeed received reinforcement because of the Depression. It was not an isolated incident, but a typical one for the time when, in 1933, the Jefferson County school board, citing pressure from the state Department of Education, discussed prohibiting the continued employment of married women. The argument was that in a time of Depression, married women should not take jobs that could otherwise go to men or single women. The editor of the Shepherdstown *Register* noted that 28 of the 115 teachers in the county were married women and that "some of them rank among the best teachers in the service."[7] The Jefferson board took no action at that time, but the mere discussion of the idea was a not-so-subtle form of pressure to persuade married women to step aside. Nationwide, three-fourths of the school boards refused to hire married women and half dismissed those already employed. State and local governments also tended to dismiss married women first. The federal government ruled that only one member of a family could hold a federal job. Because of the prejudice against working women, it is a striking fact that female unemployment rose faster than male unemployment in the early days of the Depression.[8] Later, however, in part because women worked for low-wage jobs that were traditionally female jobs, the percentage of unemployment was lower among women than among men.[9]

A 1937 study of women's work by the U.S. Department of Labor presented a rather grim view of the hours typically worked and wages earned by West Virginia wage-earning women. The majority of those who worked in hotels and restaurants worked seven-day weeks. In five-and-dime stores, most worked forty-eight hours per week or longer, in contrast to department-store workers, who worked shorter weeks. Workers in laundries and dry cleaners also tended to long hours, with a substantial number working at least sixty hours weekly.[10]

For their labors they received meager returns. Two out of three women in men's clothing factories earned less than $10 per week; workers in the pottery industry earned around $15. Department-store workers received about $12.70; five-and-dime type store workers got $11.25. Women hotel and restaurant workers took home the least earnings for their long week, only $8.50. Hotel and restaurant workers did receive some supplement to their low wages through tips, meals, and lodging.[11]

Despite the prejudices against the employment of women, New Deal agencies such as FERA, CWA, WPA, and NYA sought to provide work relief and other help for women, although most of the jobs generated by work-relief agencies were more appropriate for men, according to prevailing notions of what jobs suited what gender. A widow with three young children wrote to the state WPA director from Wolf

Creek: "You are rushing projects through right enough, but what do you expect a lady to do? We cannot get into the C.C. camps, build roads, airports etc."[12]

The New Deal relief agencies were sensitive to the need to provide work relief for women, and they also understood that it was a worn cliche to assume that the solution was simply to put needles and thread into the hands of all unemployed women. Of course, many housewives, skilled with the needle, welcomed sewing projects, and it is probably true that the needle was to unskilled women's work relief what the shovel was to unskilled men's.[13] William N. Beehler, the director of early New Deal work relief activities in the state, reflected some naivete on the topic when he told newspaper reporters he was surprised to learn that so many women needed work relief. Perhaps in an effort to be ironic he said he and most men had always thought women worked only "to earn money to buy a fur coat or a limousine." He nevertheless invited suggestions as to the kind of work projects that might be devised for women and noted that while sewing might do for some, it was unfair to expect that sewing exhausted the list of things that women might do.[14]

One of the most impressive women's work projects under FERA was a nursing program, called by one official "one of the most extensive in the United States." The program employed some 194 nurses for various services, including home nursing, supervising children's health care in FERA nursing school projects, and caring for tuberculosis patients. The WPA continued a nursing program.[15]

Some county relief offices came up with innovative ideas for dealing with the plight of unemployed women or the families of unemployed men. Alice Davis's Monongalia County relief organization set up programs for housekeeping visitors, nursery attendants, mothers' clubs and other women's projects that attracted inquiries from Ellen Woodward, FERA's director of women's programs.[16]

In Kanawha County, with a more conservative board overseeing their work, the Business and Professional Women of Charleston sponsored a women's center. Located on Capitol Street, the center employed fourteen visitors in family case work, ran sewing centers for both black and white women, and tried to prepare poor and unemployed women for jobs. It found work for some women, but most were short-term cleaning jobs. Extremely skeptical of the center's work, the Kanawha board tried to close it down with the end of the Civil

Works Administration, but the women kept the center operating for a time.[17]

When the WPA succeeded FERA in West Virginia, it hired women in some key positions and planned to create some ten thousand work-relief jobs for women. An August 1936 conference in Charleston brought together WPA women supervisors to discuss areas in which the WPA could provide employment for women, including school nutrition, sewing projects, teaching crippled children, household work, library projects, and research. By 1940 the WPA statewide school-lunch program employed 1,000 workers and a nursery program employed 193 child-care workers.[18] When the WPA went out of business in 1943, the state superintendent of schools, William Woodson Trent, feared the parsimonious legislature would fail to sustain the school-lunch program started by WPA, but when Ruth Hardman, the state director of WPA service projects, appeared before the legislature and demonstrated to them the extent of hunger among the children of the state, the legislators were appalled and readily agreed to take over financing of the school-lunch program, retaining much of the WPA personnel.[19]

Just as in private-sector employment, gender pay equity was an issue in New Deal work relief. As historian Alice Kessler-Harris has noted, both the CWA and the WPA discriminated against women in setting pay scales for relief work.[20] The Business and Professional Women's Club of Charleston protested the discrimination in West Virginia. Already at odds with the Kanawha relief board over the issue of the women's center, the women's club pointed out to the board the injustice in pay scales and called upon the board to revise work-relief pay "so that, regardless of sex, equal needs are met with equal pay." The board's chairman replied that he believed that the relief pay scales should reflect the pay scales for women in similar private employment, which were below the rates for men.[21]

A majority of West Virginia women supported the Democratic party. Insisting on "a fair share of the patronage" some one hundred members of the West Virginia Democratic Women met in Charleston in January 1933, soon after the election that put Roosevelt in the White House and the Democratic party in power in West Virginia. They urged party officials and state leaders to redeem the plank in the state party platform promising that women would share in the benefits of political victory.[22]

Did the party live up to its promise? President Roosevelt's appointment of Frances Perkins as secretary of labor served as a symbol of a new openness to the employment of women in important government work, and many middle-class women in West Virginia found employment on state and local staffs of New Deal relief agencies. Izetta Jewel Miller, the state's path-breaking woman politician of the twenties, had moved to New York and in the thirties served as a regional director of women's professional projects of the WPA.[23]

Nationally, although few women served in Congress during the decade, the percentage of women serving in state legislatures and in municipal and county governments increased.[24] In West Virginia, however, in part because of the dominance of the conservative Democrats, who tended to have traditional attitudes in gender matters, few women became candidates for elective office and relatively few served on local boards. By 1940 only one woman, Delegate Nell W. Walker of Fayette County, served in the legislature. What is more surprising—considering that in the twenties many women held the position of county welfare agent and that it was generally considered "a woman's job"—only thirteen of the fifty-five county directors of public assistance, who essentially replaced the former welfare agents, were women. Moreover, few women served on county public assistance councils, boards of education, or municipal councils.[25]

Eleanor Roosevelt took a personal interest in West Virginia and played an influential role in several projects, particularly those dealing with families and children. The best-known of her efforts in West Virginia was the Arthurdale project, but her correspondence with Alice Davis and other local relief workers makes clear that she continued to be interested in other activities of the Monongalia relief office throughout the decade. She used her influence to push the WPA to carry out West Virginia projects, persuaded wealthy friends to donate monies to local projects, and sent personal checks to help with children's Christmas parties, nursery schools, and medical care for children she met in visits to the area. When the Monongalia superintendent of schools sought her help to obtain a black high school for Morgantown, she saw to it that WPA took on the project.[26]

Lorena Hickok wrote to her in 1933 of the desperate conditions she observed in Logan County and in the town of Ward, near Charleston. In Logan County, Hickok saw families of unemployed miners squatting in an abandoned schoolhouse. The men had been fired for joining the UMWA, and sheriff's deputies came and evicted them from company houses. A baby of one of the evicted families died, and others were sick and lacked medical care. At Ward forty families of blacklisted members of the failed West Virginia Mine Workers Union had lived in tattered tents since the fall of 1931. Hickok described the sickly children and the lack of medical care and noted the bitterness of the men, most of whom, though able-bodied and willing to work, were denied work in the mines. The families were struggling on the $10.00 per month of West Virginia relief. She worried that the children were being indoctrinated in communism by the Young Pioneer group organized in the camp, "and Madame," Hickok wrote, "I do not like the Communists." She tried to describe to Mrs. Roosevelt what she had seen:

> The tents all black with soft coal dust and dampness, are huddled together along the highway, near a river. In the background, those beautiful—rather terrible hills. A little group of men sitting silent and thoughtful on a big rock. Ragged, discouraged, bitter. Women messing around, trying to do a little washing and clean the places up. A few pathetic little gardens. And those terrible looking children.[27]

Moved by Hickok's report, Mrs. Roosevelt talked to the president about the families at Ward. He told her to go to Harry Hopkins and "tell him that whatever should be done must be done and that these families must be out of tents by Christmas." Through FERA the families received attention and indeed were out of the tents by Christmas. Mrs. Roosevelt and a friend, Mrs. Leonard Elmhirst (the former Dorothy Straight), set up a clinic to try to remedy the effects on the children of the conditions in which they had lived. For two years, Mrs. Roosevelt used the income from her radio program to help pay for the clinic.[28]

The Depression in West Virginia left many dependent and neglected children in its wake, breaking down the state's antiquated system of dependent child care.[29] In the summer of 1933, Maj. Francis Turner, director of the state Department of Public Welfare, worked through the National Guard to provide summer camps for four thousand undernourished children of relief families chosen by volunteer nurses from across the state. The National Guard loaned its camps and equipment, and relief recipients made up most of the staff of the two camps, one near Morgantown and one near Charleston. The staff transported the children to the camps in school buses, the gas donated by private firms and individuals. Most private children's camps had to remain closed because of the Depression, but Turner's camps provided an innovative way to put some people to work and to give needy children nourishment. Lorena Hickok visited the camp near Charleston and wrote glowingly to Mrs. Roosevelt, "It was swell!"[30]

In late 1933 and early 1934, FERA field agent Howard Hunter judged the child-welfare problem in West Virginia to be the worst in the country. In part because so many children lacked adequate care, Hunter urged Harry Hopkins to continue federal funding for relief in spite of the failure of Governor Kump and the legislature to provide matching funds for relief.[31]

In ensuing years, the state Department of Public Welfare used FERA aid to address two critical child-care issues: the undernourishment of children in relief families and the placement of children in county poorhouses. In 1934 the department continued the camp program that Turner had started, providing longer stays for children believed to be at risk of serious disease because of malnutrition. The department established Camp Boone (later named Camp Fairchance) near Whitesville, especially for children judged by public health nurses to be pretubercular. There nearly two hundred children at a time spent at least three months receiving care designed to restore health.[32]

The problem of the county poor farm children became something of a scandal. At the beginning of the Depression, most counties still maintained poor farms for the care of the indigent. Because of the economic conditions, hundreds of families disintegrated, leaving scores of children to be cared for by the state or counties. The same conditions that caused families to break up made it difficult to find foster homes for children. Consequently, many homeless children ended up in the county poor farms. Calvert Estill, the first director of the Department of Public Welfare, estimated in 1932 that more than four hundred children suffered the indignities of poor farm life.[33] Later observers reported that children were housed in the dormitory type quarters of the poor farms with aged and mentally infirm adults. In Kanawha County alone, ninety-one children lived with some two hundred adults at the county poor farm, an institution built in the nineteenth century to house seventy-five people. Alice Davis visited a poor farm in Pendleton County and was shocked to find that children were assigned to share beds with incontinent elderly adults. Another visitor described the housing as "dilapidated and ill-arranged" and a fire hazard.[34]

After the Charleston *Gazette* ran an article detailing the conditions of the Kanawha County poor farm, Turner announced a plan to remove children from all the poor farms in the state. His department established Kamp Kump in Putnam County for the specific purpose of rehabilitating the poor farm children. There, some two hundred children removed from the county farms were fed and cared for. Afterward the department returned them to their parents or other relatives or placed them in foster homes or boarding homes until permanent homes could be found.[35]

With WPA aid, Mercer County addressed the poor farm problem in an anachronistic way touted by the agency's film *A Better West Virginia* as a model for care of the destitute. The innovative Mercer poor farm replaced the typical dormitory type lodgings with separate log cabins suitable for families and surrounded by land for family gardens. The film showed indigent families at the Mercer County poor farm toiling happily at domestic and agricultural tasks in an idyllic setting. There was, of course, no rush of counties to duplicate Mercer County's "modernized" poor farm. The coming of Social Security provided other means of addressing the problem, and mercifully, the poor farm as the basis for local care of the destitute quickly faded.[36]

In succeeding Depression years, as existing child-care institutions remained filled beyond capacity, the Department of Public Welfare expanded its summer camp and child-care center program. In 1935 the department operated camps at seven different sites including Camp Brock at Institute, on the campus of West Virginia State College, where four hundred African American children from families on relief from around the state gathered for a summer feeding and nourishment program.[37]

Two federal programs, the Civilian Conservation Corps and the National Youth Administration, helped many youthful West Virginians, and the benefits redounded to their families. President Roosevelt established the CCC by executive order early in his first hundred days. The purpose was to provide work and training for unemployed young men. Enrollees worked in camps scattered over the country and received food, shelter, clothing, medical and dental care, as well as $30 per month, part of which was to be sent home.[38] In West Virginia the CCC youth made important enduring contributions through their work in state parks, game preserves, national forests, and soil-conservation projects. They built cabins and lodges, fought forest fires, excavated trails, constructed lookout houses and towers, planted trees, and treated thousands of acres for gully erosion. By 1941 more than forty-four thousand West Virginians had served in the CCC, and its camps had been established at some sixty sites in the state.³⁹ After sixty years and more, the work of the CCC in West Virginia continues to pay dividends in the state parks and forests. More difficult to calculate but no less certain are the benefits to those who served in the CCC and their families. The popularity of the experience with enrollees is apparent in a letter written from a CCC camper at Cass, West Virginia: "God created this universe," he wrote. "He gave us spring, with its beauty of flowers, and birds and trees. Now he has given us the CCC and this man Roosevelt. For that, I praise God."⁴⁰

For all its popularity and its enduring accomplishments in conservation, the CCC did not fully address the needs of youth in a depressed economy. It offered hard work at fairly low skill levels and gave little in the way of job training. Operated by military officers, the level of discipline in the camps seemed excessive to some. Moreover, the CCC offered work only to young men. Unemployed young women also needed help.⁴¹

Offering a broader range of opportunities than the CCC, the NYA sought to provide part-time employment or full-time training projects to enable young people between sixteen and twenty-five to complete their educations and to obtain suitable work. High-school students from low-income families could earn a maximum of $6 per month, and college students $20 per month. Recipients of the student aid did library and office work, building and grounds maintenance, museum and laboratory assistance, special research, and community activities related to their studies. In its first three years of operation, the NYA in West Virginia aided twenty-five thousand high school and college students.⁴²

In 1938 more than eighty thousand West Virginians aged sixteen to twenty-five were out of school and searching for work. The NYA offered opportunities to this group in resident projects to learn farming, auto mechanics, carpentry, plumbing, and soil conservation. The NYA in West Virginia also engaged in a substantial number of construction projects, building schools, community and recreation centers, athletic fields, swimming pools, bus stops, and vocational schools. In Hardy County, for example, NYA workers built a twelve-room high school at Wardensville, eliminating the necessity of a thirty-five-mile journey to high school for local students. At New Haven in Mason County, they constructed a large youth center containing a combination gymnasium-auditorium, a community library, workshops for boys and girls, a ballroom and kitchen and living quarters for the youth leader and custodian of the property.[43]

The biggest project of NYA in West Virginia and one of the largest in the country was initiated in 1939 as war clouds grew darker in Europe and Asia and was likely inspired by concerns about the possible necessity of war mobilization. The NYA gave "work experience" to five hundred young men at the United States Naval Ordnance Plant in South Charleston. Half were West Virginians and half came from other states. The enrollees were introduced to the metal and mechanical trades, such as welding, auto mechanics, and airplane mechanics; to forges, foundries, machine shops, and electric shops. Glenn Callaghan, state director of the NYA, admitted that after completing the experience at South Charleston, "A goodly number who may desire to do so will have an opportunity to enter the United States Army or Navy schools of mechanics." However, he insisted that, though the Army and Navy were "giving splendid cooperation in placing equipment at our disposal," it was a civilian project.[44] An NYA film about the project entitled *Young Man Meets Machine* emphasized the theme of national defense.[45]

Because blacks held the least skilled and lowest-paying jobs, they suffered severely when the Depression came. The state Bureau of Negro Welfare and Statistics put the best possible face on the matter, reporting in 1932 that it could not substantiate reports that employers were pressured to fire blacks first. The bureau also maintained that "the Negro appears a little better able to 'shift' than his white neighbor under similar adverse circumstances." Moreover, black miners, according to the bureau, would more patiently bear underemployment.[46]

By 1933, however, the bureau expressed alarm about the decline of mining jobs, the occupation of some 60 percent of black male workers in West Virginia. The bureau emphasized the need to find work in other fields and called upon black leaders to organize to promote black employment in fields previously closed to black workers. Thomas E. Posey's *The Negro Citizen of West Virginia*, published by West Virginia State College in 1934, pointed out that a few black-owned businesses in West Virginia created jobs, but the Depression had also caused a decline in black ownership. "As a general rule," Posey wrote, "the income level of a Negro wage earner makes it rather difficult for him to educate his children, maintain a decent standard of living, and accumulate any larger sum of money."[47]

Black families lacked recreational facilities, but they found useful pastimes playing checkers, horse shoes, and cards and hunting and fishing. Older members of black families enjoyed church clubs, suppers, and prayer meetings. Younger groups liked dancing, and orchestras like Cab Calloway's could draw thousands when they appeared in black population centers.[48]

When the United Mine Workers of America organized the state in the spring of 1933, they took care to include black organizers, to elect African Americans to union offices, and to seek equal pay for equal work regardless of race.[49] Nevertheless, Ronald L. Lewis, in *Black Coal Miners in the United States*, shows that developments in the coal industry over the Depression decade generally affected black miners more adversely than whites. Although the United Mine Workers welcomed black miners as union members, the union also supported mechanization as a way to save the industry, even though it would cost jobs of unskilled workers, jobs held disproportionately by black miners. The West Virginia Extension Service attempted to address the problem by establishing a unique program at West Virginia State College to train blacks to operate mining machines. A black miner and former schoolteacher, Ulysses G. Carter, directed the program, which began in 1937 and continued for twenty years.[50]

The Depression presented a difficult political dilemma for African Americans in West Virginia. Traditionally inclined to the party of Lincoln, blacks had enjoyed better treatment in Republican West Virginia than in neighboring southern states controlled by the Democratic party, in spite of the racial and ethnic conflict and occasional violence of the coalfields. The state legislature had segregated the schools but had rejected legislation to establish segregation on common carriers. Black voters in West Virginia retained their suffrage rights, and because the margin of difference between Republican and Democratic registration was narrow, the black vote helped the Republican party retain control of the state.[51]

When the Depression came, blacks had to consider whether their continued allegiance to the Republican party made economic sense. Herbert Hoover gave little attention to his black supporters and some of his white appointees were openly racist. After the 1928 election, white Republicans in West Virginia regarded the black vote as representing the balance of power in the 1930 election, and they urged the White House to provide some choice black appointments. Hoover, informed that the newly-elected senator, Henry D. Hatfield, was a strong supporter and could help in the Senate, sought Hatfield's favor by naming a black West Virginian, Charles E. Mitchell, as ambassador to Liberia. Hatfield and the entire congressional delegation also strongly urged that the incumbent register of deeds for the District of Columbia, Arthur G. Froe, a popular black politician from West Virginia, be retained. Disaster struck, however, when Daniel J. Donovan, the federal auditor for the District of Columbia, charged that Froe was incompetent to carry out his duties. Hoover immediately fired Froe, just two months before the 1930 election. Hatfield threatened to fight the nomination of Froe's successor on the floor of the Senate but was eventually placated with some lesser appointments.[52]

Another event that helped to turn the tide was Hoover's nomination of John J. Parker of North Carolina for the U.S. Supreme Court. As a candidate for governor in 1920, Parker had advocated the disfranchisement of black voters. In the case of *United Mine Workers v. Red Jacket Coal and Coke* in 1927, he had upheld the use of injunctions and yellow-dog contracts to fight the UMWA. The combined forces of organized labor and the National Association for the Advancement of Colored People helped to defeat the Parker nomination. The struggle caused the NAACP to begin to appreciate the possibilities of organized political power.[53]

The election of 1932 marked the beginning of a shift of black voters from Republican to Democrat, though the very idea of a black Democrat was still anomalous and even suspicious to some white Democrats. When 250 blacks registered Democrat in Jefferson County in 1932, newspapers in both Jefferson and Berkeley commented on the switch, which the Martinsburg *Journal* said was "causing much wonderment."[54] One local editor suspected that it was a Republican plot to control the nominations of Democrats. In a none-too-subtle effort to intimidate, the editor said, "These colored voters will be watched next November, and if they vote the Republican ticket at that time, as they always do, they will be arrested."[55]

Though it is possible that the Jefferson black Democrats of 1932 were Republican stalking horses, it is more likely that they were making a deliberate choice to vote Democrat in the hopes of bringing about an improvement in their economic circumstances. If suspicious white Democrats tried to intimidate them, Republicans tried to frighten them into staying in the Republican column by parading "the ghost of Lincoln." The state Negro Democratic Committee complained of Republican statements that Roosevelt was a sick man, who if elected would soon be succeeded by the segregationist John Nance Garner. Then, "all Negroes would be carried to Texas and burned at the stake." The committee maintained that, because white Republicans were as segregationist as white Democrats, segregation was a social issue, not a political one. According to the committee, white Democratic politicians in West Virginia had a record of supporting black institutions.[56]

On election day in 1932, African American voters still honored the ghost of Lincoln; Hoover ran well ahead of Roosevelt in black districts. In Charleston, black Republican Thomas G. Nutter reported to the NAACP that "we hardly knew there were any Negro Democrats on election day, as they were so few in number and were rather quiet."[57] Roosevelt and the Democrats did not carry the black vote in 1932, but by 1936 Democrats would attract a black majority.[58]

In West Virginia, although African Americans represented only some 6 percent of the population, during the Republican era they had exerted some influence as a group that could tip the balance between the Democrat and Republican parties. The white leaders of the Democratic party understood the potential of the black vote and were pleased to cultivate the black leaders. When Governor Kump signed a bill in 1933 creating a separate black board of education, it might have been interpreted as a move by conservative West Virginia Democrats toward the more extreme Jim Crow system of the South, but the Pittsburgh *Courier*, a national African American newspaper, hailed the news as a new day for blacks in West Virginia. Noting that "for many years Negroes of West Virginia have been more successful in attaining the bi-racial ideal" than in any other state, the *Courier* contended that the creation of a separate board gave West Virginia blacks "the power to employ instructors to train their own children and to generally dictate what Negro education shall be." Though this was indeed segregation, it was "segregation de luxe." The *Courier* argued that West Virginia blacks were "making Jim Crowism as expensive to the state and as lucrative and as valuable to Negroes as possible where segregation is decreed by law." If segregation became too expensive, whites might "accept the colored brother on terms of equality."[59]

By September 1934, the Democratic Negro Executive Committee could point to several beneficial results of Democratic control in the state. In addition to the separate state board of education, the county-unit bill in education had provided that the five counties with the largest black populations would have black assistant superintendents.

Also, the patronage jobs that blacks had formerly held under the Republicans were now under Democratic control, and blacks under the new regime had been appointed to various local, county, and municipal positions and had been elected as constables, justices of the peace, members of school boards, and deputy sheriffs. Governor Kump initiated a practice carried on annually throughout the Kump-Holt years, when he sponsored a state dinner attended by some sixty high state officials and one hundred African Americans. I.J.K. Wells of Beckley, the chairman of the black Democratic committee, said the new era had led to the tearing down of "barriers of ill-will between the Negro People and the Democratic Party."[60] In 1936, when the legislature established the new public assistance–social security system, the law provided that any county having 10 percent black population would have a black assistant director of public assistance.[61]

Though black Democrats expressed satisfaction publicly, privately they complained of inadequate attention, particularly in federal patronage matters. Wells wrote presidential aide Louis Howe to say that unless black Democrats received some federal appointments as black Republicans had under Republican regimes, the trend toward the Democrats among black West Virginians would likely be reversed. A scribbled annotation on Wells's letter says simply, "File, no answer."[62] A white former county chairman in McDowell County warned Governor Kump that black Democrats in the county were not receiving adequate attention. The large African American population in the county had been solidly Republican, but in 1932, many had voted Democratic. He asked that the governor find them some "janitors jobs or elevator jobs."[63]

Early New Deal relief programs often discriminated against blacks by paying lower wages and by hiring blacks only after whites had been taken care of.[64] Some blacks, noting the many examples of discriminatory codes and practices under the National Recovery Administration (NRA), labeled it "Negro Rights Abused."[65] The Public Works Administration, established by the same legislation that set up the NRA, was much more positive in trying to give blacks fair treatment. Headed by Secretary of the Interior Harold Ickes, one of the few key New Dealers with a real commitment to racial justice, the PWA set a quota for employment of black workers. The PWA, however, which financed capital-intensive improvement projects on a matching basis with states and localities, employed fewer workers than the more labor-intensive WPA, and in West Virginia the state was slow to provide matching funds.[66]

Writing in 1934, Thomas Posey, a professor at West Virginia State College, suggested that blacks were not as fully involved as they might be during the early New Deal because they were inadequately organized and lacked knowledge of what was available. He reported, however, that "several organizations and persons are working to see that Negroes be given their full share in the new programs." One of the leading individuals in this work was Jane Spaulding, who was director of the Negro Division of the West Virginia Relief Administration. Spaulding was the president of the West Virginia State Federation of Women's Clubs, which for fifteen years had been the most constructive force in the field of private charities for African Americans in West Virginia.[67]

Evidence of black organization is found in Governor Kump's files. He received letters from groups like the Monongalia County Negro Progressive League (which sought the governor's help in obtaining a consolidated black high school and elementary school for Morgantown) and the Young Negro Democratic Association of Beckley (which wanted Kump's support for a bill to deport 6 million aliens).[68]

Early in the Depression, the faculty and administration at West Virginia State College organized a voluntary relief organization, and in the summer of 1934 the college held a conference called "the Teacher as Non-professional Social Worker in the Community." Five graduates of West Virginia State were among those given scholarships by the West Virginia Relief Administration in 1934 to study social work at the Atlanta School of Social Work.[69]

Eleanor Roosevelt was sympathetic to black issues, but her most noted project in West Virginia, Arthurdale, admitted only white families, and the other two resettlement communities in West Virginia, Red House and Tygart Valley, also were for whites only. She did hope to have communities for blacks, and in January 1934, she had Clarence Pickett of the Resettlement Administration invite leading black spokesmen to the White House for a discussion of the homestead issue.[71] During 1935 the Monongalia County relief administration completed surveys for a black subsistence homestead in West Virginia. Over one hundred families had been interviewed as prospective homesteaders, but the project never received approval in the Interior Department, which at the time had statutory responsibility for the

The New Deal and Families

homestead projects. Despite his strong support for racial justice, Interior Secretary Harold Ickes believed Arthurdale was a mistake and was unlikely to encourage a similar project for black West Virginians.[72]

The CCC provided employment for black youths, but records of the West Virginia camps indicate that African American enrollees suffered substantial discrimination in the CCC camps. The state director of conservation, Hubert W. Shawhan, protested to the CCC inspector that blacks and whites in Camp Decota, Kanawha County, used the same latrines. At a camp at Sharples, the black workers lived in the same camp as white workers but with partitioned sleeping quarters, a separate mess, and separate baths. White workers at Dunmore in Pocahontas County refused to mix with the eight "colored boys" in the camp. The camp commander reported to the inspector that they "should be transferred to a colored company where life will be more pleasant."[73]

The National Youth Administration, a part of WPA, was administered by Aubrey Williams, a white Alabamian, and gained a reputation as the New Deal agency most strongly committed to a New Deal for blacks. Williams appointed Mary McLeod Bethune as head of the NYA office of minority affairs. The highest ranking African American in the New Deal, she saw to it that the NYA gave equitable treatment to black youths.[74] Bethune visited West Virginia in 1937 to dedicate a state museum of black history built by the NYA on the campus of West Virginia State College.[75]

When the West Virginia NYA set up an all-white advisory board, the agency insisted that a black member be appointed "in order that there may be a just recognition of this group." Glenn S. Callaghan, the state director, responded quickly, appointing Dr. W.O. Armstrong, principal of Dunbar High School of Fairmont.[76] Pressured by Washington to justify the relatively few blacks in the NYA, the state NYA noted the relatively small percentage of blacks in the population but noted, "They have been especially interested in the student aid program as it provides the opportunity for a large lumber of negroes to attend school who otherwise could not."[77]

Most NYA work and training projects were open to whites or blacks but used segregated crews. At West Virginia State College, however, the NYA operated an all-black resident-youth training program, which gave training in agriculture, auto mechanics, sketching and blueprint reading, carpentry, electricity, guidance and counseling, home economics, janitorial and custodial services, masonry, moving pictures, painting, photography, plumbing, and printing.[78]

Of all the New Deal agencies, the Works Progress Administration benefitted blacks most. It gave them desperately needed jobs and provided new facilities for black communities, such as the new black high school in Morgantown, a 4-H camp in Fayette county, a new sanitarium at Denmar, and literacy classes. Through the National Youth Administration, it helped black youths to stay in school through part-time employment.[79] Black leaders in the state held a conference in Charleston when the WPA was set up in order to suggest suitable black programs. They were particularly interested in improved public school buildings, better health facilities, and better housing and slum clearance in Charleston.[80] Some black leaders complained of political discrimination in the WPA, claiming that a black political operator with no official position in the WPA, Dr. C.F. Hopson, screened all black applicants to determine whether they were Democratic voters. This charge paralleled similar charges by white Republicans.[81]

Housing was often a critical issue for families at all socioeconomic levels during the Depression. Early New Deal housing policy sought to stem the rising tide of urban middle-class mortgage foreclosures by establishing the Home Owners' Loan Corporation (HOLC). Between July 1933 and June 1935, the corporation rescued 9,139 homeowners in West Virginia, making loans of $22.9 million. Its loans allowed homeowners to extend their mortgages over longer periods, usually twenty years, rather than the usual five.[82] The HOLC, building upon established practice in appraising real estate, established uniform appraisal standards with four grades for residential neighborhoods. HOLC appraisers rated areas in the lowest grade based on not only the condition of the housing but also on the ethnic and racial makeup of the neighborhood. Fourth-rated areas of cities were marked in red on HOLC maps, making mortgages difficult to obtain.[83]

The Federal Housing Administration (FHA), set up in 1934, sought to stimulate the construction industry by insuring loans for largely white middle-class buyers of new housing. By 1940 FHA had insured mortgages amounting to $15 million for some 3,500 new houses in West Virginia. The FHA also insured loans for alterations and repairs to some eight thousand homes.[84] FHA-insured mortgages helped to continue the growth of mountaintop suburbs that had begun in the twenties and would flourish after World War II around Charleston,

Huntington, Wheeling, and smaller towns and cities. As middle- and upper-class urban dwellers fled the older residential areas in the bottomlands for mountaintop suburbs, the schism grew between the way of life of the new suburbanites and those who continued to live in the rural slums of the mountain coves and hollows, the mining camps, and the older residential areas of the cities.[85]

The FHA avoided urban slum areas and did nothing to help those who needed to renovate older housing or find low-income housing. Part of the original intent of the PWA was to provide low-rent housing, but the PWA projects tended to displace low-income slum housing with apartments too costly for low-income renters. West Virginia's towns and cities, however, reeling from the effects of the Tax Limitation Amendment, sought no housing projects under the PWA.[86]

One of the last gasps of New Deal liberalism in the Depression era was the idea of low-cost public housing championed by Senator Robert Wagner of New York. Wagner believed public housing could wipe out slums, improve low-income purchasing power, and stimulate the construction industry. Though congressional conservatives severely undermined the original concept of the sponsors, the Wagner-Steagall Housing Act became law in 1937, establishing the United States Housing Authority. The new agency could loan up to 90 percent of the value of new low-rental housing with repayment extended over sixty years at an interest rate of 0.5 percent. To qualify, cities were required to set up permanent housing commissions to administer the public housing. The new housing was to be limited to rental rates that could be afforded by low-income dwellers in the slums that would be cleared by the new housing.[87] Several West Virginia cities took advantage of the new program, including Charleston, Huntington, Martinsburg, Wheeling, and Mt. Hope.[88]

Charleston's experience in launching low-cost public housing illustrates some of the achievements and problems of the program in West Virginia. As early as 1935 the FERA conducted a housing survey that indicated that the city needed 1,410 units to replace slum housing. The survey showed that some people in the city had gathered material from the garbage dump to build shacks. In the Water Street area between Reynolds Street and Elk River, the survey listed 1,469 "dwelling units," mostly rough-built shacks and landed house boats lacking indoor sanitary facilities. The rent in the area for an average three-and-a-half room unit was $16.45 per month.[89]

With the passage of the Wagner-Steagall Act in 1937, the city administration, under a conservative Republican mayor, Daniel Boone Dawson, established a Charleston Housing Authority (CHA) to lay plans for public housing and to seek funds from the United States Housing Authority. CHA's plans for two large apartment complexes, Littlepage Terrace for white residents and Washington Manor for whites and blacks (in separate sections), were quickly approved, and by the spring of 1940, a broadly representative committee appointed by Chairman Leroy Allebach of the CHA "to take politics out of it" was interviewing the hundreds of applicants for the apartments, which rented for $15 per month, less than the average rent in the slum housing.[90] The CHA appointed two black social workers, Carrie B. Crichlow and Fannie Cobb Carter, to interview applicants for the 127 units set aside for black families in Washington Manor. Though the number of units set aside for blacks was far short of need, the efforts of the Negro Business and Professional Men's Association had assured that at least some part of the public housing would be for blacks.[91]

The policy of providing affordable housing for the poor and clearing slums generated some perplexing issues. The contract with the U.S. Housing Authority required that CHA raze units of substandard housing equivalent to the number of new apartments. Some tenants of the condemned buildings would not leave after the housing authority had bought and condemned the structures. CHA claimed they remained in their dwellings because they were then living rent free, as the CHA collected no rent. It is likely also that some of the residents did not want to be forced from their homes. Like a cruel landlord, the CHA had to evict the city's poorest dwellers, people who were pushcart salesmen, pensioners, odd-jobs men, and washerwomen. CHA helped the evicted to find housing, but the poorest of the evicted could not qualify for the new housing.[92]

Low-rent housing turned out to be inaccessible to the poorest families. Citizen committees appointed by the CHA screened the hundreds of applicants for the 470 units available in the two Charleston complexes. To qualify for residence, a family had to have an income of roughly $900 to $1,000 per year. A minimum income was thought necessary so that the family could pay the rent and expenses without undue hardship, but it did disqualify a substantial percentage of the poor. Despite the hundreds of applications, the minimum income requirement made it difficult for the CHA screening committee, chaired by Henderson Peebles, to find enough qualified residents.[93] A study of similar circumstances in Tennessee concluded that the lowest 20 percent of income earners could not qualify for the low-income public housing.⁹⁴

The number of units provided by Littlepage Terrace and Washington Manor did not begin to meet the need for low-income housing in Charleston as indicated by the 1935 FERA survey and a survey by the WPA in 1939. Between 1935 and 1940, 522 substandard dwelling units were demolished, largely in accordance with the agreement between the CHA and the USHA. By 1940, however, the Charleston Board of Realtors and some other business groups joined a nationally-orchestrated campaign to protest any further construction of low-rent housing with government funds. The board agreed that there was a need for slum clearance and a need for low-rent housing but questioned whether the CHA units really were for slum dwellers. The Charleston Realtors joined other boards of the National Association of Real Estate Boards in writing to candidates and congressmen in 1940 to protest the USHA.⁹⁵ Because of the opposition from the realtors and political conservatives who feared "the cutting edge of communism," federal appropriations for public housing dried up in 1939, and there were no further federal funds for public housing until 1949. English historian Anthony J. Badger argues that the reluctance to support low-cost public housing in the United States meant that the low-cost public housing that was built tended to isolate and stigmatize the poor, a result at odds with Senator Wagner's original dreams for public housing.⁹⁶

In the end relatively few low-rent projects were carried out in West Virginia, and expectations that the USHA projects would reform urban life went unfulfilled. Most of the USHA projects, including Littlepage Terrace and Washington Manor, filled a severe need, however, and at the end of the twentieth century still provide much of the available low-rent public housing in West Virginia. For all of its shortcomings, the USHA effort in West Virginia held much promise. It stimulated awareness of urban low-income housing needs and inspired communities to organize to deal with a problem largely ignored in the past.

The New Deal offered some paths to order for West Virginia families most buffeted by the disarray of the Depression. In addition to the work relief provided male heads of families, New Deal agencies also offered help to women, children, and young people. Opportunities for women let them help themselves and their families, though they had to settle for lower wages than men. New state welfare policies and

New Deal measures such as Social Security rescued children and the elderly from the humiliations and degradations of county poor farms. The CCC and the NYA gave needy young men and women hope and the means to stay in school or to work and learn trades. For African American families, who had to deal with discrimination as well as economic deprivation, the New Deal offered little in the way of special programs, but the relief and welfare available to whites was available to blacks as well, and blacks, moving toward the Democratic column, organized to call attention to their needs and to insist on a fair share from government programs. The HOLC and FHA provided help to middle-class families seeking to save their homes from foreclosure or trying to build a new home. The public housing program of the U.S. Housing Authority offered some hope for better housing for the working poor, but not for the very poor. Like most New Deal programs, the CCC, the NYA, and public housing stimulated community organization, but distant metropolitan bureaucracies made the critical decisions.

10
Reluctant New Dealers

Many students of the New Deal have noted that one of the reasons the New Deal fell short of its goals was that state Democratic leaders often lacked enthusiasm and gave only lukewarm cooperation.[1] In West Virginia this was particularly so. In spite of the great popularity of Franklin D. Roosevelt and the New Deal, the Democratic governors of the era, while proclaiming their loyalty to the president, often openly opposed New Deal programs. The historian James T. Patterson asserts in *The New Deal and the States* that the terms of Herman Guy Kump and his successor Homer Adams Holt "failed to bring progressivism to West Virginia and left the poverty-ridden state at odds with the Democratic party in Washington."[2] Despite the conservatism of the governors, however, the Depression and New Deal transformed politics in West Virginia by empowering some groups who had wielded little influence in the past, including organized labor and, to a lesser extent, women and African Americans. These forces pushed the Democratic party to accept reforms previously considered unthinkable, and change did come to West Virginia.[3]

In the elections of 1930 and 1932, the long Republican dominance of the state came to an end, to be replaced by overwhelming Democratic control of all branches of the government. Through most of the decade, Republicans could do little more than criticize from the sidelines or from the pages of the still-substantial Republican press in the state. The eclipse of the two-party system, however, did not mean that the New Deal had easy sledding. In fact, while the two-party system faded, it was replaced by a complicated, many-sided Democratic factionalism that reflected historic class, economic, sectional, and philosophical differences that were complicated by personal conflicts and patronage battles.[4]

Calvert Estill, who had served as the first director of the Department of Public Welfare during the Republican Conley administration and had been among the first strongly advocating taxation for relief and federal aid to the states, became a caustic critic of the New Deal as a columnist for the Ogden press. In 1939 Estill charged that the Holt administration, like its predecessor, disliked the New Deal, but, he wrote, "it has, of course, gathered at the banquet table and hovered around the flesh pots; it has gorged itself on the Roosevelt bounty—at the taxpayer expense."[5] Certainly the popularity of President Roosevelt and the burgeoning power of organized labor and other pro–New Deal elements in the state required that conservative Democrats temper their criticisms and even give occasional lip service to the ideals of the New Deal and its labor allies. The "liberal" or federal Democrats, on the other hand, while embracing the federal program and the abundant patronage opportunities that it provided, found themselves in a minority in Charleston, where the conservatives controlled the Governor's Mansion, the legislature, the Supreme Court of Appeals, and the statehouse patronage throughout the thirties. Three elected state executive officials, Superintendent William Woodson Trent, Secretary of State William Smithe O'Brien, and Treasurer Richard E. Talbott sympathized with the federal faction.[6] Despite statehouse efforts to purge them in 1936, these three remained as a beachhead of the federal faction in the state capitol. Through most of the decade, the federal faction succeeded in congressional and senatorial elections but could not take over the legislature. Voters tended to elect federal faction candidates for federal posts and statehouse candidates for the legislature.

Governor Kump's term had been tempestuous. He had faced the constitutional crisis of 1933 with energy and intelligence, but he never felt comfortable with the New Deal. He sought to promote an image of himself as fighting a lonely battle for state sovereignty against unscrupulous agents of the federal government and organized labor. In a Jackson Day dinner speech at Parkersburg on January 8, 1936, at the beginning of his final year as governor, he called for Democrats to stop fighting among themselves, but he could not refrain from his usual tactics of alliterative innuendo and vague but sweeping charges of conspiracy. Without offering any specifics, he charged that efforts had been made to interfere with the constitutional discharge of his duties. He claimed that he had "to fight every inch of the way . . . for the preservation of our statehood" during these "treacherous days." He called for the party to turn against "malevolent marauders masquerading as friends."[7] Presumably he was talking about the leaders of organized labor in the state.

Prohibited by the constitution from succeeding himself, Kump toyed with the idea of challenging Matthew M. Neely for the Senate nomination in 1936. As late as the end of March, he claimed that the decision was up to his "fellow citizens."[8] If he expected a groundswell of opinion in his favor, he never found it, nor was he likely to do so. Although he had won respect for his efforts in the 1933 crisis, he had never been a popular figure. Lashing out at his opponents emotionally and self-righteously, he had antagonized both state and federal officials as well as consumers, merchants, relief clients, schoolteachers, the Young Democrats and organized labor. Consumers blamed him for the sales tax passed by the legislature (on Kump's recommendation) as a consequence of the Tax Limitation Amendment. Merchants helped identify the governor with the tax when they deployed "Kump kans" to collect "Kump koppers."[9]

Despite his deeply conservative instincts, Kump had attempted, out of a sense of political realism, to win some New Deal credentials. The popularity of the president, the growing power of organized labor, and the desperate economic straits of the state compelled him to try to moderate his views. He had finally, after much cajoling by Harry Hopkins and other federal officials, helped to persuade the legislature to commit funds to relief. He ordered the end of the mine-guard system. He brought his former "little brain trust" back into operation to write a suitable state social security law. When Senator Holt accused him of being a member of the ultra-conservative Liberty League and opposing the New Deal, he denied the charge but hedged his answer by insisting upon his loyalty to President Roosevelt, neglecting to mention the New Deal.[10] He had hoped he might be rewarded for his efforts with a seat in the U.S. Senate, but leaders of organized labor made it clear that they would oppose him. United Mine Workers leader Van Amberg Bittner denounced him as a utilities man and dared him to run for office. Without labor's support, Kump knew that his chances were slight. Reluctantly, on April 10, while warning against "foreign freebooters who attempt to possess our state through their puppets," he announced that he would not run in 1936.[11] Though he would seek a Senate seat in 1940 and 1942, Democratic voters would deny him even a nomination.

After Kump's decision not to challenge Neely in 1936, there was talk of a unity ticket. Kump even made a "courtesy call" upon Neely in Washington. Ogden Press columnist Sam Mallison reported that unnamed unifiers had proposed a ticket that included Charles Hodges, a Morgantown newspaperman and Kump faction senate president, as governor; Neely for Senate; and Homer Holt and Kump for the Supreme Court of Appeals. Such a ticket, however, lacked geographic balance, being at once too northern and yet ignoring the northern panhandle, which had voted Democratic in 1932. By consigning Kump and Holt to long terms on the judiciary, the plan would have undermined the leadership of the statehouse faction.[12] Given the personalities involved, a unity ticket was most unlikely in any case and never materialized.

The recognized leader of the pro–New Deal, pro-labor federal faction, Senator Neely was in the middle of a remarkable political career in which he served as mayor of Fairmont, clerk of the House of Delegates, ten years in the U.S. House of Representatives, twenty-four years in the U.S. Senate, and four years as governor.[13] An old-fashioned stem-winding orator given to colorful exaggeration, Neely's attacks upon Republicans and statehouse Democrats were often replete with Biblical and literary quotations and classical allusions. He once declared, for example, that charges Senator Holt made against WPA director Witcher McCullough were "as false as the tales of Munchausen and as malicious as the schemes of Iago."[14] Reporter Sam Mallison claimed that Neely's phenomenal memory enabled him to quote verbatim long passages that he had read many years before and to remember the name of any constituent he had ever met.[15]

Not strongly committed to any particular set of ideas, Neely thoroughly loved the political game and dedicated himself to winning. Though he maintained friendships with some leading coal operators, he also understood the political importance of organized labor and took care to win labor's support.

As the senior Democratic senator and the earliest promotor of Roosevelt's candidacy in West Virginia, Neely became the chief dispenser of federal patronage in the state. Several key appointees provided Neely the main cogs in a powerful patronage machine. He named F. Witcher McCullough of Huntington as state director of the National Emergency Council and later championed McCullough as the director of the state WPA, much to the chagrin of Kump, who had wanted his own man in that position. McCullough, of course, appointed many others to positions in WPA. In 1937 Neely obtained for McCullough the position of secretary to the National Coal Commission. Another friend, Clarence Edwin "Ned" Smith, long-time editor of the Fairmont *Times*, was named as a commissioner. Neely arranged for Joseph N. Alderson, a Monroe County businessman, to succeed McCullough as WPA director. The state administrator of the Home Owners Loan Corporation, W. Vergil Ross of Bluefield, was part of Neely's group as was Walter R. Thurmond of Logan, a conservative coal operator whom Neely arranged to have appointed as state collector of internal revenue. Herbert Fitzpatrick of Huntington, the Democratic national committeeman, and most of the congressional delegation were in Neely's camp. The federal Home Owners' Loan Corporation (HOLC) was particularly useful to him as an agency that employed several of his political friends, including Rush D. Holt and other legislative liberals in the era before Holt's election to the Senate.[16] Neely used federal appointments to build an opposition to Kump in the legislature, thus giving some basis for the governor's paranoia. In 1935, Kump, who had substantial state patronage to offer, complained to a friend that Neely's agents were working the legislature, "offering Federal patronage right and left."[17]

One issue upon which Neely was uncompromising was Prohibition. A lifelong teetotaler, he opposed the repeal of Prohibition at the risk of political damage.[18] He also risked White House disapproval when he joined Huey Long in the Senate to defend the demagogic radio priest, Father Coughlin. Neely maintained that Coughlin, who had begun to attack the New Deal, was merely a misunderstood spokesman of advanced social justice.[19] Voting in this case with conservative Southerners, Neely failed to support the Wheeler-Rayburn bill, an effort to impose a "death sentence" tax on public utility holding companies and a measure strongly favored by the president.[20] On most issues, however, Neely was a dependable supporter of Roosevelt and the New Deal.

Homer Adams "Rocky" Holt, the statehouse faction candidate for governor in 1936, shared Kump's lack of enthusiasm for the New Deal. Like Kump, Holt was more oriented toward the conservative Democracy of Virginia and its fiscal conservatism than Roosevelt's New Deal. A native of Lewisburg, Holt graduated from Greenbrier Military School and attended Washington and Lee University in Lexington, Virginia. After service in the Coast Artillery, in 1920 he returned to Lexington to earn a bachelor of law degree. Holt taught briefly in the Washington and Lee law school and then established a law practice in Fayetteville. Although only thirty-two, he was elected attorney general in the Democratic sweep of 1932.[21] Campaigning as a supporter of the New Deal and a friend of the working man, Holt won the nomination in 1936 despite endorsements of his primary opponents by the leaders of organized labor and by Senator Neely.[22]

When Roosevelt's campaign manager, Postmaster General James Farley, asked state Democrats who had been convention delegates to assess the party's chances in 1936, he received generally optimistic responses, but the fractured nature of the state party became apparent. A Huntington attorney, George I. Neal, noted the division of the party into hostile camps. He contended that the "state crowd," though unpopular with the general population, retained much influence through its popularity with business. The state faction was headed by Kump and Robert Kelly, the retiring state party chairman, and Lon Kelly, Robert's father. The Kellys were members of the law firm of Brown, Jackson, and Knight, which Neal maintained was the chief firm representing the utilities. The firm's attorneys frequently attacked the constitutionality of New Deal legislation and were outspoken opponents of New Deal ideas.[23]

Many conservative Democrats expressed outrage at some of the speakers sent into the state by the Roosevelt administration. They complained that the director of the mint, Nellie Tayloe Ross, attacked the sales tax, a measure that the Kump administration relied heavily upon.[24] More alarming to the conservatives were speeches by Aubrey Williams, the top aide to Harry Hopkins in the WPA and the chief administrator of the National Youth Administration, when he visited Charleston on October 25, 1935. Speaking to a state convention of the West Virginia Education Association, Williams asserted that "Professional and intellectual honesty demand that you tell your pupils that seventy percent of our people must live below the standard of decency; that nearly half the national wealth is concentrated in the hands of less than two percent of the population; that millions now unemployed will never find jobs again; that their chances of gaining economic freedom are stacked four to one against them."[25] Williams expressed similar views before the state bar association, telling the generally conservative attorneys that "the next twenty months will see a fight to the finish between the Haves and the Have Nots."[26]

State Democratic chairman Robert Kelly reported to Farley that Williams's speech to the bar association was "the most startling address I ever heard by a responsible public official." Kelly said many staunch Democrats were turning away from the party because the White House looked only to labor leaders and social workers like Harry Hopkins and Williams. He said many state party leaders believed that the WPA would be a business, social, economic, and political failure. Farley asked Kelly for his permission to show the president his letter. He wanted Roosevelt to see what Kelly had said about Aubrey Williams's speech.[27]

Responding to Farley's query about the condition of the party in 1936, Kelly expressed some of the anti–New Deal attitudes ascribed to the statehouse faction by others. While assuring Farley that "working man, farmer, and the greater part of little business in West Virginia will vote the straight Democratic ticket," Kelly also reported that many businessmen and lawyers would oppose the president, because the New Deal had interfered with business, and because "the President's views are too loose with regard to the Constitution." Kelly condemned the "philosophy of Hopkins and Williams and some of the others." He claimed that some federal appointees were campaigning against part of the state ticket. Despite this "dark side," however, Kelly expressed confidence that the president would carry the state.[28]

Some of Farley's correspondents in 1936 worried that the Republicans were gaining ground and might win. Herman Bennett, writing for the Young Democrat Club of Charleston two months before the 1936 election, complained that the Roosevelt administration had neglected West Virginia and its conservative Democrats in the confidence that the miners' vote would carry the state. Many Democrats, however, had been put off by what they saw as radical legislation and by the feeling that the president's closest advisers were radical and undemocratic. Bennett urged Farley to send conservative speakers into West Virginia and to place a conservative West Virginian in some major political post. He suggested that Governor Kump would make a great Secretary of War.[29]

John L. Biddle of Charleston also reported that the Republicans were gaining ground. The GOP had covered the state with sunflower buttons featuring the face of Governor Alfred Landon of Kansas, the Republican presidential nominee. Billboards throughout the state displayed posters of common people saying "We do not want relief, we want a steady job. Vote for Landon and land a job."[30] Republicans took heart with the Landon campaign and the continued squabbling among the Democrats. The Charleston *Daily Mail* doubted if the "real Democrats"—Governor Kump and Attorney General Holt and their friends—

really wanted to help John L. Lewis deliver the state to Roosevelt.[31]

The state Democratic picture was further complicated by the maverick Rush Dew Holt, who had made a remarkable record for himself in his two years in the U.S. Senate. For a time the "Boy Senator" had been unhappy in Washington. No longer the focus of attention he had been as the leader of young liberals in the state legislature, he tried to rekindle the spark by continuing to speak on the same issues in Washington that had won him notice in Charleston, but other senators and the press ignored his diatribes against West Virginia utilities. Holt hit his stride in Washington and found his way back to the front pages, however, when he attacked the WPA and the senior senator from his own state on the floor of the Senate.[32]

By 1936 Holt had split with both Neely and the state UMWA leader, Van Amberg Bittner. Holt first attacked Neely for voting against the Public Utilities Holding Company Act. He then denounced one of Neely's major appointees, Walter R. Thurmond, the state collector of internal revenue, charging that Thurmond, a conservative coal operator of Logan County, had abused his position by opposing Holt's election and by working to defeat Holt's liberal colleague, Abram Lubliner, as president of the state Young Democrats. Bittner arranged a meeting between Holt and Neely on the Thurmond matter, but Holt continued to attack until Thurmond stepped down in 1937 to accept an appointment from the statehouse faction as secretary of the state Board of Control.[33]

Another major reason for the split between Holt and Neely was Holt's conviction that Neely, F. Witcher McCullough, and Harry Hopkins denied him a fair share of the federal patronage, especially in WPA. Although he attacked the WPA's patronage aspects, he was himself eager to reward his political friends. When McCullough, the state WPA administrator, favored Neely's friends for the several hundred appointive positions in the state WPA, Holt became angry and lashed out, becoming the most outspoken Democratic critic of WPA in the Senate.[34]

Holt's antagonistic position on coal industry legislation favored by both Bittner and Neely also drove a wedge between the junior senator and his chief political sponsors. Though organized labor and especially the United Mine Workers had worked mightily for his election in 1934, Holt almost immediately began offending rank-and-file union members and quarreling with Van Bittner and other UMWA officials. His most offensive action was to align himself with southern West

Virginia coal operators and to filibuster against the Guffey-Vinson Bill, the effort to enact a "little NRA" for the coal industry. By the spring of 1936, Bittner was openly denouncing Holt at UMWA meetings, charging him with "the sin of ingratitude."[35]

If any hope remained for his senatorial career by 1936, Holt burned all bridges by his election year antics. He tried to build his own organization to counter both the Neely and statehouse factions. He encouraged former road commissioner Ernest Bailey to oppose Homer Holt and L.R. Via, the federal-faction candidate, in the gubernatorial primary. More important to him was the Senate seat, and he persuaded former speaker of the House of Delegates Ralph Hiner of Franklin, to oppose Senator Neely's campaign for renomination. Neely easily vanquished Hiner in the primary despite Holt's open campaigning against his former patron.[36]

During the general campaign, Holt gave the keynote address for Father Coughlin's National Union of Social Justice convention, but he refrained from openly endorsing the organization's favored presidential candidate, William Lemke of the Union party. He endorsed Neely's conservative Republican opponent, Hugh Ike Shott, the Bluefield newspaper publisher and former congressman. In September, he visited the Republican presidential candidate, Alfred M. Landon, in Kansas. He campaigned extensively across West Virginia against Neely, but the miners and union members who had supported Holt so enthusiastically in 1934 now turned harshly against him, booing and harassing him wherever he appeared.[37] On one occasion at a meeting in the Charleston Armory, he sought to attack Neely, Witcher McCullough, and the WPA, but shouts of "Neely, Neely" made it impossible for him to be heard. After Holt walked out of the Armory, William Blizzard, vice-president of UMWA District 17 attempted to speak. Matthew Holt, the senator's brother, cut off the loudspeaker, and then the lights, but Blizzard continued to speak. Then a Holt supporter attacked Blizzard with his fists, and the meeting broke up in disarray.[38] After denouncing Neely in a speech at Welch, Holt needed police protection to escape a crowd of enraged miners. When the election was over, Neely had swamped Shott by 150,000 votes. Miners in Neely's hometown of Fairmont celebrated by hanging Holt in effigy on the courthouse square.[39]

After the 1936 election, Holt had four more years to serve in the Senate, but he no longer had any real constituency. Organized labor and both factions of the state party despised him, and he was ostracized by the national Democratic party. Writing in *Colliers* magazine in December, Democratic publicist George Creel described Holt as a "half-baked opportunist" who was detested by his Senate colleagues. Among other things, Senator Neely labeled his junior colleague "a pusillanimous political tramp."[40] Holt's apostasy represented a tremendous lost opportunity for the state labor movement, which had put so much effort into electing him. After having flexed its electoral muscles for the first time, labor, and especially the UMWA, had to be shaken when its own creation turned against it.

Despite the fissures in the state Democratic party and the concerns of some of Jim Farley's conservative West Virginia correspondents, Franklin D. Roosevelt's overwhelming popularity carried the ticket to a sweeping victory in 1936. Roosevelt helped patch the factions together for the general election by appearing with Kump, Homer Holt, and Senator Neely at the Mountain State Forest Festival in Elkins in early October. In November Roosevelt ran better in the state than he had in 1932, and Landon failed to equal Hoover's 1932 vote. With 502,333 votes, Roosevelt led all candidates in the state. Homer A. Holt followed closely behind as he easily defeated the Republican, Summers H. Sharp, for governor. Senator Neely won his Senate race, and Democrats won all six congressional seats. Democrats also won all elective state executive offices, the two seats on the Supreme Court of Appeals, and twenty of twenty-five circuit judgeships. In the House of Delegates, Democrats won eighty-two seats to the Republicans' twelve. Democrats won thirteen of fifteen West Virginia Senate seats to give them a 24-6 margin.[41]

The Tax Limitation Amendment and the Depression had compelled the Kump administration, in which Homer Holt had been the attorney general, to undertake major innovations, but Holt saw his task as governor as one of simply consolidating the substantial changes already carried out. Because his administration faced no immediate emergency, as Kump's had, Holt looked forward to a less hectic term.[42] Before it ended, however, Holt, no less than had Kump, became engaged in heated battles with educators, organized labor, and federal agencies, especially the WPA.

Like Governor Kump, Holt at first insisted that West Virginia's constitutional prohibition against the government incurring debt and the restrictions of the Tax Limitation Amendment severely limited the ability of the state and its counties and municipalities to undertake projects requiring matching funds. He ingeniously argued that PWA funds were intended for relief and that if the state or its inferior jurisdictions could not pay the 55 percent matching amount to receive the funds, they should receive the 45 percent federal funds anyway. Forty-five percent would not be as good as one-hundred percent, but it was better than nothing, he argued, and West Virginia needed the relief. He even urged Senator Neely to seek federal legislation exempting West Virginia and states with similar constitutional peculiarities from the requirements of matching grants.[43]

By 1937 the impact of the severe budgetary contraction brought about by the Depression, the Tax Limitation Amendment and the Kump administration's extreme fiscal conservatism was beginning to be felt in a variety of ways. In the twenties, the state had the benefit of road construction bonds that provided upwards of $10 or $15 million dollars annually for construction and maintenance of primary roads. Counties had floated their own bonds and also engaged in construction programs. By the mid-thirties, the proceeds of the bonds had been spent. The state was paying $7.5 million annually to retire the state bonds, and counties were paying some $4 million on their bonded debt. Meager legislative appropriations and automobile title fees provided less than $3 million dollars annually for maintenance and administration of state roads. The 1920s road system, which was not particularly well-built to begin with, crumbled from lack of adequate maintenance. As road commissioner Ernest L. Bailey had warned when Governor Kump withdrew the original WPA projects drawn up by the road commission, WPA road projects also suffered from the lack of state contribution. The WPA roads were built with a rock base with the understanding that the state road commission would supply the finished surface. Because of its scarcity of funds, however, the state could finish only a few of the WPA roads.[44]

The state education system also suffered from inadequate maintenance, lack of funds for new construction, and poor salaries for teachers and others. The counties' ability to support education was drastically curtailed by the Tax Limitation Amendment and the enabling law requirement that 30 percent of all levies had to go to debt service. Though elementary teachers in 1937 averaged $1,035, slightly more than the average in 1927, secondary teachers had seen their salaries drop from $2,119 to $1,234.[45] Other state institutions—including penal institutions, the university and state colleges, and hospitals for the treatment of tuberculosis and mental diseases—were also in various stages of deterioration and desperately needed infusions of capital to recover from what Governor Holt himself called "the parsimony and neglect" of recent years.[46]

The fiscal situation of the state improved little during the Holt administration. The recession of 1937-1938 delayed hopes of attending to postponed public needs, but the burden of bonded debt waned on both the state and local levels. The Virginia debt was finally retired at end of the decade. In 1937 the legislature approved an additional one-cent-per-gallon tax on gasoline to finance improvement and maintenance of secondary roads. Though neither the governor nor the legislature were willing to consider an attempt to repeal the Tax Limitation Amendment, both understood the need to modify the enabling law in ways to relieve some of the shackles the amendment imposed on county and municipal finances. In 1939 the legislature amended the enabling legislation to increase to 80 percent (rather than 70 percent) the amount of local levies available for current expenses rather than debt service. Holt encouraged counties to use most of the increased revenue available to them for schools. He also urged counties to take advantage of a provision in the Tax Limitation Amendment that enabled counties to provide for increased levies for schools through local referendum. Although one of the arguments in favor of the county unit system had been that it could insure uniform quality and equal opportunity throughout the state, Holt urged counties that could afford it to seek higher standards than state aid alone could provide.[47]

Holt also was less resistant than Kump to county and municipality participation in matching federal programs. The state itself found PWA useful in helping to fund a desperately needed building program for state institutions. Though Holt proved to be slightly less of a fiscal conservative than Kump, he nevertheless remained at odds with the state education association and organized labor and suspicious of federal agencies. The deep hostility between the two wings of the party, publicly moderated for the 1938 election, also continued through the Holt administration. Feelings were so intense that when the White House announced plans for a presidential visit to Arthurdale and Morgantown in May 1938, Bill Hart, editor of the Morgantown *Dominion News* and secretary of the West Virginia Young Democrats, wrote Louis Johnson, the assistant secretary of war (a West Virginian from Clarksburg), asking him to persuade the president not to come because the governor and "that gang of economic royalists who control the State Administration" would try to take advantage of the visit, sending "every knife-throwing state official . . . to bask in the reflected glory of the President." Hart's letter made it to the president's desk. Roosevelt scribbled in the margin a note to work it out by giving Neely, the leader of the federal faction, "a big place in it."[48]

At about the same time, Governor Holt complained to President Roosevelt and Harry Hopkins that the WPA worked against statehouse candidates.[49] If the WPA worked against the Holt administration in 1938, it had little impact on the outcome, because the administration candidates, in a primary election marked by a light turnout, overwhelmed the labor-federal faction, leaving Holt in a commanding position in Charleston.[50]

Unlike most of the Depression-era legislatures, the 1939 body, thoroughly controlled by Holt and the conservative faction, did its work efficiently and with relatively little conflict. Although it cut appropriations by $2 million, the legislature tried to mollify the education lobby. It enacted several measures to improve school financing, provided for free textbooks for indigent students, started funding for a teacher retirement plan, and also provided for state certification of experienced miners. As the Democratic legislators left Charleston in mid-March, the Charleston *Gazette*, which tended to give Holt better press than it had Kump, reported that many believed the sixty-day session had gone a long way to moderate factionalism and to heal party wounds.[51]

Events, however, soon dispelled any hope of an era of good feeling among the Democrats. Continued state and national economic insecurity, a civil war within the ranks of organized labor, and growing concerns about totalitarian regimes abroad created a supercharged political atmosphere that drove the contending factions of West Virginia's Democracy even further apart, leading to a caustic confrontation in the 1940 primary election.

One of the complications that arose to muddy the political waters in the state was the national split between the American Federation of Labor (AFL) and the Congress of Industrial Organizations (CIO). Basically a division between craft and industrial unions over organizational strategies, the debate led John L. Lewis, the head of the UMWA and a vice president of the AFL, to secede from the AFL in 1937 and to create a rival federation, the CIO. William Green, president of the AFL, then ordered the West Virginia Federation of Labor to purge all

CIO unions. Because the UMWA was the largest union in the state federation, most of the officers and members of the federation simply reorganized as the West Virginia Industrial Union Council, CIO. John B. Easton, who had headed the state federation since 1924, became president of the new organization, which continued to operate from the same offices in Charleston. A remnant group reorganized the state federation under the presidency of AFL loyalist Thomas Cairns.[52]

The reorganized West Virginia Federation of Labor was, without the UMWA, a mere shadow of its former self, but it was large enough to be a continuing threat to the Industrial Union Council. The biggest issue between the two was the federation's effort to organize a rival coal miners union, the Progressive Mine Workers (PMW) and the CIO's threat to organize among the craft unions. In March 1938, President William Green of the AFL came to West Virginia to open a drive to win back the miners.[53] To help organize the miners, the AFL even welcomed to the fold Frank Keeney, who had organized the rival West Virginia Mine Workers Union early in the Depression and thereafter had been blacklisted. The AFL also imported other organizers for the PMW, but they generally found a hostile reception in the state's coal camps.[54]

The AFL-CIO civil war not only divided labor but also contributed to the split in the Democratic party as Homer Holt's statehouse faction supported the AFL and the Neely-federal faction supported the UMWA and the CIO. Reflecting on the situation at the time of William Green's visit, many state newspaper editors expected a violent confrontation that would require action by the state police and the National Guard.[55] Some of the PMW organizers were indeed physically attacked, and their automobile tires were slashed, but the predicted large-scale violence never occurred, probably because the PMW could mount no serious threat to the UMWA in West Virginia. Within six months, the rival union faded.[56]

The PMW's failure in West Virginia resulted not from assaults on organizers, but from the UMWA's success in negotiating a union-shop agreement with the operators. When the two-year Appalachian Agreement in the coal industry expired in April 1939, the UMWA insisted on a union-shop provision in a new contract. The union shop provided security for the union; it required that anyone working at a given mine had to become a union member. Operators at first resisted a union-shop clause, arguing that it interfered with the right to work, and a six-week work shutdown ensued.[57]

As the stoppage dragged on, Governor Holt refused UMWA requests that the state provide relief for workers or even to request surplus commodity goods for the unemployed miners from the Surplus Commodity Corporation. When a new agreement was reached in May, some southern West Virginia companies refused to sign the new contract, objecting to the union-shop provision. Holt had remained silent throughout the contract dispute except to say that the state could provide no relief to the "voluntarily unemployed," but in July he wrote letters to all employees of the hold-out companies, guaranteeing them "the right to work" and offering "protection" if they would agree to return to work without a union contract.[58]

Holt's attitude toward relief for the miners and his direct interference in the dispute between the union and the holdout companies inspired bitter denunciations from CIO and UMWA leaders. The CIO executive board termed his action "usurpation of power." In his annual report, the state CIO president, John B. Easton, condemned "the undemocratic, un-American, and brazen attempt of the governor to turn his high office into a strike-breaking agency."[59] UMWA leaders Van Bittner and William Blizzard and Senator Neely all lambasted the governor's actions at the annual convention of the State Industrial Union Council. Neely claimed that "reactionary forces" created the spirit that moved public officials in West Virginia "to become strike breakers and recommend to you coal miners . . . that you become traitors to your organization and cover yourselves with infamy and dishonor by forsaking your principles." He urged the CIO to join forces with school teachers, farmers, and veterans to defeat the reactionaries in 1940.[60]

Holt reacted to these criticisms by preparing an extensive end-of-year "message" for all coal miners in the state. Sent to miners in the form of a pocket-sized, seventy-nine-page booklet, the message accused the leaders of the UMWA and CIO of using "Hitler tactics." Holt asserted that the complaints of Bittner, Blizzard, and Easton that he sought to hurt the UMWA were "just about as convincing as Hitler's charges that Germany was attacked by Czechoslovakia and later by Poland or Stalin's charges that Communistic Soviet Russia was attacked by little Finland—shallow pretenses for dictatorial aggression."[61]

Holt's jeremiad against the union leaders reflected a rising intensity in national political discourse. During the summer of 1938, the House Un-American Activities Committee (HUAC), under the chairmanship of Martin Dies, a rabidly anti–New Deal Democrat from Texas, allowed witnesses to make unsubstantiated charges of subversion against individuals, newspapers, and organizations, including such implausible targets as Shirley Temple, the Boy Scouts, and the Camp Fire Girls. Although many New Dealers saw the committee as a modern witch hunt, Governor Holt believed it did necessary and patriotic work "ferreting out those who would install the methods of Stalin and Hitler in America." When John L. Lewis and the United Mine Workers' leadership in West Virginia supported an effort to defeat Dies in the 1938 election, Holt cited it as evidence of the UMWA's "totalitarianism."[62]

Among other targets of HUAC was the Writers Project of the WPA, which Dies accused of promoting "class struggle and class hatred."[63] Holt, largely unsympathetic with the relief activities of the New Deal, angry at the political coloration of the WPA, and suspicious of the radical background of Bruce Crawford, the West Virginia director of the Writers Project, sought to prevent publication of *West Virginia: A Guide to the Mountain State*, the West Virginia WPA writers' contribution to the national guidebook series.[64] Claiming that the book was "propaganda from start to finish," Holt protested to WPA officials and to President Roosevelt. Calvert Estill took up the story and reported that the West Virginia *Guide* manuscript contained seditious material and "blackens the character of West Virginia industrialists and attempts to smear the honor of the state itself." National liberal journals such as *Nation* and the *New Republic* as well as syndicated columnist Drew Pearson picked up the story and ridiculed the concerns of Holt and the conservative press in West Virginia. Noting that Holt wished to eliminate from the manuscript the labor history of the state, the *New Republic*, under the title "The Nearly Perfect State," suggested that the governor wanted a fairy tale.[65]

Fearing that Holt might refuse to cooperate with other WPA projects, the WPA tried to satisfy Holt that the *Guide* was no radical plot hatched by communists or the CIO. Holt appointed Roy Bird Cook, a Charleston druggist with an avocational interest in history, to assist him in evaluating the manuscript. Cook found the manuscript troubling because it discussed such things as "the so-called armed miners' march" in Logan County and living conditions in coal camps, contained "frivolous statements such as 'tobacco spitting loafers on the steps of the Post Office in Charleston,'" and made "slurring allusions" to former governor Conley and other prominent persons in the state. In addition to concerns about the text, Holt grew indignant at pictures that showed a miner bathing over a wash tub, foreign-born miners, and robust children riding to school in the back of a truck. Such photographs, he felt, did not properly represent a state where many homes had modern plumbing, the people were proud of their Anglo-Saxon heritage, and children generally were not "herded to school like livestock going to market" but rode school buses. Despite assurances by the national staff of the Writers Project, which had reviewed the West Virginia manuscript carefully, Holt refused to approve publication until substantial changes were made, including elimination of the chapter on labor history.[66]

Holt especially objected to the account of the Hawks Nest silicosis tragedy, calling into question the use of material from a U.S. Senate investigation of the disaster, which emphasized the dereliction of the construction company hired by Union Carbide in creating a silica-filled atmosphere inside the tunnel construction site. Before being elected attorney general in 1932, Holt had been an attorney in Fayette County at the time when the tunnel was being constructed. And as attorney general, he had argued for Union Carbide before the Supreme Court in a dispute with the Federal Power Commission over riparian rights. After leaving the Governor's Mansion, Holt would again take up the legal causes of Union Carbide, eventually moving to the firm's New York headquarters as chief counsel.[67]

Crawford and his staff made all the changes Holt and Roy Bird Cook wanted, but with the prospect of a political change in West Virginia in 1940, the national staff in effect put the West Virginia manuscript in "cold storage," hoping a new governor might be more receptive to a realistic account of West Virginia history and culture.[68]

Meanwhile, Holt's Department of Archives launched a state quarterly journal, *West Virginia History*, to be under the editorship of Roy Bird Cook. According to Calvert Estill, the new journal would inoculate West Virginians against the "communistic and alien" propaganda offered by the WPA *Guide*.[69]

In the primary election of 1940 the two Democratic factions put aside all pretenses of moderation and engaged in one of the most bitterly fought primary battles in the history of the state. Governor Holt could not succeed himself and chose not to run for the Senate seat of Rush Dew Holt, but former governor Kump sought the senate nomination, and R. Carl Andrews, the state party chairman, carried the statehouse faction banner into the gubernatorial race. Senator Neely promised there would be a federal candidate for governor, and, after several months of rumors, at the last minute he filed for the office himself, sacrificing his Senate seat to take on the statehouse organization. Harley M. Kilgore, a little-known Beckley judge, received the federal endorsement for the Senate seat.[70]

The discredited incumbent, Rush D. Holt, also filed for the Senate seat. Holt had continued to oppose his own party, suggesting that it had violated the Corrupt Practices Act, attacking the National Labor Relations Board and the Home Owners Loan Corporation (which he had worked for briefly), and opposing a third term for Roosevelt. Holt had also become one of the president's chief critics on foreign policy, charging that Roosevelt was leading the country to war.[71]

Left without any clear constituency, it was certain that the "boy senator" would retire from the Senate at age 35. Possessed of a personality that seemed to preclude cooperation with anyone for very long, Holt often made enemies of those who sought to be his friends. Convinced of his own righteousness and eager to do combat, he took any disagreement on issues as a personal attack and tended to retaliate in kind. He also enjoyed being the center of attention and careened across the political spectrum from left to right with more regard for notoriety than political consistency. He often touched raw nerves and sometimes even called attention to critical issues, as in the Hawks Nest matter, which he was willing to address more frankly than any other state politician, but his reckless disregard of his political allies and his capriciousness ruined him as a politician, and his inability to cooperate and compromise doomed him as a senator.[72]

Former governor Kump, long recognized as lukewarm on the New Deal, nonetheless sought White House support for the Senate nomination, insisting to Edwin Watson, secretary to the president, that "I have never faltered in my support of him and his administration." Kump, in what was either a show of bravado or a serious miscalculation, predicted he would win the Senate nomination by an overwhelming vote and run far ahead of the ticket in the general election.[73] Roosevelt, however, made no endorsements. Though he tended to ignore impotent liberal factions and to support entrenched conservative organizations in the one-party states of the South, in West Virginia Roosevelt gave no aid and comfort to the statehouse Democrats. To challenge entrenched machines like Harry Byrd's in Virginia would be too costly, but the situation in West Virginia was different. The pro–New Deal faction led by Neely generally controlled the congressional seats and was therefore more important to Roosevelt than the governors. He could ignore Kump and Holt.[74]

The statehouse Democrats received a great boost to their chances when, in January 1940, John L. Lewis told a UMWA convention that Roosevelt faced "ignominious defeat" if renominated. Though the union convention made no endorsement, many West Virginia miners were outraged at Lewis's action. On October 25, Lewis endorsed the Republican presidential candidate, Wendell Willkie. Both the rank and file of the UMWA and the CIO in West Virginia made it clear that they enthusiastically supported Roosevelt for a third term. Van Bittner immediately sent Lewis a telegram saying "I am 100 per cent for John L. Lewis against any man living for president of the United Mine Workers of America and our great modern labor movement the Congress of Industrial Organizations, and I am 100 per cent for the reelection of President Roosevelt over Mr. Wendell Willkie." John Easton, the state CIO president, expressed similar sentiments.[75]

Why did Lewis risk his own hold over labor to oppose Roosevelt? According to Melvyn Dubofsky and Warren Van Tine, it was not a case of personal pique, as some have suggested, but rather a reflection of substantive disagreement on a range of issues. Lewis believed labor could gain no further benefits from the New Deal, which still had not ended unemployment. Moreover, Lewis strongly opposed Roosevelt's foreign policy and feared Roosevelt was leading the country to war.[76]

With Lewis's attempt to lead labor into the Willkie camp, West Virginia's conservative Democrats could now attack the leadership of the UMWA and the CIO and claim to be the legitimate Roosevelt Democrats. They sought to brand Neely Lewis's puppet, and to identify themselves with the president. As for the relatively unknown Harley Kilgore, the Senate candidate, Kump and his statehouse supporters tried to ignore him. Governor Holt was not a candidate in the election, but he led the attack against Neely, charging that Neely's last minute filing for governor was ordered by John L. Lewis. In a radio address during the Democratic primary, Holt cast the choice for voters in stark terms—it was between Americanism or Hitlerism. John L. Lewis and Neely, he claimed, "seem to approve of the principles of Hitler."[77]

Campaign advertisements and literature reflected the bitterness of the confrontation. A statehouse faction cartoon for use in newspapers ads showed Carl Andrews, Rocky Holt, and Guy Kump defending a fort labeled "West Virginia Roosevelt Democracy" against a "peanut blitzkrieg" ordered by John L. Lewis from CIO headquarters in Washington. Neely and the two leading figures of the state UMWA, Van Bittner and Bill Blizzard, charge the fort while Lewis says "Capture that first boys, and we'll polish off Roosevelt later."[78] Former governor Cornwell sent Governor Holt a master copy of a caricature showing John L. Lewis as Hitler and Neely as Mussolini. Holt thought it a "splendid" drawing.[79]

Senator Neely's campaign put out an advertisement using photographs taken during a Junior League performance showing Holt and Kump dressed as women. The ad labeled them as "Rocky-Wocky" who "in his little dress and girdle dances with 'Kumpy-Wumpy' as the bride of the public utilities and special interests" and "Kumpy-Wumpy" as "the little fairy of the big business boys."[80]

Andrews, whose only previous experience as a candidate had been when he ran for sheriff of Kanawha County, campaigned extensively across the state, promising to follow the policies put into place by Kump and Holt. Neely's active campaign lasted less than two weeks, as he quickly crisscrossed the state, promising improvements in state support for education and in the building and maintenance of highways. He also promised to increase cooperation with the federal government to secure federal aid in the improvement of public institutions, state parks, and care of the needy.[81]

The Republican primary provided fewer fireworks. The principal contests were between gubernatorial aspirants Daniel Boone Dawson, the mayor of Charleston, and Judge Lewis H. Miller of Ripley and on the senatorial side, between two Wheeling men, former congressman Carl Bachmann and state senator Tom Sweeney.[82]

When the Democratic voters went to the polls on May 14, they resolved the fight within the party in favor of the federal faction. Neely won the nomination for governor and Harley Kilgore bested Kump and the incumbent, Rush D. Holt, for the senate nomination. Republicans nominated Daniel Boone Dawson and Tom Sweeney.[83]

The Democrats, with President Roosevelt heading the ticket for a third time, again easily carried the general election, leaving Neely and the federal faction of the party in control of the statehouse for the first time. The victories of Neely and Harley Kilgore vindicated the UMWA and the CIO in their struggles with Governor Holt and their rivals in the AFL and, according to historian John Alexander Williams, brought about "an enduring realignment of the electorate."[84] In his typically colorful language, Neely rejoiced before a convention of Young Democrats that the factional strife that "bedeviled our party as boils bedeviled Job, has at last been buried in a grave so dark and deep and wide that Gabriel and his trumpet will never resurrect its wicked spirit no matter how loud and long he may blow."[85]

One more struggle between the factions remained to be fought out after the election. Ignoring strong White House pressure to name former assistant secretary of war Louis A. Johnson of Clarksburg, Neely appointed Dr. Joseph Rosier, president of Fairmont State College, to serve out his unexpired term in the U.S. Senate.[86] Governor Holt, claiming he had the right to name Neely's successor, appointed Clarence E. Martin, Sr. of Martinsburg, a conservative Democrat who could give the fading statehouse faction a foothold in the Senate. The Senate Elections Committee eventually upheld Rosier's nomination by a vote of eight to seven, and after four months of delay, the full Senate finally approved the seating of Rosier.[87]

After many years of controlling the party and eight years in the statehouse, the conservative Democrats had suffered defeat on almost all fronts. In an impassioned valedictory at a farewell banquet arranged by his friends, an embittered Governor Holt appealed to the verdict of history. He argued that the Kump-Holt administrations were among the best in the state's history but had endured unprovoked and unjustifiable attack from within the party. These intraparty conflicts were not simply matters of conflicting personalities and personal ambitions, Holt maintained, but they were basically ideological. The statehouse Democrats represented constitutional democracy based on "well-ordered reason." Their opponents, Holt argued, followed the philosophy of "modern-day European totalitarianism." The reasons Neely and the federal forces used their considerable patronage power to try to influence events in Charleston, he maintained, was that "if the totalitarian influences, disguised and covered by the Democratic banner, were to be successful in taking over . . . , it was first necessary that the leadership of constitutional government in the State be seriously impaired or destroyed."[88]

Holt's comments revealed his bitterness toward party rivals and organized labor. Though he claimed that he had cooperated with the federal government, he uttered neither the words "New Deal" nor "Franklin D. Roosevelt." The idea of organized labor seeking solutions to its problems through strikes and the organized discipline of the union shop offended his notion of "well-ordered reason." Certainly the arrogance of labor leaders like John L. Lewis alarmed business and its political allies like Holt. When Senator Neely discussed politics with the governor in terms of what the UMWA or CIO leaders found acceptable, Holt could see only "totalitarian" influence. He had no appreciation for the positive contributions of organized labor, and though he wished to be given credit for his opinion as attorney general that led to the end of the mine guard system, he failed to give credit to the United Mine Workers for helping to create the conditions that had made the system obsolete.

Although Holt threatened to use the National Guard in 1939 to protect "the right to work," unlike conservative governors in other states, he refrained from doing so. Indeed, the substantial advances of organized labor in the state provoked relatively little violence throughout the decade, and neither Kump nor Holt used police or National Guard forces in any attempts to frustrate union efforts. Given the striking changes subsequent to the National Industrial Recovery Act, the relative peacefulness of labor-management relations in West Virginia as compared to neighboring Kentucky and Pennsylvania was remarkable,[89] but in his valedictory, Holt chose to emphasize conflict rather than order.

The principal figures of the statehouse faction never won another election. Although he was only forty when he stepped down as governor, Holt never sought elective office again. In 1941 he joined the law firm chiefly identified with the Kump-Holt faction, Brown, Knight, and Jackson. He later served for a time as general counsel in the New York headquarters of Union Carbide, the firm that built the Hawks Nest tunnel.[90] Herman Guy Kump tried again unsuccessfully for a Senate nomination in 1942 and thereafter concentrated on his legal and banking interests in Elkins.[91] The day of the Bourbon Democrats in West Virginia politics was over.

Neely's election finally put into the statehouse a Democratic governor willing to cooperate fully with the federal government and the New Deal, but in so far as such a governor might have been helpful to the state in taking fuller advantage of the New Deal, 1941 was too late. Congressional support for the New Deal had begun to wane in the late thirties, and with the war-driven economic recovery, popular impatience with the New Deal grew. Increasing numbers of people were concerned about taxes, deficits, and bureaucracy and opposed to

New Deal relief agencies. National polls revealed a growing hostility to the conduct of labor leaders and resentment toward government regulation of business. The conservative tide ran strong in Congress, and the New Deal drew to a close. As President Roosevelt himself said in 1943, Dr. New Deal had been replaced by Dr. Win the War. Politics and society now entered a new paradigm.[92]

Epilogue

From Nearly Perfect to Almost Heaven

Looking back from the perspective of more than sixty years, what are we to make of the impact of the New Deal on West Virginia? Historians have long agreed that the New Deal failed to bring economic recovery before the coming of World War II, but there is disagreement over the long-term impact of New Deal policies.[1]

Numerous circumstances intervened with the passage of time to limit New Deal influence, including the difficulty of persuading state and local governments to cooperate in the implementation of New Deal policies, the rise of congressional conservatism late in the thirties, and the coming of World War II—which is described by Anthony J. Badger as "the juggernaut that ran over American society." In the postwar period, New Deal influence faded in the face of a powerful remobilization of business and conservative forces, a booming economy, and the coming of the Cold War.[2]

Though general New Deal recovery policies fell short of their goals, the relief efforts met desperate needs in West Virginia. Before the crash West Virginians were already suffering from the impact of a half century or more of heedless exploitation of their natural resources, and with the coming to the Depression unemployment rates climbed to startling levels. Outside investigators who came into the state from 1930 onward were shocked at the level of destitution they saw, whether they were representatives of the American Friends Service Committee or the Red Cross, agents of the Hoover unemployment relief office (POUR), the Reconstruction Finance Corporation, or New Deal relief agencies. Heroic private and voluntary efforts fell short of meeting relief needs. Despite the half-hearted cooperation of the Depression-era governors, the New Deal relief and unemployment programs were lifesavers for a large percentage of West Virginians who could find

Epilogue

neither work nor adequate sustenance from the land. New Deal relief and welfare policies also led to the abandonment of county poor farms and improved conditions for children and the elderly who had once shared the humiliations of the poor farms. The New Deal meant the end of county responsibility for relief, and the attempt, compromised by politics and the lack of fiscal support, to build a modern welfare system staffed by trained social workers.

One of the lasting changes the New Deal brought to West Virginia was a political realignment that swept away a long era of Republican dominance. Democrats shaped a lasting majority that relied heavily upon organized labor but also drew increased support from women and African Americans. Despite the rising power of groups that had often been ignored within the party before, conservative Democrats, more solicitous of corporations than people and committed to fiscal conservatism, controlled the party and the state throughout the New Deal era and frustrated many federal recovery and reform programs. Only in 1941, when the New Deal had lost its impetus in Washington, did the pro–New Deal Democrats take power in Charleston, too late to test the promise of state-federal cooperation.

While the conservative governors Herman Guy Kump and Homer Adams Holt resisted what they viewed as New Deal threats to state sovereignty, the ill-conceived Tax Limitation Amendment of 1932 compelled them to make basic changes in the relationship between the state and local governments. Caught in the financial and administrative morass created by the amendment, they consoled themselves by reaping the patronage bounty that fell into their hands as the state came to control many jobs once under county courts and municipal governments. The pro–New Deal faction, led by Senator Matthew M. Neely, controlled federal patronage, and the two rival patronage machines waged a bitter struggle for party dominance in which the participants on both sides often lost sight of public needs or New Deal goals. The factions' ideological differences were not nearly as dramatic as Governor Holt imagined in characterizing it as a battle between constitutionalists and totalitarians. Indeed, upon becoming governor, Neely restructured the statehouse machine, but, as historian John Alexander Williams notes, he "did not make it liberal, only less conservative."[3]

The fiscal conservatism of statehouse Democrats, in combination with the Depression, the drastic budgetary contraction imposed by the Tax Limitation Amendment, and the reluctance to find ways to use federal matching funds, needlessly starved public institutions and inhibited efforts of cities, towns, and counties to take advantage of New Deal programs. The most damaging consequences of this unbending dogmatism were in education, which struggled through the decade bereft of needed funds for adequate teacher salaries and retirement or new buildings. The West Virginia Education Association, Superintendent William Woodson Trent, and others fought for increased educational appropriations, but both Governor Kump and Governor Holt bitterly denounced the educators' efforts. Higher education also suffered, and only the idea of self-liquidating construction projects under the PWA finally opened the door late in the decade to some improvements in the decaying physical facilities of West Virginia University and the state colleges. While schools struggled, roads disintegrated, health facilities fell shockingly short of need, and the state contributed relatively little to the relief of its citizens, statehouse Democrats boasted of their successes in reducing taxes while paying off bonds and eliminating debt. Their approach to governance exemplified what political scientist V.O. Key called "an adding machine mentality" that focuses on the short-run and ignores the long-run interests of the state.[4]

Were there alternatives to the policy of fiscal conservatism followed so strictly, and by its lights successfully, by the Kump-Holt regime? To increase revenues would have required placing a heavier burden upon the economic interests of the state, many of them with out-of-state headquarters, and the argument was, of course, that enterprise and investment would thereby be discouraged. In Virginia, where the Depression had a less severe impact, the state government also followed a policy of strict fiscal conservatism, characterized as "pay-as-you go." Historian Ronald Heinemann writes that this policy, "the icon before which all future Virginia leaders had to bow," condemned Virginia to social backwardness for a generation.[5] In West Virginia, where the need was much greater, the impact of the state's fiscal policies was even deadlier. A more enlightened leadership could have found ways for the state to prevent the decay of its infrastructure and institutions. One way would have been to amend the state constitution to eliminate barriers to wider participation by the state in federal matching programs. Another road not taken was the repeal or readjustment of the Tax Limitation Amendment to remove the funding straitjacket that it imposed. Even without constitutional amendments, it would have been possible, as a minority at the time

Epilogue

advocated, to introduce greater progressivity into the tax structure and to ask more of those corporations and individuals who earned more rather than placing the burden on sales taxes. Given the recovery in the coal industry, a small severance tax might have generated funds for schools, roads, and other needs. After the debates over implementation of the Tax Limitation Amendment in 1933, however, few dared to raise the banner of tax reform, to advocate progressive taxation, or to champion severance taxes. The Tax Limitation Amendment was practically inerrant holy writ, and those who governed the state were content to preside over the impoverishment of its public sector.[6]

Although the National Industrial Recovery Act failed as macroeconomic policy, rising production and employment figures over a twenty-year period demonstrate that it and related New Deal measures revived a dying coal industry in West Virginia and brought about more reemployment than had been thought possible in the depths of the Depression. Not the least of the consequences of New Deal policy was the success of the UMWA in organizing the state's coalfields and the rise of organized labor as a major political force in the state. The old order of coal operator domination and deputized mine guards collapsed to make way for a political and social system more responsive to constitutional guarantees. Moreover, as miners received higher wages under the Appalachian contracts and suffered no restrictions on where they could spend their money, as they had under the old system of scrip and company stores, the benefits redounded to other businesses in the coalfields. Rising labor costs encouraged mining companies to transform the nature of mining by moving toward mechanized loading, hourly wages, and stricter management of work, but the feared negative impact on mining employment did not materialize until almost a decade after World War II.

Unfortunately, the UMWA leadership fell into the trap of arrogance of power. In the postwar period, John L. Lewis rejected New Deal–type approaches to worker welfare and joined with management to create a corporate welfarism that gave workers higher wages and corporate-guaranteed benefits in return for drastic cuts in employment as management, fighting the inroads of competition from more efficient energy sources, and pursuing a new, technologically based search for order, introduced a new generation of advanced labor-saving machines and mining techniques. At the same time, Lewis managed the union as his personal fiefdom, keeping financial affairs secret and condoning harsh methods to fight a rise in small, nonunion operations. Clearly, Lewis's schemes did not always benefit the coal miners or the region that had come to depend on their wages.[7]

In the fifties, mining employment collapsed, and hard times returned to the coalfields with a vengeance. From an all-time high of 126,669 employees in 1948, employment plummeted to 42,557 by 1961. Coal miners now joined farmers in a growing stream of refugees who left the state to seek work elsewhere.[8]

New Deal agricultural policies, designed primarily to help the large commercial farmer, provided little of an enduring nature for low-income mountain farmers, but subsistence agriculture as a viable way of life for large numbers of people had been doomed before the New Deal came along. The various ministrations of the New Deal in helping the poorest farmers only postponed the day of reckoning. Agencies like the Farm Security Administration, the Resettlement Administration, and the Bureau of Agricultural Economics had no dearth of ideas about what should be done to help the low-income farmers, but Congress, increasingly dominated by conservatives as the decade wore on, had little patience with such initiatives. The state Extension Service discussed the low-income farmer problem often, but, more oriented to commercial agriculture, Extension had little success in finding ways to reach subsistence farmers. The Civilian Conservation Corps did much useful work in the state and national parks and forests and in erosion prevention and soil conservation. Alone among major economic elements in the state, the low-income farmers failed to organize to improve their conditions. Nor did they present their case before the public; they appear not to have influenced the "grass roots" committees organized in several counties at the end of the decade to establish land-use plans.

As was typical in most of the country, by the mid-thirties the exodus from rural counties that had begun before the Depression resumed. During the early Depression, the farm population increased by 119,000. Beginning in 1935, however, it began to decline as jobs became available in industrial centers in other states, and some miners were able to return to the mines. By the end of the war, the farm population of 445,000 was only slightly lower than it had been in 1930, but in the fifties the depopulation of the countryside accelerated as the farm population declined by 246,000. During the same period, the population of the state declined by 145,131. By 1970 fewer than 6 percent of the state's population lived on farms.[9]

Epilogue

When the economic travails of the state resumed in the fifties, the welfare bureaucracy created by the New Deal helped to soften the blows. Sounder education and health systems and better roads might have rendered the collapse of the fifties less precipitous and more tolerable, but the combination in the postwar period of the rural exodus, the collapse in mining employment, and an inadequate and haphazard taxation system made for a severe and chronic economic predicament for the state.

By the early sixties, West Virginia had come to symbolize "Appalachia" in all its negative connotations. West Virginians debated among themselves about the condition of their state, and they reacted with anger and embarrassment when the national media began to examine its sad plight with articles like "The Strange Case of West Virginia" by journalist Roul Tunley, which appeared in the *Saturday Evening Post* in February 1960. Tunley pointed out that the state had the highest unemployment rate in the nation, three times the national average.[10] When Theodore White traveled across the state to report the 1960 presidential primary, he focused on West Virginia's poverty and described its politics as being among the most "squalid, corrupt, and despicable" in the country.[11] Resenting the litany of such criticisms from outside media over the years, many West Virginians, who were themselves bitterly critical of the state's situation, embraced as an unofficial state anthem the popular song "Take Me Home, Country Roads" when it first appeared in the autumn of 1971. The opening line, "Almost heaven, West Virginia," became a state slogan, as West Virginians delighted in the words that, for a change, painted a positive picture of the state.[12]

Historian Roger Biles, in *The South and the New Deal*, concludes that the New Deal prepared the South for the sweeping changes of World War II and afterward by modernizing agriculture, promoting healthier labor-management relations, and helping raise wages in southern industry. Although poor farmers were largely driven from the land, their circumstances improved as they found jobs in the industries of a more economically diversified and prosperous urban south.[13]

Why did West Virginia not share in these trends? At the root of many of the state's problems is an unforgiving topography that narrows economic possibilities, forcing overdependence on extractive industries that by their nature are destructive and follow historical patterns of boom and bust. The same mountains that inspire poets and songwriters attracted the timber, railroad, and coal corporations that came to the state, heedlessly devastated the environment, and eventually left workers stranded during the Depression. Those same mountains made commercially successful agriculture problematic and stood in the way of the kind of economic diversity toward which much of the South moved in the post–World War II era. In a day of large industrial plants requiring extensive square footage and spacious parking areas, the rugged topography of the state offered few attractive sites. Much land also continued to be owned by land and mining companies with out-of-state headquarters and remained unavailable for alternative uses.[14] Though they may have moved the writers of "Country Roads," West Virginia's meandering and ill-maintained two-lane highways discouraged would-be shippers in a time when other states were building four-lane highways and interstates. Roadbuilding in West Virginia's hills cost two-and-a-half times what it cost in other states.

In addition to these natural obstacles, the heritage of the Depression-era neglect of schools and medical institutions, which left in its wake extensive illiteracy and relative ill-health in the working population, discouraged would-be investors in new industry who wanted a literate and healthy potential labor force and attractive living conditions for their management and technical personnel.[15]

The prevailing concepts of progress and growth in the American economy offered no sustainable alternatives suitable to West Virginia's environment and unusual conditions. Under these circumstances, the economic diversification needed to escape its image of poverty continued to elude West Virginia in the decades after World War II.

Notes

Introduction

1. See Ambler and Summers, *West Virginia*, 389-90, 396-98, 461-62, 478-85; Rice and Brown, *West Virginia*, 233-35, 247, 266-73; Williams, *Bicentennial History*, 159-79.

2. A good brief guide to the emergence of Appalachian historical studies is Dwight B. Billings, Mary Beth Pudup, and Altina Waller, "The Emergence and Transformation of Historical Studies of Appalachia," in *Appalachia in the Making: The Mountain South in the Nineteenth Century*, ed. Billings, Pudup, and Waller, 1-24.

3. Ibid., 8-16; Kirby, *Rural Worlds Lost*, 82-87. For a good, brief discussion of the geologic and physiographic setting of West Virginia history, see Rice and Brown, *West Virginia*, 1-10.

4. Salstrom, *Appalachia's Path to Dependency*, xxiv-xxv, 83-121; quotation, 92.

5. For accounts of the impact of industrial capitalism, see Kirby, *Rural Worlds Lost*, xv-xvi, 82-87, and Ronald D Eller, *Miners, Millhands, and Mountaineers*, passim.

6. James T. Patterson called attention to the need for state studies with *The New Deal and the States*. Among the recent state and city studies are Argersinger, *Toward a New Deal in Baltimore*; Badger, *Prosperity Road*; Biles, *Memphis in the Great Depression*; Blakey, *Hard Times and New Deal in Kentucky*; Coode and Bauman, *People, Poverty, and Politics*; Heinemann, *Depression and New Deal in Virginia*. A useful collection of articles covering eleven states and two cities is Braeman, Bremner, and Brody, eds., *The New Deal*. Also useful are two recent regional studies: Biles, *The South and the New Deal*, and Smith, *New Deal in the Urban South*.

7. Robert Wiebe pioneered in the application of the organizational concept to American history in his seminal book *The Search for Order*. Louis Galambos called attention to the idea in "Emerging Organizational Synthesis in Modern American History," 279-90. Ellis W. Hawley carries the theme forward, characterizing the New Era "associationalism" of the twenties as "a search that failed" but that left structures that could be turned to New Deal purposes. The primary organizational challenges of the New Deal, Hawley suggests, were among mass-production workers, urban ethnics, and the social

welfare system (*Great War and the Search for a Modern Order,* 198-99). Gerald D. Nash's brief *The Crucial Era* outlines a comprehensive restructuring of American life. A recent interpretation strongly influenced by the organizational approach, which emphasizes business domination of key New Deal reforms, is Colin Gordon, *New Deals: Business, Labor, and Politics in America, 1920-1935.*

8. Argersinger, *Toward a New Deal,* xvi-xvii.

9. Coode and Bauman, *People, Poverty, and Politics,* 12.

10. Heinemann, *Enduring Dominion;* Blakey, *Hard Times.*

1. On the Eve

1. Jarrett, "Industrial Conditions in West Virginia."

2. Earlier boosterism is documented by Williams, *Captains of Industry.* See also Corbin, *Life, Work, and Rebellion in the Coal Fields,* 133-36.

3. Williams, *Captains of Industry,* 210-11, 245-54; and Williams, *Bicentennial History,* 131-55.

4. Hennen, *Americanization of West Virginia.*

5. A convenient guide to the growth of government and other organizations over the decade is the *West Virginia Legislative Hand Book and Manual and Official Register,* known as the *Blue Book* and issued annually. The growth of associational bureaucracy as a central theme of the era is explored in Hawley, *Great War and the Search for Modern Order.*

6. Sly, *Tax Limitation in West Virginia,* 1.

7. For a summary of editorial opinion on the state of the coal industry, see Charleston *Gazette,* Sept. 16, 1929.

8. Sullivan, "West Virginia, the Nation's Treasure Chest," 390-91; Charleston *Gazette,* Oct. 2, 1929.

9. Hawley, *New Deal and the Problem of Monopoly,* 205-6; Longin, "Coal, Congress, and the Courts," 100-130; Johnson, *Politics of Soft Coal,* 122; Vittoz, *New Deal Labor Policy,* 47-69.

10. For accounts of the hostilities between miners and operators in the postwar period, see Corbin, *Life, Work and Rebellion;* Corbin, ed., *West Virginia Mine Wars;* Daniel P. Jordon, "The Mingo War: Labor Violence in the Southern West Virginia Coal Fields, 1919-1922," in *Essays in Southern Labor History,* ed. Fink and Reed, 102-43; Lunt, *Law and Order vs the Miners;* Lon Savage, *Thunder in the Mountains.* Also of interest is the memoir of a former state attorney general, Howard B. Lee: *Bloodletting in Appalachia.*

11. Johnson, *Politics of Soft Coal,* 95, 119.

12. Coode and Bauman, *People, Poverty, and Politics,* 43-44.

13. Clarence Edwin Smith, "Coal Commission Would Increase United Mine Workers Power," Charleston *Gazette,* April 3, 1932.

14. Bernstein, *Lean Years*, 196-200; Hennen, *Americanization of West Virginia*, 99-100, 104; Lunt, *Law and Order*, 15-17.

15. Bernstein, *Lean Years*, 211; Lunt, *Law and Order*, 90-95.

16. Charleston *Gazette*, Nov. 10, 1929.

17. Ambler and Summers, *West Virginia*, 460-61; Rice and Brown, *West Virginia*, 233. Lee, *Bloodletting*, 139-40.

18. Lee, *Bloodletting*, 9-10.

19. The best account of the impact of nineteenth-century industrialism on West Virginia is Williams, *Captains of Industry*. For conflicting views on the impact of industrialism on mountain farming and society, see Kirby, *Rural Worlds Lost*, chap. 3; Eller, *Miners, Millhands, and Mountaineers*; Shifflett, *Coal Towns*. An excellent anthology of interpretive writings on nineteenth-century Appalachia is Pudup, Billings, and Waller, eds., *Appalachia in the Making*. For an interpretive account that argues in favor of "reviving and upgrading" the semisubsistence life of mountain farming, see Salstrom, *Appalachia's Path to Dependency*.

20. U.S. Department of Agriculture, *Economic and Social Problems and Conditions of the Southern Appalachians*, 40-45.

21. Ibid.; Taylor, "Depression and New Deal in Pendleton," 29. See also Shifflett, *Coal Towns*, 15, 16.

22. W.W. Armentrout, "The Low Income Farm Situation in West Virginia as We Know It," in *Proceedings of the 1940 Conference on Low Income Farms* (Morgantown: West Virginia Univ. Agricultural Experiment Station, Bulletin 299, March 1941), 12-13, in Bureau of Agricultural Economics, Records of the Appalachian Regional Office, General Correspondence, West Virginia, box 9, RG 83, NA.

23. Taylor, "Depression and New Deal in Pendleton," 72.

24. Frame, *History of Agriculture, Horticulture and Home Economics Extension from the Close of World War One to the Beginning of the "New Deal,"* pt. 2 of *Grassroots in West Virginia*, 33-36; National Child Labor Committee, *Rural Child Welfare: An Inquiry by the National Child Labor Committee Based upon Conditions in West Virginia* (New York: Macmillan, 1922), 70-71.

25. Frame, *History of Agriculture*, 1-7, 23-26.

26. Ibid., 26, 27, 65.

27. Ibid., 30-31, 65.

28. Rice and Brown, *West Virginia*, 178-79; Ambler and Summers, *West Virginia*, 346-50.

29. West Virginia Planning Board, *A Study of the People of West Virginia*, 11-14.

30. U.S. Department of Commerce, Bureau of the Census, *Historical Statistics of the United States*, Series K 17-81, Farm Population, Land in Farms,

and Value of Farm Property and Farm Products Sold, by State, 1850-1969, 458.

31. Taylor, "Depression and New Deal in Pendleton," 34.

32. Jackson, "Problems of Public Finance and Farm Taxes," in U.S. Department of Agriculture, *Economic and Social Problems*, 89.

33. The best account of the impact of deforestation on West Virginia is Ronald L. Lewis, "Railroads, Deforestation, and the Transformation of Agriculture in the West Virginia Back Counties, 1880-1920," in *Appalachia in the Making*, ed. Pudup, Billings, and Waller, 297-320. See also Ambler and Summers, *West Virginia*, 438-39; Taylor, "Depression and New Deal in Pendleton," 31. Roy B. Clarkson chronicles the heyday of the timber industry in *Tumult on the Mountains*. For a thoughtful discussion of the timber boom and its impact on Appalachia, see Eller, *Miners, Millhands, and Mountaineers*, 86-127.

34. Kirby, *Rural Worlds Lost*, 87-88.

35. Frame, *History of Agriculture*, 48.

36. Kirby, *Rural Worlds Lost*, 185.

37. Ibid., 80.

38. *Blue Book, 1937*, 604.

39. *Blue Book, 1931*, 784.

40. Charleston *Gazette*, July 3, 1932; Trotter, *Coal, Class, and Color*, 228.

41. Comstock, ed., *West Virginia Heritage Encyclopedia*, 25:206-9; clipping from Grafton *Sentinel*, Feb. 23, 1924, in box 29, Smith Papers; Effland, "Profile of Political Activists," 59:103-14.

42. *Blue Book, 1931*, 659; Effland, "Profile of Political Activists," 109-11.

43. *Blue Book, 1929*, 217.

44. Ibid., xxiv.

45. Humphreys, *Adventures in Good Living*, 58-60.

46. Conley, *West Virginia Encyclopedia*, 149-50.

47. Scotts Run Settlement House Papers, box 1, WVRHC.

48. Clipping from Clarksburg *Sunday Exponent Telegram*, Oct. 10, 1929, in Mary Behner Christopher Diary, West Virginia Department of Archives and History, Charleston.

49. West Virginia Commissioner of Labor, *Eighteenth Biennial Report of the Bureau of Labor, 1925-1926*, 9; Sullivan, "Nation's Treasure Chest," 408.

50. Conley, *West Virginia Encyclopedia*, 1019.

51. National Child Labor Committee, *Rural Child Welfare*, 70-71; Shifflett, *Coal Towns*, 17. For an excellent discussion of the problem of the "hidden labor" of West Virginia women, see Pudup, "Women's Work in the West Virginia Economy," 7-20. In the same volume of *West Virginia History*, see also Eagan, "Women's Work Never Done," 21-36; Greene, "Strategies for Survival," 37-54; Hensley, "Women in the Industrial Work Force," 115-24.

52. Corbin, *Life, Work, and Rebellion*, 92-93; *Annual Report of the West Virginia Department of Mines, 1928* (Charleston, 1928), 12-13.

Notes to Pages 19-26

53. Frame, *History of Agriculture*, 27-28; Conley, *West Virginia Encyclopedia*, 238; Humphrey, *Adventures in Good Living*, 31-32. See also Howe, "West Virginia Women's Organizations," 81-102.
54. *Blue Book, 1929*, 680-85.
55. Ibid., 705.
56. Trotter, *Coal, Class, and Color*, 3-4.
57. Quotation from Lewis, *Black Coal Miners*, 152-55. See also Posey, *Negro Citizen*, 34-36.
58. Lewis, *Black Coal Miners*, 154-55.
59. Ibid., 243-58.
60. Ibid., 216-34; *Blue Book, 1929*, 201.
61. Posey, *Negro Citizen*, 34.
62. *Report of the State Road Commission of West Virginia, July 1, 1928-July 1, 1929*, 7.
63. *Blue Book, 1931*, 801; *Blue Book, 1929*, 740, 747-48; Conley, *West Virginia Encyclopedia*, 108, 773-74.
64. McNeill, *Milkweed Ladies*, 104.
65. Rev. A.H. Rapking, "The Mission of the Country Church," *West Virginia Farm News*, Aug. 1930.
66. *Blue Book, 1929*, 732-33.
67. Nash, *Crucial Era*, 13.
68. *Blue Book, 1931*, 798.
69. *Blue Book, 1929*, 743.
70. "Rural Electrification Movement in West Virginia Marks New Milestone," *West Virginia Farm News*, June 1940, 3-7.
71. J.H. Long to C.E. Smith, July 27, 1929; C.E. Smith to J.H. Long, July 29, 1929, in Smith Papers.
72. Rice and Brown, *West Virginia*, 200-201; E.T. Crawford, Jr., "Chemical Industry in the Kanawha Valley Is Rapidly Assuming Huge Proportions," Charleston *Gazette*, June 29, 1930.
73. Williams, *Bicentennial History*, 156.
74. Charleston *Gazette*, Jan. 26, 1930.
75. Charles Town *Spirit of Jefferson*, Dec. 5, 1929.
76. Harbaugh, *Lawyer's Lawyer*, 247-48.
77. *Blue Book, 1929*, 958-1000.
78. Democratic National Committee: Correspondence, 1928-1933, "West Virginia before the Convention: Abstracts and Memos," folder A-B, box 778, FDRL.
79. "Tabulated List of West Virginia Newspapers and Periodicals," *Blue Book, 1929*, 733-38; Coffey, "Rush Dew Holt," 55-56.

2. Drought and Depression

1. Charleston *Gazette*, Oct. 25, 1929.

2. For a brief discussion that discounts the importance of the crash, see Garraty, *Great Depression*, 32. The classic account of the crash is John Kenneth Galbraith's *Great Crash*. See also Bernstein, *Great Depression*, 4-7.

3. Olson, "Depths of the Great Depression," 214-35; Williams, *Bicentennial History*, 164; West Virginia Commissioner of Labor, *Twenty-First Biennial Report of the Department of Labor*, 6.

4. Garraty, *Great Depression*, 15.

5. Skocpol and Finegold, "State Capacity and Economic Intervention," 255-78. This article deals with the "state capacity" of the federal government, but the concept would seem equally applicable to state governments.

6. Patterson, *New Deal and the States*, 26, 27.

7. Morgan, *West Virginia Governors*, 128-30; Sobel and Raimo, eds., *Biographical Directory of the Governors*, 4:1705.

8. Morgan, *West Virginia Governors*, 130; Conley, *State Papers and Public Addresses*, 1-11.

9. Conley, "Special Message, Extraordinary Session, July 12, 1932," *State Papers and Public Addresses*, 337.

10. Conley, "Inaugural Address, March 1929," *State Papers and Public Addresses*, 8.

11. Charleston *Gazette*, Jan. 1, 1930.

12. Conley, "Special Message, Extraordinary Session, November 20, 1929," *State Papers and Public Addresses*, 260-63; for a discussion of the similar dilemmas faced by other governors at this time, see Patterson, *New Deal and the States*, chap. 2.

13. "What of West Virginia in 1930?" 110-11.

14. Conley, "Biennial Message to the Legislature, Regular Session, January 14, 1931," *State Papers and Public Addresses*, 295-96. For a general account of the drought, see Woodruff, *As Rare as Rain*.

15. *West Virginia Farm News*, April 1931, 3; Woodruff, *Rare as Rain*, 5-6.

16. Charleston *Gazette*, Aug. 10, 1930.

17. Ibid., Aug. 18, 1930.

18. Badger, *New Deal*, 12.

19. Charleston *Gazette*, June 9, 1934; June 10, 1934.

20. Ibid., April 30, 1933.

21. Ibid., Aug. 12, 15, 1930.

22. Ibid., Aug. 15, 1930.

23. Ibid., Aug. 16, 21, 1930.

24. Ibid., Aug. 21, 1930.

25. Hamilton, "Herbert Hoover and the Great Drought," 867, 871-73.

26. Charleston *Gazette*, April 23, 1930; Ambler and Summers, *West Virginia*, 392.
27. Charleston *Gazette*, June 8; June 24; June 27; Grafton *Sentinel* excerpt in *Gazette*, Aug. 21, 1930.
28. Charleston *Gazette*, Aug. 21, 1930.
29. Ibid., Aug. 4, 5, 10, 1930.
30. Charleston *Daily Mail*, Oct. 28, 1930.
31. Grafton *Sentinel* editorial reprinted in Charleston *Gazette*, Aug. 21, 1930; Jones quoted in Bluefield *Daily Telegraph*, Nov. 4, 1930.
32. "Official Returns of the General Election Held November 4, 1930," *Blue Book, 1931*, 5430-5569.
33. Hugh Ike Shott to McGinnis Hatfield, Nov. 6, 1930, series 2, correspondence (1930), Shott Papers.
34. Walter S. Hallanan to Hugh Ike Shott, Nov. 8, 1930, Shott Papers.
35. Charleston *Gazette*, Feb. 8, 1931; Feb. 17, 1931; Feb. 24, 1931; Feb. 27, 1931; March 1, 1931; March 5, 1931; Charleston *Daily Mail*, Dec. 3, 1930; Feb. 2-12.
36. Charleston *Gazette*, April 30, 1931; June 6, 1931. Charleston *Daily Mail*, April 11, 1931.
37. Charleston *Daily Mail*, April 12, 1931; June 9, 1931. Lee, *Bloodletting*, chaps. 17, 18, 19.
38. Charleston *Gazette*, Dec. 7, 1930.
39. Burner, *Herbert Hoover*, 259-66; Patterson, *New Deal and the States*, 28.
40. Charleston *Gazette*, Dec. 7, 1930; Dec. 16, 1930; Dec. 17, 1930.
41. Charleston *Daily Mail*, Dec. 17, 1930.
42. Charleston *Gazette*, Feb. 4, 1931. Sobel and Raimo, *Biographical Directory of the Governors*, 4:1704.
43. Conley, "Biennial Message," *State Papers and Public Addresses*, 295-96.
44. Patterson, *New Deal and the States*, 41.
45. Conley, "Biennial Message," *State Papers and Public Addresses*, 271-326; "Legislative Enactments, 1931," *Blue Book, 1931*, 155-68; Estill, *Organization of Department of Public Welfare*, 7-10; Charleston *Gazette*, Feb. 25, 1931; March 12, 1931.
46. Conley, "Biennial Message," *State Papers and Public Addresses*, 301-5; Hodges, ed., "Legislative Enactments, 1931," *Blue Book*, 155; Charleston *Gazette*, March 12, 1931.
47. West Virginia State Road Commission, *Annual Report, July 1, 1930, to July 1, 1931*, 7; Charleston *Gazette*, Jan. 8, 1931.
48. Charleston *Gazette*, April 15, 1931.
49. Martin Cherniak, *Hawk's Nest Incident*, 168-69. For the argument that the Senate report on the Hawks Nest incident was "vicious propaganda

instigated by self-seeking politicians," see *West Virginia Review*, 13(May 1936): 229. Skidmore's novel, *Hawk's Nest* was republished in the *West Virginia Heritage Encyclopedia* (Richwood, W.Va.: n.d.).

3. A Search for Order

1. William E. Chilton to John Hawley, March 23, 1931, box 4, Chilton Papers.

2. Patterson, *New Deal and the States*, 26-27; Coffey, "Rush Dew Holt," 26; Martinsburg *Evening Journal*, March 4, 1932, 9.

3. Bluefield *Daily Telegraph*, Nov. 9, 1930.

4. Welch *Daily News*, Jan. 6, 1931.

5. Bluefield *Daily Telegraph*, Nov. 27, 1930.

6. "Narrative Report: Service and Special Projects under FERA Administration to June 1, 1935 in Monongalia County, West Virginia." Typescript in Monongalia County FERA papers, box 5, WVRHC.

7. Clarence Edwin Smith to "My Dear George," Feb. 4, 1930, Series I, Correspondence, box 7, Smith Papers.

8. Charleston *Gazette*, March 11, 1931.

9. Ibid., April 4, 1931.

10. Woodruff, *As Rare as Rain*, 162.

11. Ibid., 165-66.

12. Edmund Wilson, "Frank Keeney's Coal Diggers" in *American Earthquake*, 310-27 (based on articles originally appearing in the *New Republic*, July 1931); Thomas Tippet, "Miners Try for a Clean Union," *Labor Age* (April 1931): 5-7, reprinted in "The West Virginia Miners Union, 1931" (Appalachian Movement Press, 1972), SCMU; Bernstein, *Lean Years*, 381-85; Harris and Krebs, *From Humble Beginnings*, 234; David A. Corbin, "'Frank Keeney Is Our Leader, and We Shall Not Be Moved': Rank and File Leadership in West Virginia Coal Fields," in *Essays in Southern Labor History*, ed. Fink and Reed, 144-58.

13. Wilson, *American Earthquake*, 316.

14. Ibid., 210-14; Charleston *Gazette*, May 20, 21, 1931.

15. Pollak, "Life or Death Struggle Looms," 5-7; Tom Tippett, "W.Va. Mine Workers Carry On," 9-10, 28, reprinted in "West Virginia Miners Union, 1931" (Appalachian Movement Press, 1972), SCMU; Corbin, "Frank Keeney," 148-51.

16. Bernstein, *Lean Years*, 384; Corbin, "Frank Kenney," 148-50; Harris and Krebs, *From Humble Beginnings*, 199.

17. Ibid., Aug. 27, 1931; June 5, 7, 8, 10, 1932.

18. Charleston *Gazette*, June 24, 1932.

19. Ibid., June 5, 7, 1932.

20. Ibid., June 8, 1932.

21. Hickok to Eleanor Roosevelt, Aug. 22, 1933, "Lorena Hickok Reports," Hopkins Papers.

22. Corbin, "Frank Keeney," 157-58; Gary M. Fink, ed., John Hevener, "C. Frank Keeney," in *Biographical Dictionary of American Labor Leaders*, ed. Gary M. Fink (Westwood, Conn.: Greenwood Press, 1974), 185-86.

23. Bernstein, *Lean Years*, 547-48, n. 20.

24. Green, *Only A Miner*, 253-57.

25. Charleston *Gazette*, Dec. 17, 1930.

26. Ibid., June 11, 1931; June 15, 1931. Some five thousand people greeted Hoover the next day as his train stopped briefly in Charleston. Ibid., June 16, 1931.

27. Bernstein, *Lean Years*, 384-85.

28. Conley, "Address to Conference of State Coal Operators, October 1931," *State Papers and Public Addresses*, 187-91.

29. Longin, "Coal, Congress, and the Courts," 104; Hawley, "Secretary Hoover and the Bituminous Coal Problem," 259-63.

30. Clarence Edwin Smith, "Coal Commission Would Increase United Mine Workers' Power," Charleston *Gazette*, April 3, 1932.

31. Huntington *Advertiser*, May 27, 1932.

32. Longin, "Coal, Congress, and the Courts," 104-5; *Appalachian Coals, Inc. v. U.S.*, 288 US 344; Thurmond, *Logan Coal Field of West Virginia*, 88-89; Vittoz, *New Deal Labor Policy and the American Economy*, 66-69.

33. Charleston *Gazette*, June 10, 1932.

34. Ibid., June 19, 1932.

35. Ibid., June 22, 1932.

36. Martinsburg *Journal*, July 25, 1932.

37. Leuchtenburg, *Perils of Prosperity*, 262-63.

38. Charleston *Gazette*, Aug. 5, 1932; Huntington *Advertiser*, Aug. 4, 1932; Daniels, *Bonus March*, 182-86.

39. Huntington *Advertiser*, Aug. 5, 1932.

40. Ibid., Aug. 6, 8, 9, 11, 12, 13, 1932.

41. Charleston *Gazette*, Sept. 29, Oct. 26, 1932.

42. Ibid., Sept. 22, 1932.

43. "Preserve Food for Winter Relief," *West Virginia Farm News*, Oct. 1931, 3.

44. Nat T. Frame to Florence Ward, Aug. 10, 1931, and Esther Brucklacher, "Narrative Report for July, 1931," both in Records of the Extension Service, General Correspondence, West Virginia, 1932, RG 33, NA.

45. Brucklacher, "Narrative Report."

46. Burner, *Herbert Hoover*, 266; Morris, *Plight of the . . . Coal Miner*, vii-viii; Pickett, *For More than Bread*, 19, 20; Woodruff, *Rare as Rain*, 173.

47. Pickett, *For More than Bread*, 20-21; Woodruff, *As Rare as Rain*, 174; *Report of the Child Relief Work in the Bituminous Coal Fields*.
48. Morris, *Plight of the . . . Coal Miner*, 32-33.
49. Report, Frank W. Connor to Fred C. Croxton, April 7, 1932, in Central Files of President's Office for Unemployment Relief, Aug. 1931-June 1932, file 106, box 153, RG 73, NA.
50. Ibid.
51. Ibid.
52. Pickett, *For More than Bread*, 32-33.
53. Goodall, "Where There's a Will," 293, 306; Pickett, *For More than Bread*, 32-35.
54. Estill, *Organization of Department of Public Welfare*, 75.
55. Pickett, *For More than Bread*, 27-28.
56. Clipping in Mary Behner Christopher, Diary, Book I (Oct. 7, 1932), West Virginia State Archives.
57. Ibid.
58. Ibid.
59. Burner, *Herbert Hoover*, 276.
60. Charleston *Gazette*, Jan. 24, 1932.
61. Ibid., March 18, 1933.
62. Martinsburg *Journal*, May 22, Sept. 22, 1932.
63. Charleston *Gazette*, Feb. 9, 1932.
64. Ibid., Feb. 17; March 11, 12, 13, 1932.
65. Bluefield *Daily Telegraph*, March 4, 12, 13, 1932.
66. Ibid., March 27, 1932.
67. Martinsburg *Journal*, June 11, 14, 1932.
68. Frank W. Conner to Fred C. Croxton, report on trip to Williamson, W.Va., April 1-5, 1932, in Presidents Office for Unemployment Relief, Central Files, Aug. 1931-June 1932, box 153, RG 73, NA.
69. Martinsburg *Journal*, Jan. 26, 1932.
70. Charleston *Gazette*, Feb. 12, March 21, 1933.
71. Ibid., Dec. 4, Dec. 21, 1932, Jan. 14, 18, 1933. Paul Salstrom maintains that bartering and "voluntary reciprocity" were the essence of traditional subsistence agriculture and offered a viable alternative to the cash nexus (*Appalachia's Path to Dependency*, chap. 3).
72. Charleston *Gazette*, March 12, 1933.
73. Sistersville *Daily Review*, reprinted in Charleston *Gazette*, March 20, 1933.
74. Martinsburg *Journal*, June 14, 1932.
75. Ibid., Jan. 2, 1933.
76. Ibid., Feb. 11, 1932.
77. Charleston *Gazette*, June 24, 1932.

78. Conley, "Special Message, Extraordinary Session," July 12, 1932, *State Papers and Public Addresses*, 350.

79. Charleston *Gazette*, June 30, 1932; Wheeling *Register* editorial, reprinted in Charleston *Gazette*, July 3, 1932.

80. Charleston *Gazette*, July 12, 1932.

81. Conley, "Special Message, Extraordinary Session, July 12, 1932," *State Papers and Public Addresses*, 349-61.

82. Ibid., 356-58.

83. Henry Drury Hatfield to McGinnis Hatfield, June 27, 1932, Series III, folder 6, box 20, Hatfield Papers.

84. Charleston *Gazette*, Aug. 3, 6, 16, 17, 20, 1932.

85. Sly and Shipman, *Tax Limitation*, 1-5. See chap. 1 above for a discussion of the expanding role of state services in the twenties.

86. Sly and Shipman, *Tax Limitation*, 5-7; West Virginia State Tax Commissioner, *Biennial Report, 1929-1930* (Charleston: 1931), v, vi. The Charleston *Gazette*, Nov. 9, 1930, notes that the Democrats "will be practically obliged to start some movement to change all or part of the present unsatisfactory tax system of the state."

87. Conley, "Second Special Message, Extraordinary Session, Aug. 2, 1932," *State Papers and Public Addresses*, 265; Charleston *Gazette*, Aug. 8, 1932. For Kump's views, see Gatrell, "Kump: Political Profile," 59. United Mine Workers state leader Van Bittner endorsed Townsend and his broad tax-limitation plan in a speech in Charleston on May 1, 1932 (Martinsburg *Evening Journal*, May 2, 1932).

88. Burner, *Herbert Hoover*, 276; Patterson, *New Deal and the States*, 32.

89. Conley, "Federal Emergency Relief, A Statement for the Press," *State Papers and Public Addresses*, 551-53; Estill, *Organization of Department of Public Welfare*, 72-74.

90. Charleston *Gazette*, Aug. 28, 1932.

91. Martinsburg *Evening Journal*, Sept. 22, 1932.

92. Martinsburg *Evening Journal*, Dec. 14, 1932.

93. Ibid., Dec. 21, 1932.

94. Charleston *Gazette*, Sept. 20, 1932.

95. Huntington *Advertiser*, Sept. 1, 14, 1932.

96. Olson, "Depths of the Great Depression," 215.

97. Charleston *Gazette*, Jan. 18, 1933; Martinsburg *Journal*, Jan. 17, 1933; Estill, *Organization of Department of Public Welfare*, 83-97. Estill also resigned in January to accept a one-year contract with the American Welfare Association in Chicago. Martinsburg *Journal*, Jan. 9, 1933.

98. Estill, *Organization of Department of Public Welfare*, 81-82.

99. For details on the composition of the new legislature and some of the problems it faced, see Sly, "Way of the Legislator," 116-17.

100. Charleston *Gazette*, April 12, May 30, 1931, June 30, Aug. 28, 1932.
101. Editorial, Buckhannon *Record*, reprinted in Charleston *Gazette*, March 30, 1932.
102. Kump, "First Message to the Legislature, First Extraordinary Session, 1933," *State Papers and Public Addresses*, 49.
103. Charleston *Gazette*, Nov. 26, 1932.
104. Sly, "Way of the Legislator," 116-17; Conley, "Biennial Message, Regular Session, January 11, 1933," *State Papers and Public Addresses*, 384-427.
105. See above, n. 50.
106. Sly and Shipman, *Tax Limitation*, 9.

4. A "Jump in the Dark"

1. Despite the critical nature of the Kump era, historians have given it little attention. Albert Steven Gatrell's "Kump: Political Profile" is useful but uncritical. Gatrell's "Kump and the Fiscal Crisis" (249-84) focuses on the key period of the Kump administration. The writings of Kump's chief braintruster, John Fairfield Sly, who was a professor of political science at West Virginia University, afford interesting and analytical contemporary views of an insider. Kump's published and unpublished papers (WVRHC) provide what is probably the most thorough documentary record of any West Virginia governor. Sly wrote a useful brief summary of the Kump administration as a preface to Kump, *State Papers and Public Addresses* (v-xxiv). See also Sly, *Rebuilding in West Virginia*, Sly and Shipman, *Tax Limitation in West Virginia*; Sly, Burke, and Parry, *Indirect Taxes*.
2. Charleston *Gazette*, Oct. 24, 1929; Martinsburg *Journal*, April 1, 1932, May 2, 1932; Townsend Scrapbook (microfilm) of 1932 election; Mallinson, *Let's Set a Spell*, 203-22.
3. Shott to Philip Hager, April 7, 1932, Series 2, Correspondence, Shott Papers.
4. Martinsburg *Evening Journal*, Oct. 15, 29, 1932; Townsend Scrapbook (mircofilm) of 1932 election.
5. Gatrell, "Kump: Political Profile," 2-52; Ambler and Summers, *West Virginia*, 480.
6. Douglas B. Craig has called attention to the fact that those who dominated the national Democratic party from 1920 to 1932 were conservatives more attuned to the age of Cleveland. Although Craig does not address the question, it is likely that Democrats of that persuasion continued to control many state parties, as was the case in West Virginia. See Craig, *After Wilson*.
7. Neely to Clarence Edwin Smith, Feb. 16, 1932, box 8, Smith Papers; Martinsburg *Evening Journal*, Feb. 18, 22, 1932.

8. Neely to Chilton, Nov. 25, 1931; Chilton to Neely, Nov. 28, 1931, folder N, box 4, Chilton Papers.

9. Neely to William E. Chilton, June 20, 1931, folder N, box 4, Chilton Papers.

10. His opponents for the nomination were J. Alfred Taylor, speaker of the House of Delegates; A.J. Wilkinson, a delegate of Huntington; state senator Charles E. Hodges of Morgantown; F. Witcher McCullough of Huntington; and state senator A.C. Herold, the Senate minority leader (Huntington *Advertiser*, Sept. 20, 1932); Gatrell, "Kump: Political Profile," 57-61.

11. Gatrell, "Kump: Political Profile," 71-80.

12. Kump to John J. Cornwell, Jan. 21, 1931, box 38, Kump Papers.

13. Kump to Robert G. Kelly, July 8, 1933, folder 1, Kelly Papers.

14. Kump to John J. Cornwell, June 11, 1930; Cornwell to Kump, June 16, 1930, box 38, Kump Papers.

15. Herman Guy Kump, "Address Delivered at a Public Meeting, Buckhannon, February 23, 1932" (opening address of gubernatorial campaign) in Kump, *State Papers and Public Addresses*, 6; Kump to Robert G. Kelly, chairman, Democratic State Executive Committee, July 12, 1932, box 38, Kump Papers.

16. Gatrell, "Kump: Political Profile," 75-77.

17. For an assessment of Kump as a speaker, see Sam Mallison, "Charleston Merry-Go-Round," Martinsburg *Evening Journal*, June 8, 1933.

18. Martinsburg *Evening Journal*, Sept. 2, 1932;

19. Huntington *Advertiser*, Sept. 15, 1932.

20. Martinsburg *Evening Journal*, Sept. 16, 1932.

21. Gatrell, "Kump: Political Profile," 81-82; *Blue Book, 1933*, 645.

22. Charleston *Gazette*, Nov. 10, 1932; Martinsburg *Journal*, Nov. 9, 10, 1932.

23. Shott to E. Chase Bore, Feb. 18, 1933, Series II, Correspondence, Shott Papers.

24. Charles Town *Spirit of Jefferson*, Jan. 21, 1933; Shepherdstown *Register*, Dec. 1, 1932.

25. Gatrell, "Kump: Political Profile," 85-86.

26. Sly, *Rebuilding in West Virginia*, 1-4.

27. Kump, *State Papers and Public Addresses*, v, vii, 28-30; Gatrell, "Kump and the Fiscal Crisis," 260-61; Gatrell, "Kump: Political Profile," 102-5; Kump to W.C. Given, Commissioner of Banking, March 24, 1933, box 39, Kump Papers; Kennedy, *Banking Crisis of 1933*, 156n.

28. Gatrell, "Kump and the Fiscal Crisis," 255-56; Gatrell, "Kump: Political Profile," 96-97.

29. Kump, *State Papers and Public Addresses*, 33, 38-39.

30. Sly, Burke, and Parry, *Indirect Taxes*, 12-13.

31. Leuchtenburg, *Franklin D. Roosevelt and the New Deal*, 42-44.

32. Kump to G.K. Kump, March 16, 1933; Kump to W.C. Given, March 24, 1933, box 39, Kump Papers.

33. Leuchtenburg, *Franklin D. Roosevelt and the New Deal*, 43-44; Kennedy, *Banking Crisis*, 179-82.

34. The amendment attempted to do several things. It *classified* all general property into four classes: (i) all tangible personal property employed exclusively in agriculture and all intangible personal property; (ii) all property used by owner for residential purposes or farms used by owners or tenants; (iii) all real and personal property outside of municipalities exclusive of classes i and ii; (iv) all real and personal property inside municipalities. It also *limited* taxes on each classification: 50 cents per $100 on i; $1 on ii; $1.50 on class iii; and $2 on class iv. Maximum rates could be increased if 60 percent of the qualified voters agreed. The amendment also permitted a graduated income tax and limited the state property tax to 1 cent per $100 of assessed valuation. Sly and Shipman, *Tax Limitation in West Virginia*, 8-9, 41-42.

35. Sly, "The Way of the Legislator Is Hard," 116-17.

36. Sly and Shipman, *Tax Limitation in West Virginia*, 9.

37. The first of the tax limitation decisions was *Finlayson v. Shinnston* on March 7, 1933 (168 S.E. 479 and 113 W.Va. 434). It held that services on bonded debt contracted subsequent to the amendment must be included within the limitation.

38. Kump, *State Papers and Public Addresses*, v-ix.

39. Clipping in letter, A.N. Breckinridge to H.G. Kump, July 27, 1933, box 40, Kump Papers.

40. Martinsburg *Journal*, Jan. 10, 1933; Sam Mallison was a reporter and political commentator for the Ogden newspaper chain, and his reports often offered colorful insights into statehouse politics. For Mallison's comments on patronage, see Martinsburg *Journal*, May 2; July 20, 1933. See also Gatrell, "Kump: Political Profile," 84-85; 99-100; and Gatrell, "Kump and the Fiscal Crisis," 259-60. Kump's papers contain hundreds of letters from job seekers.

41. Martinsburg *Journal*, May 18, 1933; Neely's speech is extensively quoted in Charleston *Gazette*, May 10, 1933.

42. Kump to John J. Cornwell, June 28, 1933, box 46, Kump Papers.

43. Charleston *Gazette*, July 7, 1933.

44. Kump set forth his basic beliefs in a speech to a convention in Bluefield that opened his campaign as the Democratic nominee for governor in 1932. See Kump "Address to Democratic Judicial Convention, Bluefield, Aug. 13, 1932," *State Papers and Public Addresses*, 12-21. Factionalism had deep roots in state politics. John A. Williams has traced the nineteenth- and early twentieth-century backgrounds of West Virginia politics in his *West Virginia and the Captains of Industry*, and *West Virginia: A Bicentennial Histor* (especially

115-57), and "Class, Section, and Culture in Nineteenth Century West Virginia Politics," in Pudup, Billings, and Waller, eds., *Appalachia in the Making*, 210-32.

45. Sam Mallison provided insightful analysis of the developing split with a slant favorable to the "liberals." See his reports: May 2 and 18, July 12 and 20, Sept. 11, and Oct. 20 in the Martinsburg *Journal*. The best documentation of the factionalism in the West Virginia Democratic party (because it includes reports from both sides) is in the files of James Farley, chairman of the national Democratic party. In 1936, Farley wrote to several state Democrats asking for their political assessments, and some of the correspondents discussed the party split: See George Johnson to Farley, Aug. 18, 1936; Robert G. Kelly to Farley, Aug. 24, 1936; Charles R. Wilson to Farley, Sept. 12, 1936; George I. Neal to Farley Aug. 6, 1936, all in "Farley's Correspondence, West Virginia, Wisconsin and Wyoming, 1936," box 39, FDR Papers. See also Coffey, "Rush Dew Holt," 182-83, and Gatrell, "Kump and the Fiscal Crisis," 259-60; Gatrell, "Kump: Political Profile," 99-100.

46. Charleston *Gazette*, April 20, 1933; May 27, 1933.

47. West Virginia Department of Education, *Report, 1933-1934*, 9-10.

48. Cook, "Problems of School Finance in West Virginia," 11, 30.

49. Huntington *Advertiser*, May 17, 1932.

50. Martinsburg *Journal*, Oct. 27 1933.

51. Martinsburg *Journal*, May 11, 15, 16, 1933; Charleston *Gazette*, May 10, 13, 21, 27, 1933. See also Ambler, *History of Education*, 609-11.

52. Kump, "Address to the Convention of the Young Democratic Clubs of West Virginia, Clarksburg, May 13, 1933," *State Papers and Public Addresses*, 162; Gatrell, "Kump and the Fiscal Crisis," 273-74.

53. Martinsburg *Journal*, May 18, 21, 1933; Charleston *Gazette*, May 22, 1933.

54. Sly, *Rebuilding in West Virginia*, 6-8.

55. *Bee v. City of Huntington, Eakle v. Braxton County,* and *Snider v. Martin, Assessor* (Sept. 19, 1933), 177 S.E., cited in Sly and Shipman, *Tax Limitation in West Virginia*, 21.

56. Charleston *Gazette*, Dec. 31, 1933; Sly and Shipman, *Tax Limitation in West Virginia*, 22-23.

57. Sly, *Rebuilding in West Virginia*, 10-11; Gatrell, "Kump and the Fiscal Crisis," 281.

58. Coffey, "Rush Dew Holt," 36-46.

59. Kump to John J. Cornwell, Sept. 15, 1933, box 40, Kump Papers.

60. Memorandum to "The President" from "Mr. Hopkins," Aug. 14, 1933; Roosevelt to Kump, Aug. 14, 1933; Kump to Roosevelt, Aug. 19, 1933: box 40, Kump Papers.

61. Kump to M.H. McIntyre, Oct. 21, 1933, box 42, Kump Papers.

62. Kump to Hughes, Sept. 14, 1933, ibid.

63. Kump, "Letter to Members of the Legislature," Nov. 2, 1933, in *State Papers and Public Addresses*, 66-69.

64. Sly and Shipman, *Tax Limitation in West Virginia*, 25-26.

65. Ibid., 25-29; Gatrell, "Kump and the Fiscal Crisis of 1933," 282-83.

66. *Blue Book, 1933*, 764.

67. Sly, Burke, and Parry, *Indirect Taxes*, 36-37.

68. Charleston *Gazette*, March 1, 1934.

69. *Ibid.*, 36.

70. Charleston *Gazette*, Jan. 25, 1936; March 9, 11, 1938; Ambler, *History of Education*, 608-17.

71. "State Cities Income Down $700,000 in Last Decade," Charleston *Gazette*, Oct. 20, 1940.

72. Sly, Burke, and Parry, *Indirect Taxes*, 42-43; Sly and Shipman, *Tax Limitation*, 32-34.

73. Goodall, "Centralizing Tendencies in Government," 196-97.

74. Williams, *Bicentennial History*, 166.

75. Charleston *Gazette*, Jan. 25, 1936; Aug. 4, 1936.

76. John F. Sly to Kump, Nov. 26, 1933, box 42, Kump Papers.

77. See Kump's letters to Senator Neely and members of the congressional delegation setting forth the legal and constitutional basis for his insistence on the state's inability to participate in a matching program (Aug. 12, 1935, box 54, Kump Papers). A clear explanation of this complicated issue was offered by Governor Homer Holt ("Address before a District Convention of Rotary Clubs, Clarksburg, April 19, 1937," *State Papers and Public Addresses*, 159-67).

78. Charleston *Gazette*, Jan. 2, 1936.

79. Homer Adams Holt, "Address before a District Convention of Rotary Clubs, Clarksburg, April 19, 1937," *State Papers and Public Addresses*; Neely's views are cited in "Remarks at a Testimonial Dinner Given by A Group of Friends," December 28, 1940, both in Holt, *State Papers and Public Addresses, 1937-1941*, 159.

80. Holt, "Correspondence Relating to West Virginia's Situation with Respect to the Availability of Funds to Match Federal Grants, and Urging Senator Neely to Present the State's Case before Congress;" Press statement on "Public Works Administration Grants" (n.d.) in Holt, *State Papers and Public Addresses*, 605-13, 569.

81. Sly and Shipman, *Tax Limitation*, 33.

82. Charleston *Gazette*, Nov. 12, 26, 1939.

83. Williams, *West Virginia*, 55.

5. The Blue Eagle

1. Quoted in Nash, *Crucial Era*, 38.
2. Shepherdstown *Register*, Oct. 26, 1933.
3. Martinsburg *Journal*, Nov. 2, 1933.
4. Hawley, *New Deal and the Problem of Monopoly*, 19-148; Bellush, *Failure of the NRA*, 1-25; Leuchtenburg, *Franklin D. Roosevelt*, 54-58.
5. Hawley, *New Deal and the Problem of Monopoly*, 31-34; Leuchtenburg, *Franklin D. Roosevelt*, 57-58; Bellush, *Failure of the NRA*, 26. Hugh Johnson wrote a memoir of the NRA, *The Blue Eagle from Egg to Earth*. Also useful on Johnson's role is Ohl, *Hugh S. Johnson and the New Deal*.
6. Bernstein, *Turbulent Years*, 41-42.
7. Description by Charles Brooks Smith in Martinsburg *Journal*, Aug. 15, 1933.
8. Bernstein, *Turbulent Years*, 41-42; Dubofsky and Van Tine, *John L. Lewis*, 185.
9. Johnson, *Politics of Soft*, 168-69.
10. Coffey, "Political Chrysalis," 86; Wayne Flynt, "The New Deal and Southern Labor," in *New Deal and the South*, ed. Cobb and Namorato, 74; Johnson, *Politics of Soft Coal*, 165; Harris and Krebs, *From Humble Beginnings*, 271.
11. Blakey, *Hard Times and New Deal in Kentucky*, 158; Hevener, *Which Side Are You On?*, 100, 104.
12. Martinsburg *Journal*, June 28, 1933.
13. Lorena Hickok to Eleanor Roosevelt, Aug. 22, 23, 1933, (from Logan): "FERA Papers: August 1933," box 12, Hickok Papers.
14. Malcolm Ross, "Lifting the Coal Mines out of the Murk," 4-5; Johnson, *Politics of Soft Coal*, 166-71; Jesse V. Sullivan, "Coal Faces the Future," *West Virginia Review* 10 (July 1933): 293.
15. Hodges, *New Deal Labor Policy and the Southern Cotton Textile Industry*, 45-46.
16. Schlesinger, *Coming of the New Deal*, 144-47.
17. Bellush, *Failure of the NRA*, 97-99.
18. Martinsburg *Journal*, Sept. 13, 1933.
19. Bernstein, *Turbulent Years*, 172-78; Bellush, *Failure of the NRA*, 98-102. In 1935 the Federal District Court ruled in favor of the Weirton Steel Employee Representation Plan, and the company union established the Weirton Steel Employee Security League. In 1937 the Steel Workers Organizing Committee (SWOC) tried to organize Weirton, but the company immediately fired three hundred SWOC sympathizers. The CIO, the National Labor Relations Board, and years of litigation could not shake the hold of the company union. Posey, "Labor Movement in West Virginia," 262-75.
20. Schlesinger, *Coming of the New Deal*, 114-16.

21. Charleston *Gazette*, July 26, Aug. 2, 12, Sept. 1, 1933.
22. Martinsburg *Journal*, Aug. 1, 1933.
23. Ibid., Sept. 1, 1933.
24. Bernstein, *Turbulent Years*, 44; Johnson, *Politics of Soft Coal*, 150.
25. Bernstein, *Turbulent Years*, 44-45; Johnson, *Politics of Soft Coal*, 159-61.
26. Charleston *Gazette*, Sept. 10, 1933.
27. Bernstein, *Turbulent Years*, 44.
28. Johnson, *Politics of Soft Coal*, 150, 159-61.
29. Bernstein, *Turbulent Years*, 44-45; Johnson, *Politics of Soft Coal*, 183-84; Longin, "Coal, Congress, and the Courts," 105-6.
30. Bernstein, *Turbulent Years*, 45.
31. Johnson, *Politics of Soft Coal*, 183-84.
32. Ibid., 190-93; Longin, "Coal, Congress, and the Courts," 106. West Virginia statistics from *Blue Book, 1940*, 671.
33. Charleston *Gazette*, Oct. 1, 1936.
34. Johnson, *Politics of Soft Coal*, 190-93. See also Salstrom, *Appalachia's Path to Dependency*, 83-93; Dix, *What's a Coal Miner to Do?*, 198-99.
35. Johnson, *Politics of Soft Coal*, 184; Dix, *What's a Coal Miner to Do?*, 198-99.
36. Fairmont *Times* editorial, reprinted in Charleston *Gazette*, Sept. 17, 1936; Dix, *What's a Coal Miner to Do?*, 161, 196.
37. Longin, "Coal, Congress, and the Courts," 106; Bellush, *Failure of the NRA*, 38.
38. Charleston *Gazette*, May 24, 1934. In a chapter appropriately entitled "Workers Organizing Capitalists," Colin Gordon argues that under the NRA, operators came to recognize that the union played an important stabilizing role in the industry *(New Deals*, 104-8).
39. Beury, "Social Aspects of Coal Mines," 63-77.
40. Holt, *Thirty-Sixth Biennial Report of the Attorney General*, 195.
41. Huntington *Herald-Dispatch*, editorial reprinted in Charleston *Gazette*, Dec. 25, 1934.
42. Ambler and Summers, *West Virginia*, 462.
43. Schlesinger, *Coming of the New Deal*, 132-34.
44. "Industry and Labor Alike 'Very Well Satisfied' with Recovery Program, State Editors Declare," Charleston *Gazette*, May 27, 1934.
45. Charleston *Gazette*, June 17, 1934.
46. Ibid.
47. Bellush, *Failure of the NRA*, 30-31.
48. Leuchtenburg, *Franklin D. Roosevelt*, 68, 69; Schlesinger, *Coming of the New Deal*, 154-57.
49. Coffey, "Political Chrysalis," 82-86; Coffey, "Rush Dew Holt," 99-101; Mallison, *Let's Set a Spell*, 110-12.

50. Mallinson to Phil Conley, March 19, 1951, folder "1950-52," box 1, Mallinson Papers.

51. Coffey, "Political Chrysalis," 87-90; Notes for Kelly speech, Aug. 24, 1934, and minutes, Democratic State Executive Committee, Aug. 24, 1934, both in Kelly Papers.

52. Transcript, Clarksburg meeting of Democrats, Aug. 23, 1934, and clipping, Clarksburg *Telegram*, Aug. 23, 1934, both in Kelly Papers; Coffey, "Rush D. Holt," 97.

53. Coffey, "Rush D. Holt," 97.

54. Ibid., 103-5.

55. Ibid., 108-9.

56. Ibid., 122-25.

57. Leuchtenburg, *Franklin D. Roosevelt*, 145.

58. Hawley, *New Deal and the Problem of Monopoly*, 206-7.

59. "Coal Operators Seek NRA Continuance, Fear Guffey Measure Will Injure State," Charleston *Gazette*, July 14, 1935.

60. Hawley, *New Deal and Problem of Monopoly*, 207.

61. Ralph Hillis Baker, *National Bituminous Coal Commission*, 50-51; Charleston *Gazette*, June 2, 1935.

62. Coffey, "Rush D. Holt," 197-203.

63. See summary of editorial opinion in Charleston *Gazette*, April 25, 1937.

64. Leuchtenburg, *Franklin D. Roosevelt and the New Deal*, 150-51; Bernstein, *Turbulent Years*, 318-51.

65. Baker, *Coal Commission*, 9-10.

66. Hawley, *New Deal and the Problem of Monopoly*, 208-9.

67. Ibid., 210; See Drew Pearson and Robert S. Allen, "Washington Merry-Go-Round" in Charleston *Gazette*, Nov. 1, 1937.

68. Hawley, *New Deal and the Problem of Monopoly*, 211-12; Baker, *Coal Commission*, 80, 109-21, 169, 325-26; Charleston *Gazette*, Feb. 2, 1938.

69. Charleston *Gazette*, March 3, 6, 9, 1938.

70. Leuchtenburg, *Franklin D. Roosevelt and the New Deal*, 69.

71. Bellush, *Failure of the NRA*, 158-75; for a thorough and devastating contemporary critique, see Lyon et al., *National Recovery Administration*.

72. Theda Skocpol and Kenneth Finegold, "State Capacity and Economic Intervention in the Early New Deal," 260-67. See also the negative critique in Salstrom, *Appalachia's Path to Dependency*," 82-93.

73. Salstrom, *Appalachia's Path to Dependency*, 90-93.

74. *Blue Book*, 1940, 671.

75. Johnson, *Politics of Soft Coal*, 190.

76. *Blue Book*, 1963, 915.

77. For a different view, see Salstrom, *Appalachia's Path to Dependency*, chap. 5. For an overview of the period, see Baratz, *Union and the Coal Indus-*

try, 47-50. See also Thomas Coode and John F. Bauman, "The New Deal and Pennsylvania Coal Miners," chap. 6 in their *People, Poverty and Politics,* 133-57. On the new generation of labor saving devices, see Kirby, *Rural Worlds Lost,* 109; Munn, "Development of Strip Mining in Southern Appalachia," 87-92, and Schurr and Netschert, *Energy in the American Economy,* 310-28. For the postwar climate see Nelson Lichtenstein, "From Corporatism to Collective Bargaining," 122-30.

78. Harry G. Hoffman, "Laws Give Labor Greater Security," Charleston *Gazette,* April 28, 1940; Ambler and Summers, *West Virginia,* 462.

79. Martin Cherniak, *Hawk's Nest Incident,* 69-75.

6. A Failed Experiment in Federal Relief

1. Robert H. Bremner, "The New Deal and Social Welfare," in *Fifty Years Later,* ed. Sitkoff, 69, 70.

2. Patterson, *New Deal and the States,* 51-53, 201-7; Skocpol and Finegold, "State Capacity and Economic Intervention," 255-78; Alan Brinkley, "The New Deal and Southern Politics," in *New Deal and the South,* ed. Cobb and Namorato, 1984), 100.

3. Beehler, *Relief, Work, and Rehabilitation,* 15, 16; *Blue Book, 1933,* 54.

4. Blumberg, *New Deal and the Unemployed,* 30-44; Bremner, "New Deal and Social Welfare," in *Fifty Years Later,* ed. Sitkoff, 72.

5. Patterson, *New Deal and the States,* 53, 72; Blakey, *Hard Times and New Deal in Kentucky,* 50-52; Heinemann, *Depression and New Deal in Virginia,* 70.

6. Copy of memorandum, Hopkins to the president, Aug. 14, 1933; Roosevelt to Kump, Aug. 14, 1933; Kump to Roosevelt, Aug. 19, 1933, all in box 40, Kump Papers.

7. Charleston *Gazette,* March 29, 1933. Explaining the cut in the rate of relief, Maj. Francis Turner of the state department of public welfare said that delegations from all over the state had requested a reduction of the rate. A poll of county welfare organizations indicated that forty-one favored the reduction.

8. Kump to John J. Cornwell, Sept. 11, 1933, box 41, Kump Papers.

9. W.W. Allen to Mrs. Lauretta K. Muir, field director, Unemployment Relief Administration, Sept. 2, 1933, box 312, RG 69, FERA, West Virginia, NA.

10. Kanawha County Relief Administration, *Report, 1933* ("Administration, Project No. 20-G-1," 1), in Records of the Kanawha County Relief Administration, WVRHC.

11. Theresa White to Loretta K. Muir, Sept. 25, 1933, FERA, West Virginia, box 312, NA.

12. Copy, J. Floyd Harrison to Kump, Sept. 26, 1933, FERA, West Virginia, box 312, NA.
13. Alice O. Davis to Mrs. Muir, Sept. 27, 1933, FERA, West Virginia, box 312, NA.
14. West Virginia Official FERA, "Material Taken by Mr. Hopkins on his S.W. Trip," box 311, NA.
15. Hopkins to Major F. W. Turner, Aug. 14, 1933, West Virginia Official, FERA, "Feb., May, June, July, August, Sept., 1933," box 311, NA.
16. Hickok to Roosevelt, Aug. 23, 1933, "FERA Papers: Aug. 1933," box 12, Hickok Papers.
17. Copy, Hopkins to Kump, Oct. 3, 1933, FERA, West Virginia, box 312, NA.
18. Copy, Howard O. Hunter, "Memorandum to Mr. Bookman," Oct. 27, 1933, box 312, RG 69, FERA, West Virginia, NA.
19. Kump to M.H. McIntyre, Oct. 21, 1933, box 42, Kump Papers.
20. Hunter, "Memorandum to Mr. Bookman."
21. "Personal and Professional History" of William E. Beehler, attached to letter, F.R. Bell to Governor Kump, April 4, 1935, box 51, Kump Papers.
22. Undated clipping (Spring 1935) in letter, Beehler to Aubrey Williams, May 18, 1935, box 311, West Virginia Official, FERA, RG 69, NA.
23. Blumberg, *New Deal and the Unemployed*, 30-31.
24. Charleston *Gazette*, Dec. 10, 1933.
25. Ibid., Nov. 17, 1933.
26. Ibid., Nov. 21, 1933.
27. Memorandum, Howard O. Hunter to Hopkins, Nov. 25, 1933, "West Virginia Field Reports," box 60, Hopkins Papers.
28. Hunter to Hopkins, Jan. 19, 1934, box 313, West Virginia Field Reports, FERA, RG 69, NA.
29. Charles K. Payne to Hopkins, Dec. 15, 1933, box 313, West Virginia Official Correspondence, FERA, RG 69, NA.
30. Hunter to Hopkins, Dec. 26, 1933, box 60, West Virginia Field Reports, box 60 Hopkins Papers; Hunter to Hopkins, Jan. 19, 1934, box 313, ; West Virginia Field Reports, FERA, RG 69, NA.
31. Minutes of Staff Conference, box 49, FERA, Hopkins Papers.
32. Bremner, "New Deal and Social Welfare," in *Fifty Years Later*, ed. Sitkoff, 72-73.
33. Ralph V. Wolford to Harry Hopkins, Jan. 2, 1934, box 50, CWA, West Virginia, Complaints, RG 69, NA.
34. Charleston *Gazette*, Jan. 25, 1934.
35. Telegram, Beehler to Jasper J. Mayer, Jan. 2, 1934, box 50, CWA, West Virginia, RG 69, NA.
36. Beehler to Aubrey Williams, March 2, 1935, box 311, West Virginia Official Files, FERA, RG 69, NA.

37. Beehler to Harry Hopkins, Dec. 26, 1933, box 50, CWA, West Virginia, RG 69, NA.

38. Beehler to Harold (sic) O. Hunter, Dec. 27, 1933, clipping with no date attached, box 50, CWA, West Virginia, Official Correspondence, RG 69, NA.

39. Report on Logan County, by Beehler, Jan. 2, 1934, box 43, Kump Papers.

40. Williams to Beehler, Aug. 22, 1934, box 311, FERA, West Virginia Official Files, Aug.-Sept. 1934, RG 69, NA.

41. Letter to Senator Neely (unsigned copy), Jan. 15, 1934, box 50, CWA, West Virginia Official, RG 69, NA.

42. Martinsburg *Journal*, Jan. 26, 1934; undated clipping reporting state senate resolution calling for dismissal of Beehler (1935), box 311, W.Va. Official FERA, RG 69, NA; John S. Hall (Clerk of the House of Delegates) to President Roosevelt, Feb. 21, 1935 (copy of resolution of the House of Delegates), box 311, W.Va. Official, FERA, RG 69, NA; Charles C. Stillman to Aubrey Williams, Feb. 4, 1935, box 313, Field Agent Reports, FERA, RG 69, NA; undated clipping from Wheeling *Intellingencer* in letter, Beehler to Aubrey Williams, May 27, 1935, box 311, W.Va. Official File, RG 69, FERA, NA; Kump to Hopkins, March 15, 1935, W.Va. Finance and Statistics File, box 312, FERA, RG 69, NA. "Beehler Ouster Was Promised, Declares Holt," Charleston *Gazette*, April 12, 1935.

43. Telegram to Senator Neely, Jan. 29, 1934, box 50, W.Va. Official, CWA, RG 69, NA.

44. Quotations from Charleston *Daily Mail*, Feb. 2, 1934, clipping, box 50, West Virginia, CWA, RG 69, NA.

45. Charleston *Gazette*, Feb. 22, 1934.

46. Kump to Beehler, Dec. 20, 1933, box 50, W.Va. Official CWA, RG 69, NA.

47. Beehler to Howard O. Hunter, Jan. 8, 1934, box 50, CWA, W.Va., RG 69, NA; Beehler to Aubrey Williams, Jan. 24, 1934, W.Va. Official, CWA, box 50, NA; *Minutes of the Board, Kanawha County Relief Administration* (Dec. 20, 1933, to Oct. 28, 1934), Kanawha County Relief Administration, Records, WVRHC.

48. Beehler to Aubrey Williams, Feb. 1, 1934, box 50, W.Va. Official, CWA, RG 69, NA.

49. Beehler to Hopkins, Dec. 28, 1933, box 50, CWA, W.Va., "Complaints," RG 69, NA.

50. Copy of letter, William N. Beehler to Harry Hopkins, April 15, 1934 (submitting report on CWA), box 44, Kump Papers.

51. Beehler, *Relief, Work, and Rehabilitation*, 16.

52. Howard Hunter to Harry Hopkins, March 24, 1934, in FERA "Field Reports," box 312, NA.

53. Bremner, "New Deal and Social Welfare," in *Fifty Years Later*, ed. Sitkoff, 71.

54. Beehler, *Relief, Work, and Rehabilitation*, 29; Final Report of the Board of the West Virginia Relief Administration to Governor Kump, Dec. 31, 1935, box 56, Kump Papers.

55. Charleston *Gazette*, Feb. 19, 1935.

56. Blakey, *Hard Times and the New Deal in Kentucky*, 54.

57. Beehler, *Relief, Work, and Rehabilitation*, 47-52; Federal Works Administration, *Final Statistical Report of the Federal Emergency Relief Administration*, 294.

58. Project No. 20-E3-18, in Kanawha County Relief Administration Records, 1933-1934, WVRHC.

59. "Physical Accomplishments of CWA-FERA, November, 1933- September 1, 1935," box 311, FERA, West Virginia Official, RG 69, NA.

60. Beehler, *Relief, Work, and Rehabilitation*, 33-34.

61. Ibid.

62. Ibid., 29, 34.

63. Patterson, *America's Struggle against Poverty*, 58-59.

64. Leon Brower, "Character of Case Load of Logan County, West Virginia," special folder, box 312, FERA, State Files, West Virginia, RG 69, NA.

65. Salstrom, *Appalachia's Path to Dependency*, 118-19.

66. For a general discussion of the chronic nature of southern rural poverty and the idea that some who lived in remote areas of Appalachian Kentucky and Virginia received relief that was higher than the standard to which they were accustomed, see Mertz, *New Deal Policy and Southern Rural Poverty*, 4-5.

67. C.C. Stillman to Aubrey Williams, June 13, 1935 box 313, FERA, West Virginia, RG 69, NA.

68. For more on mountain agriculture, see chapter 8.

69. Charleston *Gazette*, Nov. 21, 1937.

70. Beehler, *Relief, Work, and Rehabilitation*, 38.

71. Charleston *Gazette*, April 21, 1935.

72. Kenneth W. Miller (assistant director of Social Service WVRA) to Josephine C. Brown (administrative assistant, FERA), Oct. 29 1934, and Beehler to Corrington Gill, Oct. 10, 1934, both in box 311, FERA, West Virginia, RG 69, NA.

73. "Statement by Kanawha County FERA and CWA Board at meeting held Tuesday night, March 20,1934," in Kanawha County Relief Administration Records, WVRHC.

74. Kanawha County Relief Administration, *Minutes of the Board*, 1:50 (Feb. 24, 1934), 1:36 (April 12, 1934); Report of the Senate Committee, undated, appended to vol. 1: Kanawha County Relief Administration Records, WVRHC.

75. Kanawha County Relief Administration Board, resolution passed Aug. 1, 1934, exhibit A in Kanawha County Relief Records, 2:141-42; see also clippings from Charleston *Gazette*, June 17, 1934, vol. 2, WVRHC.

76. Frank R. Bell to Governor Kump, April 4, 1935, box 51, Kump Papers; Charleston *Gazette*, April 10, 1935.

77. "Narrative Report: Service and Special Projects under FERA Administration to June 1, 1935, in Monongalia County, West Virginia," Papers of the Monongalia Emergency Relief Administration, box 5, WVRHC.

78. Ibid.

79. Ibid., 3-5.

80. Pickett, *For More than Bread*, 47-50; Roosevelt, *This I Remember*, 26-27.

81. W.E. Brooks to Mrs. Roosevelt, Nov. 25, 1935 (includes statement of Monongalia FERA board in support of Davis), box 2783, WPA State Series, West Virginia, RG 69, NA.

82. Eleanor Roosevelt to Davis, Nov. 23, 1935, Da 1935, box 1334, E. Roosevelt Papers.

83. Davis to Roosevelt, n.d. (Nov. 1935), Da 1935, box 1334, E. Roosevelt Papers.

84. Leuchtenburg, *Franklin D. Roosevelt*, 124.

85. Ibid.; Bremner, "The New Deal and Social Welfare," in *Fifty Years Later*, ed. Sitkoff, 73.

86. Kump to William N. Beehler, March 19, 1935, box 50, Kump Papers.

87. "Courage and Wisdom: Editors Praise Governor's Open Stand on Relief Situation and Gardens," Charleston *Gazette*, March 31, 1935.

88. Kump to Hopkins, Nov. 23, 1934, box 311, FERA, West Virginia, RG 69, NA.

89. Kump to Harry Hopkins, March 15, 1935, Finance and Statistics, box 312, FERA, West Virginia, RG 69, NA; William N. Beehler to Aubrey Williams, March 6, 1935, box 311, FERA, West Virginia, RG 69, NA; memorandum, Hopkins to Williams, July 22, 1935, box 311, FERA, West Virginia, RG 69, NA; Telegram, Kump to Hopkins, July 24, 1935, box 311, FERA, West Virginia, RG 69, NA; Williams to Kump, July 23, 1935, box 311, FERA, West Virginia, NA; Kump to Beehler, July 25, 1935, box 53, Kump Papers.

90. Kump to Beehler, Aug. 1, 1935, box 54, Kump Papers; Beehler to Williams, July 28, 1935, box 313, FERA, West Virginia, RG 69, NA; Williams to Beehler, July 30, 1935, box 313, FERA, West Virginia, NA.; Mary Amend to Williams, n.d., box 2761, WPA, West Virginia, RG 69, NA.

7. Reshaping the Welfare System

1. Patterson, *America's Struggle against Poverty*, 59-60; Leuchtenburg, *Franklin D. Roosevelt and the New Deal*, 122-23; Brock, *Welfare, Democracy, and the New Deal*, 258-59.

Notes to Pages 136-141

2. Leuchtenburg, *Franklin D. Roosevelt and the New Deal*, 124-25.
3. Sherwood, *Roosevelt and Hopkins*, 68.
4. Ibid.
5. Charles, *Minister of Relief*, 187. Patterson, *New Deal and the States*, 84.
6. The columns of these writers can be found in the newspapers of the Ogden chain but can be conveniently sampled in the clipping file in the McCullough Papers.
7. Hopkins to McCullough, June 8, 1935, box 2761, WPA State Series, West Virginia, RG 69, NA.
8. Coffey, "Rush Dew Holt," 137-38; Charleston *Daily Mail*, July 17, 1935 in box 1, book II, McCullough Papers.
9. Martinsburg *Journal*, Dec. 2, 1935.
10. Charleston *Gazette*, July 20, 1935; Fairmont *Times*, July 20, 1935 in box 2, book III, McCullough Papers.
11. Telegram, Kump to President Roosevelt, July 19, 1935, box 2787, WPA State Series, West Virginia, RG 69, NA.
12. Telegram, Kump to President Roosevelt, July 30, 1935, in box 2787, WPA State Series, West Virginia, RG 69, NA.
13. Kump to Harold Ickes, July 22, 1935; Kump to Henry A. Wallace, July 22, 1935, box 53, Kump Papers.
14. Kump to Beehler, July 23, 1935; July 25, 1935, box 53, Kump Papers.
15. Kump to M.M. Neely, Aug. 12, 1935; Robert L. Ramsay, Jennings Randolph, Andrew Edmiston, George W. Johnson, John Kee, and Joe L. Smith to Kump, Aug. 15, 1935, box 54, Kump Papers.
16. Clipping, Charleston *Daily Mail*, Aug. 22, 1935; McCullough to Hopkins, Aug. 22, 1935, box 2754, WPA State Series, West Virginia, RG 69, NA.
17. Fairmont *Times*, Aug. 28, 1935, box 3, book IX, McCullough Papers.
18. William McKell to Kump, Feb. 7, 1935; Kump to McKell Feb. 8, 1935, box 50, Kump Papers.
19. G.K. Kump to H.G. Kump, June 21, 1935, box 52, Kump Papers.
20. Huntington *Herald Dispatch*, Sept. 19, 1935, box 1, book X, McCullough Papers.
21. See editorial in Fairmont *Times*, July 16, 1935, clipping in Kump Papers, box 53; Wheeling *Register*, July 18, article and editorial, clippings in box 1, book I, McCullough Papers.
22. McCullough to Hopkins, Aug. 19, 1935, box 2754, WPA State Series, West Virginia, NA.
23. Lorena Hickok to Harry Hopkins, Nov. 3, 1935, box 68, "Lorena Hickok Reports," Hopkins Papers.
24. Quoted in the Fairmont *Times*, Oct. 14, 1935, box 1, book VII, McCullough Papers.

25. Lorena Hickok to Harry Hopkins, November 3, 1935, box 68, "Lorena Hickok Reports," Hopkins Papers.
26. Kump to President Roosevelt, Nov. 7, 1935 (two letters), box 56, Kump Papers.
27. Kump to President Roosevelt, Nov. 22, 1935, box 56, Kump Papers.
28. Kump to C.L. Allen, Acting Relief Administrator, Nov. 15, 1935, box 56, Kump Papers.
29. Martinsburg *Journal*, Nov. 14, 1935.
30. Wheeling *News Register*, Jan. 12, 1936, box 2, book XXIII, McCullough Papers.
31. Ibid.
32. Clipping, Charleston *Daily Mail*, Jan. 12, 1936, box 2, book XXIII, McCullough Papers.
33. Wheeling *Intelligencer*, Oct. 7, 1935, box 1, book XI, McCullough Papers.
34. Telegram, Holt to McCullough, Jan. 16, 1936, box 10, series VIII, R.D. Holt Papers.
35. Bittner to Holt, Nov. 13, 1935, in box 2, series VIII, R.D. Holt Papers.
36. Ibid.
37. McCullough to Holt, Feb. 13, 1936; Parkersburg *Sentinel*, Feb. 22, 1936, clipping in box 2, Book XXI, McCullough Papers.
38. Huntington *Herald Dispatch*, Feb. 18, 1936, box 3, book XX, McCullough Papers; Coffey, "Rush Dew Holt," 168-75; Charles, *Minister of Relief*, 190.
39. Huntington *Herald Dispatch*, Feb. 18, 1936, box 3, book XX, McCullough Papers.
40. Charleston *Gazette*, Feb. 22, 1936; telegram, Aubrey Williams to Rush D. Holt, Feb. 21, 1936, in box 10, series VIII, R.D. Holt Papers.
41. "Charges of Political Exploitation of the Works Progress Administration of West Virginia," report to Harry L. Hopkins from Alan Johnstone, box 52, Hopkins Papers.
42. Ibid., 1-3.
43. Ibid., 3-10; see also press release, "WPA Administrator Hopkins Finds No Irregularities in West Virginia," in Harry Hopkins to Rush D. Holt, March 10, 1936; to F. Witcher Mccullough, March 10, 1936, box 52, Hopkins Papers.
44. "Charges of Political Exploitation of the Works Progress Administration of West Virginia," 11, report to Harry L. Hopkins from Alan Johnstone, box 52, Hopkins Papers.
45. Ibid., 10.
46. Huntington *Herald-Advertiser*, March 12, 1936; Wheeling *Intelligencer*, March 12, 13, 1936; Charleston *Daily Mail*, March 12, 1936; Charleston *Gazette*, March 12, 1936, all in box 2, book XXIV, McCullough Papers.

47. Washington *Herald*, March 12, 1936, box 2, book XXIV, McCullough Papers.
48. Quoted in Martinsburg *Journal*, March 19, 1936.
49. CBS press release, March 19, 1936, in folder "Charges of U.S. Senator Holt in West Virginia," box 52, Hopkins Papers. See also Coffey, "Rush Dew Holt," 68-75.
50. Elkins *Intermountain*, Feb. 20, 1936; Parkersburg *Sentinel*, Feb. 22, 1936; in box 2, book XXI, McCullough Papers.
51. Lorena Hickok to Harry Hopkins, Nov. 3, 1935, box 68, Hopkins Papers.
52. "Report: Three District Recreation Conferences," Jan. 27-Feb. 1, 1937, box 2782, WPA State Series, West Virginia, RG 69, NA.
53. Charleston *Labor Advocate*, Sept. 20, 1935, clipping in box 1, book X, McCullough Papers; Charleston *Gazette*, March 21, 1936.
54. Charleston *Gazette*, March 21, 1936.
55. See Smith, *New Deal in the Urban South*, 209-31.
56. Report by Irene Gillooly, State Director of Service Programs, box 2774, WPA State Series, West Virginia, RG 69, NA.
57. Clyde Billups, director of Professional and Service Project, to Bruce McClure, Oct. 21, 1935, box 2773, WPA State Series, West Virginia, RG 69, NA.
58. Verna C. Blackburn to Nikolai Sokoloff, director, Federal Music Project, Sept. 6, 1936, box 2774, WPA State Series, West Virginia, RG 69, NA.
59. Verna C. Blackburn to Thadeus Rich, Sept. 20, 1936, box 2774; Federal Music Project of West Virginia, "Narrative Report, July, 1938," Box 2775, WPA State Series, West Virginia, RG 69, NA.
60. Clipping, Huntington *Herald Advertiser*, June 27 1937, in letter, Verna Blackburn to Nikolai Sokoloff, June 28, 1937, box 2774, WPA State Series, West Virginia, RG 69, NA.
61. Verna C. Blackburn to Nikolai Sokoloff, March 12, 1937, box 2774, WPA State Series, West Virginia, RG 69, NA.
62. Federal Music Project of West Virginia, "Narrative Report, June, 1938," box 2775, WPA State Series, West Virginia, RG 69, NA.
63. Blakey, *Hard Times and New Deal in Kentucky*, 65. Virginia had mountain string bands in addition to orchestras and choral groups; see Heinemann, *Depression and New Deal in Virginia*, 93.
64. Verna C. Blackburn to Nikolai Sokoloff, June 3, 1937, box 2774, WPA State Series, West Virginia, RG 69, NA; Beezer, "Arthurdale," 25; Charleston *Gazette*, Sept. 3, 1939.
65. Edward A. Chapman, WPA library consultant, "Report of Trip to West Virginia, April 4-5, 1938," box 2787, WPA State Series, West Virginia, RG 69, NA.

66. Nellie L. Glass, "Annual Report, State Wide Library Project," Sept. 25, 1940, box 2779, WPA State Series, RG 69, NA.
67. Mary Gillette Moon, regional supervisor of Professional and Music Projects, to Florence Kerr, Dec. 23, 1940, box 2773, WPA State Series, West Virginia, RG 69, NA.
68. Helen V. Wilson, West Virginia director of General Federation of Women's Clubs, to Edward A Chapman, Oct. 19, 1940, box 2779, WPA State Series, West Virginia, RG 69, NA.
69. Edward A. Chapman to Joseph Alderson, state administrator, Nov. 11, 1940, box 2779, WPA State Series, West Virginia, RG 69, NA.
70. Charleston *Gazette*, July 26, Oct. 11, 1936.
71. "Photo Story Series," WPA photographs, West Virginia, box 107, Photographic Section, NA.
72. These films are available in the film section, National Archives.
73. Thomas, "Nearly Perfect State," 91-108.
74. Schlesinger, *Coming of The New Deal*, 285-87.
75. Charleston *Gazette*, Jan. 31, 1937; May 17, 1937; Sept. 20, 1937.
76. Ibid., July 24, 1938.
77. Ibid., July 30, 1938.
78. Patterson, *America's Struggle against Poverty*, 59-60.
79. Charleston *Gazette*, Feb. 28, 1935.
80. Sly to Kump, Sept. 19, 1935, box 55, Kump Papers.
81. Martinsburg *Journal*, Nov. 13, 1935.
82. Charleston *Gazette*, June 21, 1936.
83. *Report of the Department of Public Assistance, July 1 1936 to June 30, 1938* (Charleston, 1939), 9; West, "West Virginia's Problem of Public Care," 54-55, 63.
84. Charleston *Gazette*, June 30, 1936; Heinemann, *Depression and New Deal in Virginia*, 233, n. 11.
85. Charleston *Gazette*, Oct. 2, 1936.
86. Hickok to Harry Hopkins, Nov. 3, 1935, "Lorena Hickok Reports," box 68, Hopkins Papers.
87. Charleston *Gazette*, April 7, 1935.
88. Ibid., July 2, 1936.
89. Patterson, *America's Struggle against Poverty*, 45-46. Brock, *Welfare, Democracy, and the New Deal*, 6.
90. Edith Abbott, "Don't Do It Mr. Hopkins," *The Nation*, cited by Brock, *Welfare, Democracy, and the New Deal*, 250-51.
91. Patterson, *America's Struggle*, 45-46.
92. Charleston *Gazette*, Feb. 28, 1935.
93. West Virginia, *Report of the Department of Public Assistance, 1936-1938* (Charleston, 1939), 9-11; West, "New Venture in Security," 92.

94. West, "New Venture in Security," 92; *Report of the Department of Public Assistance,* 11.

95. W.W. Morse to Irene Gillooly, WPA District V, Feb. 22, 1938, box 2788, WPA State Series, West Virginia, RG 69, NA.

96. Homer Adams Holt, "Budget Message to the Legislature, January 20, 1939," *State Papers and Public Addresses,* 70-71.

97. Charleston *Gazette,* April 26, 1939.

98. Ibid., April 13, 1939.

99. Ibid., Feb. 23, 1939.

100. Harry Greenstein, "General Relief: Another Category or a Basic Foundation for Public Welfare Administration?" paper presented at National Conference of Social Work, 1940, cited in Brock, *Welfare, Democracy and the New Deal,* 292, 326.

101. Edith Abbott, "Relief, the No Man's Land, and How to Reclaim It," paper presented at National Conference of Social Work, 1940, in Brock, *Welfare, Democracy and the New Deal,* 326-27.

102. Hearings, Senate Special Committee on Unemployment and Relief (Byrnes Committee), 75th Congress, 3d Sess., cited in Brock, *Welfare, Democracy, and the New Deal,* 330-33.

103. West Virginia, *Report of the Department of Public Assistance, July 1, 1940 to June 30, 1941* (Charleston, Nov. 10, 1941), 3.

104. Ambler, *History of Education in West Virginia,* 856-57.

8. The New Deal and Mountain Agriculture

1. Kirby, *Rural Worlds Lost,* 87. See also Eller, *Miners, Millhands, and Mountaineers,* 87-91, and Salstrom, *Appalachia's Path to Dependency,* 95-121.

2. Excellent accounts of these developments can be found in Biles, *South and the New Deal;* Daniel, *Breaking the Land;* Fite, *Cotton Fields No More;* Kirby, *Rural Worlds Lost.*

3. Worster, *Dust Bowl,* 49-63.

4. Eller, *Miners, Millhands, and Mountaineers,* 210-40; Kirby, *Rural Worlds Lost,* 47-48, 87; Salstrom, *Appalachia's Path to Dependency,* 101.

5. W.W. Armentrout, "The Low Income Farm Situation in West Virginia as We Know It," in *Proceedings of the 1940 Conference on Low Income Farms,* Agricultural Experiment Station, Bulletin 299 (Morgantown: West Virginia University, March 1941), 12-13, Bureau of Agricultural Economics, Records of the Appalachian Regional Office, General Correspondence, 1934-1945, box 9, RG 83, NA.

6. Writers Program of the Work Projects Administration in the State of West Virginia, *West Virginia: A Guide to the Mountain State,* 70.

7. Ibid.

8. George T. Blakey, *Hard Times and New Deal in Kentucky,* 104-42; Heinemann, *Depression and New Deal in Virginia,* 105-28.

9. See chapter 3.

10. "Material taken by Mr. Hopkins on his S.W. Trip in August," FERA, West Virginia, box 311, RG 69, NA.

11. Martinsburg *Journal,* March 19, 1935.

12. The poverty of mountain farmers was often ignored, but there were efforts from time to time to come to grips with the issue, sometimes in combination with the question of stranded industrial workers. Several New Deal agencies studied the question from various perspectives, and the West Virginia University College of Agriculture and the Extension Service held three conferences on the issue from 1937 to 1940. The conclusions about chronic mountain poverty in this chapter are based largely on the following selections from this contemporary literature of rural poverty in West Virginia and Appalachia: Asch and Mangus, *Farmers on Relief and Rehabilitation;* Chapman (Chair), *Report of the Committee on the Upper Monongahela Valley;* "Farm Families' Plight Studied," Charleston *Gazette,* Sept. 10, 1938 (an account of the 1938 low-income conference); "Farm Housing Survey Shows Real Needs," *West Virginia Farm News,* June 1934, 2-3; Goodrich, *Migration and Economic Opportunity;* National Child Labor Committee, *Rural Child Welfare;* Morris, *Plight of the Bituminous Coal Miner; Report of the Child Relief Work in the Bituminous Coal Fields by the American Friends Service Committee.* Several useful documents were found in Bureau of Agricultural Economics, Records of the Appalachian Regional Office, RG 83, NA: *Appalachian Land-Use Conference Tour, Thursday and Friday, November 2 and 3, 1939* (mimeographed), WV 030, box 9; C.R. Draper, "A Study of the People and Conditions in a Low-Income Farming Area in the Southern Tip of Lewis County, West Virginia" (mimeographed), General Correspondence, 1934-1945, WV Reports 184-041, box 10; *Land-Use Planning Circular for Lewis County, West Virginia, Unified County Program* (mimeographed) in General Correspondence, 1934-1945, WV 130, box 10; *Proceedings of the 1940 Conference on Low-Income Farms,* Bulletin 299(Morgantown: West Virginia University Agricultural Experiment Station, March 1941), in General Correspondence, 1934-1945, box 9.

13. Asch and Mangus, *Farmers on Relief,* 10, 42-43.

14. Lorena Hickok to Eleanor Roosevelt, Aug. 22, 1933, "FERA Papers: Aug. 1933," box 12, Hickok Papers, FDRL.

15. *Ibid.*

16. Kirby, *Rural Worlds Lost,* 91.

17. Interview with Rev. Raymond Adkins in Marshall University Oral History of Appalachia, cited by Kirby, *Rural Worlds Lost,* 122, and Biles, *South and the New Deal,* 77.

18. Kirby, *Rural Worlds Lost,* 122.

19. "Farm Housing Survey Shows Real Needs," *West Virginia Farm News*, June 1934, 2-3; Charleston *Gazette*, May 10, 1934; Humphreys, *Adventures in Good Living*, 98. Helen P. Summers, wife of West Virginia historian Festus P. Summers, directed the survey project in West Virginia. See also chapter 1 above and National Child Labor Committee, *Rural Child Welfare*.

20. Biles, *South and the New Deal*, 47-48.

21. Saloutos, *American Farmer and the New Deal*, 150; Nash, *Crucial Era*, 42.

22. Frame, *History of Agriculture*, 26.

23. See Charleston *Gazette*, May 21, 1933; Resolution of Wood County farm bureau, letters of protest to Governor Kump, Secretary of Agriculture Henry Wallace, and federal extension director C.W. Warburton from Everett S. Humphrey, president of West Virginia Farm Bureau and Mrs. J.G. Lang, president of West Virginia Farm Women, May 25, 1933; letter from officers of West Virginia State Grange to Florence M. Ward, extension service, May 29, 1933; C. W. Warburton, director of Extension Work to John R. Turner, president of West Virginia University, May 20, 1933; all in box 216, Records of the Extension Service, General Correspondence, 1933, West Virginia, RG 33, NA; Pickett, *For More than Bread*, 48; Betty Eckhardt, West Virginia Extension Service to Florence Ward, Feb. 17, 1934, box 282, in Extension Service, General Correspondence, 1934, West Virginia, RG 33, NA.

24. Everett S. Humphrey, "Our Farm Bureau Faces the Future," Address at annual meeting of the West Virginia Farm Bureau, at Jackson's Mill, August 13, 1934, reprinted in *West Virginia Farm News*, October 1934, 1, 4; Nat T. Frame, "The West Virginia Farm Bureau and the New Deal," *West Virginia Farm News*, August 1933, 2,8.

25. Gist, "Five Years of Agricultural Adjustment," 137-41.

26. *Blue Book, 1940*, 595.

27. J.O. Knapp, "How the Extension Service Is Working with Low-Income Farmers," *Proceedings of the 1940 Conference on Low Income Farms*, 16-17.

28. Saloutos, *American Farmer and the New Deal*, 261-62; Mertz, *New Deal Policy and Southern Rural Poverty*, 81.

29. J.O. Knapp, "How the Extension Service Is Working with Low-Income Farmers," in *Proceedings of 1940 Conference on Low Income Farms*.

30. Biles, *South and the New Deal*, 46.

31. Beehler, *Relief, Work, and Rehabilitation*, 33-34. Asch and Mangus, *Farmers on Relief*, 16.

32. See above, chapter 3.

33. *Report of the Child Relief Work in the Bituminous Coal Fields*, 1-10.

34. Saloutos, *American Farmer and the New Deal*, 155-56; Schlesinger, *Coming of the New Deal*, 363-64.

35. Hareven, *Eleanor Roosevelt*, 92.

36. Pickett, *For More than Bread*, 45.

37. Schlesinger, *Coming of the New Deal*, 364-67.
38. Haid, "Arthurdale," 65-67.
39. Ibid., 12-13.
40. Gilbert Love, "Mrs. Roosevelt Steps In," *Pittsburgh Press*, Oct. 24, 1933; Eleanor Roosevelt, "Why I Went to Scotts Run," Dec. 2, 1933, clippings in Christopher Scrapbook; Schlesinger, *Coming of the New Deal*, 365; Pickett, *For More than Bread*, 45-46; Eleanor Roosevelt, *This I Remember*, 26-27.
41. Eleanor Roosevelt, *This I Remember*, 26-27; Schlesinger, *Coming of the New Deal*, 364-65; Hareven, *Eleanor Roosevelt*, 94; Baldwin, *Poverty and Politics*, 68-72.
42. Pickett, *For More than Bread*, 45-46; Schlesinger, *Coming of the New Deal*, 366; Hareven, *Eleanor Roosevelt*, 94-95; Baldwin, *Poverty and Politics*, 72; Beezer, "Arthurdale," 19.
43. Schlesinger, *Coming of the New Deal*, 366.
44. Pickett, *For More than Bread*, 47.
45. Eleanor Roosevelt, *This I Remember*, 131.
46. Schlesinger, *Coming of the New Deal*, 366; Baldwin *Poverty and Politics*, 73; Saloutos, *New Deal and the Farmer*, 156-57.
47. Pickett, *For More than Bread*, 45-46, 56-57, 61; quotation in Schlesinger, *Coming of the New Deal*, 367. A good account of the education experiments can be found in Beezer, "Arthurdale," and a thorough overall account of the community's early years in Haid, "Arthurdale."
48. See chapter 7 above.
49. Baldwin, *Poverty and Politics*, 92.
50. Charleston *Gazette*, March 23, 1934.
51. Charleston *Gazette*, March 23, 24, May 20, June 6, Oct. 7, 15 1934; Long, "Red House," 93; Beehler, *Relief, Work, and Rehabilitation*, 69-72.
52. Charleston *Gazette*, April 2, 1935.
53. Ibid., May 13, 14, 1938.
54. Baldwin, *Poverty and Politics*, 73-74.
55. Beezer, "Arthurdale," 29-36; Hareven, *Eleanor Roosevelt*, 102-108; Saloutos, *American Farmer and New Deal*, 156-57; Conkin, *Tomorrow a New World*, 331.
56. Biles, *South and the New Deal*, 48-49.
57. Russell G. Ellyson, "How the Farm Security Administration is Working with Low-Income Farmers," in *Proceedings of the 1940 Conference on Low-Income Farms*, 20.
58. Martinsburg *Evening Journal*, Sept. 26, 1940.
59. Russell G. Ellyson, "How the Farm Security Administration Is Working with Low-Income Farmers," in *Proceedings of the 1940 Conference on Low-Income Farms*, 21.
60. Ibid., 21.

61. Ibid., 21-22.

62. Ibid. 22-23.

63. Biles, *South and the New Deal*, 50; Blakey, *Hard Times and New Deal*, 130.

64. A few of the FSA photographs of West Virginia scenes may be seen in the photographic essays in WPA Writers Project, *West Virginia: A Guide to the Mountain State*. The complete collection is in the Library of Congress. The West Virginia material may be viewed on microfilm reels labeled U.S. Farm Security and Office of War Information, L 1717-1729, shelf P and P 3, reel 100 and L 1730-1737, shelf P and P 3, reel 101. Several FSA photographs appear in the photo insert following page <000>.

65. Baldwin, *Poverty and Politics*, 217-21; Heinemann, *Depression and New Deal in Virginia*, 124-25.

66. Saloutos, *American Farmer and the New Deal*, 208-17; Brown, *Electricity for Rural America*, 35-58; Nye, *Electrifying America*, 287-335.

67. "Electricity Can Transform Farm Life," *West Virginia Farm News*, Oct. 1935, 3.

68. "Rural Electrification Looking Up in West Virginia," *West Virginia Farm News*, March 1937, 3, 12; Moorefield *Examiner*, Feb. 12, 1937; Saloutos, *American Farmer and the New Deal*, 218-19.

69. Charleston *Gazette*, May 13, 1937; Jan. 20, 1938.

70. Charleston *Gazette*, May 5, 1940.

71. Heinemann, *Depression and New Deal in Virginia*, 126; Blakey, *Hard Times and New Deal in Kentucky*, 140-41.

72. "Sun-Up Comes to Many Rural West Virginians," *West Virginia Farm News*, June 1938, 3; "Rural Electrification Movement in West Virginia Marks New Milestone," *West Virginia Farm News*, June 1940, 3-7.

73. Nye, *Electrifying America*, 328.

74. U.S. Department of Agriculture, *Economic and Social Problems and Conditions*, 4.

75. Ibid., 4-6.

76. Eller, *Miners, Millhands, and Mountaineers*, 226-27; U.S. Department of Agriculture, *Economic and Social Problems*, 4. According to census figures, "land in farms" declined only slightly between 1920 (9.57 million acres) and 1940 (8.91 million acres): U.S. Department of Commerce, Bureau of the Census, *Historical Statistics of the United States*, pt. I, 460.

77. Badger, *The New Deal*, 172-73.

78. *Land-Use Planning Circular for Lewis County, West Virginia, Unified County Program*, p. 2, West Virginia 130, box 10, Bureau of Agricultural Economics, Records of Appalachian Regional Office, General Correspondence, 1934-1945, RG 83, NA.

79. Ibid. One commentator on these guidelines has called them "a prescription for disaster." They were, however, in the absence of any guidelines,

a prescription to reverse the land-use disaster that had already occurred. See Salstrom, *Appalachia's Path to Dependency*, 119.

80. West Virginia Writers Project, *West Virginia*, 70.

81. "Appalachian Land Use Conference Tour, Thursday and Friday, November 2 and 3, 1939" (mimeographed), West Virginia 030, box 9, Records of the Bureau of Agricultural Economics, Records of the Appalachian Regional Office, General Correspondence, RG 83, NA.

82. Ibid., 8-9.
83. Ibid., 9-10.
84. Ibid., 11-14.
85. Ibid., 11-15.
86. Ibid., 15-20.
87. Ibid., 24-26.
88. Ibid., 25-26.

89. *Land-Use Planning Circular for Lewis County, West Virginia, Unified County Program*, pp. 1-13, West Virginia 130, box 10, Bureau of Agricultural Economics, Records of Appalachian Regional Office, General Correspondence, 1934-1945, RG 83, NA.

90. Ibid., 1. The twelve counties were Barbour, Berkeley, Harrison, Marshall, Monroe, Morgan, Pleasants, Pocahontas, Ritchie, Tyler, Upshur, and Wood.

91. C.R. Draper, *A Study of the People and Conditions in a Low-Income Farming Area in the Southern Tip of Lewis County, West Virginia*, 1-3; folder: West Virginia 184-041 Reports, box 10, Bureau of Agricultural Economics, Records of the Appalachian Regional Office, General Correspondence, 1934-1945, RG 83, NA; also cited in Salstrom, *Appalachia's Path to Dependency*, 117.

92. Draper, *A Study of the People and Conditions*, 10.
93. Ibid., 4-5.
94. Ibid., 5-6.
95. Ibid., 1-3.
96. Ibid., 12-13.
97. Ibid., 12-14.

98. "West Virginia County Land Use Planning Program, Second Annual Progress Report, for Fiscal Year Ending June 30, 1941: A Joint Report on the Progress and Accomplishments of the Cooperative Land Use Planning Program in West Virginia" (mimeographed, July 15, 1941), pp. 31-34, WV 184-01 Reports, box 10, Bureau of Agricultural Economics, Records of Appalachian Regional Office, General Correspondence, Record Group 83, NA.

99. Ibid.; in his address to the legislature in 1941, Governor Holt referred to a hesitation in some areas to form soil conservation districts as long as the federal guidelines were in effect: Holt, "Biennial Message to the Legislature, Regular Session, 1941," *State Papers and Public Addresses*, 94-95.

100. Kirby, *Rural Worlds Lost*, 80.

101. Appalachian Land Use Conference Tour, Thursday and Friday, November 2 and 3, 1939, p. 12, West Virginia 030, box 9, Records of the Bureau of Agricultural Economics, Records of the Appalachian Regional Office, General Correspondence, RG 83, NA.

102. Kirby, *Rural Worlds Lost*, 86-87.

103. Paul Salstrom maintains (*Appalachia's Path to Dependency*, 119) that New Deal policies offered no way to stop erosion "except by terminating agriculture," but agencies such as the Extension Service, the Soil Conservation Service, the Civilian Conservation Corps, the Farm Security Administration, the Bureau of Agricultural Economics, and the West Virginia Land Use Planning Committee encouraged better land use and sought alternative ways to produce income from mountain farming.

104. In 1935, West Virginia had a farm population of 569,000. By 1945 the population had declined to 445,000 and by 1969 to only 84,000. U.S. Department of Commerce, Bureau of the Census, *Historical Statistics of the United States*, pt. 1, Series K 17-81, 485. See also West Virginia Planning Board, *Report of the Coordinating Committee*, 5-6.

9. The New Deal and Families in Distress

1. George Kahle interview of Milton Levine, Huntington, December 10, 1974, Oral History of Appalachia, SCMU.

2. William Nestor interview of Mrs. Blaine Nestor, Philippi, July 8, 1974, ibid.

3. McElvaine, *Great Depression*, 175-82.

4. *West Virginia Review* 15 (Feb. 1938): 160.

5. Ware, *Holding Their Own*, 17; Nash, *Crucial Era*, 74-75.

6. Kessler-Harris, *Out to Work*, 252-55; Badger, *New Deal*, 23-24. See also, Kessler-Harris, *Woman's Wage*, chap. 3.

7. Shepherdstown *Register*, July 20, 1933.

8. Badger, *New Deal*, 23-24.

9. Kessler-Harris, *Out to Work*, 259-62.

10. U.S. Department of Labor news release, in Charleston *Gazette*, June 10, 1937; Harriet Byrne, "Women's Employment in West Virginia," in United States Department of Labor Women's Bureau, *Bulletin* 150, 1937, 1-3, cited by Hensley, "Women in the Industrial Work Force," 121.

11. Hensley, "Women in the Industrial Work Force, " 121.

12. Christine B. Campbell, Wolf Creek, W.Va., to F. Witcher McCullough, n.d., in box 2784, WPA State Series, West Virginia, NA.

13. Nash, *Crucial Era*, 77.

14. Charleston *Gazette*, Dec. 3, 1936.

15. Kathryn Trent, "Report of the Relief Nursing Service, June 1, 1935," box 2784, WPA State Series: West Virginia, RG 69, NA.

16. Alice Davis, "Narrative Report, Service and Special Projects under F.E.R.A. Administration to June 1, 1935, Monongalia County, West Virginia," box 5, Monongalia County Federal Relief Records; Ellen S. Woodward to Ethel Moreland, April 5, 1934, in box 2, ibid., WVRHC.

17. See "History of Kanawha Women's Center," box 2784, WPA, West Virginia, RG 69, NA; Charleston *Gazette*, June 10, 1934; May 12, 1935.

18. Charleston *Gazette*, Aug. 11, 1935; Aug. 12, 1936; Mary Gillette Moon, Regional Supervisor of Professional and Music Projects to Florence Kerr, Dec. 23, 1940, box 2779, WPA: W.Va., NA.

19. Ruth D. Hardman to Florence Kerr, March 29, 1943, box 2780, WPA, West Virginia, RG 69, NA.

20. Kessler-Harris, *Out to Work*, 263.

21. Dorothea Campbell, president, Charleston Business and Professional Women's Club to John T. Morgan, chairman, Board of Kanawha County Relief Administration, Sept. 24, 1934; Morgan to Campbell, Sept. 25, 1934, in Kanawha County Relief Administration Records, Minutes of the Board, vol. II, WVRHC.

22. Charleston *Gazette*, Jan. 10, 1933.

23. Ibid., Dec. 10, 1933.

24. Nash, *Crucial Era*, 78.

25. *Blue Book*, 1940, 735-39, 376-77, 378-81, 389-442.

26. Alice Davis to Malvina T. Scheider, secretary to Eleanor Roosevelt, Oct. 14, 1933; Davis to Eleanor Roosevelt, n.d. (probably Dec. 1933); Davis to Eleanor Roosevelt, Dec. 24, 1933, "Da 1933," box 1259, E. Roosevelt Papers. WPA files on Scotts Run indicate a consistent interest and involvement of the first lady throughout the decade. See Scotts Run file, box 2774, WPA State Series, West Virginia, RG 69, NA.

27. Lorena Hickok to Eleanor Roosevelt, Aug. 22, 1933, "FERA Papers: Aug. 1933," box 12, Hickok Collection, FDRL.

28. Eleanor Roosevelt, *This I Remember*, 128.

29. See above, chapter 2.

30. "Excerpts from letter to Mrs. Roosevelt, from Charleston, August 21, 1933," FERA Papers, Aug. 1933, box 12, Hickok Collection, FDRL.

31. Hunter to Hopkins, Dec. 26, 1933, box 60, West Virginia Field Reports, Hopkins Papers; West Virginia Field Reports, FERA, Box 313, RG 69, NA.

32. Beehler, *Relief, Work, and Rehabilitation*, 119.

33. Estill, *Organization of the Department of Public Welfare*, 12-13.

34. Charleston *Gazette*, June 9, 1934; Alice Davis to Eleanor Roosevelt, Dec. 24, 1933, file Da 1933, box 1259, E. Roosevelt Papers; quotation from Taylor, "Depression and New Deal in Pendleton," 54-55.

35. Charleston *Gazette*, June 8, 10, and Oct. 28, 1934; Beehler, *Relief, Work, and Rehabilitation*, 119.

36. The film *A Better West Virginia* (WPA, 1937) may be found in the Motion Picture Collection, RG 69, Acc. no. 330, NA.

37. Charleston *Gazette*, Oct. 28, 1934; Aug. 8, 18, 1935.

38. Robert H. Bremner, "The New Deal and Social Welfare," in *Fifty Years Later*, ed. Sitkoff, 70-71. The standard account of the CCC is Salmond, *Civilian Conservation Corps*.

39. "The CCC in West Virginia," Charleston *Gazette*, Feb. 10, 1938: "CCC Enrollees by Counties, 1933-1940," *Blue Book, 1940*, 632; West Virginia Reports, Division of Investigation, Camp Inspection Reports, 1933-1942, boxes 232-35, Records of the Civilian Conservation Corps, RG 35, NA. The National Parks Service film *Recreation Resources of West Virginia* (1935) depicts the work of the CCC in the state parks of West Virginia. Acc. no. III-Nav-193, reel 2, RG 48, Motion Picture Collection, NA.

40. Quoted by Salmond, *Civilian Conservation Corps*, 132.

41. Salmond, *A Southern Rebel*, 74.

42. Final Reports of Forty-Six State Offices, to July, 1943: W.Va., box 7, pp. 12-16, Records of the National Youth Administration, RG 119, NA.

43. Ibid., 16. "Radio Address by Glenn S. Callahan," delivered by the state director over radio station WMMN, Fairmont, Oct. 5, 1937, NYA Publications File, 1935-1942, box 134, Records of the National Youth Administration, RG 119, NA.

44. Final Reports: W.Va., pp. 16-19; NYA Selected Project Files, 1939-1943, West Virginia, A-12, box 17, Records of the National Youth Administration, RG 119, NA.

45. NYA film *Young Man Meets Machine*, NYA project in South Charleston, W. Va., 1940: Acc. no. 1518, RG 199, Motion Picture Collection, NA.

46. *Fifth Biennial Report of the Bureau of Negro Welfare and Statistics, 1929-1932* (Charleston, 1933), 3-5.

47. Posey, *Negro Citizen*, 89-91.

48. Ibid, 108-9.

49. Sitkoff, *A New Deal for Blacks*, 179.

50. Lewis, *Black Coal Miner*, 170-79. See Ulysses Carter Papers, WVRHC.

51. Trotter, *Coal, Class, and Color*, 3-4; Lewis, *Black Coal Miners in America*, 152; Posey, *Negro Citizen*, 36.

52. Lisio, *Hoover, Blacks, and Lily Whites*, 204, 236-37.

53. Weiss, *Farewell to the Party of Lincoln*, 16-17; Bernstein, *Lean Years*, 407-9; Lisio, *Hoover, Blacks, and Lily Whites*, 216-31.

54. Martinsburg *Evening Journal*, April 21, 1932.

55. Shepherdstown *Register*, May 12, 1932.

56. Charleston *Gazette*, Sept. 22, 1932.

57. Quoted by Weiss, *Farewell to the Party of Lincoln*, 31.

58. Weiss, *Farewell to the Party of Lincoln*, 3-4.

59. Quotes from Pittsburgh *Courier* as reprinted in Charleston *Gazette*, July 7, 1933.
60. Posey, *Negro Citizen*, 43-53.
61. Charleston *Gazette*, June 21, 1936.
62. I.J.K. Wells to Louis Howe, Feb. 5, 1934, OF 300, "West Virginia A-Z," box 32, FDR Papers.
63. Thomas H.S. Curd to Governor Kump, Aug. 4, 1933, box 41, Kump Papers.
64. Weiss, *Farewell to the Party of Lincoln*, 58-59.
65. Ibid., 56-58.
66. Ibid., 51-53.
67. Posey, *Negro Citizen*, 106.
68. Rev. H. J. Sawyers, Monongalia County Negro Progressive League, to Kump, June 20, 1935, William Woody, chairman of Young Negro Democratic Association of Beckley, to Kump, June 24, 1935, box 52, Kump Papers.
69. Posey, *Negro Citizen*, 107.
70. Weiss, *Farewell to the Party of Lincoln*, 65-66.
71. Pickett, *For More than Bread*, 49.
72. "Narrative Report, Service and Special Projects under F.E.R.A. Administration to June 1, 1935," box 5, Monongalia County Federal Relief Records, WVRHC. For Ickes role, see Saloutos, *American Farmer and the New Deal*, 156-57. Hareven, *Eleanor Roosevelt*, 96-98.
73. See reports of T.J. McVey on Camp Dunmore, n.d., Camp Decota, March 19, 1934; J.J. McEntee, assistant director, CCC, to T.J. McVey, March 23, 1934; CCC report on Camp Sharples, July 18, 1938, all in Records of the Civilian Conservation Corps, Division of Investigations, Camp Inspection Reports, 1933-1942, box 233, RG 35, NA.
74. Sitkoff, *A New Deal for Blacks*, 80-81.
75. Charleston *Gazette*, Sept. 26, 1937.
76. John J. Corson, assistant director NYA to Glenn S. Callaghan, state director, NYA, Sept. 17, 1935; Callaghan to Corson, Sept. 20, 1935, in Administrative Correspondence with State and Territorial Directors, West Virginia, July 1935-Jan. 1936, box 34, RG 119, NYA, NA.
77. NYA Administrative Report, July-Sept. 1936, box 54, RG 119, NA.
78. *Resident Youth Training Project Sponsored and Operated by West Virginia State College* (Institute: West Virginia State College, n.d.), NYA Publications File, 1935-1942, box 134, RG 119, NA.
79. Weiss, *Farewell to the Party of Lincoln*, 168; press release, n.d., box 2784, WPA: W.Va., RG 69, NA.
80. Charleston *Gazette*, July 3, 1935.
81. Charleston *Gazette*, Jan. 26, 1936.
82. *Blue Book, 1940*, 110; Badger, *New Deal*, 239.
83. Jackson, *Crabgrass Frontier*, 196-203.

84. Charleston *Gazette*, April 1, 1940.
85. Badger, *New Deal*, 239; Williams, *Bicentennial History*, 177.
86. Badger, *New Deal*, 241; McElvaine, *Great Depression*, 303.
87. Smith, *New Deal in the Urban South*, 174; Charleston *Gazette*, Feb. 5, 1938.
88. Charleston *Gazette*, April 7, 1940.
89. Ibid., Jan. 27, 1938.
90. Ibid., May 26, 1940.
91. Ibid., Sept. 8, 1940; Jan. 27, 1938.
92. Ibid., Sept. 3, 1939.
93. Ibid., May 24, 26, 1940.
94. Smith, *New Deal in the Urban South*, 180.
95. Charleston *Gazette*, March 31, 1940; Sept. 6, 1940.
96. Badger, *New Deal*, 241-42. On the "ghettoization" of public housing, see also Jackson, *Crabgrass Frontier*, 219-30.

10. Reluctant New Dealers

1. Useful summaries of these views are found in John Braeman, Bremner, and Brody, eds., *New Deal*, ix-xiii; Argersinger, *Toward A New Deal in Baltimore*, xiii-xiv; Patterson, *New Deal and the States*.
2. Patterson, *New Deal and the States*, 155.
3. See chapter 5 for a discussion of the reforms achieved subsequent to labor's success in organizing the state. See chapter 9 for a discussion of the role of women and African Americans in Democratic politics.
4. An excellent account of the historical background is John Alexander Williams, "Class, Section, and Culture in Nineteenth Century West Virginia Politics," in *Appalachia in the Making*, ed. Pudup, Billings, Waller. See also Williams's *West Virginia: A Bicentennial History*, 115-73. When compared to one-party regimes of the South, the West Virginia system of the thirties appears sui generis. In his classic study of the one-party South, V.O. Key felt that the components of the race-driven, one-party systems of the South were not truly parties but transient factions. The factions in West Virginia fought largely over patronage, but they did seem to have real philosophical differences. On characteristics of one-party factionalism, see Key, *Southern Politics in State and Nation*, 298-316. See also Alan Brinkley, "The New Deal and Southern Politics," in *New Deal and the South*, ed. Cobb and Namorato, 101.
5. Martinsburg *Journal*, July 7, 1939.
6. Clipping, political report by Sam Mallinson, Wheeling *Intelligencer*, Oct. 9, 1935, O'Brien Papers.
7. Charleston *Gazette*, Jan. 9, 1936.
8. Ibid., March 29, 1936.
9. Noting the Kump Kan phenomenon, J.N. Hicks of the Berkeley Young

Democrats had cards printed up that read "Kump Kans Keep Kiddies in Klasses." J.N. Hicks to Kump, April 23, 1934, box 43, Kump Papers.

10. Martinsburg *Journal*, Sept. 27, 1935.
11. Charleston *Gazette*, April 11, 1936.
12. Martinsburg *Journal*, May 1, 1935.
13. It is a tragedy of West Virginia history that most of Neely's personal papers and records were apparently destroyed. Much of the story of West Virginia Democratic politics in the first half of the twentieth century could be told in a Neely biography. Extant letters in other collections suggest that he was a man of considerable wit and humor who lived and breathed politics. A brief account of his life and career can be found in the memorial addresses delivered in the Senate at the time of his death: U.S. Senate, *Memorial Services Held in the Senate and House of Representatives of the Unites States Together with Remarks Presented in Eulogy of Matthew Mansfield Neely, Late a Senator from West Virginia.* For a time during the Depression years, he corresponded regularly with William Edwin Chilton, former senator and publisher of the Charleston *Gazette*, whose papers are in the West Virginia and Regional History Collection, West Virginia University. A small collection of Neely Papers may also be found there. Former reporter Sam Mallinson (a self-described Taft Republican) wrote an interesting recollection of "The Man from Fairmont" (*Let's Set a Spell*, 99-156.)
14. Excerpts from Neely speech, in letter from F. Witcher McCullough to Col. Lawrence Westbrook and Harry Hopkins, May 25, 1936, WPA, West Virginia, box 2755, NA.
15. Mallinson, *Let's Set a Spell*, 99-104.
16. Coffey, "Rush Dew Holt," 84; Charleston *Gazette*, Nov. 1, 1937.
17. Kump to R.S. Reid, Jan. 8, 1935, box 49, Kump Papers.
18. Mallinson, *Let's Set a Spell*, 100-101.
19. Martinsburg *Journal*, May 5, 1935.
20. Charleston *Gazette*, May 9, 1936.
21. Holt, *State Papers and Public Addresses*, v-vi; Morgan, "Homer Adams Holt," *West Virginia Governors*, 148-61.
22. Charleston *Gazette*, May 13, 1936.
23. George I. Neal to James A. Farley, Aug. 6, 1936, OF 300, box 39, "Farley's Correspondence, WV, Wisc., and Wyo.," FDR Papers.
24. Herman Bennett to James A. Farley, September 19, 1936, "Farley's Correspondence," OF 300, 1936 Campaign, West Virginia, FDR Papers.
25. Aubrey Williams, "Two American Traditions," speech before the State Education Association, Charleston, Oct. 25, 1935, in *Addresses and Publications, Book I, 1934-1937*, 29-30, Williams Papers.
26. Quoted in Bennett to Farley, Sept. 19, 1936, FDR Papers.
27. Robert Kelly to James A. Farley, Oct. 29, 1935, Farley to Kelly, Nov. 12, 1935, file 3, Kelly Papers.

28. Robert Kelly to James H. Farley, Aug. 24, 1936, OF 300, "Farley's Correspondence, WV, Wisc, and Wyo," box 39, FDR Papers.
29. Herman Bennett to Farley, Sept. 19, 1936, ibid.
30. John L. Biddle to Farley, Sept. 15, 1936, ibid.
31. Charleston *Daily Mail*, Nov. 1, 1936.
32. Clipping from Wheeling *Intelligencer*, box 2, book XXIII, McCullough Papers.
33. Coffey, "Rush Dew Holt," 140-41, 152-56.
34. Ibid., 156-61. Regarding Holt's attacks on the WPA, see chapter 7, above.
35. Coffey, "Rush Dew Holt," 195-97.
36. Ibid., 190. For an interesting account of Neely on the campaign trail during the primary, see *Charleston Gazette*, May 9, 1936.
37. Coffey, "Rush Dew Holt," 208.
38. Clipping, *Labor Advocate* (1936), box 2755, WPA, West Virginia, RG 69, NA.
39. Coffey, "Rush Dew Holt," 208-15.
40. Ibid., 216-18, 208.
41. *Blue Book, 1937,* 715-34. See photograph in insert following page 100.
42. Holt, *State Papers and Public Addresses*, 5.
43. Holt, "Correspondence Relating to West Virginia's Situation with Respect to the Availability of Funds to Match Federal Grants, and Urging Senator Neely to Present the State's Case before Congress," *State Papers and Public Addresses*, 605-13.
44. Holt, "Inaugural Address, Charleston, January 18, 1937," *State Papers and Public Addresses*, 8-9. See also "Shall the Farmer Be Eternally Mud-Bound and Handicapped Economically, Financially, and Socially?" *West Virginia Farm News*, Dec. 1938, 3, 11.
45. Holt, "Address before Convention of State Education Association, Clarksburg, November 4, 1937," *State Papers and Public Addresses*, 230-40.
46. Holt, "Inaugural Address, Charleston, January 18, 1937," *State Papers and Public Addresses*, 7.
47. Holt, "Address before a District Convention of Rotary Clubs, Clarksburg, April 19, 1937," 157-67; "Address before Convention of State Education Association, Clarksburg, November, 1937," 230-40; "Press Statement on Accomplishments of 1939 Legislature," *State Papers and Public Addresses*, 81-82.
48. Bill Hart to Louis Johnson, May 21, 1938, "West Virginia, National Democratic Committee, 1932-1945," OF 300, box 32, FDR Papers.
49. Homer Holt to Stephen Early, May 11, 1938, "West Virginia, Democratic National Committee, 1933-1945," OF 300, box 32, FDR Papers; Homer Holt to Harry Hopkins, May 9, 1938, "Confidential Political File, 1938-1940,"

box 121, Hopkins Papers. For reports on the 1938 campaign in West Virginia, see Mary H. Brown to James Farley, Oct. 24, 1938, Andrew Edmiston to Farley, Oct. 24, 1938, "Election Forecasts 1938: New York-Wyoming," OF 300, box 41, FDRPL.

50. Charleston *Gazette*, Aug. 8, 1938.
51. Charleston *Gazette*, March 12, 1939.
52. Harris and Krebs, *From Humble Beginnings*, 318-19; Posey, "Labor Movement," 152-54.
53. Charleston *Gazette*, March 11, 1938.
54. Harris and Krebs, *From Humble Beginnings*, 332-33.
55. See summary of state editorial opinion in Charleston *Gazette*, March 20, 1938.
56. Harris and Krebs, *From Humble Beginnings*, 333.
57. Robert H. Zieger, *John L. Lewis*, 114-15.
58. Charleston *Gazette*, April 11, 14, May 14, Aug. 27, 1939. For the text of Holt's note, see Holt, "A Message to the Miners of West Virginia, December 15, 1939," *State Papers and Public Addresses*, 403-404.
59. Quoted in Charleston *Gazette*, Aug. 27, 1939.
60. Ibid., Aug. 29, 1939.
61. Holt, "A Message to the Miners of West Virginia, December 15, 1939," *State Papers and Public Addresses*, 392-93.
62. Leuchtenburg, *Franklin D. Roosevelt*, 280-81; Holt, *State Papers and Public Addresses*, 449; Thomas, "The Nearly Perfect State," 92-93.
63. Leuchtenburg, *Franklin D. Roosevelt*, 280.
64. During the early Depression, Bruce Crawford edited and published *Crawford's Weekly*, a crusading, left-wing labor newspaper in Norton, Virginia. Before becoming director of the West Virginia Writers Project, Crawford had served editor of the Bluefield *Sunset-News*. Thomas, "Nearly Perfect State," 93-94.
65. Ibid., 91-108.
66. Thomas, "Nearly Perfect State," 99-103.
67. Ibid., 107-8; Cherniak, *Hawk's Nest Incident*, 108-9. See also chapter two, above.
68. The book, including the controversial chapter on labor, was published in 1941, after Neely became governor. Thomas, "The Nearly Perfect State," 98-104.
69. Ibid., 97.
70. Charleston *Gazette*, Feb. 3, March 3, April 13, 1940; Williams, *Bicentennial History*, 167; Maddox, *Senatorial Career of Harley Martin Kilgore*, 1-21.
71. Jack Stinnett, "Rush D. Holt's Five Years Show 'How Not to Be Senate Success,'" Martinsburg *Journal*, Dec. 17, 1940; Coffey, "Isolation and Pacifism," 1-14.

72. These characterizations of Holt are the author's own but rely heavily on material in Coffey, "Rush Dew Holt," 180-81 and passim. For Holt's role in the Hawks Nest matter, see Cherniak, *Hawk's Nest Incident,* 78.

73. Kump to Franklin D. Roosevelt, April 13, 1940, Kump to Edwin Watson, April 22, 1940, "West Virginia Democratic National Committee, 1933-1945," OF 300, box 32, FDR Papers.

74. For a discussion of Roosevelt and his dealings with the southern Democratic organizations, see Alan Brinkley, "The New Deal and Southern Politics," in *New Deal and the South,* ed. Cobb and Namorato, 101.

75. Charleston *Gazette,* Feb. 1, Oct. 27, 1940; John B. Easton to John L. Lewis, Oct. 27, 1940, West Virginia Industrial Union Council Archives, box 3, WVRHC.

76. Dubofsky and Van Tine, *John L. Lewis,* 361-62. For a similar view, see McFarland, *Roosevelt, Lewis, and the New Deal,* 113-16.

77. Holt, "The Democratic Primary of 1940: A Radio Address, April 20, 1940," *State Papers and Public Addresses,* 447-57.

78. Cartoon in f. 6, box 2, H.A. Holt Papers.

79. It is unclear if this cartoon was used in the campaign. See f. 6, box 2, H.A. Holt Papers.

80. Ibid.

81. Charleston *Gazette,* April 29, 1940; f. 6, box 2, H.A. Holt Papers.

82. Charleston *Gazette,* March 31, 1940.

83. Charleston *Gazette,* May 15, 16, 1940.

84. Williams, *Bicentennial History,* 167.

85. Neely, *State Papers and Public Addresses,* 185.

86. "Memorandum for the President," by E.M.W. in OF 300, box 32, FDR Papers. Neely said that "he promised Rosier's wife and children that he would support their father." Neely probably appointed Rosier rather than an experienced politician with the idea that he might wish to return to the Senate himself after two years. He did attempt to return in 1942 and was defeated by the Republican, Chapman Revercomb. Morgan, *West Virginia Governors,* 171.

87. Rice and Brown, *West Virginia,* 272; Maddox, *Senatorial Career of Harley Martin Kilgore,* 30-41.

88. Holt, "Remarks at a Testimonial Dinner Given by a Group of Friends," *State Papers and Public Addresses,* 510-11.

89. On Kentucky's troubles, see Hevener, *Which Side Are You On?*

90. Thomas, "Nearly Perfect State," 105 Williams, *Bicentennial History,* 163; "Homer Adams Holt," *Biographical Directory of Governors,* ed. Sobel and Raimo, 1706-7.

91. Morgan, "Herman Guy Kump," *West Virginia Governors,* 147.

92. Brinkley, *The End of Reform,* 137-46; McElvaine, *The Great Depression,* 306-11.

Epilogue. From Nearly Perfect to Almost Heaven

1. See, for example, Biles, *South and the New Deal*, and Salstrom, *Appalachia's Path to Dependency*.

2. Badger, *New Deal*, 310; Lichtenstein, "From Corporatism to Collective Bargaining," 128-29; Bernstein, *Great Depression*.

3. Williams, *Bicentennial History*, 169.

4. Key, *Southern Politics in State and Nation*, 27, quoted by Heinemann, *Depression and New Deal in Virginia*, 179.

5. Heinemann, *Depression and New Deal in Virginia*, 179.

6. In 1953, Governor William Casey Marland proposed a severance tax on coal and other minerals. The coal industry rallied a determined opposition to defeat the plan. Lutz, *From Governor to Cabby*, 41-59.

7. Dubofsky and Van Tine, *John L. Lewis*, 500-509; Lichtenstein, "From Corporatism to Collective Bargaining," 142-43.

8. *Blue Book, 1987*, 1050. For discussions of postwar trends in the West Virginia coal industry, see Kirby, *Rural Worlds Lost*, 109, and Munn, "Development of Strip Mining," 87-92. For a discussion of the postwar changes in the coal industry, see Dubofsky and Van Tine, *John L. Lewis*, 494-95.

9. U.S. Department of Commerce, Bureau of the Census, 458; *Blue Book, 1987*, 1005; Williams, *Bicentennial History*, 178.

10. Tunley, "Strange Case of West Virginia," 19-20, 64-65.

11. White, *Making of the President 1960*, 116.

12. Williams, *Bicentennial History*, 187-88.

13. Biles, *South and the New Deal*, passim.

14. Tom D. Miller, *Who Owns West Virginia?* (Huntington *Herald Advertiser and Herald-Dispatch*, 1974), cited by Williams, *Bicentennial History*, 203. See also Lutz, *From Governor to Cabby*, 178-81.

15. Tunley, "Strange Case of West Virginia," 65; Ben A. Franklin, "Appalachia Grant Will Fight Resistance to Change," *New York Times*, Jan. 6, 1967.

Bibliography

Primary Sources

MANUSCRIPT COLLECTIONS

Franklin D. Roosevelt Library (FDRL), Hyde Park, New York.
    Lorena Hickok Papers
    Harry Hopkins Papers
    Eleanor Roosevelt Papers
    Franklin D. Roosevelt Papers
    Aubrey Williams Papers
Special Collections Division (SCMU), William E. Morrow Library, Marshall University, Huntington.
    Frank Witcher McCullough Papers
    Oral History of Appalachia
    West Virginia Miners Union (articles)
West Virginia and Regional History Collection (WVRHC), West Virginia University Library, Morgantown.
    Ulysses Carter Papers
    William Edwin Chilton Papers
    Mary Behner Christopher Scrapbooks
    Andrew Edmiston, Jr., Papers
    Howard Mason Gore Papers
    Walter Simms Hallanan Papers
    Henry Drury Hatfield Papers
    Homer Adams Holt Papers
    Rush Dew Holt Papers
    Kanawha County Relief Administration, Records, 1933-1934
    Robert G. Kelly Papers
    Herman Guy Kump Papers
    Samuel T. Mallinson Papers
    Matthew Mansfield Neely Scrapbooks (microfilm)
    Monongalia County Federal Relief Records
    William Smithe O'Brien Papers
    Scotts Run Community Center (scrapbooks)
    Hugh Ike Shott Papers
    Clarence Edwin Smith Papers
    Thomas C. Townsend Scrapbook (microfilm)

Franklin Trubee Papers
William Woodson Trent Papers
George Selden Wallace Papers
West Virginia League of Municipalities Papers, 1935-1940
West Virginia State Industrial Union Council, CIO, Archives
Writers Program Papers, WPA

West Virginia Department of Archives and History, Charleston.
Mary Behner Christopher Diary

West Virginia State College, Institute.
Special Collections

Library of Congress, Music Division, Recording Laboratory.
"Songs and Ballads of the Bituminous Miners," sound disc, recorded and edited by George Korson, LCN R65-2144.

National Archives, Washington, D.C.
Bureau of Agricultural Economics, Records of the Appalachian Regional Office, RG 83.
Civilian Conservation Corps Records, RG 35.
Civil Works Administration Records, RG 69.
Extension Service Records, RG 33
Federal Emergency Relief Administration Records, RG 69.
National Recovery Administration Records, RG 9
National Youth Administration Records, RG 119.
Motion Picture Collection
"A Better West Virginia." WPA, 1937. Acc 330, RG 69.
"Flood Special." WPA, 1936. Acc. 330, RG 69.
"The State Parks of West Virginia." CCC and Dept. Int., 1935. Acc III-Nav-193, RG 48.
"Young Man Meets Machine." South Charleston, W.Va., NYA, 1940. Acc 1518, RG 119.
"Youth Lends A Hand—A Study of Volunteer Work Camps." Harmon Foundation/American Friends Service Committee, 1940. Includes "Idle Mining Camp" (Scotts Run). Acc NN 368-14.
President's Office for Unemployment Relief, R.G. 73
Works Progress Administration Records. RG 69

UNITED STATES GOVERNMENT PUBLICATIONS

(All published in Washington, D.C., by the Government Printing Office unless otherwise indicated).

Asch, Benita, and A.R. Mangus. *Farmers on Relief and Rehabilitation.* Works Progress Administration, Division of Social Research, Monograph VIII. 1937; New York: Da Capo Press, 1971.

Chapman, Oscar L. (chair). *Report of the Committee on the Upper Monongahala Valley, West Virginia.* 1935.

Bibliography

Department of Agriculture. *Economic and Social Problems and Conditions of the Southern Appalachians.* 1935.
Department of Commerce, Bureau of the Census. *Historical Statistics of the United States: Colonial Times to 1970.* Bicentennial ed., pt. I, 1975.
Federal Works Administration. *Final Statistical Report of the Federal Emergency Relief Administration.* 1942.
National Youth Administration. *Final Report for the State of West Virginia.* 1943.
United States Senate. *Memorial Services Held in the Senate and House of Representatives of the United States Together with Remarks Presented in Eulogy of Matthew Mansfield Neely, Late a Senator from West Virginia.* 1958.

WEST VIRGINIA STATE DOCUMENTS
(All published in Charleston unless otherwise indicated)
Beehler, William N. *Relief, Work, and Rehabilitation: West Virginia Relief Administration, August, 1932 to November 1, 1934.* 1934.
Blue Book (*West Virginia Legislative Hand Book and Manual and Official Register*). Vols. 13-25, 1928-1941 (not published in 1932).
Bureau of Negro Welfare and Statistics. *Biennial Report. 1927-1942.*
Burke, Stephen Patrick. *Yardsticks for Social Planning.* 1935.
Commissioner of Labor. *Eighteenth Biennial Report of the Bureau of Labor, 1925-1926.* 1926.
―――. *Twenty-First Biennial Report of the Department of Labor.* 1933.
Conley, William Gustavus. *State Papers and Public Addresses.* 1933.
Department of Agriculture. *West Virginia: America's New Vacationland*, ed. Ross B. Johnston. 1930.
Department of Education. *Biennial Report of the State Superintendent of Free Schools.* 1932-1938.
Department of Public Assistance. *Report of the Department of Public Assistance.* 1936-1941.
Department of Public Welfare. *Biennial Report of the State of West Virginia Department of Public Welfare, July 1 1934 to July 1, 1936.* 1936.
Estill, Calvert L. *Organization and Activities of the State of West Virginia Department of Public Welfare, July 1, 1931 to January 1, 1933 and of the State of West Virginia Unemployment Relief Administration, August 19, 1932 to January 1, 1933.* 1933.
Holt, Homer Adams. *State Papers and Public Addresses: Homer Adams Holt, Twentieth Governor of West Virginia, January 18, 1937 to January 13, 1941.* Comp. William E. Hughes. Jarrett Printing, n.d.
―――. *Thirty-Sixth Biennial Report and Official Opinions of the Attorney General of the State of West Virginia, July 1, 1934-June 30, 1936.* 1936.
Kump, Herman Guy. *State Papers and Public Addresses: H.G. Kump, Nine-*

teenth Governor of West Virginia, March 4, 1933-January 18, 1937, comp. James W. Harris, Jr. Charleston, 1937.

Sly, John Fairfield, Stephen Patrick Burke, and V. Frank Parry. *Indirect Taxes: Sharing the Costs of Government.* West Virginia University Bureau of Government Research, Public Affairs Bulletin no. 9. Morgantown, 1934.

———. *Rebuilding in West Virginia: Fifteen Months of Legislation, (1933-1934).* West Virginia University Bureau of Government Research, Public Affairs Bulletin no. 8. 1934. Morgantown, 1934.

——— and George A. Shipman. *Tax Limitation in West Virginia: Relief to the Farm and Home.* West Virginia University Bureau for Government Research, Public Affairs Bulletin no. 8. Morgantown, 1934.

West Virginia Planning Board. *Report of the Coordinating Committee in the Field of Agriculture and Rural Life.* July 1, 1946.

———. *A Study of the People of West Virginia.* 1937.

West Virginia Road Commission. *Report of the State Road Commission of West Virginia, July 1, 1928-July 1 1929.* 1929.

West Virginia Writers Project. *West Virginia: A Guide to the Mountain State.* American Guide series. New York: Oxford University Press, 1941.

NEWSPAPERS

Complete runs of the Democratic Charleston *Gazette*, the largest circulation paper in the state, and the Martinsburg *Journal*, an Ogden Press Republican newspaper of the eastern panhandle, were read for the period 1929-1941. Numerous other newspapers were consulted for particular episodes or periods, as noted.

PERIODICALS

West Virginia Farm News, 1928-1941.
West Virginia Review, 1928-1940.
West Virginia School Journal, 1928-1941.

OTHER CONTEMPORARY PUBLISHED SOURCES

Becker, Paul. "Red House." *West Virginia Review* 17 (Nov. 1939): 42.

Beury, William. "The Social Aspects of Coal Mines." In *Proceedings of the West Virginia Coal Mining Institute, Twenty-Seventh Annual Meeting, Bluefield, West Virginia, December 5-6, 1933,* 63-77. Morgantown, 1933.

Conley, Philip Mallory. *West Virginia Encyclopedia.* Charleston: West Virginia Publishing, 1929.

Cook, Roy Bird. "Our New Governor—Homer A. Holt." *West Virginia Review* 14 (Dec. 1936): 98, 123.

Cook, William Cassius. "Problems of School Finance in West Virginia." *West Virginia School Journal* 60 (April 1932): 11, 30.

Crawford, Bruce. "A Guide to West Virginia." *West Virginia Review* (Oct. 1939): 10-11, 20.

"Electricity Can Transform Farm Life. *West Virginia Farm News* (Oct. 1935): 3.

Elmore, Earle L. "How National Defense Preparations Affect West Virginia." *West Virginia Review* 18 (Oct. 1940): 14-15, 31.

"Farm Housing Survey Shows Real Needs." *West Virginia Farm News* (June 1934): 2-3.

Frame, Nat Terry. *Grassroots in West Virginia: Agriculture and Rural Life*. Part 2, *History of Agriculture, Horticulture, and Home Economics Extension, From the Close of World War One to the Beginning of the "New Deal"*. Inwood, W.Va., n.p., n.d.

———. "The West Virginia Farm Bureau and the New Deal." *West Virginia Farm News* (Aug. 1933): 2, 8.

Gist, R.H. "Five Years of Agricultural Adjustment in West Virginia." *Proceedings of the West Virginia Academy of Science* 10 (1939): 137-41.

Goodall, Cecille. "Centralizing Tendencies in Government." *West Virginia Review* 11 (April 1934): 196-97.

———. "A New Era of Leadership in West Virginia." *West Virginia Review* 10 (March 1933): 164-67.

———. "Where There's a Will . . ." *West Virginia Review* 11 (July 1934): 293, 306.

Goodrich, Carter. *Migration and Economic Opportunity: The Report of the Study of Population Distribution*. Philadelphia: Univ. of Pennsylvania Press, 1936.

Harris, T.L. "Public Welfare in West Virginia." *Proceedings of the West Virginia Academy of Science* 10 (1936): 181-89.

Humphrey, Everett S. "Our Farm Bureau Faces the Future." *West Virginia Farm News* (Oct. 1934): 1, 6.

Jarrett, Howard S. "Industrial Conditions in West Virginia at a Glance." *West Virginia Review* 6 (Dec. 1928): 83; 7 (Jan. 1929): 108.

Johnson, Hugh. *The Blue Eagle from Egg to Earth*. Garden City, N.Y.: Doubleday, Doran, 1935.

Laing, James T. "Negro Migration to the Mine Fields of West Virginia." *Proceedings of the West Virginia Academy of Science* 10 (1936): 177-81.

Long, Eloise Campbell. "Red House." *West Virginia Review* 12 (Dec. 1934): 89, 93.

Lyon, Leverett S., et al. *The National Recovery Administration, Analysis and Appraisal*. Washington, D.C: Brookings Institution, 1935.

Morris, Homer Lawrence. *The Plight of the Bituminous Coal Miner*. Philadelphia: Univ. of Pennsylvania Press, 1934.

National Child Labor Committee. *Rural Child Welfare: An Inquiry by the National Child Labor Committee Based upon Conditions in West Virginia*. New York: Macmillan, 1922.

National Committee for Defense of Political Prisoners. *Harlan Miners Speak: Report on Terrorism in the Kentucky Coal Fields.* 1932; New York: Da Capo Press, 1970.

Parker, Glen Lawhon. *The Coal Industry: A Study in Social Control.* Washington, D.C.: American Council on Public Affairs, 1940.

Pollak, Katharine H. "Life and Death Struggle Looms in Coal Fields of West Virginia." *Labor Age* (Nov. 1931): 5-7.

Posey, Thomas Edward. *The Negro Citizen of West Virginia.* Institute: Press of West Virginia State College, 1934.

"Preserve Food for Winter Relief." *West Virginia Farm News* (Oct. 1931): 3.

Rapking, A. H. "The Mission of the Country Church." *West Virginia Farm News* (Aug. 1930): 3, 7.

Regier, C. C. "Our Fundamental Social Problem." *Proceedings of the West Virginia Academy of Science* 8 (March 15, 1933): 1564-69.

Report of the Child Relief Work in the Bituminous Coal Fields by the American Friends Service Committee, September 1, 1931-August 1, 1932. 1932.

Ross, Malcolm. "Lifting the Coal Mines Out of the Murk." *New York Times Magazine* (Oct. 1, 1933): 4-5.

"Rural Electrification Looking Up for West Virginia." *West Virginia Farm News* (March 1937): 3, 12.

"Rural Electrification Movement in West Virginia Marks New Milestone." *West Virginia Farm News* (June 1940): 3-7.

"Shall the Farmer Be Eternally Mud-Bound and Handicapped Economically, Financially, and Socially?" *West Virginia Farm News* (Dec. 1938): 3, 11.

Sly, John F. "The Way of the Legislator Is Hard." *West Virginia Review* 10 (Jan. 1933): 116-17.

Sullivan, Jesse V. "Coal Faces the Future." *West Virginia Review* 10 (July 1933): 293.

———. "The TVA and West Virginia Industry." *West Virginia Review* 12 (Jan. 1935): 110-11, 127.

———. "West Virginia, the Nation's Treasure Chest." *West Virginia Review* 6 (July 1929): 390-91, 408.

Stutler, Boyd B. "West Virginia's Magnificent State Capital." *West Virginia Review* 9 (July 1932): 401-3, 426.

"Sun-Up Comes to Many Rural West Virginians." *West Virginia Farm News* (June 1938): 3.

Tippet, Thomas. "W.Va. Mine Workers Carry On." *Labor Age* (Nov. 1931): 9-10, 28.

Trapnell, Edward R. "The Businessman and the Farmer." *West Virginia Review* 18 (Nov. 1940): 46, 54.

Trent, William Woodson. "All Levies within the Limit." *West Virginia School Journal* 62 (Oct. 1933): 16.

West, Mabel Ann. "A New Venture in Security." *West Virginia Review* 15 (Dec. 1937): 76-77, 91-92.

———. "West Virginia's Problem of Public Care." *West Virginia Review* 15 (Nov. 1937): 54-55, 63.

What of West Virginia in 1930?" *West Virginia Review* 7 (Jan. 1930): 110-11.

Secondary Works

Ambler, Charles Henry. *A History of Education in West Virginia.* Huntington: Standard Printing, 1951.

Ambler, Charles Henry, and Festus Paul Summers. *West Virginia, The Mountain State.* Englewood Cliffs, N.J.: Prentice-Hall, 1958.

Argersinger, Jo Ann. *Toward a New Deal in Baltimore: People and Government in the Great Depression.* Chapel Hill: Univ. of North Carolina Press, 1988.

Badger, Anthony J. *The New Deal: The Depression Years, 1933-1940.* New York: Hill and Wang, 1989.

———. *North Carolina and the New Deal.* Raleigh: North Carolina Department of Cultural Resources, 1981.

———. *Prosperity Road: The New Deal, Tobacco, and North Carolina.* Chapel Hill: Univ. of North Carolina Press, 1980.

Baldwin, Sidney. *Poverty and Politics: The Rise and Decline of the Farm Security Administration.* Chapel Hill: Univ. of North Carolina Press, 1968.

Baker, Ralph Hillis. *The National Bituminous Coal Commission: Administration of the Bituminous Coal Act, 1937-1941.* Baltimore: Johns Hopkins Univ. Press, 1941.

Baratz, Morton S. *The Union and the Coal Industry.* 1955; Port Washington, N.Y.: Kennikat Press, 1973.

Beezer, Bruce G. "Arthurdale: An Experiment in Community Education." *West Virginia History* 36 (Oct. 1974): 17-36.

Bellush, Bernard. *The Failure of the NRA.* New York: W.W. Norton, 1975.

Bernstein, Irving. *A Caring Society: The New Deal, the Worker, and the Great Depression.* Boston: Houghton-Mifflin, 1985.

———. *The Lean Years: A History of the American Worker, 1920-1933.* Boston: Houghton-Mifflin, 1960.

———. *Turbulent Years: A History of the American Worker, 1933-1941.* Boston: Hougton-Mifflin, 1970.

Bernstein, Michael A. *The Great Depression: Delayed Recovery and Economic Change in America, 1929-1939.* New York: Cambridge Univ. Press, 1987.

Biles, Roger. *The South and the New Deal.* Lexington: Univ. Press of Kentucky, 1994.

Blakey, George T. *Hard Times and New Deal in Kentucky, 1929-1939.* Lexington: Univ. Press of Kentucky, 1986.

Blumberg, Barbara. *The New Deal and the Unemployed: The View from New York City.* Lewisburg, Pa.: Bucknell Univ. Press, 1979.

Bradford, Richard H. "Religion and Politics: Alfred E. Smith and the Election of 1928 in West Virginia." *West Virginia History* 36 (April 1975): 213-24.

Braeman, John, Robert H. Bremner, and David Brody, eds. *The New Deal: The State and Local Levels.* Columbus: Ohio State Univ. Press, 1975.

Brinkley, Alan, *The End of Reform: New Deal Liberalism in Recession and War.* New York: Alfred A. Knopf, 1995.

Brock, William R. *Welfare, Democracy, and the New Deal.* Cambridge: Cambridge Univ. Press, 1988.

Brown, D. Clayton. *Electricity for Rural America.* Westport, Conn.: Greenwood Press, 1980.

Burner, David. *Herbert Hoover: A Public Life.* New York: Alfred A. Knopf, 1978.

Charles, Searle F. *Minister of Relief: Harry Hopkins and the Depression.* Syracuse: Syracuse Univ. Press, 1963.

Cherniak, Martin. *The Hawk's Nest Incident: America's Worst Industrial Disaster.* New Haven: Yale Univ. Press, 1986.

Clarkson, Roy B. *Tumult on the Mountains: Lumbering in West Virginia, 1770-1920.* Parsons, W.Va.: McClain Printing, 1964.

Cobb, James C., and Michael Namorato, eds. *The New Deal and the South.* Jackson: Univ. Press of Mississippi, 1984.

Coffey, William E. "Isolation and Pacificism: Senator Rush D. Holt and American Foreign Policy." *West Virginia History* 51 (1992): 1-14.

———. "Political Chrysalis: The United Mine Workers Union in the Election of 1934." *West Virginia History* 45 (1984): 79-87.

———. "Rush Dew Holt: The Boy Senator, 1905-1942." Ph.D. diss., West Virginia University, 1970.

Comstock, Jim, ed. *West Virginia Heritage Encyclopedia.* Richwood: Comstock, 1974-1976.

Conkin, Paul K. *Tomorrow a New World: The New Deal Community Program.* Ithaca: Cornell Univ. Press, 1959.

Coode, Thomas H., and John F. Bauman. *People, Poverty, and Politics: Pennsylvania During the Great Depression.* Lewisburg, Pa.: Bucknell Univ. Press, 1981.

Coode, Thomas H., and Dennis Fabbri. "The New Deal's Arthurdale Project in West Virginia." *West Virginia History* 36 (July 1975): 291-308.

Coode, Thomas H., and Agnes M. Riggs. "The Private Papers of West Virginia's 'Boy Senator,' Rush D. Holt." *West Virginia History* 35 (July 1974): 296-318.

Corbin, David Alan. *Life, Work and Rebellion in the Coal Fields: The Southern West Virginia Miners, 1880-1922.* Urbana: Univ. of Illinois Press, 1981.

———, ed. *The West Virginia Mine Wars: An Anthology.* Charleston: Appalachian Editions, 1990.

Bibliography

Craig, Douglas B. *After Wilson: The Struggle for the Democratic Party, 1920-1934.* Chapel Hill and London: Univ. of North Carolina Press, 1992.

Daniel, Pete. *Breaking the Land: The Transformation of Cotton, Tobacco, and Rice Cultures since 1980.* Urbana and Chicago: Univ. of Illinois Press, 1985.

Daniels, Roger. *The Bonus March: An Episode of the Great Depression.* Westport, Conn.: Greenwood, 1971.

Dix, Keith. *What's a Coal Miner to Do?: The Mechanization of Coal Mining.* Pittsburgh: Univ. of Pittsburgh Press, 1988.

Dubofsky, Melvyn, and Warren Van Tine. *John L. Lewis: A Biography.* New York: Quadrangle, New York Times, 1977.

Eagan, Shirley C. "Women's Work, Never Done: West Virginia Farm Women, 1880s-1920s." *West Virginia History* 49 (1990): 21-36.

Effland, Anne Wallace. "A Profile of Political Activists: Women of the West Virginia Suffrage Movement." *West Virginia History* 49 (1990): 103-14.

Eller, Ronald D. *Miners, Millhands, and Mountaineers: Industrialization of the Appalachian South, 1880-1930.* Knoxville: Univ. of Tennessee Press, 1982.

Fink, Gary, and Merl E. Reed, eds. *Essays in Southern Labor History: Selected Papers, Southern Labor History Conference, 1976.* Contributions in Economics and Economic History, no. 16. Westport and London: Greenwood Press, 1977.

Fishback, Price V. *Soft Coal, Hard Choices: The Economic Welfare of Bituminous Coal Miners, 1890-1930.* New York, Oxford: Oxford Univ. Press, 1992.

Fite, Gilbert C. *Cotton Fields No More: Southern Agriculture, 1865-1980.* Lexington: Univ. Press of Kentucky, 1984.

Flynt, Wayne. "The New Deal and Southern Labor." In *The New Deal and the South.* Ed. James C. Cobb and Michael Namorato. Jackson: Univ. of Mississippi Press, 1984.

Forbes, Harold. *West Virginia History: A Bibliography and Guide to Research.* Morgantown: West Virginia Univ. Press, 1981.

Fraser, Steve, and Gary Gerstle, eds. *The Rise and Fall of the New Deal Order, 1930-1980.* Princeton: Princeton Univ. Press, 1989.

Galambos, Louis. "The Emerging Organizational Synthesis in American History." *Business History Review* 44 (Autumn 1970): 279-90.

Galbraith, John Kenneth. *The Great Crash, 1929.* Boston: Houghton Mifflin, 1954.

Garraty, John A. *The Great Depression: An Inquiry into the Causes, Course, and Consequences of the Worldwide Depression of the Nineteen-Thirties, As Seen by Contemporaries and in the Light of History.* New York: Harcourt, Brace, Jovanovich, 1986.

Gatrell, Albert Steven. "Herman Guy Kump: A Political Profile." Ph.D. diss., West Virginia Univ., 1967.

———. "Herman Guy Kump and the West Virginia Fiscal Crisis of 1933." *West Virginia History* 42 (Spring-Summer 1981): 249-84.

Gladwin, Lee A. "Arthurdale: Adventure into Utopia." *West Virginia History* 28, no. 4 (July 1967): 305-17.

Gordon, Colin. *New Deals: Business Labor and Politics in America, 1929-1935.* New York: Cambridge Univ. Press, 1994.

Green, Archie. *Only a Miner: Studies in Recorded Coal Mining Songs.* Urbana: Univ. of Illinois Press, 1972.

Greene, Janet W. "Strategies for Survival: Women's Work in the Southern West Virginia Coal Camps." *West Virginia History* 49 (1990): 37-54.

Hadsell, Richard M., and William E. Coffey. "From Law and Order to Class Welfare: Baldwin-Felts Detectives in the Southern West Virginia Coal Fields." *West Virginia History* 40 (Spring 1979): 268-86.

Haid, Stephen Edward. "Arthurdale: An Experiment in Community Planning." Ph.D. diss., West Virginia University, 1975.

Hamilton, David E. *From New Day to New Deal: American Farm Policy from Hoover to Roosevelt.* Chapel Hill: Univ. of North Carolina Press, 1991.

———. "Herbert Hoover and the Great Drought of 1930." *Journal of American History* 68 (March 1982): 850-75.

Harbaugh, William H. *Lawyer's Lawyer: The Life of John W. Davis.* New York: Oxford Univ. Press, 1973.

Hareven, Tamara. *Eleanor Roosevelt: An American Conscience.* New York: Quadrangle Books, 1968.

Harris, Evelyn L.K., and Frank J. Krebs. *From Humble Beginnings: West Virginia State Federation of Labor.* Charleston: West Virginia Labor History Publishing Fund, 1960.

Hawley, Ellis W. *The Great War and the Search for Modern Order: A History of the American People and Their Institutions, 1917-1933.* 2d ed. New York: St. Martin's Press, 1992.

———. *The New Deal and the Problem of Monopoly: A Study in Economic Ambivalence.* Princeton: Princeton Univ. Press, 1966.

———. "Secretary Hoover and the Bituminous Coal Problem." *Business History Review* 42 (Autumn 1968): 247-70.

Heinemann, Ronald L. *Depression and New Deal in Virginia: The Enduring Dominion.* Charlottesville: Univ. of Virginia Press, 1983.

Hennen, John C. *The Americanization of West Virginia: Creating a Modern Industrial State.* Lexington: Univ. Press of Kentucky, 1996.

Hensley, Frances S., ed. *Missing Chapters II: West Virginia Women in History.* Charleston: West Virginia Women's Commission, 1986.

———. "Women in the Industrial Work Force in West Virginia, 1880-1945." *West Virginia History* 49 (1990): 114-24.

Hevener, John W. *Which Side Are You On? Harlan County Coal Miners, 1931-1939.* Urbana: Univ. of Illinois Press, 1978.

Hickok, Lorena A. *Reluctant First Lady.* New York: Dodd, Mead, 1962.
Hodges, James A. *New Deal Labor Policy and the Southern Cotton Textile Industry, 1933-1941.* Knoxville: Univ. of Tennessee Press, 1986.
Howe, Barbara J. "West Virginia Women's Organizations, 1880s-1930 or 'Unsexed Termagants . . . Help the World Along." *West Virginia History* 49 (1990): 81-102.
Humphreys, Gertrude. *Adventures in Good Living: West Virginia Extension Homemakers Council.* Parsons: McClain Printing, 1972.
Jackson, Kenneth T. *Crabgrass Frontier: The Suburbanization of the United States.* New York: Oxford Univ. Press, 1985.
Jenrette, Jerra. "Labor Management Conflict in the Eastern Panhandle: Perfection Garment Company Battles the ILGWU." *West Virginia History* 52 (1993):109-26.
Johnson, James P. *The Politics of Soft Coal: The Bituminous Industry from World War I through the New Deal.* Urbana: Univ. of Illinois Press, 1979.
Kennedy, Susan Estabrook. *The Banking Crisis of 1933.* Lexington: Univ. Press of Kentucky, 1973.
Kessler-Harris, Alice. *Out to Work: A History of Wage-Earning Women in the United States.* New York: Oxford Univ. Press, 1982.
———. *A Woman's Wage: Historical Earnings and Social Consequences.* Lexington: Univ. Press of Kentucky, 1990.
Key, V.O. *Southern Politics in State and Nation.* New York: Alfred A. Knopf, 1949.
Kirby, Jack Temple. *Rural Worlds Lost: The American South, 1920-1960.* Baton Rouge and London: Louisiana State Univ. Press, 1987.
Lee, Howard B. *Bloodletting in Appalachia: The Story of West Virginia's Four Major Mine Wars and Other Thrilling Incidents of Its Coal Fields.* Morgantown: West Virginia Univ. Press, 1969.
Lewis, Ronald L. *Black Coal Miners in America: Race, Class, and Community Conflict, 1780-1980.* Lexington: Univ. Press of Kentucky, 1987.
Leuchtenburg, William E. *Franklin D. Roosevelt and the New Deal, 1932-1940.* New York: Harper and Row, 1963.
———. *The Perils of Prosperity, 1914-1932.* Chicago: Univ. of Chicago Press, 1958.
Lichtenstein, Nelson. "From Corporatism to Collective Bargaining: Organized Labor and the Eclipse of Social Democracy in the Postwar Era." In *The Rise and Fall of the New Deal Order, 1930-1980,* ed. Steve Fraser and Gary Gerstle, 32-54. Princeton: Princeton Univ. Press, 1989.
Lisio, Donald J. *Hoover, Blacks, and Lily Whites: A Study of Southern Strategies.* Chapel Hill: Univ. of North Carolina Press, 1985.
———. *The President and Protest: Hoover, Conspiracy, and the Bonus Riot.* Columbia: Univ. of Missouri Press, 1974.
Longin, Thomas C. "Coal, Congress, and the Courts: The Bituminous Coal

Industry and the New Deal." *West Virginia History* 35 (Jan. 1974): 100-131.

Lunt, Richard D. *Law and Order vs the Miners: West Virginia 1906-1933*. Charleston: Appalachian Editions, 1992.

Lutz, Paul F. *From Governor to Cabby: The Political Career and Tragic Death of West Virginia's William Casey Marland, 1950-1965*. Huntington: Marshall Univ. Library Associates, 1996.

McElvaine, Robert S. *The Great Depression: America 1929-1941*. New York: Times Books, 1984.

McFarland, Charles K. *Roosevelt, Lewis and the New Deal, 1933-1940*. Fort Worth: Texas Christian Univ. Press, 1970.

McJimsey, George. *Harry Hopkins, Ally of the Poor and Defender of Democracy*. Cambridge: Harvard Univ. Press. 1987.

Macmahon, Arthur W., John D. Millett and Gladys Ogden. *The Administration of Federal Work Relief*. 1941; New York: Da Capo Press, 1971.

McNeill, Louise. *The Milkweed Ladies*. Pittsburgh: Univ. of Pittsburgh Press, 1988.

Maddox, Robert Franklin. *The Senatorial Career of Harley Martin Kilgore*. East Rockaway, N.Y.: Cummings and Hathaway, 1997.

Mallinson, Sam T. *Let's Set a Spell*. Charleston: Education Foundation, 1961.

Mangione, Jerre. *The Dream and the Deal: The Federal Writers Project, 1935-1943*. New York: Avon Books, 1972.

Melosh, Barbara. "Recovery and Revision: Women's History and West Virginia." *West Virginia History* 49 (1990): 3-6.

Mertz, Paul E. *New Deal Policy and Southern Rural Poverty*. Baton Rouge and London: Louisiana State Univ. Press, 1978.

Mitchell, Broadus. *Depression Decade: From New Era through New Deal, 1929-1941*. New York: Harper and Row, 1969.

Morgan, John G. *West Virginia Governors, 1863-1980*. Charleston: Charleston Newspapers, 1980.

Munn, Robert F. "The Development of Strip Mining in Southern Appalachia." *Appalachian Journal* 3 (Autumn 1975): 87-92.

Nash, Gerald D. *The Crucial Era: The Great Depression and World War II*. 2d ed. New York: St. Martin's Press, 1992.

Nye, David E. *Electrifying America: Social Meanings of a New Technology, 1880-1940*. Cambridge, London: MIT Press, 1991.

Ohl, John Kennedy. *Hugh S. Johnson and the New Deal*. Dekalb: Northern Illinois Univ. Press, 1985.

Olsen, James S. "The Depths of the Great Depression: Economic Collapse in West Virginia, 1932-1933. *West Virginia History* 38 (April 1977): 214-35.

———. *Saving Capitalism: The Reconstruction Finance Corporation and the New Deal, 1933-1940*. Princeton: Princeton Univ. Press, 1988.

Pavlick, Anthony L. *Towards Solving the Low-Income Problem of Small Farm-*

ers in the Appalachian Area. West Virginia Univ. Experiment Station, Bulletin 499T. Morgantown, June, 1964.

Parrish, Michael E. *Anxious Decades: America in Prosperity and Depression, 1920-1941.* New York: W.W. Norton, 1992.

Patterson, James T. *America's Struggle against Poverty, 1900-1980.* Cambridge: Harvard Univ. Press, 1986.

———. *The New Deal and the States: Federalism in Transition.* Princeton: Princeton Univ. Press, 1969.

Penkower, Marty. *The Federal Writers' Project: A Study in Government Patronage of the Arts.* Urbana: Univ. of Illinois Press, 1988.

Pickett, Clarence E. *For More than Bread: An Autobiographical Account of Twenty-Two Years Work with the American Friends Service Committee.* Boston: Little, Brown, 1953.

Piven, Frances Fox, and Richard Cloward. *Poor People's Movements: Why They Succeed, How They Fail.* New York: Pantheon, 1977.

Posey, Thomas Edward. "The Labor Movement in West Virginia, 1900-1948." Ph.D. diss., University of Wisconsin, 1948.

Pritchard, Arthur C. " 'In West Virginia I Had More Freedom:' Bruce Crawford's Story." *Goldenseal: West Virginia Traditional Life* 10, no. 1 (Spring 1984): 34-37.

Pudup, Mary Beth. "Women's Work in the West Virginia Economy." *West Virginia History* 49 (1990): 7-20.

Pudup, Mary Beth, Dwight B. Billings, Altina L. Waller, eds. *Appalachia in the Making: The Mountain South in the Nineteenth Century.* Chapel Hill and London: Univ. of North Carolina Press, 1995.

Roosevelt, Eleanor. *This I Remember.* New York: Harper and Brothers, 1949.

Rice, Otis K., and Stephen W. Brown. *West Virginia: A History.* 2d ed. Lexington: Univ. Press of Kentucky, 1993.

Salmon, John. *The Civilian Conservation Corps, 1933-1942: A New Deal Case Study.* Durham: Duke Univ. Press, 1967.

———. *A Southern Rebel: The Life and Times of Aubrey W. Williams.* Chapel Hill: Univ. of North Carolina Press, 1983.

Saloutos, Theodore. *The American Farmer and the New Deal.* Ames: Iowa State Univ. Press: 1982.

Salstrom, Paul. *Appalachia's Path to Dependency: Rethinking a Region's Economic History.* Lexington: Univ. Press of Kentucky, 1994.

Savage, Lon. *Thunder in the Mountains: The West Virginia Mine War, 1920-1921.* Pittsburgh: Univ. of Pittsburgh Press, 1990.

Schlesinger, Arthur, Jr. *The Coming of the New Deal.* Boston: Houghton Mifflin, 1958.

Schurr, Sam H., and Netschert. *Energy in the American Economy, 1850-1975: An Economic Study of Its History and Prospects.* Baltimore: Johns Hopkins Univ. Press, 1960.

Searle, Charles F. *Minister of Relief: Harry Hopkins and the Depression.* Syracuse: Syracuse Univ. Press, 1963.

Sherwood, Robert E. *Roosevelt and Hopkins: An Intimate History.* New York: Harper and Brothers, 1948.

Shifflett, Crandall A. *Coal Towns: Life, Work, and Culture in Company Towns of Southern Appalachia, 1880-1960.* Knoxville: Univ. of Tennessee Press, 1991.

Simon, Richard Mark. "The Development of Underdevelopment: The Coal Industry and Its Effect on the West Virginia Economy, 1880-1930." Ph.D. diss., University of Pittsburgh, 1978.

Sitkoff, Harvard. *A New Deal for Blacks: The Emergence of Civil Rights as a National Issue.* New York: Oxford Univ. Press, 1978.

———. *Fifty Years Later: The New Deal Evaluated.* Philadelphia: Temple Univ. Press, 1985.

Skocpol, Theda, and Kenneth Finegold, "State Capacity and Economic Intervention in the New Deal." *Political Science Quarterly* 97 (Summer 1982): 255-78.

Smith, Douglas L. *The New Deal in the Urban South.* Baton Rouge: Louisiana State Univ. Press, 1988.

Sobel, Robert, and John Raimo, eds. *Biographical Directory of the Governors of the United States, 1789-1978.* Vol. 4. Westport, Conn: Meckler Books, 1978.

Soule, George. *Prosperity Decade: From War to Depression: 1917-1929.* New York: Harper and Row, 1968.

Taylor, John Craft. "Depression and New Deal in Pendleton: A History of a West Virginia County from the Great Crash to Pearl Harbor." Ph.D. diss., Pennsylvania State University, 1980.

Thomas, Jerry B. "'The Nearly Perfect State': Governor Homer Adams Holt, the WPA Writers' Project and the Making of *West Virginia: A Guide to the Mountain State.*" *West Virginia History* 52 (1993): 91-109.

Thurmond, Walter R. *The Logan Coal Field of West Virginia: A Brief History.* Morgantown: West Virginia Univ. Library, 1974.

Tindall, George Brown. *The Emergence of the New South, 1913-1945.* Vol. 10 in *A History of the South.* Baton Rouge: Louisiana State Univ. Press, 1967.

Trotter, Joe William, Jr. *Coal, Class, and Color: Blacks in Southern West Virginia, 1915-1932.* Urbana: Univ. of Illinois Press, 1990.

Tunley, Roul. "The Strange Case of West Virginia." *Saturday Evening Post,* Feb. 6, 1960, 19-20, 64-65.

Vittoz, Stanley. *New Deal Labor Policy and the American Economy.* Chapel Hill: Univ. of North Carolina Press, 1987.

Ware, Susan. *Beyond Suffrage: Women in the New Deal.* Cambridge and London: Harvard Univ. Press, 1981.

Bibliography

———. *Holding Their Own: American Women in the 1930s.* Boston: Twayne, 1982.

Weiss, Nancy. *Farewell to the Party of Lincoln: Black Politics in the Age of FDR.* Princeton: Princeton Univ. Press, 1983.

Whisnant, David E. *Modernizing the Mountaineer: People, Power, and Planning in Appalachia.* Boone, N.C.: Appalachian Consortium Press, 1980.

Wiebe, Robert. *The Search for Order, 1877-1920.* New York: Hill and Wang, 1967.

Williams, John Alexander. *West Virginia: A Bicentennial History.* New York: W.W. Norton and Company, 1976.

———. *West Virginia and the Captains of Industry.* Morgantown: West Virginia Univ. Press, 1976.

Wilson, Edmund. *An American Earthquake: A Documentary of the Jazz Age, The Great Depression and the New Deal.* Garden City: Doubleday, 1958.

Woodruff, Nan Elizabeth. *As Rare as Rain: Federal Relief in the Great Southern Drought of 1930-1931.* Urbana: Univ. of Illinois Press, 1985.

Worster, Donald. *Dust Bowl: The Southern Plains in the 1930s.* New York, Oxford: Oxford Univ. Press, 1979.

White, Theodore. *The Making of the President, 1960.* New York: Atheneum House, 1961.

Zieger, Robert H. *John L. Lewis, Labor Leader.* Boston: Twayne, 1988.

INDEX

Abbot, Edith, 155, 157
African Americans, 19-21, 199-206; state institutions for, 20; businesses owned by, 21; schools for, 24, 194; desire for music project in Wheeling, 149; camp for children of, 197; in coal mining, 199; and recreation, 200; as members of the UMWA, 200; and Depression politics, 200-203; and assistant director positions in public assistance, 203; and NRA, 203; in McDowell County, 203; and PWA, 203-4; survey for subsistence homestead for, 204; in CCC, 205
Agricultural Adjustment Act of 1933, 2; lack of attention to poor farmers, 165; benefits to West Virginia farmers, 166; declared unconstitutional, 166
agriculture. *See* farming in West Virginia
Alderson, Joseph N., 215
Alfriend, John S., 24
Allebach, Leroy, 208
Allen, C.L., 139, 143; hired as state relief administrator, 135
Amalgamated Association of Iron, Steel, and Tin Workers, 95
Amend, Mary, 123
American Emergency Force (AEF), 52
American Federation of Labor (AFL), 223-25
American Friends Service Committee (AFSC), 54-57; Appalachian children's feeding program, 55; development of supplemental employment, 55-56; chairmaking and quilting, 56; West Virginia relief organization, 57; in Monongalia County, 168
American Legion, 58-59
Andrews, Carl, 227, 229, 230
Appalachia: ambiguity of term, 2; and study by U.S. Department of Agriculture, 179; West Virginia as symbolizing negative connotation of, 239; historiography of, 241 n 2
Appalachian Agreement, 1933, 98
Appalachian contracts, 224, 237
Appalachian Electric Power Co., 23
Armstrong, Dr. W.O., 205
Arthurdale, 170-74; musical activity at, 149; and racial exclusivity, 204. *See also* subsistence homesteads
Atlanta School of Social Work, 204

Babcock, Col. George D., 147
Bachman, Carl, 230
back to the land movement, 60, 162
Badger, Anthony J., 209, 234
Bailey, Ernest L., 138, 140, 219, 221
Baltimore, Md., 4
Bane, Frank, 154
banking: decline of, in twenties, 16; bank failures, 27; crisis in, 77; New Deal legislation on, 78
Barbour County, 175
Barbour Power Co., 177
Barkley, Alben, 104
barter systems, 60-61, 250 n 71
Bauman, John, 4
Beckley, 204
Beckley *Post-Herald*, on National Industrial Recovery Act, 106
Beehler, William N.: as West Virginia relief administrator, 118;

background, 118-19; as political lightning rod, 119; addresses members of Unemployed League, 119; place in state history, 119; described, 120; and CWA, 120; defends Logan County welfare administrator, 122; removal sought, 123; denies charges of Republicanism, 124; defended by Harry Hopkins, 124; on work relief, 126; and Kanawha County board, 130; fired, 135; on work relief for women, 192
Behner, Mary, 18
Bell, Frank R., 130, 131
Bennett, Herman, 217
Berkeley County, 58, 59, 65, 66
Berkeley Woolen Mills, 95
Bernstein, Irving, 9
Berry vs Fox, 85
Bethune, Mary McLeod, 205
Better West Virginia, A (WPA film), 197
Beury, William, 100
Biddle, John L., 217
Big Sandy River Basin, 181
Biles, Roger, 239
Bittner, Van Amberg: negotiates deal at Scotts Run, 49; on Thomas C. Townsend, 71; opposes Guy Kump, 73; described, 92; on UMWA's success in southern West Virginia, 93; and coal code negotiations, 97; on NRA, 102; and Rush D. Holt, 104, 106, 143-44, 218; dares Kump to run for Senate, 213; denounces Gov. Homer Holt, 225; supports Roosevelt for president, 229. *See also* United Mine Workers of America
Black, Hugo, 104
Blackburn, Verna, 148, 149
black lung disease, 108
blacks. *See* African Americans
Black Thursday, 27
Blakey, George T., 4
Blakey, Dr. Roy, 61

Blizzard, Reese, 38
Blizzard, William, 219, 225
Bluefield, 59
Bluefield *Daily Telegraph*, 35
Bonus Expeditionary Force (BEF), and West Virginians, 51-53
Boone County, 46-47
Brant, Scott A., 47
Brooks, Harry L., 36, 37
Brooks, William E., 58, 133
Brookwood Labor College, 45
Brown, Herbert, 51, 53
Brown, Izetta Jewel, 16-17. *See also* Miller, Izetta Jewel
Brown, Knight, and Jackson, 24, 104, 215, 232,
Bruchlacher, Esther, 54
Buckhannon *Record*, 68
Bureau of Agricultural Economics (BAE), 180-85
Burke, Stephen P., 153, 154
Business and Professional Women of Charleston, 192-93
Byrd, Harry Flood, 76, 228
Byrd, Mrs. Percy, 25
Byrne, W.E.R., 37

Cabell County, 53
Cabin Creek, 43
Cairns, Thomas, 224
Calhoun County, 128, 161
Callaghan, Glenn, 199, 205
Camp Boone, 196
Camp Brock, 197
Camp Fairchance, 196
Carmody, John, 177
Carter, Doak, 52-53
Carter, Fannie Cobb, 208
Carter, Ulysses G., 200
charity, 128-29
Charleston: and new capitol, 7; and twenties building boom, 24; and bonus marchers, 53; and Community Chest, 58; and Reconstruction Finance Corp., 66; and use of matching funds, 90; and NRA, 96; and NRA birthday parade, 102; and private charity, 129; and PWA

projects, 152; public housing in, 207-9, mentioned, 226
Charleston Armory, 219
Charleston Board of Realtors, 209
Charleston *Daily Mail*, 25, 217
Charleston *Gazette*: on problems of coal industry, 8; circulation, 25; quoted on American Legion unemployment campaign, 59; attacks Gov. Conley, 68; laments triumph of "unholy alliance" on tax legislation, 86; on Francis Turner, 155; on conditions of county poor farm, 197; on 1939 legislature, 223
Charleston Housing Authority, 208
Charleston Young Democrat Club, 217
Charles Town, 24, 166
chemical industry, 23-24
Cherniak, Martin, *The Hawk's Nest Incident*, 111
Chesapeake and Potomac Telephone Co., 24
chestnut blight, 14
children in West Virginia: report on rural child labor in 1922, 12-13; condition of, in coalfields, 44; study of their welfare urged, 121; lives disrupted by Depression, 190; hunger among, 193; care of undernourished, 195; summer camps for, 195-96; care of, called worst in country, 196; in county poor farms, 196. *See also* West Virginia Board of Children's Guardians
Chilton, William E., 17, 42, 84, 103
C.H. James and Son, 21
churches, 22
cities: populations, 19; and technological change, 22. *See individual cities by name*
Civilian Conservation Corps (CCC): in Greenbrier County, 183; projects of in West Virginia summarized, 197-98; work assessed, 198, 238; and racial discrimination in, 205
Civil Works Administration, 119-27; as experiment in work relief, 119; and wages in Kanawha County, 120; end of, ordered by President Roosevelt, 121; earnings of workers in, 127; studies rural housing, 164-65
Clark, Mrs. Friend, 58
Clarksburg *Exponent*, 8
Clay County, 161
coal industry in West Virginia: problems in twenties, 8-11; in Monongalia County, 43; and NRA, 97-99; and stripmining, 99; and mechanization, 99; and snowbirds, 99; and change in nature of mining, 100; employment figures, 109; decline in mining employment in fifties, 109, 237-38; and national decline of employment in, 109
Coal Valley News, 123
Cold War, 234
collective bargaining. *See* National Industrial Recovery Act; National Labor Relations Act
Collins, Justus, 32
Committee of One Hundred, 38
committee on efficiency and economy, 76
communists, 45, 49, 195
Community Chest, 58
company houses, 195
conference of governors (1930), 33
Congress of Industrial Organizations (CIO), 223-26, 229, 230
Conley, William Gustavus, 3, 25-41, 46-69; quoted, 6, 30; as governor, 6; background, 29-30; inaugural address, 29; advocates constitutional reforms, 30; and special sessions, 30, 62; and drought of 1930, 32-33; stops investigation of state police, 37; on seriousness of Depression, 39; and veto of Democratic bills, 40; and West Virginia Miners Union, 45-46; and

Index

hunger marchers, 47; and coal miners, 49; urges stabilization of coal industry, 50; and Bonus Army, 51; urges retrenchment, 61; calls for tax limitation amendment, 62; seeks new taxes for unemployment relief fund, 63; names state relief board, 65; applies for Reconstruction Finance Corporation aid, 67; as lame duck, 67; attacked by newspapers, 67-68; injured by furnace explosion, 68; assessment of, 69; imposes banking restrictions, 77
constitutional commission, 64
construction, 64
Coode, Thomas, 4
Cook, Morris L., 177
Cook, Roy Bird, 226
Cook, William Cassius, 82
Coolidge, Calvin, 25
cooperatives, 177-78
Corbin, David Alan, quoted, 48
Cornwell, John Jacob, 6, 33, 74, 82, 230
corporate welfarism, 237
Coughlin, Father Charles, 21
Country Life Movement, 12
"Country Roads," 239, 240
county agents, 167
county poor farms, 32, 196, 235
county welfare boards, 18, 65, 122
Coy, Wayne, 144-45
Craig-Botetourt Electric Cooperative, 178
Crawford, Bruce, 226-27
Creel, George, 220
Crichlow, Carrie B., 208
Croxton, Fred C., 44, 55
cultural life, in cities, 22

Daniel Boone Hotel, 24
Danilevsky, Nadia, 133
Darrow, Clarence, 101
Davis, Alice: on danger of relief population becoming unemployable, 116; on conditions of relief clients in coal camps, 116-17; as Monongalia relief director, 132; forced to resign, 133; introduces Eleanor Roosevelt to Scotts Run, 170; Eleanor Roosevelt's correspondence with, 194; visits Pendleton County poor farm, 196
Davis, John W., 24
Davis, Mrs. T.J., 16
Davis-Kelley Bill, 50
Dawson, Daniel Boone, 90
Dawson, William M.O., 29, 208, 230
"Death of Mother Jones," 48
Democratic Women's Club, Kanawha County, 75
Denmar Sanitarium, 206
Depression: and conditions in West Virginia, 27-28; and economic theory, 28
Devan, R.P., 46
Diamond Department Store, 24
Dickinson, Charles C., 50
Dies, Martin, 226
diseases, statistics of, 32
Division of Subsistence Homesteads, 170
Dix, Keith, 99, 100
Donaldson, Walter, 150
Draper, C.R., 185-86
drought of 1930, 27, 31-33
Dubofsky, Melvyn, 229
Du Pont, 23
Duty (Mingo County), 55-56

Easton, John, 39, 65, 224, 225, 229
education: impact of Depression on, 42; and county unit system, 80, 87; and teacher salary reductions, 87; and lack funding, 221; effect of fiscal conservatism on, 236
Eleanor. See Red House Garden Farms, Inc.
elections: of 1928, 25, 200; of 1930, 34-36, 200-201; of 1932, 71-75, 201-2; of 1934, 103-5; of 1936, 142, 219, 220; of 1938, 222-23; of 1940, 223, 227-31
electrification, 23; and New Deal

efforts, 176-78; benefits of, for farm family, 178-79
Elkins, 220, 232
Eller, Ronald D, 179
Ellyson, Russell G., 174
Elmhirst, Mrs. Leonard (Dorothy Straight), 168
Emergency Relief and Construction Act, 64
Estep, Clarence L., 50
Estill, Calvert: as advocate of federal relief, 3; praises work of American Friends Service Committee, 57; as administrator of state relief board, 65; testifies before Congress, 67; resigns as director of Department of Welfare, 113; as journalist and critic of New Deal, 138; on number of children in county poor farms, 196; on Holt administration, 211; on "seditious" nature of *West Virginia: A Guide to the Mountain State*, 226; on *West Virginia History* as antidote to communistic propaganda, 227

factionalism, Democratic, 255 n 45; roots of, 72-73; Kump-Neely rivalry, 80-82; in 1934 Clarksburg meeting, 104; complicates relief administration, 124; and fight over WPA, 137; summarized, 196; factions described, 212; leaders of statehouse faction, 216; in Holt administration, 222; and defeat of conservative Democrats, 231
Fairmont, 23, 219
Fairmont coalfield, 43, 108
Fairmont State College, 231
families, 189-210; and New Deal, 190; in abandoned schoolhouse, 194
Farley, James, 216
Farm Bureau Federation, 165
farm-forest communities, 179
farming in West Virginia, 11-16, 160-88; in 1929, 11; typical small farm, 12; bipartisan farm bloc, 13; sources of income, 14; effects of Tax Limitation Amendment, 88; as different from South, 160; decline in size of farms and income, 161; nonagricultural sources of income, 161; farmers' need for relief, 161; in southwestern counties, 163-64; technological change, 166; farm women's organizations, 167; decline of farm population, 238. *See also* subsistence farmers; subsistence homesteads
Farm Security Administration (FSA), 174-76; and plight of rural poor, 176; efforts assessed, 176
Federal Emergency Relief Act (1933), 113
Federal Emergency Relief Administration (FERA), 112-35; as experiment, 112; and conflict with state relief administrations, 114; agents urge continued funding of West Virginia, 114; field agent reports, 115; and control of relief administration in West Virginia, 118; work summarized, 125-30; effectiveness of, 129-30; help for low-income farmers, 167-68; work relief for women, 192; survey of Charleston housing, 207
Federal Housing Administration (FHA), 206-7
fiddle-making, 149
Finegold, Kenneth, 108
fiscal conservatism, 221, 235. *See also* "pay-as-you-go"
Fitzpatrick, Herbert, 215
five-and-dime store workers, 191
floods: of 1932, 27, 62; of 1936, 150
food preservation campaign (1931), 53, 55
Forth, R.F., 33
Foster, William Z., 49
4-H club, 13
Fox, Fred L., 89

Index

Frame, Nat Terry, 12, 165, 166
Francis, James Draper, 50, 97
Friends. *See* American Friends Service Committee
Froe, Arthur G., 201

Garner, John Nance, 202
Garnett, Alfred Willis, 155
Garraty, John A., 28
Gates, Anna Johnson, 16
Given, Waitman C., 78
Godlove, Bud, 56
Goldberg, Rabbi Ariel, 129
Goff, Guy, 34
Good Roads Movement, 21
Gore, Howard Mason, 11; on twenties, 6; elected governor, 14; appointed chair of drought relief committee, 33; and unemployment committee, 39, 44
Grafton *Sentinel*, 35
Grant County, 164
Gray, Lewis Cecil, 179
Green, Archie, 48-49
Green, William, 223, 224
Greenbrier County, 183
Greenstein, Harry, 157
Greve, Belle, 58
Grimes, Bushrod, 171
Guffey, Joseph, 105
Guffey bill, 105-6
Guffey-Snyder Act, 106
Guffey-Vinson Act (1937), 107, 219

Haid, Stephen, 169
Hallanan, Walter S., 36
Hampshire County, 177
Hardman, Ruth, 193
Hardy County, 177, 198
Hardy County Light and Power Assoc., 177
Harlow, John, 46
Harper, Minnie Buckingham, 16
Harpers Ferry, 24
Harris, Winthrop, and Co., 27
Harrison Rural Electrical Assoc., 178
Hart, Bill, 222

Hart, Walter, 141
Hatfield, Henry Drury: "waves bloody shirt" in election of 1930, 34-35; "out of town" to bonus marchers, 51; opposes "paternalism," 63; faces reelection, 103; denounces New Deal, 104; helps African Americans get federal appointments, 200
Hatfield, Joe, 37
Hatfield, Maginnis, 101
Hatfield, Tennis, 36, 37
Hawks Nest Tunnel, 41, 227
Hawley, Ellis, 92
Heater, Claude, 150
Heinemann, Ronald L., 4, 236
Hennen, John: *The Americanization of West Virginia*, 7
Herold, Anderson C., 123
Hickok, Lorena: on West Virginia Mine Workers Union, 47-48; calls on president to assume dictatorial powers, 93-94; reports on relief conditions in West Virginia, 117; visits Gov. Kump, 141; on West Virginia political situation, 141; on F. Witcher McCullough, 146; on Maj. Francis Turner, 154; on conditions in Logan County, 163, 194; visits Scotts Run, 169-70; on families living in tents, 195; on summer camp for poor children, 196
higher education: reduction of salaries in, 61; effects of tax limitation amendment, 87; neglect of needs, 221; and PWA funds for buildings, 236
highways, 240. *See also* road building
Hill, Edward Tyler, 20
Hiner, Ralph, 219
Hines, Lewis, 12
historiography, of New Deal and states, 240 n 26
Hitchman Coal and Coke vs Mitchell, 9-10
Hodges, Charles, 214

Holt, Homer Adams: on Tax Limitation Amendment, 89; as attorney general, legal opinion on mine guards, 101; accompanies Gov. Kump to meeting in Washington, 139; attempts to censor *West Virginia: A Guide to the Mountain State*, 151; as governor, calls for cuts in Dept. of Public Assistance budget, 212, 215-16, 220-32, 235; background, 215; elected governor, 220; attitude toward matching funds, 221; conservatism, 222; urges counties to increase local levies, 222; complains to president of political interference by WPA, 223; on labor's "Hitler tactics," 225; and 1939 work stoppage, 225; approval of House Un-American Activities Committee, 226; and Hawks Nest, 227; and 1940 election, 229; tries to name successor to Neely in Senate, 231; farewell banquet, 231; assessed, 232

Holt, Matthew, 144, 219

Holt, Rush Dew: opposes Kump program, 81; in House of Delegates, 84; and election of 1934, 103; wins senate nomination, 104; elected to U.S. Senate, 104-5; as "boy senator," 105; opposes Guffey-Snyder bill, 106; estrangement from Democratic liberals, 143, 146; attacks WPA, 144, 146; on Johnstone report, 145; and Huey Long, 146; and opposition to, by conservative Democrats, 146; accuses Kump of Liberty League membership, 213; and employment by HOLC, 215; and split with Neely and Bittner, 218; and coal industry legislation, 218-19; seeks reelection, 228; assessed, 228; loses in 1940 primary, 230

home demonstration agents, 17

Home Owners Loan Corporation (HOLC), 206, 215

Hoover, Mrs. B.M., 123

Hoover, Herbert: carries West Virginia in 1928 election, 25; and drought of 1930, 32-34; opposes federal relief, 37-38; looks to Red Cross for relief, 44; signs relief bill, 64; campaigns in West Virginia, 72; last months of presidency, 76; and African Americans, 200-201

Hopkins, Harry: pressures Gov. Kump, 85, 114-15, 117-18; appointed relief administrator, 112; urges states to provide relief for women, 113; urges states to use FERA money for work relief, 113; on stranded populations, 121; and creation of New state organization for WPA, 137; and politics in WPA, 137; opposes federal direct relief, 158; shocked at rural relief load in West Virginia, 161; condemned by Robert Kelly, 216-17

Hopson, Dr. C.F., 206

Horner, Lynn S., 35

hospitals, 221

hotel and restaurant workers, 191

House Un-American Activities Committee, 226-27

Howe, Louis, 169, 203

Hughes, William E., 85

Humphrey, Everett S., 54, 166

Humphreys, Gertrude, 164

hunger marchers, 46-47

Hunter, Howard C.: quoted on Kump's "sob story," 117; names Beehler West Virginia relief administrator, 118; despairs of governor and legislature, 120; says counties in permanent collapse, 120; reports on changes in West Virginia relief administration, 120; praises Kump, 125; on child welfare, 196

Huntington: and bonus marchers,

Index

52-53; seeks RFC aid, 66; and New Deal matching funds, 90; therapeutic center for hospital, 147; WPA musical pageant, 149; WPA orchestra, 149; business failures in, 189; and mountaintop suburbs, 207

Huntington *Herald-Dispatch*, 25, 101

Ickes, Harold: heads PWA and resettlement projects, 91-92; slowness to push work projects forward, 119; scrupulousness in spending funds, 151; on Arthurdale, 171; support for racial justice, 205

Ireland Community, 185

Jackson, Naaman, 37
Jackson's Mill, 13, 32, 150, 178
Jacksonville Agreement, 1924, 8
Jarrett, Howard, 6, 37
Jefferson County, 201
Jefferson County school board, 190-91
Johnson, Gen. Hugh S., 92; lack of negotiating skills, 97; denounces NRA opponents, 102; resigns, 103
Johnson, Louis A., 103, 222, 231
Johnstone, Allen, 145
Jones, Dr. Harriet B., 16
Jones, James Elwood, 34-36
Jones, Luther, 123

Kamp Kump, 197
Kanawha City, 47
Kanawha County, 66; and relief needs, 115; and conservative relief board, 192; poor farm children in, 196
Kanawha County Relief Administration: reorganized, 124; concerns about radicalism, 130; and guide for "visitors," 130; attacks Beehler and WVRA, 131; conservatism of, 192; opposes gender pay equity, 193

Kanawha Valley Bank, 24, 138
Keeney, Frank, 44-48, 224
Kelley's Creek Colliery Co., 45
Kelly, Robert G.: and planning for 1932 campaign, 73; handles appointments for Kump administration, 80; as attorney for railroad, mining, and power interests, 81; and 1934 Democratic party fight, 104; as leader of statehouse faction, 216; expresses anti-New Deal views, 217
Kelsey, Mary, 55
Kenna, Joseph N., 85
Kennedy, Duncan, 97
Kennedy, Tom, 97
Kentucky, 4, 49, 93, 114, 149, 178
Kessler-Harris, Alice, 193
Key, V.O., 236
Keynes, John Maynard, 28
Khaki Shirts of America, 53
Kilgore, Harley M., 228-30
Kirby, Jack Temple: on mountain slums, 15; on impact of back-to-the-land movement, 128; on post-industrial landscape of Appalachia, 160; quotes West Virginia woman on love for land, 187
Knapp, J.O., 166, 167
Koontz, Arthur B., 103
Kump, Herman Guy, 3; supports Tax Limitation Amendment, 64; early life, 72; conservative views, 72; nominated for governor, 73; on tax relief, 74; as campaigner, 75; elected, 75; and "little brain trust," 76; develops legislative program, 76-77; inaugurated, 77; and Tax Limitation Amendment, 77, 89; and banking crisis, 78; and hearings on recapture of corporate property taxes, 78; and job seekers, 80; as Bourbon Democrat, 81; and federal patronage concerns, 81; reacts to school lobby, 83; and legislative opposition, 84; orders state police to

stand ready, 84; recalls legislature, 1933, 85; approves sales tax, 87; goes to Washington, 97; and end of mine guard system, 101; remarks at NRA birthday celebration, 102; warns Rush D. Holt, 104; presents case to president, 114; says state cannot appropriate relief funds, 114; reduces relief rolls, cuts payments, 115; warns president of grave consequences of special session, 115; and FERA, 117, 125; appeals to White House, 118; makes commitment to seek relief funds, 120; on need for party control of welfare boards, 124; seeks to control relief administration, 125; says "public bounty must end," 134; opposes hiring "outside people" to administer relief, 134; fires Beehler, hires C.L. Allen to administer state relief, 135; and WPA, 138, 139; complains of federal interference, 139; concern over New Deal excesses, 140; on "spending orgy," 140; as characterized by opponents, 140-41; protests to Roosevelt, 141-42; expresses concern over relief load, 142; questions impact of relief programs, 156; and separate black board of education, 202; and African American Democratic dinner, 203; and black organizations, 204; term assessed, 212-14; and New Deal, 213; runs for U.S. Senate, 213, 228-29; refrains from use of force in labor disputes, 232; concentrates on business interests in Elkins, 232; historiography of, 252 n 1
Kump, Kerr, 140

Laing, A.W., 65
Laing, John, 8
land abuse, 179

Landon, Alfred M., 217, 219
land use planning, 180-87
laundry and dry cleaner workers, 191
League for Industrial Democracy, 46
Lee, Howard B.: on coalfield oligarchy, 11; restores rule of law to Logan County, 37; halts evictions at Wacomah Fuel Co., 47
Lenroot, Katharine, 65
Lesage Community Tractor Service, 182
Leuchtenburg, William E., 108
Levine, Milton, 189
Lewis, John L.: sends organizers to West Virginia, 92; calms strike fever, 98; supports mechanization, 100; leaves AFL, 218; creates CIO, 223; endorses Willkie for president, 229; succumbs to arrogance of power, 237-38
Lewis, Ronald L.: *Black Coal Miners in the United States*, 200
Lewisburg, 166
Lewis County: characteristics of, 183; as demonstration area for land use planning, 183-85; and survey of "C" area, 184-86
Liberty League, 213
libraries, 61, 150
Lincoln County, 57, 128, 162
liquor stores, 89
Littlepage Terrace, 208, 209
Logan *Banner*, 122
Logan County, 36-37, 94, 163, 194; study of relief in, 127
Long, Huey, 215
Long, Joseph H., 23, 104
Lorentz, Pare, 176
Lubliner, Abram J., 81, 218

MacArthur, Gen. Douglas, 52
McCullough, Frank Witcher: as state chairman of national emergency committee, 102; appointed secretary of National Coal Commission, 107; appointed

Index

state WPA administrator, 138; suggests to Hopkins an attack on Kump, 139-40; disavows candidacy for political office, 144; as part of Neely political machine, 214; favors Neely's friends for WPA appointments, 218

McDowell County, 161, 163; and county court, 42-43; courtesy deputies disbanded, 101; relief needs in, 116; rise of coal mining unemployment in, 117; and black Democrats, 203

McDowell County Colored Republican Organization, 20

McGovran, T.Y., 60

McGovran, Thomas H., 72

McIntyre, Marvin, 85, 118

McKell, William, 140

McKinley, T.C., 38

Mallison, Sam, 254 n 40; reports strain on governor from job seekers, 80; on advice to Rush D. Holt in 1934, 103-4; as critic of New Deal, 138; reports on proposed Democratic unity ticket, 214

manufacturing, 28

Marshall College, 129, 189

Martin, Clarence E., Sr., 231

Martinsburg, 51, 58, 60, 166; relief efforts in, 66; and NRA excitement, 96-97; public housing, 207

Martinsburg *Journal*, 93

Mason, Maude, 66

Mason County, 187, 198; land use project in, 182

matching funds: Gov. Kump's views on, 139, 256 n 77, 259 n 74; Gov. Holt's views on, 221-22

medical care plan, 175

medical problems, 115, 116

melon production, 181-82

Mercer County, 43; poor farm, 197

Miller, Izetta Jewel, 194. *See also* Brown, Izetta Jewel

Miller, Lewis H., 230

mine guard system, 101

Mingo County, 55, 161, 162, 163

Mitchell, Charles E., 201

Monongahela National Forest, 31, 183

Monongahela Valley, 56

Monongahela West Penn Public Service Co., 23

Monongalia Council of Social Agencies, 43, 53, 54

Monongalia County: needs of relief population, 116-17; and Appalachian children's feeding program, 168; Eleanor Roosevelt's interest in, 194

Monongalia County Negro Progressive League, 204

Monongalia County relief organization: cooperation with state and federal authorities, 132; and community organizations, 132; as democratic and rehabilitative model, 133; and work for unemployed women, 192; and planning for a black homestead community, 204

Moorefield, 166

Morgan, Ephriam, 34

Morgantown, 56, 57, 61; black high school, 206

Morgantown *Dominion News*, 101, 141

Morris, Homer, 55

Morrow, J.D.A., 97

mothers pension funds, 17

Moundsville state prison, 40

Mountaineer Craftsmen's Cooperative Association, 56, 171

Mountain State Forest Festival, 220

mountaintop suburbs, 206

Mt. Hope, 207

municipalities: and ill-effects of Tax Limitation Amendment, 88

Murray, Philip, 97

Myers, James, 57

Nation, 226

National Association for the Advancement of Colored People, 201

National Bituminous Coal Commission, 107, 214-15
National Child Labor Committee, 12
National Conference of Social Workers, 157
National Guard, 195
National Industrial Recovery Act, 91-111; and right to organize, 92; positive consequences for West Virginia, 100-110; political consequences of, in West Virginia, 103-5, 110; held unconstitutional by Supreme Court, 105; criticisms of, by scholars, 108; and social reforms in West Virginia, 110; assessed, 237. *See also* National Recovery Administration
National Labor Board, 95-96
National Labor Relations Act, 106
National Labor Relations Board, 106
National Miners Union, 45, 49
National Recovery Administration, 92-111; and codes of fair competition, 96; and national campaign for NRA standards on wages and hours, 96; and negotiations of industrial codes, 97; and improvements in labor-management relations, 99; and creation of new problems in coal industry, 99; and difficulties of enforcing coal code, 100; and critics of, 102; and support from miners and operators in West Virginia, 100; and recovery of coal industry in West Virginia, 98-99; ends, 105
National Recovery Review Board, 101, 102
National Union of Social Justice, 219
National Youth Administration, 197-99; projects in West Virginia, 198-99; and blacks, 205
Neal, George I., 216
Neale, M.L., 151
Neely, Matthew Mansfield, 17; and election of 1930, 34-35; and Bonus Army, 51; supports New Deal liberalism, 82; and 1932 election, 72-73; characterized, 214; and federal patronage, 214; and 1936 election, 219-20; on "reactionary forces," 225; files for governor, 228; opposed by Gov. Holt, 229; and 1940 election, 230; elected governor, 232; as leader of pro<n>New Deal faction, 235; sources for biography of, 280 n 13; attempt to return to the U.S. Senate, 283 n 86
Negro Business and Professional Men's Association (Charleston), 208
Nestor, Blaine, 189
New Deal: and banking crisis, 78; first hundred days, 91; economic ambivalence of, 92; and West Virginia coal industry, 92-111; and change of care of poor and unemployed in West Virginia, 158; and mountain agriculture, 166-88, 238; and programs for poor farmers, 167-68; and family, 189-210; and housing, 206-9; and attitude of state Democratic leaders, 211; waning of, 232-33; impact on West Virginia summarized, 234-40
New Haven, 198
New Republic, 226
newspapers, 25-26. *See also* by name
Nicholas *Chronicle*, 80
North Carolina, 178
Norton, Wilbert Henry, 85
nursing, 126, 192
Nutter, Thomas G., 202

O'Brien, William Smyth, 212
O'Conner, R.E., 49
Ogden, Hershel C., 20, 34
Ogden newspapers, 73, 138
Oglebay Park, 149
Ohio River basin, 181
Old Hickory Club, 88

Index

O'Neill, Charles, 97
organizational thesis, 7, 241 n 7
organized labor, 110

Parker, John J., 10, 201
patronage, 80; and benefits to statehouse faction of Tax Limitation Amendment, 88-89; M.M. Neely as chief federal dispenser of, 214-15; and Rush D. Holt, 218, 254 n 40
Patterson, James T., 3; *The New Deal and the States*, 211
"pay-as-you-go," 90, 236
Payne, Charles K., 65
Payne, John Barton, 44
Pearson, Drew, 107, 226
Peebles, Henderson, 208
Pendleton County, 12, 196
Pennsylvania, 4, 9
pensions for aged poor, 40
Perkins, Frances, 194
Philippi, 189
photographers, 175
Pickett, Clarence, 168, 204
Pinecrest Sanitarium, 152
Pittsburgh *Courier*, 202
Poff, Nellie, 43
Point Pleasant, 166
political cartoons, 229-30
political system of West Virginia, 279 n 4
Pollard, John Garland, 76
population, West Virginia: decline of, in rural counties, 14; characteristics of, 19
population removal, proposed, 179
Posey, Thomas E.: *The Negro Citizen in West Virginia*, 199; on lack of black organization, 204
Potomac Light and Power Co., 177
President's Emergency Committee on Employment (PECE), 38
President's Office for Unemployment Relief (POUR), 54
Preston County, 170
Princeton, 59
Progressive Mine Workers, 224

Prohibition, 215
property tax, 15
public finance. *See* Tax Limitation Amendment
public housing, 207-10
public service commission, 177-78
Public Utilities Holding Company Act, 218
Public Works Administration (PWA): established, 92; and Harold Ickes, 119; focus on capital-intensive projects, 151; and matching fund requirements, 151; and projects in West Virginia, 151-52; and low-rent housing, 207; and state institutions, 222
Putnam County, 172, 197

Quakers. *See* American Friends Service Committee

Radenbaugh, Francis Irvine, 17
Raleigh County, 162; courthouse, 152
Randolph, Jennings, 35
Randolph County, 123, 164
Reconstruction Finance Corp., 66
Red Cross, 43, 44, 65, 66
Red House Garden Farms, Inc., 127; WPA band at, 149; described, 172-73; on 1939 land use tour, 182; and racial exclusivity, 204. *See also* subsistence homesteads
Reedsville Experimental Community. *See* Arthurdale; subsistence homesteads
rehabilitation of counties: study needed, 121; groundwork laid, 127; efforts of FSA, 174-75
relief: efforts of local governments, 42-43; needs in rural counties, 116, 128, 162; inadequacy of, in West Virginia, 128. *See also* Civil Works Administration; Federal Emergency Relief Administration; West Virginia Department of Public Assistance; West Virginia Relief Administration; Works

Progress Administration
Reorganized United Mine Workers, 45
Republican party, 24, 26; loss of dominance in West Virginia, 211, 194. See also elections
Republican regime of twenties, 7
Resettlement Administration, 174
resettlement communities. See subsistence homesteads
Revercomb, Chapman, 283 n 86
Richberg, Donald, 92, 102
Riffner, William, 51
right to work, 225, 232
road building: and good roads movement, 21-22; as unemployment relief, 40, 59-60, 65; by WPA, 145-48, 221
Rollins, Lawrence E., 190
Roosevelt, Eleanor: and Alice Davis, 133; in Monongalia County, 133, 170; and subsistence homesteads, 168; interest in West Virginia, 194-95; and Logan clinic, 195; and black subsistence homestead idea, 204
Roosevelt, Franklin D., 25; and bank holiday, 78; on need for experimentation, 91; intervenes to urge coal code, 98; and support for idea of federal relief, 112; orders end of CWA, 121; decries dole, calls for federal work-relief, 124; on relief and role of the states, 136; and subsistence homesteads program, 168; quoted on West Virginia tent colony, 195; popularity of, 211; on West Virginia factions, 203, 229
Rosenbloom, Benjamin, 35
Rosier, Dr. Joseph, 231, 283 n 86
Ross, Nelly Tayloe, 216
Ross, Shirley, 63
Ross, W. Vergil, 215
Rural Electrification Administration (REA), 176-78
rural housing, conditions of, 164
rural poverty, 270 n 12
rural relief, 162

St. Albans bridge, 152
Sale, Graham, 103
Salstrom, Paul: *Appalachia's Path to Dependency*, 2; on impact of NRA on Appalachia, 108; faults "high" relief payments, 127; on barter economy, 250 n 71; on New Deal and soil erosion, 275 n 103
Salvation Army, 43
Saturday Evening Post, 239
saw mill towns, 183
Schecter Poultry case, 105
school-lunch program, 193
Scotts Run: Methodist settlement house at, 18; and Presbyterian mission, 18; and UMWA, 49; and arrival of first mechanical coal loaders, 99-100; and Eleanor Roosevelt, 133, 169-70; described, 169
Secrist, Walter, 48
segregation, 200, 202
Shaffer, E.E., 43
Sharp, Summers H., 220
Sharples, 205
Shaver, Clem, 103
Shepherdstown, 24, 75, 205
Shepherdstown *Register*, 191
Sherwood, Robert E.: *Roosevelt and Hopkins*, 137
Shipman, George, 153
Shott, Hugh Ike, 35-36, 72; on experience in Congress, 75; runs for U.S. Senate, 219
silicosis fund, 110-11
Silver, Grey, 33
Skinner, Mary, 65
Skokpol, Theda, 108
Skuce, Tom, 56
slum clearance, 208
Sly, John Fairfield, 64; quoted, 69; and "little brain trust," 76; and tax hearings, 78; quoted on "jump in the dark," 79; drafts report on welfare services, 153; drafts welfare act, 153
Small businesses, 189

Smith, Alfred E., 25
Smith, Charles Brooks, 119, 138
Smith, Clarence Edwin "Ned": quoted, 9, 23, 43; opposes Davis-Kelley Bill, 50; appointed to Coal Commission, 107; as part of Neely faction, 215
Smith, Joe L., 35
Smith, John W., 38, 39
Smity, Dr. Mary, 54
Snyder, J. Buell, 105
Social Security Act, 112, 152
Social Services Union (Martinsburg), 58
social workers, 129, 158
soil conservation, 180-82
Soil Conservation Service, 183
songs of labor movement, 48-49. *See also individual titles*
South Charleston, 199
Southern Tenant Farmers Union, 167
South Side bridge, 147
Spaulding, Jane, 204
Splash Beach, 47
state capacity, 28
Staunton, Sue, 17
Stein Brothers and Boyce, 27
Stillman, C.C., 128
stock market crash, 27
stranded populations: and FERA, 121; subsistence communities as a panacea, 163; of mining and timber workers, 163, 170; in southern Lewis County, 184
Stribling, Mary, 61
"Striker's Orphaned Child, The," 48
subsistence farmers: lack of organization, 11-12; relief needs, 116; and their farms, 161; and lack of mobility in Appalachia, 162; and electrification, 178-79; decline of, 187. *See also* farming in West Virginia; Farm Security Administration; subsistence homesteads
subsistence homesteads, 173-74. *See also* Arthurdale; Red House

Garden Farms; Tygart Valley
Sullivan, Jesse, 18
Summers, Festus Paul, 1
Supplemental Emergency Relief Act, 86
Surplus Commodity Corp., 225
Sutherland, Mabel, 54, 122, 163
Sweeney, Tom, 230

Taggart, Ralph E., 97
Talbott, Richard E., 212
taxes: property, 15; consumer sales, 70, 83, 213, 237; gross sales, 80, 83; income, 83; gasoline, 222; severance, 237. *See also* Tax Limitation Amendment
Tax Limitation Amendment, 70-90, 236; and rejection of "narrow" classification, 63-64; and adverse judicial decisions on implementing legislation, 79; and revenue loss to local government, 79; ill-effects of, 87-88; and patronage benefits, 88-89; sanctity of, 89; impact on education, 221; details of, 254 n 34
tax relief, 7; as issue in 1932 election, 74
Taylor, J. Alfred, 29, 103
teachers: salary cuts, 42; oppose county-unit bill, 82; unemployed, given work relief, 126; hired by WPA adult education and literacy program, 150; salaries, 221. *See also* education; higher education
tenant farmers, 174
Tennessee, 178, 208-9
Tetlow, Percy, 97
Thurmond, Walter R., 218
timber industry, 15, 244 n 33
Tippet, Tom, 46
Togery, The, 189
Townsend, Thomas C., 64, 71-72
Townsend Revolving Old Age Pension Club, 143
transients, 126
Trent, William Woodson, 82; attacks underfunding of schools,

87; and school lunch program, 193; as part of federal faction, 212; fights for increased appropriations, 236
Tuckwiller, Ross, 183
Tugwell, Rexford, 174
Tunley, Roul, 239
Turner, Maj. Francis, 113, 118, 260 n 7; quoted, 117; and child-care issues, 155; and children's camps, 195
two-party system in West Virginia, 211
Tygart Valley resettlement community, 168, 204. *See also* subsistence homesteads

unemployment, in 1933, 117; impact of, 190
unemployment committee, 38, 39
Unemployment League of West Virginia, 119-20; and strike of CWA workers, 121-22; marches on relief headquarters, 122; seeks investigation of WPA, 143
Union Carbide and Chemical Corp., 23, 41, 227, 232
union shop, 224-25
United Mine Workers of America (UMWA): and problems of twenties in West Virginia, 8-10; and Frank Keeney, 44-45; organizing drive, 1933, 92-94; and struggle in Kentucky, 93; rise in membership, 93; and acquiescence by operators, 94; and mechanization of mining, 99-100; and Rush D. Holt, 104, 218-20; advocates stronger stabilization law for industry, 105; and labor's civil war, 224-26; work stoppage of 1939 and Gov. Holt, 225; John L. Lewis and arrogance of power, 237
United Mine Workers Journal, 98
United Mine Workers v Red Jacket Consolidated Coal and Coke, 10, 201

United States Department of Labor, 191
United States Elections Committee, 231
United States Housing Authority, 207-9
United States Naval Ordnance Plant (South Charleston), 199

Van Tine, Warren, 229
Via, L.R., 219
Virginia, 4, 114, 161, 236
Virginia debt, 222
volunteers, and New Deal relief work, 126-27

Wagner, Robert, 95, 207
Wagner Act. *See* National Labor Relations Act
Wagner-Steagall Housing Act, 207
Walker, Nell, 194
Wallace, Henry, 91
Ward, 194
Wardensville, 198
Ware, Susan, 190
Warrum, Henry, 105
Washington Manor, 208
Waters, Walter W. 52
Wayne County, 116, 128, 181
Webster County, 128
Weir, Ernest T., 95-96
Weirton Steel Employee Security League, 257 n 19
Weirton Steel strike, 95-96
Welch, 219
welfare system, West Virginia, 119
Wells, I.J.K., 203
"We Shall Not Be Moved," 48
West Virginia: A Guide to the Mountain State, 147, 181; opposed by Gov. Holt, 226-27
West Virginia Agricultural Extension Service, 12; orientation to small family farm, 167; program to train black mining machine operators, 200; lack of success in reaching subsistence farmers, 238

Index

West Virginia Better Libraries Movement, 150
West Virginia Board of Children's Guardians, 17, 32
West Virginia Bureau of Agriculture, 14
West Virginia Bureau of Labor, 18
West Virginia Bureau of Negro Welfare and Statistics, 199
West Virginia Civil Works Administration, 113, 119-25
West Virginia Coal Operators Assoc., 18
West Virginia Dairymen's Association, 91
West Virginia Department of Archives, 227
West Virginia Department of Education, 191
West Virginia Department of Public Assistance, 153-58; control of, by statehouse faction, 137; and federal grants-in-aid under social security, 153; and Children's Bureau, 153; and county councils, 154; and growth of case load, 156; functions of, 156; requires able-bodied relief clients to work for state, 157
West Virginia Department of Public Welfare, 40, 113, 195-97
West Virginia Education Association, 216; advocates county unit, 82; seeks increased appropriations for education, 236
West Virginia Farm Bureau, 12, 165; and cooperative movement, 13; and *Farm News*, 13; and Cooperative Marketing Act of 1922, 14
West Virginia Farm Women's Bureau, 15
West Virginia Federation of Labor, 39, 71, 223-24
West Virginia Federation of Women's Clubs, 150
West Virginia Grange, 165
"West Virginia Hills," 48

West Virginia History, 227
West Virginia Industrial Union Council, CIO, 224-25
West Virginia Legislature: 1929, 39; 1929 extraordinary session, 30; 1931, launches investigations, 36; 1931, depression measures of, 39-40; 1932 special session, 62-63; 1933, first extraordinary session, 80-83; 1933, second extraordinary session, 85; 1933, tax bill survives court challenge, 86; 1933, investigates Beehler, 122; and 1936 election, 220; and Holt administration, 222; in 1939, 223
West Virginia Mine Workers Union, 44-49; and 1931 strike, 46; members blacklisted, 195
West Virginia Negro Democratic Executive Committee, 201-2
West Virginia Public Welfare Act of 1936, 153
West Virginia Relief Administration, 113, 125; and attempts to maintain political neutrality, 124; and work relief, 126; Negro Division of, 204
West Virginia Review, 30, 190
West Virginia School for the Deaf and Blind (Romney), 152
West Virginia State College, 197, 200, 205-6
West Virginia State Federation of Women's Clubs (African American), 204
West Virginia state land-use planning committee, 186
West Virginia Supreme Court of Appeals, 25, 84, 85, 220
West Virginia University: urged to set up school of social service, 129; establishes sociology and public welfare departments, 158; decaying facilities of, 236
West Virginia Workers Compensation Commission, 11
West Virginia Writers Project, 151.

See also *West Virginia: A Guide to the Mountain State*; Works Progress Administration
West Virginia Young Democrats, 83, 222
Wheeler-Rayburn bill, 215
Wheeling, 90; and WPA music festival, 149; and desire of "colored people" for music project, 149; and film on 1936 flood, 150; mountaintop suburbs, 207; and 1940 election, 230
Wheeling *Intelligencer*, 106
White, Albert Blakeslee, 34
White, Theodore, 239
white collar unemployed, 113
Williams, Aubrey, 128, 139, 141, 144, 216-17
Williams, John Alexander: on "confluence of power," 24; on spoils benefits of liquor stores, 89; on "inferiority complex" resulting from fiscal parsimony, 90; on impact of 1940 election, 230; on restructuring of statehouse machine, 235
Williamson conference, 1932, 55
Willkie, Wendell, 229
Wilson, Edmund, 45
Wilson, Milburn L., 168, 171
women, 16-19, 190-94; and nineteenth amendment, 16; organizations of, 19; on farms, 19; as relief administrators, 122-23; prejudices against employment of, 191-92; and compensation, 191; and work relief for, 191-92; and Democratic party, 193-94; in government, 194
Wood County, 164
Woods, Col. Arthur, 38, 44
Woodward, Ellen, 192
Works Progress Administration, 136-59, 206; criticism of, 137; investigation of, 144; and political patronage, 146; and report of politics in, 146-47; and work projects, 147-48; and cities, 148; and music projects, 148; and municipal bands, 148-49; and art centers, 148; and statewide library project, 150; and adult education, 150; and films on West Virginia, 150; and writers project, 151, 226-27; and women's work relief, 192-93; and African Americans, 206
World War II, 234
WWVA, 23

Yager, Mary L., 17, 32
Yost, Lenna Lowe, 17
"Young Man Meets Machine," 199

www.ingramcontent.com/pod-product-compliance
Lightning Source LLC
Chambersburg PA
CBHW071314150426
43191CB00007B/624